Paris, City of Dreams

Paris, City of Dreams

Napoleon III, Baron Haussmann,
and the Creation of Paris

Mary McAuliffe

ROWMAN & LITTLEFIELD
Lanham • Boulder • New York • London

Published by Rowman & Littlefield
An imprint of The Rowman & Littlefield Publishing Group, Inc.
4501 Forbes Boulevard, Suite 200, Lanham, Maryland 20706
www.rowman.com

6 Tinworth Street, London SE11 5AL, United Kingdom

Distributed by NATIONAL BOOK NETWORK

British Library Cataloguing in Publication Information Available

Library of Congress Cataloging-in-Publication Data

Names: McAuliffe, Mary Sperling, 1943– author.
Title: Paris, City of Dreams : Napoleon III, Baron Haussmann, and the Creation of Paris
  / Mary McAuliffe.
Other titles: Napoleon III, Baron Haussmann, and the creation of Paris
Description: Lanham : Rowman & Littlefield, [2020] | Includes bibliographical
  references and index. | Summary: "Traces the profound transformation of the
  City of Light during Napoleon III's Second Empire, as he and Georges Haussmann
  completely rebuilt Paris in less than two decades."— Provided by publisher.
Identifiers: LCCN 2019045560 (print) | LCCN 2019045561 (ebook) | ISBN
  9781538121283 (cloth) | ISBN 9781538121290 (epub)
Subjects: LCSH: Paris (France)—History—1848–1870. | Urban renewal—France—
  Paris—History—19th century. | Napoleon III, Emperor of the French, 1808–1873—
  Influence. | Haussmann, Georges Eugène, baron, 1809–1891—Influence. | Paris
  (France)—Social life and customs—19th century.
Classification: LCC DC733 .M48 2020 (print) | LCC DC733 (ebook) | DDC
  944/.36107—dc23
LC record available at https://lccn.loc.gov/2019045560
LC ebook record available at https://lccn.loc.gov/2019045561

♾™ The paper used in this publication meets the minimum requirements of
American National Standard for Information Sciences—Permanence of Paper
for Printed Library Materials, ANSI/NISO Z39.48-1992.

For Mavyn, Jay, and Tyler

~

Contents

Illustrations

~

Acknowledgments

When I began writing about Paris, with *Dawn of the Belle Epoque*, I had no idea that more books would follow, creating what amounts to a history of Paris during the eventful years of the Third Republic. Now, *Paris, City of Dreams* creates a prequel to the four that follow, an unexpected development that has opened up new vistas for me and, I hope, for my readers.

Throughout this entire process, I have been grateful for the support I have received from the New York Public Library, which has provided me, as a resident scholar, with a place in its much-coveted Wertheim Study Room. Without this, my research in the NYPL's vast resources would have been far more difficult. Special thanks to Melanie Locay, the NYPL's research study liaison, for her ongoing support and assistance in matters large and small. I have also appreciated aid from of a number of the NYPL's fine research librarians, especially Fernando Martinez and Deirdre Donohue.

In Paris, I am grateful for the assistance of Bérengère de l'Epine at the Bibliothèque historique de la ville de Paris, as well as the introduction that Juliette Jestaz gave me to this research treasure. Also in Paris, I would like to extend my thanks to Gilles Thomas for his remarkable insights into the history of Paris and his accompanying on-site trips, especially his introduction to the Petite Ceinture. My thanks as well to the staunch crew of ASNEP (l'Association Sources du Nord—Etudes et Préservation), led by Gérard Duserre and Jean-Luc Largier, for sharing their extraordinary knowledge of the history of Paris's water and its ancient aqueducts, which I have been privileged to visit. Thanks, too, to our good friend Ray Lampard, who has made our stays in Paris especially enjoyable and who has braved Paris traffic to cart us around to various historic locales.

Here in the United States, I am grateful for the assistance of our friend Robin Taff in helping me to decipher the mysteries of triangulation and spot heights that plagued Baron Haussmann all those years ago. I am especially grateful to my daughter, Mavyn Holman, for responding to my cries for help on this and numerous other subjects that cropped up as the book progressed. Her ongoing support has been invaluable.

Special thanks goes to my longtime editor, Susan McEachern, who has patiently held my hand through a series of books that now extend from the Revolution of 1848 to World War II. Similarly, I am grateful to Jehanne Schweitzer, who has so diligently served as production editor for each and every one of these books.

Last, my thanks to my husband, whose aid in this and all my other books and articles has been immeasurable. Jack McAuliffe, as everyone who knows him is quick to acknowledge, is someone who makes things work—and who is a pleasure to work with as well. It has been a delight exploring Paris with him over these many years.

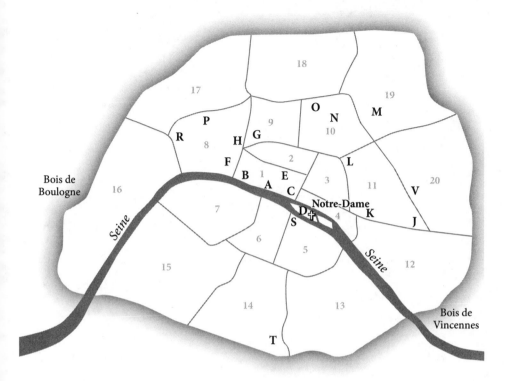

PARIS, 1860–1870
Key

A. Palais du Louvre
B. Palais des Tuileries
C. Place du Châtelet
D. Ile de la Cité and Notre-Dame
E. Les Halles
F. Place de la Concorde
G. Opéra Garnier
H. Place de la Madeleine
J. Place de la Nation (originally Place du Trône)
K. Place de la Bastille
L. Place de la République (originally Place du Château d'Eau)
M. Parc des Buttes Chaumont
N. Gare de l'Est
O. Gare du Nord
P. Parc Monceau
R. Arc de Triomphe and Place de l'Etoile
S. Sorbonne and Latin Quarter
T. Parc Montsouris
V. Père-Lachaise Cemetery

Paris's twenty arrondissements, as established in 1860, are indicated by number

© J. McAuliffe

~

Introduction

Paris—the Paris that inspires so many dreams—is a recent creation, the product of a charming playboy with imperial visions and his invaluable ally, a hard-driving bureaucrat with an extraordinary ability to get things done. The playboy was a Bonaparte, the nephew of France's first emperor, and his dedicated right-hand man was Georges Haussmann. Together they completely rebuilt Paris from the ground up—from below the ground, counting the new water and sewer system—and created the city that Paris is today.

This breathtaking achievement had its origins on December 10, 1848, when Louis-Napoleon Bonaparte, nephew of Napoleon Bonaparte, was elected president of France's Second Republic. He did not remain in elected office for long. Three years later, on December 2, 1851, he carried out a bloody *coup d'état*, which a plebiscite of France's adult male voters overwhelmingly endorsed. This in turn led, a year later, to Louis-Napoleon's proclamation of the Second Empire and his assumption of the title of Napoleon III (having granted Napoleon I's son, who died young, the title of Napoleon II). His reign lasted eighteen years, until he led France into a catastrophic war with Bismarck's Prussia and was deposed and replaced by the Third Republic.

Politically, it was not a glorious time for Paris or for France. During these almost two decades of imperial rule, Napoleon III imposed an authoritarian government that severely limited freedom of assembly, speech, and publication, all the while claiming to act on behalf of the common man. Yet those who most benefited from the Second Empire were not the workers but rather

1

those new men of commerce, banking, and the railroads, whose sudden wealth led to a gaudy era of excess, in which the emperor led the way.

Still, Napoleon III's vision included a better Paris for one and all, and this meant a complete overhaul of the city, much of which at the outset of his reign still resembled the Paris of medieval times. Paris in the early 1850s was a densely packed metropolis, with narrow, winding, and often filthy streets lined by ancient and decaying housing. This was a Paris that Victor Hugo could rhapsodize over, but it also was a hellhole for those stuck there, especially in the eastern and central portions of the city. Napoleon III had a better idea for Paris, one that would improve the city's housing and sanitation as well as encourage commerce by providing broad and wide avenues connecting the recently built railway stations with one another and with the city's center. Napoleon III had a vision, and he soon found the man to carry it out—Georges Haussmann.

During the seventeen years that Haussmann served as the emperor's prefect of the Seine, he tore up an astonishing amount of old Paris, both above and below ground, introducing a modernized water and sewer system as well as those broad and wide avenues lined with uniform apartment buildings that have since become known as "Haussmann buildings." Uniformity was prized, not only as aesthetically desirable but also as an economical approach to rebuilding the huge swaths of the city that were being razed. This destruction and rebuilding of course displaced the poor, who could no longer afford to live in these cleaned-up areas, but order and prosperity marched together, as far as both Haussmann and his emperor were concerned. The fact that these broad streets made it far easier for troops to march—and far more difficult for the workers of Paris to build barricades—was an added incentive.

And yet, even while the emperor imposed his vision on Paris, a number of Parisians, especially the young, refused to comply with the restrictions that the empire imposed. Young artists such as Edouard Manet, Berthe Morisot, and Claude Monet, as well as young writers such as Emile Zola, Gustave Flaubert, and the poet Charles Baudelaire, resisted the constraints imposed by government censorship and entrenched institutional taste, even while politicized students and teachers such as Georges Clemenceau and Louise Michel linked up with a growing number of Parisians who were anxious to end imperial rule. And while Eugène Viollet-le-Duc staunchly resisted the stultifying influence of the all-powerful Ecole des Beaux Arts as he restored Notre-Dame de Paris to its former glory, the rising young photographer Nadar discreetly thumbed his nose at the palace—although not at those clients it provided.

Nadar had risen to prominence after a lengthy stint among the poor young artists, writers, and musicians of the Latin Quarter, who now became known as bohemians, after Henry Murger's publication of *Scenes from Bohemian Life*. Murger based his stories on his own hard experience as a starving writer in a Paris garret, and his book bestowed the name "Bohemian" on those who similarly eked out an existence dedicated to the creative arts. Yet not all young artists of this time were inclined to suffer, and even while resisting the rules, young Sarah Bernhardt did what was necessary to ensure her own comfort as she began what would turn out to be a long and glittering career, embracing an acting and life style that was distinctly her own.

While young Parisians were at the forefront of resistance to Napoleon III's empire, defiance was not limited to the young. From his exile outside of France, Victor Hugo continued to fire literary broadsides at Louis-Napoleon, scathingly labeling him as "Napoléon le Petit," while Hugo's longtime friend Alexandre Dumas kept just shy of the censors at home and dove into the fight for Italian unification abroad.

It was a time of vast change—a change that was not limited to the enormous physical transformation occurring in Paris. Supported by the emperor, a network of railways grew during these years to encompass the nation, while back in Paris—the vortex of all this upheaval—innovative forms of banking and money-lending were buoying an upsurge in industry, creating new wealth even while attracting a growing number of poverty-stricken workers to the city in search of jobs.

Even more deeply, change was occurring in the very way people looked at and understood the world around them, as railroads revolutionized mobility, the telegraph and rotary press modernized communications, and photography transformed ways of viewing people and places. What would soon be known as Impressionism in art and Naturalism and Realism in literature would create their own cultural revolutions, leading the way into the era of the Belle Epoque. But first, a devastating war had to be fought, a siege endured, and an uprising of Paris's workers overcome. Napoleon III's empire began in bloodshed and ended with more bloodshed. But the Third Republic that rose from the empire's ashes would endure, sometimes shakily, for seventy years.

As for the man who claimed the title of Napoleon III, he has been forgotten, in the way that embarrassments in history are largely forgotten. He led France into a devastating defeat against a newly unified Germany, and therefore there is no memorial to him in Paris save for the small (and easily overlooked) area in front of the Gare du Nord called the "Place Napoléon III."

Yet this was the man who created the Paris that is so beloved today. Paris, that city of dreams, has survived Napoleon III into the twenty-first century, and perhaps it can be said that this Paris, the Paris he created, is his lasting memorial.

Barricade at the Rue Saint-Martin in Paris, French Revolution of February 1848. © SZ Photo / Bridgeman Images

CHAPTER ONE

~

From Barricades to Bonaparte

(1848–1851)

The barricades went up the night of February 23–24, 1848. Victor Hugo, on one of his regular tramps through Paris's streets, asserted that there were some 1,574 of them, made up of 4,013 trees and more than fifteen million paving stones. His friend Alexandre Dumas, who was similarly drawn to turmoil, had already concluded that "the Prince protects us, it is true, but our real protector is the people. Within three days there will still be a great people, and there won't be any small princes."[1]

He was right. The king, Louis-Philippe, fled Paris for London on the morning of February 24 disguised as "Mister Smith," leaving his palace and kingdom to the mob. Eighteen years before, in July 1830, a similar mob had exuberantly ushered out the last of the unpopular Bourbon monarchs and ushered in this same Louis-Philippe, the Bourbons' Orléanist cousin, whose personal history and even appearance promised a change toward comforting moderation and prosperity. This stout bourgeois king, or Citizen-King as he was known, maintained happy relations with his subjects until the 1840s, when the economy began to sour.

Bad harvests, food shortages, rising prices, and growing unemployment now heightened the absence of liberty that the king's subjects had hitherto been willing to tolerate. But no longer. It was in fact the specific curtailment of freedom of association (and its close relation, freedom of speech) that provided the spark that set off February's 1848 revolution. Cleverly working around the regime's restrictions on meetings, which were banned, reformers had settled on holding large-scale banquets, during which toasts served as a vehicle for political speeches. The regime failed to appreciate this distinction and banned one especially large banquet scheduled during January 1848. The organizers moved the date to February 22, charged an admission fee, and encountered similar opposition from the authorities. But now the small shopkeepers and craftsmen who had subscribed to the banquet were irate. They had paid their money and—having seen their voting rights recently curtailed, even while they suffered from a worsening economy—were determined to gain admission to the now-forbidden banquet.

The crowds grew, as workers demanding both work and bread joined in. Even the National Guard, largely made up of petty bourgeoisie with grudges to spare, went over to the reformers. A bad situation rapidly spiraled out of control when soldiers began shooting into the crowd. The dead were loaded onto carts and pushed through the streets of Paris to spectacular effect. By February 24, Paris was in open revolt, and the king fled.

What was left was a provisional government, whose attempts to mollify the workers quickly led to a number of concessions, including the right to work, the right to organize in unions, a ten-hour day (much shorter than the usual), and abolition of debtors' prisons—in addition to establishing universal adult male suffrage and, of course, proclaiming a Republic, the second one since France's great Revolution of the 1790s.

It was at this point that Louis-Napoleon Bonaparte arrived on the scene.

Louis-Napoleon, born in 1808—the son of Hortense de Beauharnais (daughter of Napoleon Bonaparte's wife Josephine, by Josephine's first marriage) and Louis Bonaparte, younger brother of Napoleon Bonaparte—was the product of a scheme to provide Napoleon and the now-infertile Josephine with an heir. This scheme was successful, in that Hortense and Louis produced two sons, but the couple had a dismal marriage. Louis-Napoleon's detractors have contended that in fact his father was Hortense's lover, the dashing Charles-Joseph, Count of Flahaut, who in turn was the illegitimate son of Prince Talleyrand. Those defending Louis-Napoleon have carefully tabulated calendar dates and locations of the parties concerned and concluded in favor of his legitimacy, which now seems to be widely accepted among those still interested in the question. Unaware, however, of parentage problems until later in life, little Louis-Napoleon enjoyed a childhood ensconced in imperial splendor at the Tuileries, Saint-Cloud, and Fontainebleau, thoroughly cosseted and spoiled by his mother and his maternal grandmother, Josephine.

Like both Hortense and Josephine, young Louis-Napoleon was a charmer, and he maintained his ability to captivate throughout his life. Certainly he was not a warrior leader in the image of his uncle: Louis-Napoleon's military exploits were embarrassingly slight and came to unfortunate ends, although everyone who knew him insisted that he looked good on a horse. Instead, exiled (along with the rest of the Bonapartes) from France after Waterloo, he focused on seducing women, spending money, and enjoying himself. At the same time, this playboy-prince took considerable pride in his name and never ceased to dream that someday he would rule France.

This dream, as well as a longing for a dashing military role, led Louis-Napoleon into two abortive coup attempts, the second of which landed him in a French military prison where he studied, wrote, and consorted with a mistress, with whom he had two children before he eventually escaped for London. But his prison stay had not been without benefit, for during those long years he had widely published his political ideas—including a growing concern for the poor—in numerous articles and pamphlets. His *L'Extinction du paupérisme*, a study of the causes of poverty in France, was especially popular, going into multiple editions and drawing numerous reformers and workers to his cause.

His cause became ever clearer with the deaths, first, of his older brother; then of Napoleon Bonaparte's only son, the young Duke of Reichstadt; and, last, of Louis-Napoleon's father. These deaths left Louis-Napoleon as the foremost Bonaparte claimant to France's imperial throne. By the 1840s, this had become markedly more significant, for Emperor Napoleon Bonaparte had surged back into popularity in France, signaled by the 1840 return of his ashes to Paris, where he was interred with great ceremony in the Invalides. The Bonaparte name was now one that Louis-Napoleon could flaunt with pride in his native land.

This opportunity presented itself in February 1848, as revolution toppled yet another French monarch. Returning to Paris two days after Louis-Philippe fled France, Louis-Napoleon met with members of the Provisional Government and assured them that he was devoted to their cause. These leaders were, however, understandably wary and urged him to return to England as soon as possible, reminding him that the law of exile was still in effect. Louis-Napoleon gracefully acceded to their wishes and returned to London. There, he wrote his ardent supporter, the self-styled Count de Persigny, that "at present the people believe in all the fine words they hear. . . . There must be an end of these illusions before a man who can bring order . . . can make himself heard."

Even more to the point, he told a friend, "I have wagered the Princess Mathilde [Bonaparte] that I shall sign myself Emperor of the French in four years."[2]

～

Louis-Napoleon was right. Very quickly, conflict began to appear between the revolutionary workers and the far more conservative bourgeoisie. National Workshops, the provisional government's solution to the unemployment problem, were proving unsatisfactory to everyone: government-sponsored public works did not supply enough jobs, leaving too many workers unemployed, hungry, and angry, while the bourgeoisie complained of handouts to lazy workers.

Street demonstrations from both sides provided an uneasy background to the April elections for a Constituent Assembly. Louis-Napoleon did not run. "So long as the social condition of France remains unsettled," he wrote a friend, "I feel my position in France must be very difficult, tiresome and even dangerous."[3] The electoral turnout was huge (making use of printed voting slips for the first time in French history) and resulted in a victory for a liberal Republic—a middle way between social revolution and monarchical reaction. The deputies now reproclaimed the Republic, making May 4, 1848, the official birth of the Second Republic.

But the workers still had grievances and revolted, first in Rouen, then in Paris, where they invaded the Assembly chamber itself. As the earlier spirit of reconciliation faded, attitudes became increasingly polarized. By-elections in early June brought a troubled Victor Hugo into the Constituent Assembly, backed by a committee of moderates.[4] Hugo's politics thus far had favored the monarchy—although after being elevated to the peerage in 1845 and entering the Senate, he had spoken out against the death penalty and social injustice. During the February 1848 riots, he had supported a regency for Louis-Philippe's grandson. But now what? He did not like what he saw emerging from the political right.

The June by-elections also brought Louis-Napoleon Bonaparte into the Assembly, although with becoming modesty. Claiming that his friends had announced his candidacy without his approval, he won in all four departments (including Paris) in which his name was placed, without so much as waging a campaign. Although some strongly urged that he be disqualified (on the grounds that the law banning him from France was still in effect), the majority admitted him to the Assembly. But then, on his own initiative, Louis-Napoleon sent a letter of resignation, prompting many later to wonder whether this was genuine hesitation or whether he was simply waiting for a better moment.

The ax was now about to fall on the National Workshops. A June decree gave workers a choice between enlisting in the army or departure for hard labor in the provinces. Workers rose up in a massive revolt (later called the "June Days"), with barricades going up, bullets whistling, and intense fighting between the army—under a relentless General Cavaignac, joined by a heavily bourgeois National Guard—and the increasingly desperate workers.

The young poet Charles Baudelaire took part in the street fighting, siding with the workers and using his own rifle to fire at government troops. Shooting from the government's side was Gustave Flaubert, also in his twenties. According to his friend, the writer Maxime Du Camp, Flaubert "shouldered a fowling piece [and] joined the ranks of my company [in the National Guard]." Baudelaire and Flaubert escaped injury, but Du Camp was wounded and had a long convalescence.[5]

Victor Hugo, who at the time lived in the once-elegant but increasingly decrepit Place Royale (now the Place des Vosges) in the heart of the insurrection, unsuccessfully attempted to return to his family before learning that they had escaped unharmed. Sent with other representatives to inform the insurgents that their cause was a lost one and that General Cavaignac was in control, he ended up leading a contingent of the Republican Guard against a series of barricades, directing cannon fire, taking prisoners, and contributing to the deaths of countless insurgents, whom he considered heroic but tragically misguided.

Hugo told himself that he was engaged in nothing less than "saving civilization." Yet what he saw on those June days and nights seared itself into the unforgettable memory that he recorded in *Les Misérables*—a vision of one of the largest barricades of this 1848 insurrection, "the biggest street-war in history." This barricade was not to be confused with his own story's far smaller barricade of 1832, but was instead the gargantuan one that stretched across the main road leading into the Faubourg Saint-Antoine, the sight of which "conveyed a sense of intolerable distress which had reached the point where suffering becomes disaster." Distress ennobled it, for this monstrosity was both "a pile of garbage, and it was Sinai."

Conflicted about the role he had played in this tragedy, Hugo added, "These are popular upheavals which must be suppressed. The man of probity stands firm, and from very love of the people opposes them." Well, in any case, he had done so, and a bitter memory lingered. With a sigh, he concluded, "Duty is burdened with a heavy heart."[6]

⁓

"For two days," Maxime Du Camp later wrote, "the contest was a doubtful one, but finally the cause of civilization carried off the victory, and General Cavaignac was proclaimed the savior of the country."[7]

Order was quickly reestablished, and the reprisals began. Executions proceeded smartly, and about fifteen thousand men were arrested, piled into improvised prisons, and deported to Algeria, France's recent colonial conquest. At the Assembly's insistence, the National Workshops were completely dissolved, and General Cavaignac—a republican, albeit a stern one—became leader of the Republic, at least until a president could be elected.

The young scholar Ernest Renan, then studying in Paris, wrote to his sister after touring the worst affected areas: "In Rue Saint-Martin, Rue Saint-Antoine, and the part of Rue Saint-Jacques stretching from the Pantheon to the docks, there was not one house that had not been lacerated by cannon fire. Some you could literally see through." Maxime Du Camp noted proposals "to take up all the paving-stones of Paris, macadamize the streets so as to close the era of revolution forever."[8] He was specifically referring to certain quarters of the city, for by now, the contrast was clear between eastern Paris, where the insurgency had erupted, and the more bourgeois neighborhoods in the city's west.

Order was returning, and with it, suppression. Leftists Adolphe Blanqui and François-Vincent Raspail were already in jail, and others, including Louis Blanc, now escaped to London. A new law abolished the recent reform that had established a ten-hour working day in Paris, now lengthening it to twelve hours, and a series of regulations served to muzzle the press—"silencing the poor," as one irate lawmaker called it.[9] In addition, Paris—where the position of mayor had been briefly restored after its disappearance during the long years of postrevolutionary monarchy—once again lost its mayor and its autonomy, and the prefect of the Seine again became the capital's chief executive.

Louis-Napoleon considered all of this with interest and, after careful consideration, decided to stand in the September 1848 by-elections. He swept the five departments where he was a candidate (one more than those he had won in June), and he chose to represent the department of the Seine. When he arrived in Paris on September 24 at the Paris embarkation point of the Great Northern railway (now the Gare du Nord), he carried with him a color-coded map of Paris—his plan for renewing the great city—along with dreams for improving the lot of workers and the entire nation.

The Assembly welcomed him and suspended the banishment order. Even Victor Hugo was enthusiastic: "The man just named by the people as their representative," he proclaimed, was in his eyes a worthy heir of the great Bonaparte; "his candidacy dates from the time of Austerlitz."[10] Louis-Napoleon informally subscribed to a number of the progressive ideas that then were circulating, which held in common an optimistic view of the emerging industrial revolution and its promise for one and all. Jobs and riches could be had for worker and bourgeoisie alike if only the old way of doing things could be cleared away and replaced with the new. Regarding Paris in particular, Louis-Napoleon was thoroughly convinced that misery and mobs would disappear if only the narrow, festering streets could be demolished and broad thoroughfares created in their place, letting sunshine in and allowing the free flow of commerce as well as the activities of daily life.

The Provisional Government had already chalked up several potential public works in Paris, largely to satisfy the job requirements of the short-lived National Workshops. These included the completion of the northern wing of the Louvre Palace (the wing begun under Napoleon Bonaparte) and the continuation of the Rue de Rivoli (another Napoleon project). This had stalled in its eastward course alongside the Louvre's uncompleted northern wing, reaching only a point even with Napoleon's nearby Arc du Carrousel. Nothing for the moment came of these plans, but the government did in fact make a significant change in the law on compulsory purchases (eminent domain) that would have huge impact in Paris's future: this now allowed the city to purchase the entire portion rather than just the precise area of land directly affected by whatever public works were involved.

Louis-Napoleon believed in the socialistic philosophies of his age, and he dreamed of initiating major public works that would foster progress and benefit one and all. But unlike those who had ardently supported the National Workshops or something like them, he believed in the necessity for good, solid organization. Indeed, his distaste for the National Workshops did not so much derive from a horror of handouts to what the bourgeoisie regarded as the undeserving poor as it recoiled from the sheer disorganization that riddled the project.

He firmly believed that he could do better, and in late October, when the Constituent Assembly set December 10 as the date for the presidential elections, Louis-Napoleon immediately announced that he would run.

At last, on November 4, 1848, the Second Republic had a constitution. This document, which the Constituent Assembly overwhelmingly approved, provided for a single Legislative Assembly and a president with full executive powers, both to be directly elected by universal male suffrage. This president would serve a four-year term and, most importantly—especially for those who cast a worried glance in the direction of Louis-Napoleon Bonaparte—would not be eligible for reelection.

It quickly emerged that Louis-Napoleon's main opponent would be none other than General Cavaignac, who was widely favored to win. Cavaignac, of course, was by then known as the man who had "gunned down the workers," and Louis-Napoleon—who had made no public pronouncement whatever following the riots—is supposed to have remarked (at a London dinner party in the riots' aftermath): "That man [Cavaignac] is clearing the way for me."[11]

But Louis-Napoleon would benefit not only from worker support but also from the forces on the right—those conservatives (such as King Louis-Philippe's former prime minister, Adolphe Thiers) who had always been un-enthusiastic about the Republic. Bonaparte easily promised them whatever they wanted and, according to historian Maurice Agulhon, "seemed to be a mediocre, simple-enough fellow whom it would be easy to maneuver in the corridors of power."[12]

Certainly the general atmosphere in Paris had changed and not in Cavaignac's favor. Maxime Du Camp noted this upon his return to Paris after an absence of several months. As he put it, "I was astonished at the change which had taken place in my absence. General Cavaignac, when I left Paris, was a great man—a savior of society. . . . Our French weather-cock had had time to turn, and it was 'Cavaignac is a revolutionary just like the others.'" Reaction, he added, "'was setting in' with a will."[13]

Louis-Napoleon's right-hand man, Persigny, campaigned as he had in September, using the ample funds provided by Louis-Napoleon's faithful (and wealthy) mistress, Lizzie Howard, to flood the streets of Paris and all the major French cities with posters, leaflets, and placards, in addition to match-boxes with the candidate's portrait, medals on red ribbons with his effigy, and miniature French flags bearing his name. Persigny also bribed journalists to insert articles favorable to Louis in newspapers otherwise hostile to the candidate and paid street singers to sing songs acclaiming him. It was new, it was modern, and the public loved it. The public also took to Louis-Napoleon personally, despite (and perhaps even because of) his lack of polish as a speaker. Whereas Cavaignac was aloof and military in demeanor, Louis-Napoleon exuded charm and connected instantly with ordinary people. Riding through Paris on horseback, he took pleasure in greeting crowds in the streets and talking with soldiers in the barracks.

Still, it came as a surprise to most seasoned politicians when this Bonaparte upstart, as many derisively called him, demolished Cavaignac on election day, December 10. Louis-Napoleon had promised peace as well as prosperity, and having thus reassured those who dreaded another Bonaparte on the loose in Europe, he found his base among a large majority who favored a return to order under an approachable leader with a pleasant smile—especially one with a legendary name.

Ten days later, he took the oath of office, swearing "to remain faithful to the democratic Republic." He then read a brief speech in which he extolled the Republic and again promised it his complete loyalty.

According to Victor Hugo, many representatives were reserved in their applause, not knowing whether they were witnessing "a conversion or a perjury."[14]

Victor Hugo adored Paris and had done so ever since he could remember. The youngest son of an officer in Napoleon Bonaparte's army, Hugo was born in 1802 in Besançon, near the Swiss border, but arrived in Paris soon after, when his mother, a confirmed royalist, left Major Hugo to his mistress and his wars. Settling in Paris with her three sons, Madame Hugo acquired a lover of her own, who actively plotted against Bonaparte until ending up facing a firing squad.

In the midst of this turbulent family life, young Victor went back and forth between mother and father (now a general), between royalist and Napoleonic sympathies, and between Paris, Italy, and Spain. Even Paris offered little stability during his early years, as one home depressingly followed another. But in the midst of this unsettled life, young Hugo began to write and found that he was good at it, winning a major prize when he was fifteen and (with his older brothers) founding a literary review that he filled with torrents of poetry and prose.

Yet even these successes could not distract from the Hugo family's mounting troubles, including the unmistakable evidence that Victor's brother Eugène was going mad. On the day of Victor's wedding to Adèle Foucher, Eugène permanently slipped into insanity and spent the rest of his brief life in confinement.

Life for young Victor Hugo was already looking a lot like one of his emotion-packed novels. Still, there were more serene moments, and by his midtwenties, he was beginning to achieve a literary reputation and the income to go with it. He now began to write plays and made his triumphal debut at the Comédie-Française with *Hernani*, where it prompted riots with its daring new Romantic style.

But it was the 1831 publication of Hugo's remarkable novel *Notre-Dame de Paris* that really announced his arrival as a literary star. Huge, sprawling, and fairly dripping with emotion, this dark Romantic tale quickly became a best seller and was translated into countless foreign languages, including English, where (much to Hugo's dismay) it was retitled *The Hunchback of Notre-Dame*. Passionately drawn to the medieval architecture and poverty-mired inhabitants of this ancient cathedral quarter, Hugo turned his novel into a demand for social justice as well as an elegy to the past. In the process, he saved Notre-Dame, for his book prompted a surge of public attention to the dying cathedral, resulting in the enormous restoration efforts that followed.

Given his considerable earnings from *Notre-Dame de Paris*, Hugo now could afford to move his family to 6 Place Royale (now the Place des Vosges), the most well-known of his many Paris residences. Here in this beautiful seventeenth-century square—which Hugo shrugged off as too modern and architecturally uninteresting—he lived for sixteen years in the height of Gothic comfort. It was now that he established his liaison with actress Juliette Drouet that would last the rest of his life, while his wife, Adèle, turned to Hugo's friend, the writer and critic Charles Augustin Sainte-Beuve.

This could not have been the happiest of households, and indeed, after an 1847 visit, Charles Dickens gave a memorable description. From Hugo's wife ("who looks as if she might poison [Hugo's] breakfast any morning when the humor seized her") to his daughter (whom Dickens suspected "of carrying a sharp poignard in her stays"), Dickens was struck by the family's over-the-top creepiness, ensconced "among old armor, and old tapestry, and old coffers, and grim old chairs and tables."[15]

Still, Hugo seemed content in this remarkable setting and continued to pour out torrents of words, including the initial portion of *Les Misérables*. Revolution and imperial coup would drive him from his home and his country long before the final version of the book would appear.

⌣

Seventeen-year-old Edouard Manet, writing to a friend in February 1849, asked: "How do you feel about the election of L[ouis] Napoleon[?]" He then added, "For goodness sake don't go and make him emperor." Soon after, Manet wrote to his father: "So you've had more excitement in Paris; try and keep a decent republic against our return, for I fear L[ouis] Napoleon is not a good republican."[16]

At this time, young Manet was aboard a naval training ship bound for Rio de Janeiro, having acquiesced to family insistence that he find a career, any career, after the young man's poor school record negated any possibility of following his father (a distinguished lawyer in the Ministry of Justice) in the law. Young Edouard reluctantly agreed to give up his dream of becoming an artist and took the naval exams but failed them. Then, after a change in navy regulations made it possible to reapply after making a voyage south of the Equator in the merchant marine, Edouard's determined father signed him up on a vessel bound for Rio. Edouard made the best of it and seemed to enjoy the voyage, crossing the equator on January 22, 1849, with the usual crossing-the-line rituals, and finding suitably exotic entertainment in tropical Rio. After his return to Paris in June, though, Edouard again dashed his father's hopes by once again failing the naval entrance exams. At long last, Manet *père* gave in to his son and agreed to let him go to art school.

This meant either studying at the Ecole des Beaux-Arts, with its Academy of Painting and Sculpture, or entering a private atelier. The former offered a highly formalized and classical training, largely with members of the Académie des Beaux-Arts, and emphasized drawing the human figure and copying Old Masters in the Louvre. The aim here was to win special competitions—the most exalted being the Prix de Rome. Instruction in private ateliers, on the other hand, could be less rigid, and among these, the ateliers of Charles Gleyre and Thomas Couture were the most prominent.

In time, Charles Gleyre would attract young Claude Monet, Pierre-Auguste Renoir, Frédéric Bazille, and Alfred Sisley. But now, Edouard Manet opted for Thomas Couture, and in January 1850 he entered Couture's atelier—located just inside what then was the Farmers-General wall, at the foot of Montmartre.

∽

Louis-Napoleon began his presidency of the Second Republic with a certain amount of discretion. Despite his long history of proclaiming himself heir to the Empire, he went through the motions of swearing loyalty to a constitution that forbade him from seizing what he had always regarded as rightfully his.

Some of his first steps were to reinforce his image as benefactor of the people. Envisioning huge green spaces for the city as well as a major road-building program, he soon ordered work to begin on the Bois de Boulogne. Paris at that time had four public parks: the Luxembourg Gardens, the Jardin des Plantes, the Tuileries gardens, and the gardens of the Palais Royal, all in the city's center. But Louis-Napoleon saw a need for parks on the city's growing outskirts. The lands of the Bois de Boulogne, immediately to the west of

Paris, belonged to the state, but the new president soon provided for their transfer to the city free of charge, on condition that they be turned into an area for public walking and relaxation. Louis-Napoleon's idea, based on his years in London, was to create a curving watercourse there modeled on Hyde Park's Serpentine. It was, in theory, a pleasing idea, and Louis-Napoleon eagerly awaited the outcome, as teams of workmen set to digging.

But before long, the new president began to take other steps, these ones carefully calibrated to consolidate his power. Soon after assuming the presidency, Louis-Napoleon formed a government of former royalist notables and cronies, completely excluding any republicans. And, working to curb resistance in the Legislative Assembly, whose large republican majority still distrusted him, he and the Assembly's right wing forced through spring elections. These, which (like the presidential election) were based on universal male suffrage, installed a legislature more to Louis-Napoleon's liking, delivering a crushing victory for the bourgeois party of order (the order of obedience rather than the order of law). No matter that the leaders of the right regarded Bonaparte as an adventurer and an illegitimate one at that; they and he shared a fear of a democratic upsurge. While these leaders of the right dismissed any possibility that he could rule without them, Bonaparte saw things entirely differently and was quite willing to accept their help until he no longer needed them.

In the meantime, this new majority for the French right had an immediate impact on affairs far from home, for Louis-Napoleon—whose sympathy with Italian unification and independence dated from his youth, when he and his brother fought with Italian revolutionaries against Austrian domination in northern Italy—now agreed with the strongly Catholic French right to support the temporal power of the pope. The papacy had dominated much of central Italy for centuries, but now the Papal States were under attack from nationalists inspired by the same waves of reform and revolution that had swept France and other countries in 1848. In early 1849, Italian nationalists under Giuseppe Mazzini declared a Roman Republic, and the pope fled Rome. Louis-Napoleon's conservative Catholic backers now strongly urged him to go to the pope's aid. Despite his sympathy for the revolutionaries, Louis-Napoleon was not about to risk his own political power. The French army attacked Rome, ousted the republicans, and welcomed back the pope.

Since this military action was directly in contradiction to the French constitution (which stated that the Republic "respects foreign nationalities just as it expects its own nationality to be respected . . . and never employs its forces against the liberty of any people"), the political left attempted to protest, with peaceful demonstrations. But these protests failed. The Parisian workers, still traumatized by the bloody days of June 1848, did not show up, and in those cities—such as Lyon—where they did, they were brutally repressed. "No one could say that the Government erred on the side of leniency," Maxime Du Camp observed, adding that from 1849, "the prisons were crowded with political journalists." For his part, a newly authoritarian Louis-Napoleon proclaimed that "it is time that the good took heart and the bad trembled."[17]

The tide of revolution had definitely turned. French forces turned a subdued Rome back to the pope, who embarked on severe repression. Soon after, Austria retook an insurgent Venice and crushed the Hungarian revolution. Later, Maxime Du Camp wrote that "as early as . . . June, 1849, the more sagacious spirits foresaw what the end would be, but neither Flaubert nor myself suspected anything."[18]

In October 1849, Louis-Napoleon announced that he was forming a ministry that would be accountable to him alone and that henceforth the Assembly would be narrowly limited in its legislative responsibilities—meaning that it would be dependent upon the direction of the president. Victor Hugo, who had believed that Bonaparte was preferable to Cavaignac, now saw the light and, in a speech to the Assembly, denounced the regime's brutality. With this dramatic switch, he found himself in the company of a growing network of international socialists, including revolutionaries from the popular uprisings that had recently swept Europe. Hugo even chaired an international peace conference in Paris in August 1849.

But Hugo and those now fearing for the Republic could do little or nothing to stop the train of events, especially since conservatives in the Assembly were still willing to put up with almost anything from Bonaparte so long as they got what they wanted in return. In particular, this meant the establishment of control over public education by the Roman Catholic Church, a longed-for event that became law (the Falloux law) in March 1850. Church-run public education had always appealed to the party of order, whose clerical ties were strong, but it became essential now with the introduction of universal male suffrage. Who, indeed, would teach the workers and the peasants? Who would guide them in their opinions? With the Falloux law, the Church rather than the State became that mentor, in public as well as spiritual affairs—giving rise to hard-fought opposition that would last through the rest of the century.

A last-ditch effort on the part of the left came in the spring 1850 by-elections, as the left put up the writer Eugène Sue for one of the Paris districts.

Sue, raised in wealth, had wandered extensively in Paris's slums and, in the early 1840s, had conveyed his appalled reaction in a wildly popular series of novels, *Les Mystères de Paris* (*The Mysteries of Paris*). It was Sue who introduced readers to the horrors of the *tapis-franc*, a word that—"in the slang of theft and murder," as Sue put it—signified "a drinking shop of the lowest class."[19] These foul dens were in turn run by degraded beings called "ogres" or "ogresses," depending on their sex, and attracted the lowest of the low. Sue's readers descended with him into the depths of these places where in real life they would never, ever dream to go and cried out for reform—as he meant them to.

It was as a reformer that Sue took his seat in the Assembly in 1850, after an overwhelming victory. But his victory—and that of Sue's left-wing Paris colleagues—signaled a still-resilient element of resistance among Paris workers that alarmed the thoroughly bourgeois party of order. These now determined to do something about the dangers of universal suffrage and set to work to restrict the number of those eligible to vote. The outcome, a law of May 31, 1850, did the job nicely, establishing numerous requirements, including the necessity of having paid a personal tax; of having committed no offense, no matter how trivial; and of having stayed at one address throughout the prior three years—the latter being an impossibility for those in search of work. This law easily passed, and the result was exactly what the political right desired: it reduced the electoral body by almost one third. Although no one knew for sure that all of these votes would have gone to the left, it was generally accepted that the left now had no chance of winning the 1852 elections.

The atmosphere of revolution was rapidly disappearing in Paris, as streets were repaved and houses rebuilt. Even the trees of liberty, planted with much ceremony during the revolution's early days, were now uprooted. Social life resumed, with elegant receptions for those in high society and crowded cafés along the boulevards for lesser mortals.

Louis-Napoleon, still a bachelor at forty, enjoyed his pleasures, and Lizzie Howard—the *maîtresse en titre*, or official mistress, as some snidely called her—was only one of a bevy of women with whom he dallied. The Palais de l'Elysée, where he lived (making a point of not moving into the Tuileries, where his uncle Bonaparte had resided) now glittered with splendid balls and receptions. Louis-Napoleon was creating a court around him, and he was looking more and more like an emperor-in-waiting. He flooded army leaders with flattering attention, made regular appearances throughout the country (where he said the right things in the right places), and began to encourage revision of the constitution—in particular, that bothersome section limiting his presidency to one term.

Royalists as well as liberals became increasingly alarmed, especially when, in early 1851, Louis-Napoleon formally requested that the Assembly revise the constitution so he could be elected for another term—on the grounds that this was of the utmost importance, to allow him to continue his mission of doing good and improving the lot of the people. A constitutional revision needed a three-quarters majority to pass, and as Louis–Napoleon toured the provinces, trying to drum up support outside of Paris, Victor Hugo did his utmost to prevent passage, giving an especially thrilling July speech to the Assembly that introduced his famous slam: "Just because we had Napoléon le Grand," he demanded, "do we have to have Napoléon le Petit?!"[20]

Hugo turned back the tide—Louis-Napoleon just missed getting the 75 percent vote he needed to change the constitution. Although the president could do nothing about Hugo, who as a legislator was legally immune, he could and did take other steps of petty revenge, going after Hugo's son Charles, who edited the influential and by now strongly anti-Bonaparte newspaper, *L'Evénement*. Charles, although dramatically defended in court by his father, was convicted of contempt and sentenced to six months in the bleak Conciergerie. Soon after, Hugo's other son, François-Victor, was sentenced to nine months for having urged the government (in *L'Evénement*) to extend political asylum to foreigners, and *L'Evénement* itself was shut down.

But Louis-Napoleon still did not have the constitutional amendment he wanted, and in lieu of this, he began to consider stronger measures. "The President wanted to suppress the Assemblée, the Assemblée to suppress the President," wrote Maxime Du Camp. "No one knew when the crisis would occur, but all were sure that it was inevitable."[21] Rumors of conspiracy flooded Paris, even as Louis-Napoleon considered a September coup but was discouraged by advisers who reminded him that all the leftist representatives in the Assembly would be away from Paris at the time, having gone to their districts for their parliamentary recess. Wait, they advised him, until these representatives returned to Paris in November, so they could be more easily rounded up.

Louis-Napoleon, in his best friend-of-the-people mode, now proposed the repeal of the repressive May 1850 election law. The party of order was appalled, while the republicans were in a flurry, not knowing which way to turn. In the end, most on the left were persuaded that the principal danger remained with the party of order. As Victor Hugo observed in his notebook: "I am not particularly alarmed by the Elysée [Louis-Napoléon], but I am worried about the [conservative] majority."[22] The president's proposal was roundly defeated, doing him no harm whatever but adding significantly to confusion and unrest among the legislators.

One night in late November, the Count de Morny invited Maxime Du Camp to show the president the photographs he had recently taken while in Egypt. Du Camp was an early and enthusiastic amateur photographer, and— as he put it—"at that time [my photographs] were an object of interest, for I was the first to reproduce in this manner the different architectural monuments of Cairo, the ruined temples on the banks of the Nile, the various points of view at Jerusalem."[23] At that time, the Count de Morny himself was also an object of considerable interest, being no less than Louis-Napoleon's illegitimate half-brother.

De Morny, whose illegitimacy was both uncontested and unregretted, was the love child of Louis-Napoleon's mother, Hortense, and the Count de Flahaut. He was three years younger than Louis-Napoleon, and the two had never met until 1849, although Louis-Napoleon learned of his half-brother's existence soon after their mother's death. Described as both "ruthless and charming," de Morny had fought "with great distinction" in North Africa before exchanging his military career for an equally successful (and undeniably ruthless) one in business, making a huge fortune through a series of lucrative but arguably unscrupulous speculations. Although a loyal supporter of the former monarch, Louis-Philippe, Morny had never confused loyalty with his best interests, and after Louis-Philippe's ouster, he quickly navigated to his half-brother's side. Their first meeting was not warm, as the two brothers figuratively paced around one another, sizing each other up. But it ended with Louis-Napoleon observing, "You have a great future to play in the future of France. . . . I will have need of you." Morny in turn declared his devotion, and the pact between them was sealed.[24] Morny quickly became one of Louis-Napoleon's closest advisers.

And so when the Count de Morny asked Maxime Du Camp to show his collection of photographs to the president, whom he thought they might interest, Du Camp promptly appeared on the agreed evening in late November at Morny's Champs-Elysées residence. There, President Louis-Napoleon graciously received him and several others and questioned Du Camp knowledgably about the history surrounding some of the photographs. As the president was leaving, he told Du Camp: "I am at home always on Mondays; I shall hope to see you."

Soon after, Du Camp dined in town with Morny and several others, and in the course of the evening, Morny asked him, "Shall you go to the Elysée on Monday?" Although flattered, Du Camp replied with some hesitation and a shrug. But Morny pressed him. "Do come," he told him. "It will interest you."

Accordingly, on Monday, December 1, 1851, Maxime Du Camp went to the Elysée Palace at about nine in the evening. Noting that there were not many present at the reception, he was interested to see one of Louis-Napoleon's most loyal officers approach the president, who advanced toward him and held him by the button of his coat while speaking with him in low tones for nearly twenty minutes. When the officer left the room, someone joked that the fellow had gone out "as if he was the bearer of a State secret."

As Du Camp soon realized, this was the absolute truth. Louis-Napoleon had confided his project to the man, "and that very night the blow was to be struck."[25]

Louis-Napoleon Bonaparte, future Emperor Napoleon III, here as president of the Second French Republic. Photograph by Gustave Le Gray, 1852. © PVDE / Bridgeman Images

CHAPTER TWO

~

Blood and Empire

(1852)

After leaving the Elysée Palace at about half-past ten, Maxime Du Camp headed for the Opéra Comique, where he arrived just in time for the second act. "The house was thronged," he noted, "and ladies in full dress displayed their neck and shoulders under the light of the chandeliers." In one of the boxes, he could see the Count de Morny, a notorious womanizer, "engaged in fixing a fair young girl with his opera glasses." She, in turn, was "doing her best to attract attention in the balcony."

For the moment, nothing in Paris seemed to have changed. After the Opéra, Du Camp accompanied the poet and critic Théophile Gautier home, walking slowly along the boulevard. "A few cabs drove past us, the ground floor rooms of the great restaurants were brilliant with light, and some few belated pedestrians walked along near us smoking cigars or humming." When the two parted, it was just past one o'clock in the morning, and no soldiers or policemen were in sight.

Du Camp was therefore astonished when he reached home to find his friend Louis de Cormenin waiting for him. The Viscount de Cormenin, a leading republican jurist and political figure, had played a major role in drawing up the Second Republic's constitution. Ardently opposed to tyranny and committed to freedom of religion and universal suffrage, Cormenin nonetheless had defended Louis-Napoleon after the latter's ill-fated 1836 coup attempt in Strasbourg. Now he told Du Camp, "Something extraordinary is going on."

"Just now," Cormenin went on, "at about 12 o'clock, as I passed through the Rue Vieille-du-Temple, I saw that the public printing offices were guarded by a company of the Garde Municipale." He tried to get an explanation but was brushed off. "You will see that tomorrow they will be firing in the streets of Paris," he told Du Camp, who thought he was exaggerating. But the next morning, Du Camp's servant breathlessly informed him that during the night the walls of Paris had been covered with posters, the National Assembly had been dissolved, and several generals had been arrested; regiments of soldiers were marching through the streets.[1]

Similarly, that same morning, Victor Hugo was awakened by his servant, who burst in with the news that sixteen representatives had been arrested in their beds and sent to prison. Not only that, troops now occupied the National Assembly, guards were established in the bell towers, unknown persons had punctured the municipal drums, and the walls of Paris were covered with posters. These proclaimed that the Assembly was plotting a *coup d'état* and that, in response, President Louis-Napoleon vowed to protect all of France's citizens from such skullduggery and restore universal suffrage. In the meantime, Paris was under a state of siege.

The *coup d'état* had taken place.

Louis-Napoleon picked December 2 (or the night of December 1–2) for the coup because it was the anniversary of Napoleon I's coronation. It was also the anniversary of Napoleon Bonaparte's greatest victory, the Battle of Austerlitz. Louis-Napoleon chose this date as a sign of Bonaparte destiny.

His planning was precise and began with what amounted to a vast propaganda operation, starting with the huge number of posters plastered everywhere on the walls of Paris (Cormenin was right about the secrecy at the public printing offices). These posters announced the dissolution of the Assembly and the preparation of a new constitution. They also announced that the new constitution would be ratified by a plebiscite re-endowed with universal suffrage. Louis-Napoleon had thus been careful to outflank his republican opponents on the left and now was just as careful to arrest leading republicans as well as any other significant opponents, all of whom were taken by surprise, many in bed. Those republican members of the Assembly who remained for the moment at liberty protested this gross infringement on the constitution (members of the Assembly were legally protected from arrest) but to no avail: Louis-Napoleon had the support of the army, and the constitution of the Second Republic was now just a piece of paper.

The response was at first subdued but soon became violent. On the first day, Parisians seemed stunned, but by the day after, resistance began. It was on the third day that popular resistance exploded, urged on by republican leaders, including Victor Hugo and Victor Schoelcher, who formed a small resistance committee that urged the people to the barricades. It was now that Louis-Napoleon struck. "The repressive measures—or shall I say aggressive measures?—were brutal," wrote Du Camp. "The soldiers let loose upon the boulevard fired at random, and did not spare their ammunition." Victor Hugo was even more explicit, quoting a bystander who "had not taken three steps on the sidewalk, when the troops, who were marching past, suddenly halted, faced about towards the south, leveled their muskets, and, by an instantaneous movement, fired upon the affrighted crowd." Appalled, the man threw himself facedown on the pavement as "the firing continued uninterruptedly for twenty minutes, drowned from time to time by a cannon shot."[2]

Young Edward Manet and his friend Antonin Proust were among the crowds rioting on the streets and were arrested. They spent the night in the police station. Two days later, they visited Montmartre Cemetery, where the bodies of some of the rioters were buried in a common plot, heads gruesomely above the dirt so that family members could identify them.

Nineteen-year-old Gustave Eiffel, who had arrived in Paris from Dijon two years before to continue his education (at the Latin Quarter's Collège Sainte-Barbe), wrote his mother that "from two till five o'clock we heard the sound of roaring cannon-fire; that was truly sinister. At a given signal everybody stopped and listened and in the general silence we could hear the distant muted sound of cannon-fire; it was frightening." Even though there was little activity in his district, "all the streets are occupied by soldiers."[3]

The brothers Edmond and Jules de Goncourt, residing on the other side of town (on Rue Saint-George, in what is now the 9th arrondissement), watched soldiers fire at people in windows, police "kicking men in the chest, [and] cuirassiers making terrifying charges, pistol in hand, at any cry of 'The Republic for ever!'" The Goncourts' response, while swallowing their anger "with a lot of shame," was to remain "as silent as a carp." After all, it was the safest thing to do.

"On the Day of Last Judgment," they wrote soon after (as always, in the singular voice), "when God the Father . . . questions me about everything to which I have lent the complicity of my eyes, he will doubtless ask me: 'Creature whom I made human and good, have you by any chance seen the bullfight at the Barrière du Combat with five great famished bulldogs tearing to pieces some poor, thin old donkey incapable of defending itself?' To which I will reply, 'Alas, no, Lord, I have seen something worse than that: I have seen a *coup d'état.*'"[4]

By December 4, the resistance was crushed.

⌒

The Goncourts, who began their famous journal on December 2, 1851, were especially dismayed by the coup's impact on their first novel, which was due for publication that very day. With Paris under martial law, their literary debut—which they had greatly anticipated—went almost completely unnoticed. In part, this was the result of their title, *En 18 . . .* , which their terrified printer thought could refer to 18 Brumaire, the date of Napoleon I's *coup d'état*. The frightened man threw all of the Goncourts' promotional posters in the fire and made unapproved cuts of a political nature. According to him, "we had made the most dangerous allusions, six months before, to the events which had just taken place."[5] In any case, with soldiers on the streets, few buyers were to be found, and the book sold only sixty copies—much to the Goncourts' despair.

Alexandre Dumas, who was surprised by the coup, decided that—despite his republican sympathies—it was not worth dying for the cause. But he did make an attempt to defend those in danger. On December 3, responding to rumors that were circulating about a price placed on Victor Hugo's head, he wrote a mutual friend: "Today at six o'clock 25,000 francs have been promised to the person who arrests or kills Hugo. You know where he is. Under no circumstances must he go out."[6]

Despite the danger, Hugo had remained in hiding in Paris, reluctant to abandon his sons, who still were imprisoned in the Conciergerie. But his friends insisted that he get out and had arranged an escape route. Hugo finally agreed, departing from the Gare du Nord for Brussels on the evening of December 11, disguised with a heavy beard, a cloak with upturned collar, and a cap pulled down over his eyes. Befitting his impoverished look, he rode in a second-class carriage and brought with him merely an orange and a ham sandwich.

Alexandre Dumas shortly followed him out of the country, accompanied by his son and pursued not by police but by debt collectors, in the wake of a December 11 judgment of bankruptcy against him. Dumas *fils* dearly loved his father, who had managed to go through several fortunes without a thought to the future, assuming that yet another hit play or serialized novel, like his *The Three Musketeers* or *Count of Monte Cristo*, would save the day. Dumas's lucrative literary production continued to be amazing, but so did his inability to regulate his life. As the son put it, "My father is a great big child whom I had when I was a little boy."[7]

The ranks of exiles swelled as it became clear that the new regime was introducing a compulsory oath of loyalty for those holding public office—something that the Second Republic had abolished as monarchical and adverse to liberty. Those university professors with republican sympathies who had not yet been banished now fled the country, while those who remained—such as the revered historian Jules Michelet—suffered the consequences. Michelet, who had previously been deprived of his chair at the Collège de France, was now relieved of his position as director of the National Archives. Henceforth, he would have to earn his living entirely by writing. Fortunately, he was prolific.

In addition, the regime rounded up a huge number of suspects, assuming that any republican could be arrested on the grounds of having been a potential insurgent, an accomplice of insurgents, or even a source of inspiration for insurgency. With prisons overflowing, justice was summarily dispatched, without allowing evidence for the defense or any appeals. Repression and abolition of rule of law were the order of the day. Looking back, Maxime Du Camp simply commented, "Revolutions produce despotism and despotism produces revolutions. In France," he added, "the oscillations of the political pendulum are excessive; scarcely ever does it pause in the middle where safety and strength are only to be found."[8]

Charles Merruau, who became general secretary of the Seine prefecture after the coup (and thus was among those whom Victor Hugo labeled as "shipmates of a pirate"), later wrote: "Up to the present, since 1789, France, by the weight of its habits and customs, has not been able to raise itself above Caesarism; institutions, such as they are, seem of little consequence for the French; instead, men [charismatic leaders] are everything in their eyes."[9]

Louis-Napoleon, the man of the hour, now took the title "Prince-President" and immediately submitted a new constitution to a vote by universal male suffrage. To prevent any mischance, the voting—by open ballot for the military, by paper ballot for civilians—was done under considerable surveillance. Although resistance persisted in Paris and other large towns (in Paris, out of some 300,000 registered voters, only 133,000 voted in favor, while 80,000 opposed and 80,000 abstained), the result was overwhelmingly in favor of the new constitution. Consequently, with the plebiscite's blessing, Louis-Napoleon could now claim the presidency for a ten-year term, with ministers who depended upon him alone and with other governmental bodies, including a legislature, that now served essentially as rubber stamps. The new prince-president announced the results with much pomp, maintaining the he had "only departed from legality in order to return to the law." And then, perhaps admitting some discomfort with his methods, he added, "More than seven million votes have just absolved me."[10]

Louis-Napoleon quickly made use of the full powers he had been granted, promulgating the constitution and establishing what amounted to an autocracy, even while paying lip service to democracy. In addition to demanding oaths of loyalty for those holding public office, he introduced a wide range of measures to reinforce his position, including repression of the press. His touch was deft: he saw no need for censorship per se, which was unpopular. Instead, the system he imposed consisted merely of a series of warnings. An article considered offensive would draw a warning; after a limited number of warnings, the newspaper would be suspended. Maxime Du Camp, who soon ran afoul of the system, later wrote that it effectively operated as self-censorship: "The pen had to be held suspended over the paper before one dared write a word." He added that, while the system technically applied only to political journalism, it indirectly "reached and ruined many writers who wrote artistic and dramatic criticism, novels, or scientific articles for newspapers," especially as the number of newspapers became limited. The result was that editors, fearful of reporting on politics or anything of any substance whatever, resorted to reporting gossip and scandal—and, of course, finance.[11]

In addition to muzzling the press, Louis-Napoleon subjected taverns and public houses to licensing, on the grounds that they could become hotbeds of opposition politics. He also took stringent measures to ensure that universal suffrage produced only the correct results, by providing voters with official candidates. This meant that after the public was notified of an official candidate, the government would openly campaign for this individual, provide him with public speaking facilities, and issue publicity on his behalf. Any opponent who dared to run could expect considerable harassment—including subtle and no-so-subtle threats to the well-being of the offending party and his family.

On January 1, 1852, evidently pleased with developments, the newly minted prince-president departed from the Elysée Palace for the Tuileries Palace, the residence of the first Bonaparte. It was not difficult to see what was coming.

～

Despite the winds of political oppression, France and the French were not inclined to object so long as the economy was going strong. Louis-Napoleon had in fact already put considerable pep into a sluggish economy through his enthusiastic backing of economic expansion, in which his vision for a reconstructed Paris played a central role. "I want to be a second Augustus," he had written in 1842, from his prison fortress of Ham, "because Augustus . . . made Rome a city of marble."[12] By opening up the dark and narrow tangle of streets of central Paris and replacing aged and sinister tenements with attractive housing blocks, he intended to create a city that was far more welcoming to commerce as well as a pleasanter place in which to live. This meant, to his way of thinking, the necessity of creating unimpeded east-west arteries on both the Right and the Left Banks as well as a central route leading directly from the northern to the southern gates of the city. It also meant connecting the warehouses and passenger stations of the new railroads—not only with each other, but with the city's vital center. In that era of booming new industrialization, the magic word was "railroads."

Already Paris had a scattering of embarkation points and stations around its outskirts, marking the end points of several different railway lines. Unfortunately, these were not connected, nor were they linked in any meaningful way with the center of Paris. Predecessors of the Gare du Nord, Gare de l'Est, Gare de Lyon, Gare d'Austerlitz (originally the Gare d'Orléans), Gare Montparnasse, and the Gare Saint Lazare existed but remained awkwardly unconnected and difficult to reach, whether for freight or passengers.

Complicating matters, in the 1850s, Paris was still a walled city. Its innermost wall, the Farmers-General wall, was merely a tax barrier, built to collect customs for incoming goods (Métro lines 2 and 6 now follow its original course around the Right and Left Banks). But the city's outermost wall, the massive Thiers fortifications—named after then–prime minister Adolphe Thiers—was a bristling defensive wall that had just been completed shortly before the outburst of the 1848 revolution (the ring road, the Périphérique, follows its course around Paris's current city limits). The Thiers fortifications included sixteen forts built outside the wall's perimeter, and there was some concern in higher echelons that in time of war, it might be difficult to connect and supply these. As a result, the idea for a *chemin de ceinture*, or circular railway, began to win support.

By 1851, it had also become clear that it would be a good idea to link the various warehouses of the railway lines then entering Paris. And so in 1851, responding to military need as well as commercial opportunity, Louis-Napoleon signed a decree authorizing the creation of a seventeen-kilometer Right Bank *chemin de ceinture*, which was to run along the interior of the Thiers fortifications and link several important railway lines.

This little railway would for the time being carry only freight, but within a decade, it would carry passengers as well.

Piece by piece the little circular railway expanded, soon completing the circuit around the city and extending spurs to major commercial ventures such as the slaughterhouses of La Villette. By the 1860s, its glory days as a passenger railway began, and by the turn of the century, it would carry almost forty million passengers a year. Familiarly known as the Petite Ceinture, or Little Belt, its demise only came with the twentieth century's construction of the Métro system. But in its heyday, the Petite Ceinture was a necessary— and beloved—part of the fabric of Paris.[13]

⌒

Railroads had become all-important, and entrepreneurs and investors flocked to the opportunity they offered. Among these up-and-coming businessmen, some of the most colorful were the Pereire brothers, who rose from obscurity to challenge the mighty House of Rothschild.

Born in Bordeaux, into a family of Jewish Portuguese immigrants, the older Pereire brother, Emile, decided in 1822 to pursue his fortunes in the far bigger metropolis of Paris. Soon Emile's younger brother, Isaac, joined him, and the two proceeded to work closely together throughout their careers— with the exception of a brief period of chilliness after Isaac (then a widower) fell in love with and proposed to Emile's sixteen-year-old daughter, who of course was Isaac's niece. Under the Napoleonic Code, Emile's consent was requisite for such a marriage, and Emile was uncomfortable with the close relationship. But the marriage took place and seems to have been happy as well as fruitful, producing three children. In any case, the brothers soon decided to let bygones be bygones and resumed working together.

In their early Paris years, Isaac first worked as a journalist, while Emile became a broker at the Bourse, the French stock exchange. During this time, they became followers of Count de Saint-Simon, whose doctrines reflected the buoyant optimism of the age. Saint-Simonians were enthusiastic about the emerging Industrial Revolution, seeing in it the potential for a new social order. This, they agreed, would be achieved rationally, through science and industry, and would benefit all humanity, especially the poor. Saint-Simon's promised land was utopian, but it was so firmly based on logic, method, and rationality that it appealed to a number of scientists as well as industrialists. These followers of Saint-Simon did not aspire to sainthood: the businessmen and industrialists in particular had every expectation of becoming rich, even very rich; they simply thought that it was possible to do so and benefit humanity at the same time.

The Pereire brothers were especially attracted to what Saint-Simonians had to say on the need to develop new and better forms of transportation, whether to increase people's mobility or to foster better circulation of goods. By the 1830s, the newest of the new in transportation was the railroad, aided by the invention of the steam engine. The French had been slow to follow the English with their railroads, but by the 1830s, the Pereire brothers were among the first in France to sense the possibilities, especially given the climate favorable to major business enterprises once Louis-Philippe was on the throne. After visiting England to study the technical problems of construction, the Pereires decided to build a short railroad line (nineteen kilometers) from Paris to Saint-Germain, which would be the first passenger line in France.

Before proceeding, it was necessary to persuade the government to grant a railway concession. Isaac undertook what amounted to a major public relations campaign, overcoming objections from powerful political figures such as Adolphe Thiers, whom Félix Nadar later lampooned for proclaiming to all and sundry that "the wheels will slip without ever advancing"—and when the wheels did not slip, Thiers refused to back down, affirming just as strongly that this newfangled mode of transportation could only be used for short distances.[14] In addition to benighted politicians, another major hurdle was those whose land was threatened by expropriation. Fortunately for the Pereires, a recent (1833) law had facilitated expropriations in the public interest, and the Pereires got what they wanted—a concession for ninety-nine years. Then came the challenge of convincing the bankers, especially Baron James de Rothschild, to invest in their project. Rothschild, who for a time had employed Emile, was at first hesitant. After all, the Pereires were relative youngsters (Emile in 1835 was thirty-five and Isaac was in his twenties), while Rothschild, although still in his forties, was a king in his extensive and powerful realm of banking and finance.

Of course, it had not always been that way. The Rothschilds, like the Pereires, were Jewish but originated in the heavily circumscribed ghetto of Frankfurt. From there, the Rothschild patriarch, Mayer, had seen business opportunities when the French invaded Germany during the 1790s, and Britain's subsequent wars with France created even more financing opportunities for Mayer Rothschild and his five sons. "It is better to deal with a government in difficulties than with one that has luck on its side," Mayer advised his sons, and he also told them that "if you can't make yourself loved, make yourself feared."[15] By 1825, the five Rothschild brothers were well established in Vienna, Frankfurt, and Naples, as well as in London and Paris, and although each son had his own bailiwick, the family stuck together to create a single multinational entity. With riches came status, and Jacob Rothschild became the Baron James de Rothschild, Austrian consul general in Paris, chevalier of the French Legion of Honor, and, after his elder brother's death, leader of the Rothschild clan—a formidable figure in French as well as international finance.

In 1835, James de Rothschild came on board with the Pereires, along with two other investors, and continued his support when the Pereires increased their ambitions and lengthened their railway line, first to Versailles, then to Rouen and Le Havre. Soon the Pereires embarked with Rothschild on their Chemin de Fer du Nord, linking Paris with Lille and Brussels, which became France's first grand line—inaugurated in 1846 with a fine ceremony from the new Gare du Nord. Attending the festivities was an impressive sprinkling of dukes and celebrities, including Victor Hugo and Alexandre Dumas, while in Lille, there was a banquet for two thousand and a performance of *Chant des chemins de fer* (*Song of the Railroads*), a cantata for tenor and six-part chorus written for the occasion (and conducted by) the renowned composer Hector Berlioz.

At this time, James de Rothschild was still heavily involved in financing the Pereires' projects, but tensions between the two parties were beginning to emerge. Rothschild had a way of taking credit for their mutual success as his own personal triumph, the result of his foresight, while for their part, the Pereires were not shy about their own accomplishments. Relations between Rothschild and the Pereires continued to deteriorate, in part because the Pereires, whom Rothschild viewed as parvenus, had the temerity to buy an estate near his own country château. But more fundamentally, strain between the parties grew because they embraced different goals: Rothschild wanted to avoid risk, while the Pereires continued to push for growth.

As 1848 approached, James de Rothschild worried about the possibility of turmoil ahead, although he did not foresee the magnitude of what was coming. A stagnant economy and a seething mass of unhappy people meant trouble, and this kind of trouble signaled danger for the Rothschilds—largely because revolutions cause government bonds to plummet in value, and the Rothschilds held a large proportion of their immense wealth in the form of bonds. The Rothschilds did in fact suffer financially from the tsunami of revolution in France and throughout Europe in 1848–1849 but managed to survive, mainly by pulling together, as they always had. Still, they (and James in particular, as head of the "firm") emerged with an increased preference for risk avoidance, even if it meant lower profitability. In the long run, according to James, it made sense.

Not only did France's 1848 revolution pummel the value of bonds, but the emergence of joint-stock and limited-liability companies now weakened some of the Rothschilds' financial hegemony. The Pereires, in particular, who had once been dependent on the Rothschilds for financing, now had other opportunities for raising money, and they were about to use them.

The Pereires could not have picked a better time to embark on expansion. Louis-Napoleon had, like them, a long history of interest in the theories of Saint-Simon, which promised a rising tide of prosperity for all in return for industrial investment—a happy outcome that most certainly would reinforce Louis-Napoleon's own rule. Accordingly, promptly after his *coup*, the prince-president took steps to encourage industrial expansion, especially on behalf of those fearless buccaneers who were embarked on railway building throughout France.

Louis-Napoleon did not have to start from scratch. For a decade during the railroads' pioneer days, the state had assumed the role of handling railroad infrastructure, while private companies received the responsibility for installing track, stations, and other components of superstructure. Since that time, the state had also maintained the right to control concessions and operating leases. Louis-Napoleon, realizing that he had in hand the proverbial goose with the golden eggs, was liberal in handing out these concessions: in early 1852, soon after his *coup*, he freely dispensed concessions for new lines, including the Lyon-Mediterranean and the Paris-Lyon, granting companies generous (usually ninety-nine-year) operating leases in order to allow them to spread their initial costs over time. By 1857, he had awarded twenty-five railroad concessions, with thirty more to follow during his remaining years of rule.

Not surprisingly, after a period of stagnation between 1848 and 1851, figures for railway investment now boomed, increasing fivefold in the next five years. And the Pereire brothers were positioned to take advantage of it. Instead of relying on Rothschild money, they now devised a new source of income to rival the wealth of the Rothschilds themselves.

In November 1852, Louis-Napoleon (in his last days as prince-president of the Second Republic) signed the decree authorizing the creation of Crédit Mobilier, a new form of financial institution promoted by the ever-inventive Pereire brothers. Originally called the *Banque des grands travaux*, until the finance minister objected to the word "bank" in its title, this institution—a joint stock venture—was formed to lend money not only to governments but to new or developing industrial companies as well as to businesses engaged in trade or public works. Furthermore, it would receive its capital, not from bankers such as Rothschild, but through a large volume of bonds issued to the general public. It was a brilliant idea and one which, given the shares' face value of only 500 francs, was calculated to appeal to a broad spectrum of investors. The Pereires would not have to supply a cent.

Whether or not Crédit Mobilier was intended as a direct challenge to Rothschild financial power, it certainly was a response to James Rothschild's alliance with the Pereires' competitor, Paulin Talabot, together with Rothschild's moves to freeze out the Pereires from financial support for their own railway ventures. The Pereires now found a ready ally in Louis-Napoleon, who faced considerable opposition from the highly conservative French banking sector, which had no interest whatever in his Saint-Simonian goals. The prince-president viewed Crédit Mobilier as a welcome promoter of the kind of business expansion and infrastructure development that he so keenly wanted and did not even bother to consult the Banque de France on the subject. He was also unmoved by Rothschild's warnings of the dangers of joint stock companies in general and one run by the Pereires in particular. Louis-Napoleon, who was well aware of the Rothschilds' preference for the previous Orléanist monarchy, merely shrugged at their warnings, leaving relations icy between him and James de Rothschild for years.

Crédit Mobilier opened brilliantly, with its 500-franc shares immediately soaring in value. At their peak, in early 1856, they were trading at close to 2,000 francs. Crédit Mobilier soon was financing railways, coal mines, and gas companies, among its many large-scale enterprises, most especially including the rebuilding of Paris, which it undertook through its Compagnie Immobilière. It would not be long before Crédit Mobilier would be in a position to threaten the Rothschilds not only in France but throughout Europe and beyond.

⁓

The Pereires found an ally in Louis-Napoleon, but Louis-Napoleon found a valuable ally in the Pereires as well. As Louis-Napoleon's longtime right-hand man, the Count de Persigny, later remarked, it was necessary to find "an instrument that would free the new regime of the domination that financiers usually exercised over governments," especially since established financial interests were so hostile toward Louis-Napoleon and his goals. Without

Crédit Mobilier, he added, Louis-Napoleon's policies "would not have been as bold and free from restrictions as they were."[16]

These bold policies centered on the prince-president's long-desired goals for Paris, which he continued to push ahead. Already started on the Bois de Boulogne and the eastward extension of the Rue de Rivoli, in early 1852, he took up the challenge of creating a north-south route through the city, beginning at the current Gare de l'Est and bringing this new route, called the Boulevard de Strasbourg, as far as the Grands Boulevards, where they became the Boulevard Saint-Denis. And this was only the beginning. There was so much more he wanted to do! Yet most unfortunately, he was running out of money.

It was Persigny, now minister of the interior, who came up with the idea that these huge public works should be regarded as an investment, as "productive expenditure." As he put it, the enormous expenditures on public works necessary to transform Paris "would certainly help the city's finances by producing a huge movement of business and wealth into the capital." In not too many more months a new face at Louis-Napoleon's side, Georges Haussmann, would make the same argument, taking the credit for this discovery, which laid the basis for the glory and the opulence of the Second Empire.

But in the meantime, Louis-Napoleon's current prefect for the Seine, Jean-Jacques Berger, was of a far more conservative bent and was unwilling to proceed without the cash in hand. Louis-Napoleon needed money for the great remodeling of Paris that he had only just begun, and it was to the Pereire brothers that he soon turned.

Now comfortably ensconced in Brussels, Victor Hugo kept up his opposition to Louis-Napoleon. In March 1852, he went to war on the prince-president's plan to pull down the ancient church of Saint-Germain l'Auxerrois to make way for the extension of Rue de Rivoli to the Hôtel de Ville and beyond. Hugo promptly published an outraged article in the *Revue des Deux Mondes* titled "Guerre aux Démolisseurs!" (War on the Wreckers). The church, which stood across from the Palais du Louvre and had served for centuries as its parish church, entered history in 1572 when its bell tolled the signal for the infamous St. Bartholomew's Day Massacre. More concerned with opening a perspective on the Louvre colonnade than with history, Louis-Napoleon had not anticipated the amount of opposition that Hugo could and did stir up. At last, the prince-president gave in and altered his plans, and the church was saved.

But Hugo was not through with Louis-Napoleon. That July he published *Napoléon-le-Petit* (*Napoleon the Little*), a scathing attack on the prince-president and the authoritarian government he had established. "Ever since the second of December, 1851," Hugo wrote, "a successful ambush, a crime, odious, repulsive, infamous, unprecedented, considering the age in which it was committed, has triumphed and held sway." Before that date, Hugo continued, leaders of the right had openly said of Louis-Napoleon, "He is an idiot." But, Hugo added ominously, "they were mistaken." Indeed, this man "knows what he wants, and he goes straight to it; through justice, through law, through reason, through honor, through humanity, it may be, but straight none the less."

Characterizing Louis-Napoleon as someone who "lies as other men breathe," Hugo condemned him as one who would do anything to achieve his ends. Yet Hugo refused to make a great man of the prince-president, even if an evil one: "Though he has committed enormous crimes," Hugo concluded, "he will remain paltry. He will never be other than the nocturnal strangler of liberty."[17]

Paltry, Louis-Napoleon may have been, in Hugo's eyes and in those of others, but the prince-president was still dangerous, and Hugo knew it. Anticipating trouble as soon as the book was published, Hugo left Brussels for the Channel Island of Jersey, where he brought his family (and his mistress) to safety around him. There, he did everything in his power to smuggle a tiny edition of *Napoléon-le-Petit* into France, where it arrived by the thousands, whether in bales of hay, fishing boats, hollowed-out blocks of wood, or trunks with false bottoms. Even balloons were used to float the tiny book-bomb into Louis-Napoleon's France. Helpful tourists came up with numerous ploys to bring the banned book into the country, but customs officers became alert to the problem, leading to long lines, interrogations, and even the occasional strip search at the border.

Hugo regarded all this with satisfaction. "My function," he said, "is somehow sacerdotal. I have taken the place of the magistracy and the clergy. Unlike the judges, I judge, and unlike the priests, I excommunicate."[18]

⌒

Despite the repression, by late March 1852, life as usual had resumed in Paris, where the state of siege was lifted and railway speculation now enthralled. Louis-Napoleon entertained thousands at magnificent balls in the Tuileries and the Ecole Militaire and provided glitter for the masses with a magnificent fireworks display on August 15, the date of his imperial uncle's birth. As the prince-president shrewdly noted, "The future belongs to apathetic people."[19]

Those prepared to work hard and harness the winds of change on their own behalf were already thriving in Louis-Napoleon's Paris. One of these was Aristide Boucicaut, son of a Norman hatter, who had made his way to Paris and worked his way into a position of some responsibility at a small store there. In 1852, having saved or borrowed 50,000 francs, he joined with another willing businessman to open the Left Bank shop the Bon Marché, which at first sold only linens and notions and had a total of twelve employees. Boucicaut soon made fundamental changes, introducing fixed prices as well as a policy of exchanges and refunds—novel practices that appealed to the practical side of the ladies who shopped there. He also invested heavily in newspaper advertising and introduced seasonal sales. Yet as Emile Zola later recognized, in *Au Bonheur des dames* (*The Ladies' Paradise*), female shoppers were especially enchanted with the delightful ambiance that Boucicaut's Le Bon Marché offered. For in this agreeable place, they could browse amid a wide range of tempting merchandise, displayed in an appealing manner. Immersed in this pleasantly seductive atmosphere, goods that one didn't really need suddenly became irresistible, and Le Bon Marché quickly profited. By 1860, Boucicaut had increased the store's annual income from 500,000 francs to five million.

Boucicaut's timing was impeccable, for in 1852 the great boom period of the Second Empire was just beginning, and consumerism—a novel concept for the newly affluent bourgeoisie—was on the rise. So was the inclination to be entertained, and for some time long lines had been forming to see *La Dame aux Camélias* (*The Lady with the Camellias*), which opened at Paris's Vaudeville theater in early February.

The play's author, Alexandre Dumas *fils*, had hurried back to Paris soon after depositing his famous father in Brussels, since he was anxious to attend rehearsals for *La Dame aux Camélias*. After all, it was his first play, which he had adapted from his novel of the same name, and the story was dear to his heart. Dumas *fils*, who was every bit as romantic as his father, although far less flamboyant and self-indulgent, wrote *La Dame aux Camélias* in memory of the beautiful courtesan Marie Duplessis, who had inspired the great tragic love affair of his youth.

When Dumas *fils* met her, Marie Duplessis was young and lovely, emanating the sort of fragility that virtually demanded protection. She had taken to reckless expenditure and drinking to combat her boredom and unhappiness, which her admirers did everything to alleviate. Her demands grew in proportion to their willingness to fulfill them, yet she remained unhappy. Even their roses left her cold. Perhaps she was allergic to roses, or perhaps not, but they made her dizzy. Only camellias, which are odorless, would do.

Dumas, who was but twenty at the time, fell helplessly in love with Marie Duplessis and became eager to provide the protection she needed. But most unfortunately, he did not possess the requisite fortune, and Duplessis was accustomed to going through fortunes. Of course Dumas's father was one of the century's most successful playwrights and novelists, with an income to match, but Dumas *père* was in his own way as irresponsible with money as was Marie Duplessis. No matter how much money Dumas *père* made (and it was a lot), he always managed to outspend his income. An epic womanizer (much like his friend Victor Hugo), he spent freely, was an easy target for loans, and supported not only his current mistresses but also those who had come before.

Dumas *fils* possessed neither his father's taste for adventure nor his gargantuan appetite for life. But he did have this one love, and he desperately wanted to keep her for himself. It was not to be. Not only was Marie Duplessis a devourer of fortunes, but she suffered from a disease of the lungs, which the nineteenth century viewed with romantically infused trepidation. If pretty young girls had to die in nineteenth-century novels, this was the way to do it, and by the time young Dumas met her, Marie Duplessis was in an advanced state of consumption.

Tender and compassionate in his love, young Dumas won her over and seems to have dreamed of reforming her. Yet reform proved impossible. Even worse, as Dumas's debts began to mount, he came to realize that Duplessis was being false to him. Finally, the wounded young man left the beautiful courtesan. Months later, hearing that she was very ill, he wrote to beg her forgiveness, but she never replied. Although by now a pale ghost of her former self, she continued to make the rounds of all the stylish places as her illness progressed. After a long and difficult decline, Marie Duplessis finally died.

Young Dumas was devastated by the news, and upon learning of her death, wrote his novel about her, *La Dame aux Camélias*. In it, he portrayed the Lady of the Camellias as he would have liked her to have been. Marie Duplessis never would have recognized herself as a penitent who renounces her degrading life for the man she loves. But the story was heartrendingly romantic, and it was an enormous hit. It became an even bigger hit when Dumas turned it into a play.

Soon after, Giuseppe Verdi turned the story into *La Traviata* (*The Fallen Woman*), which debuted at Venice's La Fenice opera house in March 1853.

By this time, pitiful deaths of beautiful young girls had become a staple of romantic literature, gobbled up by a public avid for comfortable tears. A related theme, first popularized by Henry Murger in his *Scènes de la vie de bohème* (*Scenes from Bohemian Life*), was any tale involving the romantic suffering of impoverished artists, preferably ones who eked out their existences in the garrets of Paris's Latin Quarter. In time, Giacomo Puccini would turn Murger's stories into his opera *La Bohème*, but by the 1850s *Scènes de la vie de bohème* had already reached an enthusiastic audience, first in the form of stories, then as a play, and finally as a book that appeared in 1851. In the process, the term "bohemian" became shorthand for a particular lifestyle, one dedicated to the creative arts. Although this lifestyle was reputed to be lively, romantic, and carefree, Murger made it plain that, despite moments of humor, hope, and bravado, it was a bleak life, threaded with sadness and crushing poverty.

Murger based his stories, and his book, on his own hard experience as a starving writer in a Paris garret, where he and fellow writers, musicians, and artists (and the women who lived with them) eased the troubles of their day-to-day existence with good-natured camaraderie, sharing what little they had just to get by. The "water drinkers," they joshingly called themselves, since they barely had enough money to buy wine. Love, devotion, and sex played a pivotal role in this difficult existence, but dreams of creative achievement were what pulled these artists and intellectuals forward, along with a determination not to betray their particular vision for mere money. Art for Art's Sake was their creed.

Although the term "bohemian" had already come to describe the unconventional lifestyles of an earlier era's young Romantics, and also referred to gypsies and nomadic peoples, it was Murger who permanently stamped the word "bohemian" with the meaning of an artistic subculture that thrived, or at least persisted, in dense urban settings—especially in Paris. As he put it, "Today, as in the past, any man who enters the path of Art, with his art as his sole means of support, is bound to pass by way of Bohemia." And bohemia, for Murger as for so many others, could only exist in Paris, the Paris of the Latin Quarter: "Bohemia," he stated, "neither exists nor can exist anywhere but in Paris."

Yet Murger was not enamored with bohemian life. "Bohemia is a stage of the artist's career," he wrote; "it is the preface to the Academy, the Hospital or the Morgue."[20] He knew whereof he spoke. Murger, the son of a concierge, had lived the life of a starving writer and indeed used himself as the model for Rodolphe in *Scènes de la vie de bohème*. His life had been replete with hardship but not because he wanted it so. His novel—unlike Puccini's opera—ends not with Mimi's death but with the characters renouncing their bohemian ways and entering bourgeois society, finding acceptance in official circles and learning to pay their debts. By this time, rather than return to their old haunts, they are quite prepared to reject their former principles and threadbare past for warm lodgings and a good meal.

"I no longer care for anything but what is good and comfortable," one of the characters declares.[21] Bohemia may have been fine for a moment but not for a lifetime.

∿

Paris's Left Bank bohemia rubbed side by side with the poorest of the working or nonworking poor. And islanded in the midst of all this deprivation was the Sorbonne.

Founded in 1257 by a high-ranking clergyman, Robert de Sorbon, its original purpose was to provide a small college to lodge poor students at the University of Paris. The university itself, founded in 1200, owed its existence to town-and-gown tensions, student protests, and the monarch's decision to grant the students certain rights and protections. These relied heavily on enforcement by the powerful Roman Catholic Church, under whose jurisdiction the students now came. This bothered few, as the concept of the separation of church and state was yet a long way off. Indeed, to be a student in those days was to be a cleric, albeit a lowly one. For years this jumble of religiously affiliated but dismaying worldly students trooped through Paris, annoying their teachers and creating havoc in the local taverns. But in the end, everyone usually managed to sort things out.

And then, in the thirteenth century, members of the newly formed Dominican and Franciscan orders showed up. These newcomers, who had originated as mendicant, or begging, orders, had little in common either with those destined to become priests or those who would become members of monastic orders. The Dominican and Franciscans friars were teaching orders, and they brought with them some of the most brilliant teachers of the age, including young Thomas Aquinas. Conflict soon erupted between them and the University's theology faculty (then located at Notre-Dame), and the University attempted to expel the newcomers. Before long, the fracas reached the Vatican, leading to excommunication and a temporary shutdown of the University.

It was then that Robert de Sorbon began looking at real estate on the Left Bank. He purchased several properties, intent on turning them into endowed lodgings for poor students—specifically for those who were not Dominican or Franciscan friars. Sorbon, not coincidentally, was chaplain to the king, Louis IX (known to history as St. Louis), who supported this project. After all, the Dominicans and Franciscans came under the direct authority of the pope, and despite his saintliness, Louis was no pushover when it came to protecting his royal prerogatives. Sorbon's project offered a way of quietly opposing the friars without direct confrontation.

Given this royal seal of approval, the College de Sorbon, or the Sorbonne, prospered. Instead of competing with the Theology Faculty, it supported it by providing room and board for its poorest students. In time, Sorbon's college replaced the cloister of Notre-Dame as the official seat of the Faculty of Theology, and by the seventeenth century, the Sorbonne had become an established power in theological circles. It had also clearly outgrown its by-now shabby facilities, and Cardinal Richelieu—Louis XIII's powerful prime minister, who was also Chancellor of the Sorbonne—replaced the Sorbonne's medieval structures with a far larger and grander arrangement, whose centerpiece was an impressive Baroque chapel that would eventually house Richelieu's own magnificent tomb.

Not surprisingly, the Sorbonne's theologians did not adapt well to the increasingly secular and scientific world of the Enlightenment, and by the time of the Revolution, its Faculty of Theology had earned a well-deserved reputation for flint-hard conservatism. This conservatism did not sit well with the Revolutionaries, who shut down the entire university, including the Sorbonne. They had only just begun to set up their own secular and scientifically oriented educational system when Bonaparte came to power—bringing the university under his own imperial supervision, kicking out all references to the Enlightenment, and restoring the Faculty of Theology. But this was not the same as restoring the Sorbonne, which for a time was occupied by a group of artists who had just been evicted from their residence in the Louvre.

Soon after returning to power, the Bourbon monarchs expelled these artists once again, and the Sorbonne now became the seat of the Faculties of Letters and Sciences as well as the Faculty of Theology. But the goal of the hidebound Bourbons was not simply to restore the Sorbonne, or even to expand its mission, but to bring the Faculties of Letters and Sciences under the influence of the Sorbonne's conservative Faculty of Theology. In this, it was only partly successful, and by the time Louis-Napoleon surveyed the scene, resistance to clericalism in the Sorbonne was rising.

But what especially drew Louis-Napoleon's attention to the Sorbonne was its location, in the heart of a tangle of dark and tiny streets occupied not only by students but by a dense jungle of Paris's poor. This was one of those Paris quarters that had erupted with the most violence during the bloody days of June 1848, and it remained a hotbed of sullen anger and bitterness, prone to insurrection. Louis-Napoleon viewed the entire area as a blight that needed to be eradicated, and from the outset, he prepared for major demolition, not only to aerate the quarter and improve sightlines and traffic flow but to prevent future barricades from going up.

Specifically, his plan—on which he embarked in 1852—was to pierce through the Rue des Ecoles, to make it a grand east-west thoroughfare on the Left Bank parallel to the Rue de Rivoli on the Right Bank. As a bonus, this urban cleanup would also isolate the Sorbonne, making it "a monumental independent island, with easily controlled access" in case of future turmoil nearby.[22]

It would be a major undertaking, but Louis-Napoleon had no qualms about what he was doing. After all, he already was exercising the powers of an absolute monarch, and he expected that soon he would hold the imperial title as well.

～

In preparation for his final power grab, Louis-Napoleon decided to visit southern France, where Bonapartism had never been popular and where the population needed some careful persuading. Proceeding along a ceremonial route lined with troops shouting "Long live the Emperor!" and brightened with entertainment and festivals, the prince-president made a series of important speeches in which he assured his audiences that he had only their welfare in mind and that under his rule France would always remain a bastion of peace and prosperity. With a significant nod to the Church, he also placed religion and morality in the same praiseworthy category.

In Bordeaux, Louis-Napoleon received an especially regal welcome, engineered by its prefect, Georges Haussmann, who made exactly the kind of impression on the prince-president that he had hoped for. Clearly, those around Haussmann knowingly nodded, this particular prefect could anticipate reaping great benefit from the red carpet he had so magnificently unfurled.

But now, eyes were riveted on the prince-president, who had almost reached his long-sought-for imperial crown. With all potential opposition quashed, Louis-Napoleon took this final step upon his return to Paris that autumn, revising the constitution to take the title of Emperor—as Napoleon III, out of respect for his deceased cousin, Bonaparte's son, who had been known in certain quarters as Napoleon II.

Presenting this momentous (but hardly unexpected) event before the voting public for its ratification, the new emperor was gratified to receive an overwhelming vote of approval. With this in hand, he proceeded to make his official proclamation of the Second Empire on December 2, 1852, the anniversary of his coup as well as of the duo of dates recalling the first Bonaparte.

Napoleon III's Second Empire was about to begin.

Baron Georges Haussmann. Photograph by Pierre Pepetit, circa 1850. © Selva / Bridgeman Images

CHAPTER THREE

~

Enter Haussmann

(1853)

Georges-Eugène Haussmann, who was about to become the second most powerful man in the empire, was French, despite his Germanic name. Born in 1809 in Paris, not far from l'Etoile (now Place Charles-de-Gaulle), he came from a family that, many years before, had relocated from the Rhineland to France, where at that time they found the freedom to practice their Protestant religion. The Haussmanns kept their Lutheran faith throughout the years, even after the revocation of the Edict of Nantes in 1685 led to widespread religious persecution in France. Despite his minority status, Georges Haussmann remained a Protestant throughout his life.

Haussmann followed in the family footsteps in his career as well as his religion—his grandfather had been a public administrator before becoming commissar to the revolutionary armies of the Rhine, and his father had become a war commissar and quartermaster during the Napoleonic wars. Haussmann's maternal grandfather, also of German Protestant origins, fought in the American Revolution before serving on Bonaparte's general staff, where he was made a baron of the empire. He was in the service of Prince Eugène de Beauharnais (son of Empress Josephine) when his grandson Georges-Eugène was born. "Eugène" was added to the child's name in honor of the prince, who agreed to serve as his godfather.

Raised in the home of his paternal grandparents, Haussmann later recalled that it was his grandfather who brought him up. "Thanks to a great aptitude for impressions common to all children," he wrote in his memoirs, "I was influenced by the methodical habits and orderly principles that reigned in the

45

house of that truly wise man, much as in his clear, sensible, and well-ordered mind." It was to this upbringing that Haussmann attributed "the sense of duty, the calm firmness, and the indefatigable perseverance that have given me the ability to deal with so many obstacles."[1]

Clearly a serious young man, Haussmann focused on his studies at Paris's prestigious Collège Henri-IV, where he was top in his class, and then attended the Collège Bourbon (now the Lycée Condorcet), where he passed the baccalaureate with flying colors. Still, life was not always easy for him. Not only did he suffer from delicate health, but he also endured taunts and snubs for his Germanic name as well as for his religion. Years later, he confessed in his memoirs that, "coming as I did from a family that had had to endure many trials to keep its faith, and having been brought up in a dissident community surrounded by an often intolerant Catholic majority, I learned from childhood to detest persecution . . . and to respect . . . all sincere beliefs, whether religious or political."[2]

By the age of seventeen, young Haussmann was ready to enter law studies at the Ecole de Droit, where he kept up the hard work. But he took his nose out of the law books long enough to broaden his horizons by attending lectures at the Sorbonne and the Collège de France—lectures in philosophy, mathematics, and physics, as well as in geology and music. This rigorous schedule prepared him well for the diverse challenges in the career of his choice, in public administration, and during the reign of Louis-Philippe, he methodically climbed the administrative ladder, moving from one administrative post to another, honing his organizational and management skills along the way.

By the time of Haussmann's impressive welcome for Louis-Napoleon in Bordeaux in 1852, he had married wealthily, had fathered two daughters, and was living comfortably in the Bordeaux area, where he was prefect. He had earned a reputation for tirelessly exploring the geographical areas for which he was responsible and for introducing many improvements—whether draining swamps or building roads, canals, and suspension bridges. He had learned to organize parties and balls (a skill that would serve him well in the future) and had made important connections, with an ever-constant eye on advancement. He had also earned a reputation for being curt, inconsiderate, and arrogant, and he was not shy about pulling strings or letting his ambition show.

Admired but not loved, Haussmann had been promoted to the rank of officer in the Legion of Honor just before the 1848 revolution broke out. There was talk of a high-level prefect appointment, but the revolution put all that temporarily on hold, even as the Assembly became increasingly wary of Parisian autonomy and restored the old system, in which the prefect of the Seine, rather than a mayor, served as chief executive of the capital.

Soon after Louis-Napoleon's election in 1848, Haussmann met with the prince-president, during which he expressed his idolization of Prince Eugène and his long-held Bonapartism, which had been a fundamental part of his upbringing. Louis-Napoleon assured him that he would indeed be rewarded, and two appointments quickly followed, neither of which was to Haussmann's liking but in which he once again proved his loyalty and his worth. Then, immediately following the *coup d'état*, he met with the Count de Morny, who did not waste words but asked him, "Monsieur Haussmann, are you with us?" Haussmann promptly replied: "My life belongs to the Prince; use me without reservation."[3]

Still another appointment followed, this time to Bordeaux and the Gironde, where there was serous unrest following the 1851 *coup*. Acting with characteristic firmness, Haussmann issued strict orders, including the threat to shoot any rebel who carried a weapon. Having thus repressed insurgence, Haussmann now delivered the vote for his prince-president, who received the presidency for an extended ten-year term. Haussmann then prepared a royal welcome for Louis-Napoleon in Bordeaux, as the prince-president prepared to seize the imperial crown.

Following Louis-Napoleon's proclamation of empire in 1852, Haussmann once again delivered the vote for his master—under circumstances that understandably favored the incumbent. Haussmann's reward came shortly after, in June 1853, when the emperor appointed him prefect of the Seine.

〜

There remained one more major job opening for the newly proclaimed Napoleon III to fill, and that was for empress. An emperor clearly needed an empress—of that, few were in doubt. Even Louis-Napoleon, who thoroughly enjoyed his bachelor status, was reluctantly inclined to agree. His regime was a personal one, and he already was forty-four years old; if he should disappear without a direct heir, his empire would likely collapse. With this in mind, Louis-Napoleon's entourage went about with perhaps unseemly haste to secure a bride for the new emperor—a task complicated by the fact that none of the leading royal houses of Europe were interested in an alliance with the heir of their old enemy Bonaparte.

Lizzie Howard, Louis-Napoleon's faithful and supportive mistress, seems to have dreamed of marriage, but clearly she would not do: a mistress, especially one of insignificant birth, could not make the leap to such an exalted position.

And so it was that Eugenia de Montijo, a beautiful twenty-six-year-old Spanish countess, entered the competition for the new emperor's hand.

Eugenia, daughter of the late Count of Montijo, arrived at the imperial court with her mother in October 1852, shortly before the proclamation of empire. She immediately turned heads, not the least that of Louis-Napoleon. Eugenia was a striking auburn-haired beauty, whose mother—herself a beautiful woman, with a history of many lovers—was determined to find good marriages for both of her daughters. The older had already married wealthily in Spain; now the mother, Maria Manuela, had her eye on Louis-Napoleon for her second daughter.

But this daughter was hardly a pushover and, on an earlier visit to Paris, had coolly brushed off Louis-Napoleon's advances. Now, she was determined to hold out for marriage. Louis-Napoleon, judging that, at the advanced age of twenty-six, Eugenia was getting too old for husband-hunting, at least at the rarified level on which she was operating, renewed his stratagems but without success. One story, of an overheard conversation between the two at the château of Compiègne, had Louis asking, "What is the way to your heart?" To which she replied, "By the church, Sire."

By this time, most of the court and a good part of Paris knew that Louis-Napoleon was mad for Eugenia and that she was holding out. Adding to the difficulties, Louis's ministers and close associates were opposed to the match. As the Count de Morny put it, "If [the emperor] couldn't find a royal princess, why couldn't he at least have chosen a French countess, not a Spanish one!" Similarly, the Count de Persigny did his best to derail the match, circulating pamphlets smearing both Eugenia and her mother.

Desperate to bring Louis-Napoleon to a decision, Eugenia and her mother decided that they would inform the emperor that they intended to leave Paris. Arriving at a court ball on the arm of the Baron James de Rothschild, Eugenia was brought to a table reserved for the wives of Louis Napoleon's ministers, one of whom angrily told her that there was no room at the table for a foreign adventuress. Overhearing this fracas, Louis-Napoleon rescued Eugenia and her mother by inviting them to join him on the imperial dais. He then led Eugenia to the dance floor, after which they left the ballroom for his study. There, she told him that she was prepared to live dangerously by his side, but she would no longer stay at the court to be insulted. At this, the emperor at last proposed.

Writing her sister with the news, Eugenia (soon to be known as Eugenie) confided that the Emperor "has been so noble, so generous with me, he has shown me so much affection that I am still overcome." She then added, "He has struggled with the Ministers and conquered." For his part, Louis-Napoleon announced the news to a packed assembly of his Senate, Legislature, and

Council of State. "I have chosen a woman I love and respect," he told them, "rather than one unknown to me or an alliance which would involve sacrifices as well as advantages. In a word, I put independence of mind, a warm heart and domestic happiness above dynastic interests."

They married within two weeks, on January 30, 1853, at the great cathedral of Notre-Dame. Eugenie, wearing white velvet and a diamond crown, curtseyed low to the crowd at the door when she arrived—a surprising action but a brilliant one, which immediately won them over. Upon the couple's emergence from the cathedral, the crowd cheered.

Empress Eugenie, portrait by Franz Xaver Winterhalter. © Bridgeman Images

But not everyone was persuaded. "We are living in a society of adventurers," reported the British ambassador, Lord Cowley, to London. "The great one of all," he continued, "has been captured by an adventuress."[4]

~

Napoleon III, the recently wedded adventurer, now embarked on what would become an era of stunning prosperity and expansion. Unquestionably authoritarian, he nonetheless seemed genuinely concerned for the well-being of his people: as he said in his December 2, 1851, proclamation, he aimed to "bring the age of revolutions to a close by satisfying the legitimate needs of the people." Not that it was ever easy to see into Louis-Napoleon's mind: Zola referred to him as "the enigma, the sphinx," and the emperor's cousin, Princess Mathilde Bonaparte, who had been briefly engaged to him in their youth, remarked to the Goncourts that, "if I had married him, I would have broken open his head to discover what was inside it."[5]

Genial and charming to all, Louis-Napoleon was rarely roused to anger and, given his reputation as an inveterate womanizer, had been brushed off by many as a lightweight in the course of his somewhat erratic career. But this particular lightweight was politically adroit and remarkably nimble. By successfully navigating the dangerous shoals of the 1848 revolution and Second Republic, he had at last established himself as emperor—over a restored empire, as he was careful to point out. And now he was determined to fulfill France's greatness—not by foreign conquest, like his uncle, but by pushing and propelling his nation into the modern age.

Napoleon III's Second Empire gave pride of place to economic development, on the assumption that a booming economy would provide wealth and well-being for all. And at the heart of this grand vision was the emperor's plan to remake Paris. Even before his declaration of empire, he had dreamed dreams, creating that color-coded map of the city with his priorities for change and demolition arranged by hue. Choosing what he viewed as a middle course between reaction and revolution, he took command of the ship of state and began to remake the city even before he claimed the imperial title.

Over the centuries, other rulers had undertaken massive building projects, largely as a means of accommodating Paris's growth while providing for its security. This meant an ever-larger series of defensive walls, going back to the third-century Gallo-Romans, who walled what now is the Ile de la Cité, and twelfth-century King Philip Augustus, whose wall, anchored by the Louvre fortress, girdled both sides of the Seine. By the late fourteenth century, the burgeoning city was pushing hard against the confines of Philip's outdated wall, even as English enemies were pressing from without. A new wall then went up, encircling a far larger portion of the Right Bank, which had emerged as the commercial center of Paris (the students on the Left Bank were left to fend for themselves). This was anchored at its easternmost point by a new fortress, the Bastille. Two centuries later, as civil warfare engulfed France, Louis XIII extended this wall, creating a new and larger shell for the prospering Right Bank city within.

The Sun King, Louis XIV, demolished these walls, declaring that they no longer were necessary in the wake of his decisive defeat of all his enemies. This left what became the Grands Boulevards on the traces of the former bulwarks, stretching in a semicircle from what now is the Place de la Madeleine in the west to the Place de la Bastille in the east. But the defensive walls were much missed by royal tax collectors, as they had served to stop smugglers from evading the traditionally steep royal tariffs on incoming goods. The royal solution was a new wall around Paris, one whose sole purpose was to buttress the royal tax collectors—also known as tax farmers, or the Farmers-General. This wall, known as the Farmers-General wall, went up in a hurry in the 1780s, ringing Paris with more than sixty tollhouses linked by a substantial wall, roughly circular in shape and more than fifteen miles in circumference.

Although the wall's tollhouses were architect-designed and beautiful, Parisians were not impressed, and when revolution broke out, they destroyed all but four.[6] But the Farmers-General wall managed to survive, since Napoleon Bonaparte and subsequent regimes found it, and the income it collected, useful. So this somewhat-battered relic was still standing when Louis-Napoleon Bonaparte assumed the imperial crown.

By this time, Paris had continued its surge outward, into areas such as Passy, Montmartre, and Belleville. In the 1840s, reflecting this new ring of growth, the government under King Louis-Philippe enclosed Paris within yet a larger and more bristling wall. Named after France's then-premier, Adolphe Thiers, the Thiers Fortifications with their sixteen forts now stood ready to withstand all comers as Louis-Napoleon began his reign.

Of course, other rulers throughout French history had sought to beautify and improve Paris, perhaps none more so than rough and gruff Henri IV, with the creation of his beautiful Place des Vosges in the Marais and his harmonious and elegant western entrance to the city— featuring massive additions to the Seine-side Louvre and the completion of the Pont Neuf, or New Bridge, as well as the creation of Place Dauphine.

Napoleon Bonaparte had also entertained visions of Paris: "I intend to make Paris the most beautiful capital in the world," he once remarked, and he set about this task with dizzying focus and energy. He was responsible for the stone embankments around the Ile de la Cité and along a portion of the Right and Left Banks. He added four more bridges, including the popular footbridge linking the Ile de la Cité and the Ile Saint-Louis, as well as the stone Pont d'Austerlitz and Pont d'Iéna (both named in honor of his victories) and an iron footbridge, the Pont des Arts, linking the Louvre and what now is the Institut de France. He began work on the Louvre's massive northern wing and started the new Rue de Rivoli, from the Place de la Concorde. Not about to leave his place in history to chance, he did not overlook monuments dedicated to his own glory, including his work on the Vendôme Column, the Arc de Triomphe, and the Arc du Carrousel, as well as his makeover of the Church of La Madeleine and the Palais Bourbon in a style more in keeping with the neoclassical tastes of the time.

In addition to monumental fountains (especially the large sphinx-bedecked Fontaine du Palmier in the Place du Châtelet), Bonaparte planned a vast imperial city on the site of the current Place du Tracadéro and the Palais de Chaillot, visualized as extending all the way to the Bois de Boulogne— a grandiose scheme that fell by the wayside after Waterloo.

Bonaparte's successors, Louis XVIII and Charles X, completed the Bourse (the neoclassical structure housing the stock exchange) as well as a network of canals (the St-Denis and the St-Martin) that connected the wide-swinging loops of the Seine. They also continued work on the Madeleine and resumed construction on the Arc de Triomphe while commissioning several new bridges, including the Pont de l'Archvêché (at the tip of the Ile de la Cité) and a pedestrian bridge linking the Right Bank to the Ile de la Cité (now replaced by the Pont d'Arcole).

King Louis-Philippe's prefect of the Seine, Claude-Philibert de Rambuteau, completed work on the Arc de Triomphe, the Madeleine, the Hôtel du Quai d'Orsay, and several town halls and improved prisons and hospitals. He paved streets; built public fountains, sidewalks, and drains; and planted trees. Under Rambuteau's direction the quays and the Seine's retaining walls were extended, and gas was supplied to customers through concessions to private companies. Perhaps most striking, Rambuteau decided to cut directly into the urban fabric with a straight and wide street (since named in his honor) that required a large number of compulsory purchases, through an ancient slum to the north of Les Halles. He thus, not by chance, eradicated the very streets where the uprising of 1832 took place—the one that Victor Hugo so memorably commemorated in Les Misérables.

Still, by the time Louis-Napoleon came to power, Paris remained a city of just under a million people hemmed in by the old toll wall and living in tall, narrow houses lining dark and often filthy streets. More than one-third of the city's inhabitants were crammed into the city's small and concentrated center, where they fought for survival or simply eked out their lives. Traffic throughout the city was impeded by the tolls placed on the city's bridges, and although several squares—including the Place des Vosges, the Place Vendôme, and the Place de la Concorde—broke up the dense urban fabric, the Grands Boulevards were crowded, and even the Champs-Elysées was still only a dusty road between the Place de la Concorde and the Rond-Point. Beyond, the Arc de Triomphe simply marked l'Etoile, one of the entrances through the toll wall, while beyond the toll wall stretched a ring of rural communes, themselves encircled, or in some cases even bisected, by the Thiers fortifications.

This was a city marked by an almost savage divide between opulence and poverty, with as many as 650,000 impoverished residents (workers and unemployed) out of a population of just under a million. Perhaps 180,000 Parisians were of the various ranks of the middle class, or bourgeoisie, while the remaining population was largely made up of domestic servants who resided with their employers. Already, western Paris was the abode of the well-to-do, while the poor clung to life in the eastern and central portions of town.

Thus, while Paris by Napoleon III's reign had become France's center of banking and finance as well as of industry and manufacturing, its opulence was pockmarked by large areas of dirt- and disease-infested slums that bred regular outbreaks of cholera. This dense tangle of streets, dark and congested, was a nightmare for anyone trying to cross the city, whether in horse-drawn carriage, on horseback, or by walking. Men carried goods on their backs or in handcarts or wheelbarrows, dodging horses and carriages (in 1853, some six thousand horse-drawn carriages traversed the Grand Boulevards in a twenty-four-hour period). Traffic was impeded by the warren of small streets—"impenetrable labyrinths," as one historian has called them[7]—that one had to traverse in order to get anywhere. All this intensified as the city's population continued to rise.

Adding to the difficulties in getting from one point to another, the railway stations (the Gare du Nord, the Gare de l'Est, the Gare de Lyon, the Gare Montparnasse, the Gare Saint Lazare, and the Gare d'Orléans, now the Gare d'Austerlitz) were unconnected with one another and difficult to reach from the center of town. Something had to be done to link them and to provide access to the city center. Other forms of transportation were just as hamstrung, with six-horse stagecoaches thundering into stations that were difficult to reach and completely inadequate to handle the traffic. Even the Seine was overcrowded, with rafts now having to stop outside of town, and large shipments of hay, wheat, and wine piling up, waiting for delivery.

Louis-Napoleon saw the railway stations as the true gateways of the city, and he was intent on providing north-south and east-west transportation arteries as well as green spaces throughout every part of Paris. And yes, he wanted to open up areas that had been bastions of insurrection and to facilitate troop movement—on wider streets that could not be easily blockaded by a few mattresses and a pile of junk. Order and prosperity marched together to his way of thinking, and he was convinced that his *grands travaux* would achieve what the National Workshops had failed to do, offering a solution to economic crisis. In the process, the cleanup of ghastly slums would, to his view, improve the morals of the people who lived in them.

Louis-Napoleon had already begun the work but was stymied by his then-prefect of the Seine, a cautious bureaucrat by name of Jacques Berger, who—much to his employer's exasperation—was unwilling to fund such grandiose plans on credit. Unlike Berger, Louis-Napoleon strongly believed that the development of amenities and infrastructure in Paris would pay for itself by having a multiplier effect upon the economy as a whole. In this, he was supported by Persigny. And soon, he would be supported by Georges Haussmann.

Although Louis-Napoleon had long nurtured his dreams, he needed someone to carry them out. Georges Haussmann would be his great organizer, the one who would push, prod, and transform dreams into reality.

Haussmann first saw the map—the original map that Louis-Napoleon had created when in exile and had brought with him to Paris after his election—in a private tête-à-tête with the emperor immediately after being sworn in as prefect. After displaying an appropriate amount of enthusiasm, he warned the emperor that although the people of Paris would in the main be supportive of this kind of improvement, he might well encounter opposition, especially from the powerful and wealthy *haute bourgeoisie* (upper middle class). Louis-Napoleon seemed neither surprised nor disturbed by this observation and replied that he would simply override any opposition by dissolving the conservative and potentially stiff-necked municipal council and creating a more supportive body in its place. Haussmann, who well knew the emperor's power but understood the dangers of creating enemies at the outset, warned him to be cautious and wait until such steps were absolutely necessary (in the end, Haussmann prevailed over the councilors, and the council remained). And then, after an exhausting and somewhat troubling day, Haussmann moved into to his suite of offices and living quarters in the Hôtel de Ville.

Work on the Hôtel de Ville, the town hall for all of Paris, had been completed just before the 1848 revolution, and Haussmann's apartments, in the wing facing the Seine, were luxurious and included several reception rooms on the first floor.[8] The first floor also featured a large Festive Hall, facing east in an adjoining wing overlooking the main courtyard, the Cour Louis XIV, which for the moment featured a statue of the Sun King. After Haussmann's arrival, this particular effigy would give way to a monumental staircase, providing an impressive entrance to the Festive Hall—in time for Queen Victoria's visit.

Other buildings and annexes soon followed the new prefect's arrival, for the Hôtel de Ville had nowhere near the number of offices necessary to accommodate the functions of the Seine prefect, whose responsibilities stretched beyond the city of Paris and included the districts of Saint-Denis and Sceaux. In addition to his primary responsibilities, Haussmann took great care to decorate these offices and meeting rooms with appropriate murals, carvings, and ceiling paintings.

The new prefect also set up a private study next to his bedroom, with an internal staircase leading directly to his first-floor office. This setup functioned as a kind of war room, for Haussmann kept a secretary on duty round-the-clock (often working late into the night to come up with the figures or clarifications that the prefect urgently needed for the following day). It was in his private study that Haussmann set up a unique map of his own, mounted on casters, that he could consult at any moment.

This map was the result of Haussmann's appalled discovery that Paris did not have an up-to-date official survey map. Roadbuilding in Paris had always proceeded informally, and this way of doing things was now creating a huge mess with the Rue de Rivoli extension as it slowly made its way toward the Hôtel de Ville. Most unfortunately, when this much-ballyhooed east-west artery reached the tower that remained from the ancient Church of Saint-Jacques de la Boucherie, workers were surprised to discover that the variations in land height between the road and its surrounding area were far greater than anyone had anticipated, being off by several feet. This was an astonishing difference, and something that immediately raised the question of how to join the new Rue de Rivoli with the streets attempting to cross it, as well as with its access to the Pont Notre-Dame, whose entrance was already sufficiently steep to cause comment. Even the stability of the tower of Saint-Jacques de la Boucherie was threatened, and there was talk about having to pull it down.

Soon Haussmann found the man he wanted to provide the kind of technical support he needed—Eugène Deschamps, a Paris architect and land surveyor to whom Haussmann later (and uncharacteristically) paid tribute as "a man of unrivaled merit," who demonstrated his "unquestionable superiority" for the seventeen years he spent by the prefect's side. In talks with section heads and lower-level civil servants (whom Haussmann, to his credit, had worked with throughout his career), the prefect had spotted Deschamps as someone with the kind of knowledge and preference for plain speaking that he needed. At the time, Deschamps's survey office formed an insignificant part of the *voirie de Paris* (Paris Department of Transport), which in turn was buried deep in the bureaucracy along with a number of other offices dealing with the city's infrastructure. Haussmann doubled the size of Deschamps's office, placed him in charge, and promoted the office to a far more prominent place on the organizational chart. Within a few years, the once-lowly Department of Transport would become a major department responsible for all official maps and surveys for the City of Paris.

Deschamps's new responsibilities were breathtaking: as Haussmann later put it in his memoirs, "I formed the plan to make M. Deschamps my immediate assistant for the principal and certainly the most arduous part of the great project for which I had assumed responsibility." Deschamps's job, first, was to "draw up the whole new system of major roads that were needed throughout Paris in order to implement the emperor's program." Next, "while this vast program was being carried out," his job would be "to study carefully the route of each section in the smallest detail." At that point, he would decide which properties the government would take over, in compulsory purchases (expropriation), and finally—in a function requiring the utmost sensitivity and discretion—Deschamps would estimate the value of these properties. In all of these duties, Haussmann relied on the "integrity of [Deschamps's] character" and "the reliability of his work."[9] Haussmann would not be disappointed in his choice.

Not surprisingly, given the disaster that the Rue de Rivoli project had become, Haussmann immediately asked Deschamps to prepare a survey for the entire area of Paris as contained within the Farmers-General wall. This enormous project required that Paris be divided into a multitude of adjacent triangles, minutely measured and fitted together into divisions and then into a general map of the city. This map showed the alignments of the old roads and—as the program proceeded—the lines where new roads would go. It also recorded spot heights. Haussmann had this survey map made up on large sheets on a scale that he could accommodate, on casters, in his private study. He would soon publish a smaller reproduction (still a cumbersome five feet by eight) and an even smaller reproduction for the general public.

In the past, Haussmann had found good people to work for him, and his ability to spot talent was especially noteworthy here. Eugène Deschamps would play a primary role in creating the Paris of the Second Empire. And it was his map, not the emperor's map, that would dominate Haussmann's thinking, as well as the confines of the prefect's study, where Haussmann could pull it out at any moment, day or night, to consult it. In the seventeen years during which Georges Haussmann consulted this detailed map, as it changed and grew, there never occurred a single mistake.

~

When Haussmann came into office, preliminary sections of the emperor's projects were already under way, including the beginning of the great north-south axis, christened the Boulevard de Strasbourg, which in 1853 was completed between the Gare de l'Est and the Grands Boulevards. The emperor's longed-for redevelopment of the Latin Quarter around the Rue des Ecoles and the Sorbonne had also begun, as had the eastward push of the Rue de Rivoli.

What Haussmann now faced was the completion of these daunting projects, which revolved around the objective of a grand cross of thoroughfares in the heart of Paris (east-west and north-south, or *"la Grande Croisée de Paris,"* as he put it).[10] These featured the extension of the Rue de Rivoli toward the Bastille; the parallel continuation of the Rue des Ecoles along the Left Bank; and the continuation of the north-south artery from the Boulevard de Strasbourg down to Châtelet and beyond, bisecting the Rue de Rivoli, the Ile de la Cité, and the Left Bank.

In addition, as if Haussmann didn't have enough to do, the emperor had already launched two other major projects: construction of the huge central markets of Les Halles and the development of the Bois de Boulogne.

Plus, the emperor was concerned about Paris's inadequate water supply as well as the city's clearly overwhelmed sewage system. Problems with the horse-drawn omnibus system also drew his attention, and something needed to be done about the price of bread.

And, oh, yes—the emperor was deeply interested in throwing some lavish parties. Haussmann, of course, was expected to make these happen—and as grandly as possible.

Haussmann started out with his wrecking ball on the slum that had grown up, astonishingly, around the Place du Carrousel, between the Louvre and the emperor's own Palais des Tuileries, and spread northward to the adjacent quarter that now encompasses Rue Saint-Honoré and the Place du Palais Royal. This dismal area consisted of a web of dark and fetid lanes lined with a crowd of ancient and crumbling abodes—"dangerous little streets," as Félix Nadar later recalled, "suffocated, dark and humid."[11] According to the decree declaring this in the public interest, those slums along the northern side of the Louvre were to be replaced with arcaded houses—which indeed happened. The Rue de Rivoli that Haussmann created is one long extension of arcaded buildings, a straight line being, in the words of urban geographer and historian Michel Carmona, "part of France's heritage in aesthetics and regulatory practices."[12]

Those with a yen for the past—including most notably Victor Hugo—mourn the loss of all those ancient buildings. But the question remains whether it was possible to do anything but clear out the accumulation of filth and desolation that they had become, especially given the timetable and overwhelmed budget that Haussmann had to work with. Describing a similar area just to the east, which for the moment remained intact, Alexandre Dumas *père* described a "sticky, sinister staircase" emerging at the foot of a wall: "You are afraid to put a foot on the slippery steps, or a hand on the rusted rail," he told the intrepid visitor and then directed this prospective explorer to scramble up, where in the darkness he would feel a window with iron bars similar to those of prison windows. Across the blackness, on the right, was a boardinghouse offering overnight lodgings with coffee and water. But some could not afford even this simple fare and huddled from the icy cold in the shelter of these dark walls. It was here, Dumas told his readers, that the poet Gérard de Nerval hanged himself in the cold and dark.[13]

Of course, Haussmann was not concerned with the death of Nerval or the desperate poverty of those who lived in these sinister quarters. The question of renovation never occurred to the prefect, who took "great satisfaction" in clearing out the area between the Louvre and the Palais des Tuileries and leveling the area between the Louvre and Rue Saint-Honoré to the ground.

⁓

In the wake of the wrecking ball, the Place du Palais Royal gradually emerged, while between the Louvre and the Church of Saint-Germain-l'Auxerrois, a new esplanade fully revealed the east-facing colonnade of the Louvre for the first time since the Sun King had it built. The Place du Carrousel also revived, laid out as gardens that would be officially inaugurated in 1857.

But Haussmann had an emperor on his heels, and he could not take time out to enjoy what he had already accomplished. In the process of continuing the extension of the Rue de Rivoli, he soon encountered the knotty problem of the difference in ground levels. This he neatly solved by razing most of the surrounding neighborhoods, which also solved the problem of the land levels around the tower of Saint-Jacques de la Boucherie.[14] It was Haussmann who placed the statue of Blaise Pascal in the tower, to commemorate the experiments in air pressure and vacuum that Pascal had carried out there.

Unfortunately, the surplus land left over from Haussmann's expropriations along the Rue de Rivoli was not proving a hot sale item, as few were interested in buying. Who could yet be sure whether these areas, razed but not yet rebuilt, would be worth the investment? It was at this point that the Pereire brothers stepped in as head of a banking syndicate willing to pay the city some seven million francs for the unsold land. The only condition, Haussmann told them, was that all the building they planned to do on this land had to be completed by May 1, 1855—the scheduled opening of Paris's first World's Fair.

In the meantime, the first stone of Napoleon III's major addition to the northern wing of the Louvre—alongside the Rue de Rivoli—had been laid. Its Rue de Rivoli façade would be completed by that all-important 1855 date.

Everyone, it seemed, was in a hurry.

Just to the north of Haussmann's major works on the Rue de Rivoli lay the huge food markets of Paris, Les Halles. Since the twelfth century, when Philip Augustus built two market halls on this site, it had served as a major source of food for Parisians. Unfortunately, by the time Louis-Napoleon seized the imperial crown, it had become cramped and derelict, much like its slum-ridden surroundings.

Others before Louis-Napoleon had studied and debated the problem, but it was the emperor who lit the proverbial fires beneath a host of slow-moving bureaucrats to get a move on. Haussmann, who needed no prodding, entered office just after the first demolitions (some 147 houses) had begun and pressed successfully for even further demolition and roadwork. But the main problem was architectural: the emperor hated what his architect, Victor Baltard, had come up with as a replacement for the old market halls. Baltard, a prestigious architect and Prix de Rome winner, had designed eight pavilions, the first of which was completed just before Haussmann took office. Heavy, grandiose, and made of stone, it looked every inch the "Halles fortress" that derisive Parisians called it. The emperor agreed: what he had in mind was the sort of glass-covered metal frame that had become popular ever since the British had presented the Crystal Palace to the world in 1851, at their World's Fair. "What I must have are huge umbrellas," the emperor told Haussmann and sketched out what he envisioned.

Haussmann was careful to preserve the sketch. He then elaborated, adding a broad road connecting traffic between the Church of Saint-Eustache, at the north of Les Halles, and the Place du Châtelet to the south, with the eight pavilions distributed around it. He then handed the whole thing over

The sole surviving Baltard pavilion from Les Halles, constructed under Napoleon III. Now located in Nogent-sur-Marne. © J. McAuliffe

to Baltard, who was a friend (and fellow Protestant). "Quickly get me a draft following these basic ideas," he told him. Just remember, he added, "iron, iron, nothing but iron!"[15]

The use of iron rather than stone was of course heresy to a classical architect such as Baltard (an attitude that Gustave Eiffel would encounter almost thirty years later when he proposed his all-iron tower for the 1889 World's Fair). Baltard protested, but at last he came up with the design that Haussmann—and the emperor—asked for. It would remain a graceful presence for more than a century.[16]

～

One of the persistent questions surrounding the Paris that was now emerging concerns the uniformity of its architecture—of what has become known as the "Haussmann building." Although the twentieth and twenty-first centuries have embraced this architecture as quintessentially Parisian, in its best sense, contemporaries were less enthused. As one journalist and writer, Alfred Delvau, bluntly put it, these new houses of the Second Empire were "cold, colorless, as regular as barracks and as sad as prisons in the middle of streets aligned like infantrymen, . . . lamentable in their regularity." Another contemporary, J.-E. Horn, described these structures as "half palace, half-barracks."[17]

Although such regimentation may well have appealed to someone as devoted to order as was Haussmann, architectural historian Pierre Pinon argues that it did not result from specific regulation. Instead, he speculates that this type of housing simply caught on during the Second Empire—illustrated in architecture reviews and reproduced by countless anonymous architects who, in turn, were designing for masses of equally anonymous residents. Many Haussmann-style buildings were rental properties, a new form of investment that burgeoned during these years. Given the circumstances, standardized design was valued; individuality was not. Haussmann-style structures, which went up in blocks, were easy enough to build, were easy enough to copy, and stood to make money. Naturally, they became popular.

Yet constraints did exist and had existed since the eighteenth century, establishing a very-French proportion between the height of a building and the width of its street. In 1853, as the demolition and building frenzy was under way, the rule was simply put: use the width of a street as a measure to establish the height of the buildings constructed along it, applying the principle that one building not be any larger than any other.

By 1859, the rule would be more clearly defined, keeping the principle of a proportion between the width of the street and the height of the building but defining maximum heights, depending on the street's width. For streets and boulevards of more than twenty meters wide or greater, the height could be greater than twenty meters but without in any case exceeding a total of five floors above the *rez-de-chausée* (ground floor), including the mezzanine. The roof ridge, or tallest part of the roof, could not exceed a height equal to half the depth of the building, including projections and cornices. As for the façade facing the public street, its projecting eaves could not exceed a forty-five-degree angle.

In addition, the terms of sale of the land parcels, personally signed by Haussmann, typically required that the houses in each housing block have the same floor heights and façades and that these façades be made of cut stone with identical balconies, cornices, and moldings. The goal was that the houses would form an "architectural ensemble."

For above all, uniformity was prized—not only as aesthetically desirable but also as an economical approach to rebuilding the huge swaths of the city that were now being razed. The long straight lines of the newly pierced streets and boulevards left deep strips of expropriated property that developers like the Pereires were now grabbing up. Haussmann-style buildings, all in a row, suited these developers exactly.

A Haussmann-style building, Boulevard de Courcelles. The buildings along this street, bordering Parc Monceau, are considered some of the most beautiful of Paris's Haussmann-style buildings. © J. McAuliffe

～

Haussmann generally took the position of making happen whatever the emperor wanted, but in one instance, he balked. This was the emperor's much-desired plan to open up the Rue des Ecoles as a major Left Bank thoroughfare. The street was located along the slopes of Mount Sainte-Geneviève, where Haussmann feared it could not be broadened sufficiently to safely carry the large volumes of traffic that the emperor had in mind. In its place, Haussmann recommended another route, on level ground closer to the Seine. This would become the Boulevard Saint-Germain.

As for the Bois de Boulogne, by the time of Haussmann's arrival at the prefecture, it was clear that the project was a mess. Louis-Napoleon had dreamed of providing Parisians with a green space starring a sinuous water-course. But unfortunately the previous prefect, Berger, had seriously under-estimated the river's gradient, which left the upper portion dry while the lower level had become a swamp. Taking the situation in hand, Haussmann decided to divide the river into two lakes separated by a waterfall—not what the emperor had in mind but nonetheless a happy solution that has worked well to this day. By the following year, the emperor and empress would in-augurate the first stage of the Bois de Boulogne's waterworks, which brought water from the Seine along an artificial canal to supply not only the upper and lower lakes that had prompted this change of plan but also other streams and lakes throughout the park.

Haussmann had saved the day, but as with the disasters-in-waiting involv-ing the Tour Saint-Jacques de la Boucherie, he realized that he could not go on without reliable technical assistance. He now reached into his memory of men he had worked with in previous prefectures and recalled the civil engineer Adolphe Alphand, with whom he had worked most successfully in Bordeaux. Within a few months, Alphand joined the Seine prefecture as head of a newly created Walks and Horticulture Department. Haussmann now had two exceptional men, Deschamps and Alphand, by his side.

Still, Haussmann—although not a modest man—never forgot the role of Louis-Napoleon in creating the new Paris that already was emerging. "Alone," he later wrote in his memoirs, "I would never have been able to pursue, nor especially to bring to its successful conclusion, the mission that [the emperor] demanded of me." And he added, "I merely carried it out."[18]

Charles Merruau, who at the time was general secretary of the Seine prefecture, added his voice to Haussmann's: "The broad guidelines and the system [of the transformation of Paris]," he wrote in his memoirs, "were fixed in the prince's mind since the days of his presidency, and, for many essential points, well before that."[19]

～

There were other major works going on throughout Paris, most especially at the eastern end of the Ile de la Cité, at the great cathedral of Notre-Dame. This had been covered in scaffolding and under restoration for almost a de-cade by the time Napoleon III and Eugenie were married there in early 1853.

Dedicated in 1163 under the dynamic guidance of Maurice de Sully, Bishop of Paris, Notre-Dame by the early 1800s had survived the Revolution but was in terrible shape—aging, dark, and neglected. Revolutionary mobs had made off with or destroyed anything within reach, but there had also been destructive acts of a more calculated sort, most notably the mutilation of the cathedral's grand central portal, which had been hacked apart to make way for processionals. Moreover, as one authority has pointed out, "the masonry was in a lamentable state throughout the building."[20]

It was Victor Hugo who took note and did something about it. His 1831 novel, Notre-Dame de Paris (the original title of The Hunchback of Notre-Dame), made a cause célèbre of the dying cathedral, and responding to popular demand, the government of King Louis-Philippe agreed to underwrite a huge restoration program. In 1843, the young architectural team of Jean-Baptiste Lassus and Eugène Viollet-le-Duc won the competition to lead this all-important project. Both men, much like Victor Hugo, were enthusiasts of Gothic rather than neoclassical Greek and Roman architecture, and both were dedicated to remaining true to the original concept behind Notre-Dame. Of the two, though, it was Viollet-le-Duc whose imprint on the cathedral would be the greatest.[21]

Although still only thirty years old and with no degree in architecture when he set to work on Notre-Dame, Viollet-le-Duc had already established himself in the field of architectural restoration. Grandson of an architect and son of the governor of royal residences, Viollet-le-Duc had enjoyed a life filled with art and literature as well as the privilege to follow his own (strong) inclinations. A renegade from his youth, he had flat-out refused to attend the Ecole des Beaux-Arts, on the grounds that it was tied too rigidly to neoclassicism and churned out unimaginative architects. Instead, he got the practical experience he wanted at an architectural firm and then traveled, drew extensively (buildings and their ornamentation), and began to be known for his restoration work, starting with the abbey church of Vézelay and moving on to Sainte-Chapelle in Paris (where he worked with Lassus), as well as the chapel at the Château d'Amboise that held Leonardo da Vinci's tomb.

The restoration of Notre-Dame, which was Viollet-le-Duc's largest and most important project to date, drew upon his talents for meticulous research as well as for informed inspiration. He made careful drawings and took photographs of the damaged sculptures, whether on the façade or the interior, most of which had to be removed and re-created from scratch by a large team of sculptors. All those years of careful observation and drawing allowed him to fill in the blanks where only blanks remained, whether gargoyles on the drain spouts and chimeras on the cathedral roof or statues of saints throughout the structure. He rebuilt entire sections of the cathedral, repaired and replaced windows, and positioned a taller and more ornate spire over the transept, which had been removed for safety reasons a half-century before. That spire in particular may have taken "many liberties with the thirteenth-century design," but in the end, it has evoked admiration for being nothing short of "spectacular, in terms of its detailing and harmonization with the building."[22]

The work would go on for more than a decade, and some would complain that not all of Viollet-le-Duc's work was accurate and that his imagination sometimes got the better of him. As Erlande-Brandenburg points out, Viollet-le-Duc's invention became bolder as the project progressed, "due both to increasing familiarity with the building and to [his own] growing national stature." Yet such was the genius of Lassus and Viollet-le-Duc that "the [architectural] interventions they made are not always apparent, even to the practiced eye."[23]

Others may disagree. But whether or not the restored Notre-Dame is the Notre-Dame of the thirteenth century, Lassus and especially Viollet-le-Duc saved the cathedral—as had Victor Hugo.

A bad wheat harvest, which drove up the price of bread, prompted the emperor to tell Haussmann to do something about lowering bread prices (Haussmann, wary of the dangers of price caps, instead established a Bakery Trade Fund financed by the bonds it issued). But despite the price of bread, the population of Paris was generally content that year, distracted from their loss of liberties by rising profits and employment. As the English writer Bayle St. John caustically put it, in his contemporary observations of Napoleon III's Paris: "Fine masonry is certainly an excellent substitute for liberty."[24] And Zola would in time dramatize this boomtown atmosphere in his novel *La Curée* (*The Kill*, or *The Spoils*), where his major protagonist, the ruthless Aristide Rougon (who has taken the name "Saccard"), arrives in Paris in 1853 prepared to get rich quick—rich and powerful.

Saccard does not receive his longed-for rewards immediately, but the fortuitous death of his first wife and his marriage to a wealthy (and pregnant) young woman in need of a husband starts to bring in "the kill"—which Zola likens to the reward given to the dogs after a successful hunt. There were a lot of spoils to be handed out in Napoleon III's Paris, and Saccard, strategically placed (by his scheming brother) in the city's planning permission office as assistant commissioner of roads, realizes that he can make good use of his insider information on the houses and buildings due for demolition—buildings whose owners will be well recompensed. He only needs some capital to buy up these properties before their status becomes known, and he will be a rich man. Thus equipped with the second wife's dowry as capital, Saccard's career in speculation begins.

There is no question of where Zola's sympathies lie (or do not lie) in this vivisection of the Second Empire's new Babylon. His very description of the house that Saccard builds, overlooking Parc Monceau, is a peon to vulgarity.

Among its sculptured swags of flowers and branches can be seen "balconies shaped like baskets full of blossoms, and supported by great naked women with straining hips, with breasts jutting out before them." Around the roof runs a balustrade punctuated by "urns blazing with flames of stone." And the structure's interior is, if possible, even more laden with gilt and display. The money practically clanks as one walks through this *nouveau riche* paradise—and that was the idea.

Saccard's young second wife, cast into this life of excess, first heard the name of "Saccard" with "the brutal cadence of two rakes gathering up gold," and Saccard has done exactly that, raking in his take from the emperor's, and Haussmann's, plan to transform Paris. Zola had his own views on Persigny and Haussmann's theory of productive expenditure and those who took advantage of it. As one of Saccard's guests remarks, at a suitably sumptuous dinner: "You see, everything is fine so long as you make money by it." While another guest grandly observes: "Let those brawlers of the opposition say what they will; to plough up Paris is to make it productive."[25]

Alexandre Dumas *père* had another view of Paris, and from the outset, he had filled his life with an endless series of mistresses, lovers, and one-night stands. Age did not slow him down. Although his appetites may not have reached the cosmic levels of his friend Victor Hugo, they nonetheless remained impressive, in tandem with his prodigious literary output. When Rodin, in his original monument honoring Hugo, placed the sexually explicit splayed legs and crotch of Iris, messenger of the gods, hovering above the head of the seated Hugo, he was pinpointing the source of Hugo's creative energy. He might well have done the same for the senior Alexandre Dumas.

Dumas was the son of a flamboyant Napoleonic general, who in turn was the son of a minor French nobleman and a Haitian slave. After falling out of favor with Bonaparte, the general died young, leaving his family destitute. On the distaff side, Dumas's mother was the daughter of a failed French innkeeper. These were not the most promising of beginnings, but despite this, Alexandre Dumas managed to rise from abject poverty into fame and wealth as one of the century's most successful playwrights and novelists.

His recipe for success included sheer persistence, nerve, and brutally hard work—added to eye-catching flamboyance, a vivid imagination, and the ability to give his audience the kind of entertainment it craved. Excitement, derring-do, and romance all poured from Dumas's prolific pen, the very instrument that won him his first job in Paris as a lowly copy clerk. Most fortunately for him, his employer was the powerful Duke of Orléans, who would eventually become king.

Dumas made good use of this connection, as well as every other he could find, to realize his burning ambition to become a playwright. Working and maneuvering, he at last made his mark with an historical drama, *Henri III and His Court*, a romantic blockbuster that dared to break with the stultifying conventions of the time. Other successful plays followed, and then came his historical novels—just as the Paris press was beginning to publish new novels in serial form. *The Three Musketeers* first appeared in this serialized format in 1844, as did many of Dumas's subsequent novels, including *The Count of Monte Cristo* (1844–1845).

No one could have written as many plays and novels as Dumas did without assistance, especially in the days before word processors or typewriters: even though he was a notorious workaholic, Dumas unhesitatingly made use of collaborators. But it was Dumas himself, with his wit, rapid-fire dialogue, and unfailing ability to tell a good story, who wrote the final versions and gave these works their characteristic pizzazz. Readers loved them and could hardly wait for the next episode to appear.

Along the way, Dumas and Victor Hugo became friends, two literary giants who got along rather than colliding with one another. As an inside joke, Dumas even placed his extraordinary villainess, Lady de Winter, at no. 6 Place Royale (the name of the Place des Vosges during d'Artagnan's time)—Victor Hugo's own address.

Perhaps it was not surprising that Dumas *père* found Brussels empty after Hugo's departure for the Channel Isles. But his considerable debts preoccupied him, and until he discharged them, he kept clear of Paris. Not until spring of 1853 did he manage to return to Paris (after settling with some 153 creditors), but he still had to keep publishing to survive and in the process managed to offend both the Church and Napoleon's censors. When these powers stopped publication of the writer's understandably provocative memoirs, Dumas simply sidestepped and founded his own daily newspaper, *Le Mousquetaire*, in which he planned to publish what he liked.

It was an enormous endeavor—run on a financial shoestring, unhampered by administration of any recognizable sort, and held together only by Dumas's sheer energy and joy in climbing the next mountain. Although he quickly surrounded himself with his usual cadre of young collaborators, Dumas provided the core copy, and late in the year, after the first issues appeared, the plaudits began to roll in. The poet Alphonse de Lamartine, now retired from politics, told him: "You are superhuman. My opinion of you is an exclamation mark. There have been studies to determine the nature of perpetual motion. You have created perpetual astonishment!" The historian Jules Michelet wrote that he was "so impressed by your indomitable talent which bends and bends again before so many absurd obstacles, and not less by your heroic perseverance." And early in the new year came the best of all, from Victor Hugo: "I read your newspaper," he wrote Dumas. "You are giving us back Voltaire, a supreme comfort for the humiliated and silent France."[26]

The Goncourt brothers, for their part, had already run afoul of the censors with their literary journal, *L'Eclair*, for which they were summoned to the police court in February. *L'Eclair* was being prosecuted for a December 1852 issue in which the Goncourts had described "in a whimsical fashion" some of the shops lying along their route from home to office, including a story of a particular nude artifact. "Behind this incredible, puerile pretext for the prosecution there were hidden reasons," the brothers speculated in their journal for February 20. "There were underhand intrigues, secret instructions from the powers-that-be to the judges, the hand of the Ministry of Police," and a welter of other factors that, "in a Byzantine Empire, bring the storm-clouds down on a decent man's head."

The storm clouds descended, and the Goncourts were summoned to appear in police court on February 2, in the particular chamber "whose complaisance had won it the honor of specializing in press trials and political convictions." When the brothers presented themselves, they were directed to take their places on the bench, which was normally reserved for thieves and gendarmes. Never before had a journalist been required to sit on the bench. One of their friends, the writer Alphonse Karr, told them that they didn't stand a chance of acquittal. "I know the presiding judge, too," he added— "I've had the misfortune to sleep with his wife."[27]

The Goncourts' lawyer defended them ably, representing the brothers as a couple of decent young men, and cited as a commendable character trait the fact that they had employed the same elderly housekeeper for twenty years. This fact seemed to impress those in the courtroom, and the brothers began to have hope for a favorable verdict. But then the court postponed the case, swinging the tide back once again in favor of conviction.

Some years later, the Goncourts would learn that a former mistress of the Goncourt brother Jules had at one time, in her duties as a midwife, performed an abortion on this particular judge's mistress, who was his wife's chambermaid. This was the same judge, they noted, who had been trying them for offending public morals.

But irony aside, there were serious considerations at hand, and it was with considerable interest that, during the intervening week, the Goncourts learned of a change of judges. This new one happened to be a relative of a friend's wife, who spoke to him on their behalf. Other friends did the same.

Still, when the Goncourts stood to hear the verdict, it was with surprise and relief that they learned that although admonished, they were acquitted.

No harm had been done—except that a literary journal was now closed forever and its editors would tread far more warily in the future.

At home, things were going well for Louis-Napoleon's new empire. He had moved quickly to choose an empress, appoint a prefect, and set in motion all the financial and earth-moving requirements necessary to create the Paris of his dreams.

He had assured his people—and the world—that he was disinterested in conquest and had promised that his empire would be an empire of peace. But soon Louis-Napoleon would be at war, and it would be a bloody one.

This particular war's roots lay most improbably in the Holy Places of Jerusalem, which for centuries had been under the care of contending Roman Catholic and Greek Orthodox monks. These proved unable to cohabit peacefully and instead argued over who should have the keys to which doors in the Church of the Holy Sepulcher. For over a century, the Roman Catholic monks had received French protection, but this had waned during recent years—that is, until Louis-Napoleon decided to take the matter very seriously and, with the backing of the French Roman Catholic Church as well as his army, demanded full restoration of the Roman Catholic monks' rights.

By this time, Palestine was part of the vast but decaying Ottoman Empire, which Czar Nicholas I memorably called "the sick man of Europe." Like vultures, Russia and France began to circle around. Russia wanted Constantinople and a foothold in the eastern Mediterranean, while Louis-Napoleon, despite his talk of peace, was deeply interested in extending French influence in the eastern Mediterranean, with dreams of a canal through the isthmus of Suez.

One thing quickly led to another, and by autumn of 1853, Russia and the Turks were at war. The French and even the British realized the dangers of a Russian presence in the eastern Mediterranean and by January 1854, combined British and French naval fleets were entering the Black Sea.

On March 30, 1854, Britain and France—upending centuries of mutual hostility—jointly declared war on Russia.

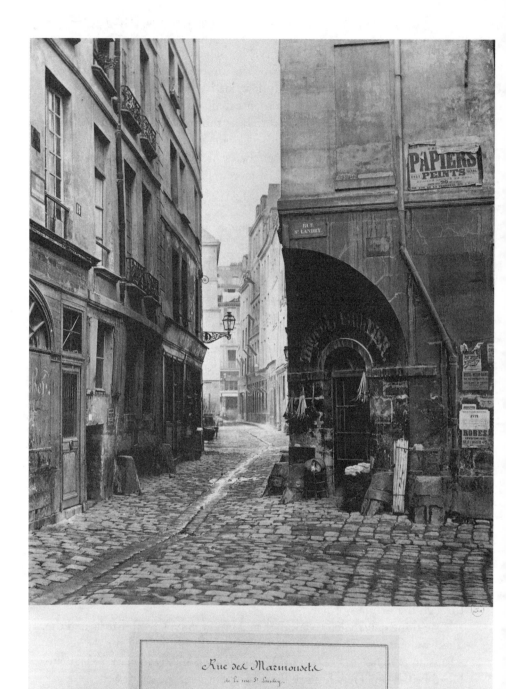

Old Paris. Rue des Marmousets, from Rue Saint-Landry. Photograph by Charles Marville. © Musée de la Ville de Paris, Musée Carnavalet, Paris, France / Bridgeman Images

CHAPTER FOUR

~

A Nonessential War

(1854)

At first the French greeted the Crimean War with enthusiasm. A patriotic tide swept the country—a tide that Louis-Napoleon was happy to ride. After all, despite his earlier promises of peace, what was a Bonaparte without a great victory in war to seal that close bond with his people? The army, too, was eager to join the fray, having for too long been denied the opportunity for glory.

Perhaps, as has been conjectured, Louis-Napoleon was playing the long game and looking to secure the support of Britain in breaking up the entente between Russia, Prussia, and Austria.[1] But that may be giving too much credit to the emperor, who was known more for his charm than his subtlety. Going to war so early in his reign was a risky move, especially with the nation just emerging from a decade of economic doldrums. Now, under imperial rule, France was fully committed to economic expansion at home, and there certainly was no extra money to throw into foreign adventures.

Still, the opening months of the war looked promising, as the allied French and British forces soon pressed the Russians to withdraw from the Balkan principalities of Moldavia and Wallachia and retreat into their own lands. By now, public war fever had reached such a pitch that it was impossible to end the war with these victories, and France and Britain now chose to continue the war by invading the Crimea. Preparing to attack Russia's formidable port and naval base at Sebastopol, they fought and won the Battle of the Alma— which, in a flood of patriotism back home, gave its name to a new stone bridge being erected across the Seine (Pont de l'Alma, dedicated in 1856).

But by winter, the war had deteriorated into a stalemate at Sebastopol, where the Allies placed the port city under siege. There, a brutal winter, coupled with outbreaks of cholera, led to the kind of misery that no one had anticipated. The heroic but futile charge of the British Light Brigade was only one of many bloody encounters that failed to end the mess. The war was rapidly turning into a disaster for both sides.

In the meantime, back in Paris, Haussmann followed his emperor's wishes and proceeded to entertain Parisians with a series of sumptuous balls and festivities. In addition to the balls that the emperor began to hold on a weekly basis, the prefect opened the new year with a bash at the Hôtel de Ville for one thousand elegantly attired guests, who partook of a lavish array of food and drink accompanied by music and dancing. Similarly, on Napoleon Bonaparte's birthday in August (which Louis-Napoleon faithfully observed), Haussmann marked the occasion with early morning cannon fire from the Invalides and an escort vessel in the Seine. He entertained Parisians throughout the day, starting with water tournaments along the Seine followed by free admission to all the theaters and a military show on the Champ de Mars before some 200,000 spectators.

The war was not forgotten, but it had not yet turned ugly. Late in the afternoon, Haussmann glorified what still could be depicted as a glorious war by sending up a huge balloon adorned with the gilded names of France's allies in front of the Ecole Militaire. There were acrobatics and mime shows throughout town, and by early evening a band of two hundred musicians began to play in the gardens of the Tuileries. Bands also played in front of the Hôtel de Ville, while from the Tuileries to the Place de la Concorde, and all along the Champs-Elysées to l'Etoile, stretched a triumphal route of arches decked in greenery lit by more than one thousand gas candelabras shimmering in the night.

Nightfall brought fireworks, with depictions of Napoleon I, War, and Peace. People went to bed that night filled with the comfortable expectation of victory and peace in far-off lands, for no one had any doubt but that affairs were going well for France in the Crimea.

While French troops were dying miserable deaths at Sebastopol, the emperor's plans for Paris continued unabated, faithfully carried out by Georges Haussmann. "It is impossible to walk out without noticing some new change," Bayle St. John noted. "Even old Parisians are obliged to study the map of their city anew."[2]

Construction was now under way on the Rue de Rivoli from the Louvre to the Hôtel de Ville, while the legal provision for the street's last extension, between the Hôtel de Ville and the Place de la Bastille, was signed that September. But problems already were emerging along the proposed route, which was to continue its arrow-straight journey eastward, bypassing Rue-Saint-Antoine. At that time, Rue Saint-Antoine was the ancient winding street that now bears the name Rue François-Miron; all along it, shopkeepers wanted to keep this as the main thoroughfare rather than substitute the straight one that Haussmann proposed, even if it meant widening the street. After all, business was at stake, and the new route threatened to drain business from the old one.

Yet Haussmann was deaf to their pleas and drove the Rue de Rivoli straight on from the Hôtel de Ville, as planned. He then renamed the original Rue Saint-Antoine as Rue François-Miron, while the new eastward extension of the Rue de Rivoli became Rue Saint-Antoine, all the way to the Place de la Bastille.

In the process, Haussmann built, on an enlarged Place Baudoyer, the town hall of what now is the fourth arrondissement—the largest of all the town halls that he built throughout Paris, since it was meant to serve as a kind of annex to the Hôtel de Ville, which functioned as the town hall for all of Paris.

The Right Bank's east-west thoroughfare was now complete, or was about to be, linking the Place de la Concorde with the Place de la Bastille. In time, it would continue (along Rue du Faubourg Saint-Antoine) all the way to what now is the Place de la Nation, in eastern Paris.

Haussmann now turned to the north-south axis, which the Boulevard de Strasbourg had already opened from the Gare de l'Est as far as that section of the Grands Boulevards known as the Boulevard Saint-Denis. Louis-Napoleon had already decided that this broad north-south route should meet up with the Rue de Rivoli at the Tour Saint-Jacques and continue on to the Place du Châtelet, crossing the Seine to the Ile de la Cité. From there, it would proceed south to the Observatoire, which was located just beyond the southern tip of the Luxembourg Gardens, and then would continue on to what then was the Barrière de l'Enfer in the city walls (now Place Denfert-Rochereau).

Originally called the Boulevard du Centre, this major north-south axis would soon acquire a new name on its Right Bank, thanks to the outcome of the Crimean War. But that was yet to come. In the meantime, this route was strongly opposed by those who thought it should proceed along a widened Rue Saint-Denis or Rue Saint-Martin, both of which were ancient roadways going back to medieval and even Roman times.

Haussmann retorted that if he took either of these routes, it would require years to cut through the urban fabric that had grown up around them. This new route, unfolding between the ancient ones, could proceed relatively unimpeded through gardens, courtyards, and low-rise buildings, spreading to what then was an impressive width of ninety-eight feet. Nonetheless, "it ripped open Old Paris," he later agreed, "with its riots and barricades, . . . piercing this almost impenetrable maze with a large central roadway."[3] Moreover, the resulting roadway would not only be wide, but it would be straight, unlike the narrow and somewhat meandering Rues Saint-Martin and Saint-Denis that flanked it. Haussmann could also do some chest-thumping by asserting that this route allowed him to spare buildings of historical merit, such as the abbey church of Saint-Martin des Champs.

Unfortunately, Haussmann could not get everything as ramrod straight as he liked, and as his north-south artery approached the Seine and the Ile de la Cité, the dome of the Sorbonne stood out in the distance, obstinately unaligned with the approaching boulevard. Given this dismaying prospect, Haussmann finally proposed placing a new building at the water's edge, to house the commercial courts of Paris (the Tribunal de Commerce, formerly located in the Bourse). This rose across from the Palais de Justice, where it provided some visual heft and balance—including its own dome—to the southward perspective from across the Seine.

Haussmann was now embarked on a multitude of projects, including major roadways to and from Les Halles as well as three major crossroads (Rue Réaumur, Rue de Turbigo, and Rue Etienne Marcel) between Rue Saint-Denis and Rue Saint-Martin, in addition to starting to develop the Left Bank's Saint-Marcel and Gare d'Orléans (now Gare Austerlitz) quarters. He also was taking initial steps to construct the future Boulevard Malesherbes from Place de la Madeleine northwest toward what now is Parc Monceau. While fully occupied with these projects, he took special interest in the new Left Bank east-west artery, which (to his relief) no longer focused on Rue des Ecoles and now would extend along what would become the Boulevard Saint-Germain.

In particular, Haussmann homed in on the crossing of Boulevard Saint-Germain with the north-south artery, which occurred at Boulevard Saint-Michel. This, following the Right Bank crossing of the north-south roadway with the Rue de Rivoli at Tour Saint-Jacques, would create a second major crossing, completing what Haussmann majestically called "*la Grande Croisée de Paris.*" To celebrate this in an appropriate manner required a major architectural statement, and Haussmann now ordered the creation of Place Saint-Michel, to the south of Pont Saint-Michel, where the north-south artery entered the Left Bank. Work here, to enlarge what had been a simple meeting place of several ancient streets, would begin the following year.

At the same time, Haussmann was paying great attention to two major sites on the Right Bank: the Place de la Concorde and the Place de l'Etoile, the latter being the western gateway in the Farmers-General wall where Napoleon Bonaparte placed his Arc de Triomphe. Between the two ran the Champs-Elysées, which in recent years had changed from a country road to a more urbanized one but still amounted to only a modest roadway, even though one planted with trees.

Louis-Napoleon had given the job of redesigning the Place de la Concorde to Jacques-Ignace Hittorff, who had been at work on the project ever since the reign of Louis-Philippe. It was he who placed statues representing major cities of France at each of the octagonal Place's eight angles, and it was he who saw the possibilities in the obelisk that Egypt offered France and had it erected (a difficult and dangerous project) at the Place's center, in line with the Champs-Elysées and the Arc de Triomphe. Hittorff was also responsible for the two fountains framing the obelisk, as well as for the streetlamps and commemorative columns throughout the enormous square. It could and should have marked a triumph for the architect, except for the fact that, most unfortunately, Georges Haussmann could not stand him.

On various projects around town, Haussmann took special glee in thwarting Hittorff, but it was at the Place de la Concorde where Haussmann's differences with Hittorff became virulent. The emperor, who was fond of festivals and parades, had already realized that, as then constituted, the Place de la Concorde was a potential death trap for crowds—much as it had been in pre-Revolutionary times, when the grand celebration commemorating the marriage of Marie-Antoinette and then-dauphin Louis had ended in more than one hundred fatalities. Other crowd-related tragedies had marked the spot over the years, and Louis-Napoleon wanted the problem of traffic and crowd flow resolved, especially with a World's Fair coming up.

Now that the obelisk and fountains were in, thanks to Hittorff, the available open space had shrunk even further. Worse, the Place contained flower borders located somewhat below ground level. These had the merit of being part of Ange-Jacques Gabriel's original design, but they doubtless threatened to upend unwary pedestrians. The question was, which would go—the obelisk or the flower beds? Haussmann voted for the obelisk, but Hittorff stood firm. The two brought their squabble to the emperor, who decided against the flower beds.

Haussmann said little at the time, but he was not happy. Taking his revenge where he could, he lowered the lamps from the tall stands that Hittorff had provided in the Place de la Concorde, claiming that they were too high. And he soon found other spots where he could make life difficult for Hittorff, especially in the developing areas to the west of the Place de la Concorde, including the Place de l'Etoile, the Champs-Elysées, and the Bois de Boulogne.

From the outset, Haussmann had placed special emphasis on plans for developing the Place de l'Etoile (now Place Charles-de-Gaulle). At that time, the Arc de Triomphe—completed under Louis-Philippe's monarchy—rose just outside the city limits, behind the Etoile tollhouses of the Farmers-General wall. It was a solitary spot, and Louis-Napoleon's concept for it, originally developed when he still resided in London, was to open up several new avenues there. He foresaw the Avenue de l'Impératrice (Avenue of the Empress, now Avenue Foch), Avenue Kléber, and Avenue Friedland, the latter two resonating with memories of the first Bonaparte's military victories.

But Haussmann did not believe the emperor was thinking in sufficiently grand terms and instead proposed the twelve-armed star and huge circular space that the Place de l'Etoile indeed became. In particular, Haussmann wanted the whole layout to be symmetrical, with identical or similar houses around the circumference, while a circular road would enclose the Arc de Triomphe and link the radiating avenues.

No detail was too small for Haussmann. Of course the tollhouses and the toll barrier would go, following which he wanted the strip of land bordering the Place and its sides to be enclosed in railings that were to be identical in height and decoration. He insisted that there be no buildings within fifty-two feet of the Place itself and that all the houses facing it be similar, with façades and all ornamentation made of freestone (as would be the bases of the iron railings). The houses' roofs were to be made of zinc, with two slopes linked by a cast iron channel that opened discreetly into the attics. Other rules regulated the houses' levels and alignments, while the prefect saw fit to issue instructions for keeping the railings and façades clean as well as for planting the flower beds that he required between the buildings and the railings (prior approval necessary). No trade signs whatever would be allowed, and in a similar manner, no trade could be practiced in this space without Haussmann's specific approval.

Haussmann and Hittorff battled on the height of the homes built around the periphery, with the emperor once again backing Hittorff. But on the whole, Haussmann's plan won out, and he was delighted with it: "This beautiful design," he later wrote in his memoirs, "which I am very proud to have thought up," was what he considered to be "one of the greatest successes of my administration."[4]

While Haussmann considered the Place de l'Etoile his masterpiece, the emperor viewed the Bois de Boulogne as the jewel in his crown and pushed for results accordingly.

By 1854, the unfortunate mess left by the river venture had vanished, replaced by two lakes separated by a waterfall, as Haussmann had recommended. That spring, the emperor and empress inaugurated the first stage of the Bois's waterworks, to great pomp and ceremony. Soon after, Haussmann brought in Gabriel Davioud (replacing Hittorff) to design the chalets and other structures throughout the park. In the years that followed, Davioud would create a distinctly Parisian look in the city's parks and public spaces, with his street benches, pavilions, fences, and lampposts, as well as his fountains—in particular the grandly gushing Saint-Michel fountain in the newly emerging Place Saint-Michel.

But the Bois de Boulogne still lacked a major access route from the Place de l'Etoile. Hittorff had proposed a wide avenue, the widest so far in Paris, but Haussmann was contemptuous, arguing that it was banal and not nearly wide enough. By this time, some were beginning to take notice of what gossips already were calling Haussmann's "megalomania," and the Legislature uncharacteristically stepped in. Eventually, Haussmann had to scale back some of his requirements for this avenue, although the resulting roadway was still uncommonly ample. With more than a little political acumen, Haussmann proposed that it be called the Avenue de l'Impératrice (Avenue of the Empress).

Still, Haussmann had ideas for the Bois de Boulogne that were far more grandiose than what even the emperor had in mind. Haussmann wanted to extend the Bois to include the plain of Longchamp and other land right down to the Seine and encountered resistance from the top—at least until the emperor's half-brother, the Duke de Morny, suggested a clever way to get what Haussmann had in mind. The Jockey Club (of which Morny was a prominent member) regularly held races on the Champ-de-Mars, which annoyed the military authorities. After all, this was traditionally military territory, fronting the Ecole Militaire; the young cadet Napoleon Bonaparte had marched on this spot, and in due course he had inspected his troops here. Morny's idea was to build a racetrack on the plain of Longchamp, where facilities would be better for everyone. The emperor thought the idea made sense, but he feared that it would take time to acquire the land in question, since it would extend the Bois de Boulogne all the way to one of the Seine's wide-swinging loops. But he underestimated Haussmann, who moved quickly. Development began in little more than a year.

By April 1857, the new racetrack at Longchamp was inaugurated, to great success, drawing large numbers of Parisians to the Bois de Boulogne. Best of all, thanks to Haussmann's quick resale of the land that the city did not keep, it ended up in costing the city virtually nothing.

Money—the quest for it and the making of it—was at the heart of the huge midcentury upheaval taking place in Napoleon III's Paris. Re-creating the city was an expensive undertaking that required heavy borrowing—especially since Napoleon and those closest to him realized that raising taxes was politically out of the question. Bolstered by Persigny and Haussmann's belief in productive expenditure, the emperor came to embrace the idea of credit in order to pay for the enormous public works that now were under way.

Credit provided the main financial underpinning, but sale of excess land along proposed routes afforded another major source of funding. Such lands became the commodity on which the men at the center of this hub—like the Pereires and Zola's Saccard—built and speculated. Paris under Napoleon III was being turned into a vast money machine, where every shovelful of dirt promised gold to someone along the line.

By 1854, the Pereires had created the Compagnie Immobilière de Paris, which permitted not only the construction and utilization of housing on the parcels of land they acquired but the rental and resale of these lands.[5] The brothers' Compagnie Immobilière snapped up land along the Rue de Rivoli and adjoining streets, as well as in what would become the Opéra quarter and westward toward the plain of Monceau and the Champs-Elysées. Capping it all, in 1854, the Pereires decided to get into the business of hotel building and began to erect a luxury hotel, the Grand Hôtel du Louvre. This they did with their typical energy, pushing construction to finish in time for the great 1855 World's Fair.

Wherever they looked, the Pereires saw opportunity. They proposed to link the Gare Saint-Lazare to Auteuil in southwest Paris by a frequent passenger omnibus, which they linked with the operation of the Petite Ceinture. This omnibus line opened in March 1854, connecting various parts along the Petite Ceinture, even as the Petite Ceinture itself rapidly expanded. Only the brothers' efforts to create a Compagnie Générale Maritime, a shipping company entrusted with the transport of mail to North America, failed to make money, having proved far more complex than they had anticipated. Its day would come but not until the next century.

⌒

In addition to relying on handy sources of funds like the Pereires, the French government under Napoleon III began to issue large-scale loans directly to the public. The first of these, floated in March 1854, was highly successful, reaching almost 100,000 subscribers who in turn provided 468 million francs. Subsequent loans brought in even more francs from an ever-larger pool of subscribers. This dramatically increased the funding for the city and state but also dramatically increased the specter of bankruptcy for those inclined to worry about these new financial schemes.

Nevertheless, bankruptcy did not disturb the sleep of many during these early bonanza years of the Second Empire. Napoleon III's government inspired confidence in business circles, especially as it did its best to facilitate business's activities, whether by turning a blind eye to inconvenient regulations or by encouraging consolidation and monopolies, especially throughout the ever-expanding network of railroads. Much as the Pereires and other big businessmen had hoped, the State under Napoleon III had become the bulwark of large-scale capitalism.

⌒

This rising economic tide was supposed to lift all boats, and Louis-Napoleon, in his 1844 pamphlet, *The Extinction of Pauperism*, had already gone on record for wanting to improve the lot of workers and the poor. After coming to power, he did not forget his earlier sympathies, taking an interest in workers' housing, which was becoming an ever-greater problem as tenements in central Paris were being eradicated. This destruction was in a good cause, of course, to make way for new roads and better housing, but better housing on cleaner streets was unfortunately well out of financial reach for these neighborhoods' former residents.

While still prince-president, Louis-Napoleon committed to supporting a scheme for decent workers' housing, donating his own funds as well as those confiscated from the family of the deposed Orléans monarch, Louis-Philippe. The first fruits of this endeavor, opened in late 1851, was a large complex

Present-day interior view of the top floor of one of the buildings of the Cité Napoléon (1851), originally constructed as workers' housing. Its interior design, including its glass roof, remains unchanged. © J. McAuliffe

called the Cité Napoléon, still located at 58 Rue de Rochechouart at the foot of Montmartre. Made up of several buildings grouped around a garden courtyard, it contained more than two hundred small subsidized apartments that were priced within the range of what workers could pay.

Although the buildings themselves were unattractive (likened to a barracks), their interiors were unusually light and airy, with open double staircases leading to floors arranged along wide corridors and a glass roof overhead. Each unit contained a kitchen and was heated and ventilated. Each floor had water pumps and toilets (this was well before the era of private bathrooms), and the buildings contained communal laundries and children's nurseries.

Unfortunately, the idea behind this well-meaning but ultimately unsuccessful endeavor was that, through careful management of the tenants' lives and surroundings, they could be improved out of poverty. There were many restrictions, most especially a ten o'clock curfew, as well as police surveillance. Louis-Napoleon wanted to place at least one of these housing blocs in each of Paris's arrondissements, and in 1856 he subsidized the construction of a similar housing bloc on Boulevard Diderot, near the Gare de Lyon. The following decade he made yet another attempt, on Avenue Daumesnil.[6] But the poor of Paris did not want to be regimented, and in any case, the supply of workers' housing was woefully inadequate.

Haussmann was especially hostile to the idea of workers' housing. In an 1857 letter to Persigny, he was dismissive of "these houses built and resold at a loss by the Emperor," these habitations "rented on the emperor's dime."[7] But then again, Haussmann was not especially sympathetic to workers in general and was deeply opposed to giving workers the vote. Universal suffrage, as far as he was concerned, was simply another of the emperor's nonsensical ideas.

As for the displaced workers of central Paris, they simply moved to cheaper quarters on the city's outskirts, where they would inhabit tenements and slums that were as bad as the ones being destroyed.

~

It was around this time that the Goncourts reported that their cousin Pierre-Charles Laurens, Comte de Villedeuil, had been overheard to pray nightly, hands clasped: "O Lord, . . . let the Emperor stay in power so that my dividends may increase, and let the rise in Anzin Coal shares be maintained."[8]

It was Villedeuil who had started the ill-fated literary journal *L'Eclair* with the Goncourts—and who had memorably accepted two hundred bottles of champagne as part of a loan from his moneylender. This champagne had so quickly gone bad that the editors decided to hold an impromptu office party, inviting everyone they could think of, including passersby and a young man by the name of Nadar, who had just begun a series of caricatures for the review.

Nadar, whose real name was Félix Tournachon, was born in Paris in 1820—innocent times, as he later put it, when "the customs were gentle, the hearts simple"; that is, "a murder would last us for two years: the conversations around it were satisfying."[9] An illegitimate son of an unsuccessful bookseller from Lyon, Nadar by his late teens had grown into a skinny and irrepressible beanpole, immediately recognizable by his bright blue eyes and carrot-colored hair. Living the Bohemian life in a series of insalubrious rooms in the Latin Quarter, he became a good friend of Henry Murger and part of the gang that provided inspiration for Murger's *Scènes de la vie de bohème*.

Later in life, Nadar described himself as "a real daredevil, always looking for tides to swim against, bracing public opinion, unreconciled to any sense of order."[10] This born rebel was a likable rogue, with a wide circle of friends who valued his honesty, loyalty, and unfailing good spirits. It was one of these friends who had invented Nadar's nickname, changing Tournachon to Tournadard, then Tournadard to Narard, and at length flipping Narard to Nadar.

By the 1840s, Nadar had won a reputation as a brilliant self-publicist, and when the Goncourts met him, his artistic talents had taken him in the direction of caricature, where he first made his name. But by 1854, after his marriage, Nadar found himself pulled into the fledgling art of photography through his younger brother, Adrien, a lost soul whom Nadar hoped to establish in this promising new field. Nadar paid for his brother's training and helped him set up a photographic studio at 11 Boulevard des Capucines, with the understanding that the brothers would collaborate (although Adrien had other ideas).

By this time, Nadar had become sufficiently interested in photography that he asked a friend for instruction and then bought his own equipment. After Adrien kicked him out of what was intended to be their joint studio, Nadar set up a rudimentary darkroom and began to solicit business through newspaper ads. The career of one of the greatest photographers of the century was about to begin.

∽

While Haussmann was spending vast sums on new roads and development schemes, including the beginning of a new water and sewage system that would prove to be one of his greatest contributions, ten-year-old Sarah Bernhardt was attending the Augustine convent school of Grandchamp, near Versailles.

Born on the Left Bank of Paris, Bernhardt was the eldest daughter of a pretty Dutch courtesan who had clawed her way out poverty and into the arms of a series of wealthy protectors, one of whom (we do not know which) was Sarah's father. The convent school had promised "to form the students by inspiring them to a solid, enlightened piety, [and] . . . to contribute, as much as possible, toward making their company agreeable and their virtues sweet."[11] But it was a lost cause. Little Sarah was trouble from the start.

She sat on the convent wall and imitated the bishop when he delivered a funeral oration below. She shocked the nuns with her foul language, slapped one sister who tried to comb her tightly curled hair, and cursed another who tried to exorcise her evil spirits by flinging holy water on her. She repeatedly ran away from school and had already showed a reckless disregard for propriety as well as an insatiable need for attention.

Where, the good sisters wondered, would it all end?

THE RECEPTION OF THE QUEEN BY THE EMPRESS IN THE VESTIBULE OF THE PALACE OF ST. CLOUD.

Reception of Queen Victoria by Empress Eugenie at the Château de Saint-Cloud (engraving). Private collection. © Look and Learn / Illustrated Papers Collection / Bridgeman Images

⌐∽

CHAPTER FIVE

A Queen Visits
(1855)

Despite nothing but bad news as the siege of Sebastopol dragged on, Napoleon III did not want to alarm the public. Instead, he went ahead with celebrations for the new year that were even more over-the-top than those for the one before. Like its predecessor, the extravaganza that Haussmann held in the Hôtel de Ville garnered praise, especially for the fountain expressly built for the courtyard, whose waters cascaded down the grand stone staircase and into a pool below. The six thousand guests enthusiastically agreed that the whole effect was magical—an evening filled with enchantment.

But the war continued as miserably as ever, and public opinion was growing testy. In April, Napoleon III decided that he would do what his uncle would have done and announced that he would sail for the Crimea to assume control of the French forces there. Eugenie, no shrinking violet, insisted that she would accompany him—at least as far as the civilized outposts of Constantinople.

The British were terrified by the news that Bonaparte's nephew would be leading his troops into battle, even if it was alongside British soldiers. The French also had reason to be unsettled by the news. Their emperor may have looked impressive on a horse, but his previous military experience (two quickly extinguished coup attempts plus some youthful hijinks in Italy) was not reassuring. Still, the British were sufficiently dismayed by the prospect of another Bonaparte at the head of an army that they quickly decided upon a diversionary tactic and invited the emperor and empress to visit Britain instead. Louis-Napoleon couldn't resist. He loved London (ever since his residence there while exiled from France). In addition, he would get to meet the queen.

Louis-Napoleon may not have been much of a soldier, but he was unrivaled as a charmer, and within even the limited time that a five-day visit allowed, he won over Queen Victoria, Prince Albert, and their growing brood of children. Count Maurice de Fleury, who attended Louis-Napoleon during this state visit, recalled that "the Queen gave a very moving adieux, and it was with tears that her daughter, the Princess Victoria, threw herself into the arms of the Empress Eugenie." Everyone cried, starting with the queen's children and extending to the queen herself and her attendants. As for Prince Albert, he, too, seemed quite moved by the occasion.[1]

Benjamin Disraeli, by now a leading figure in the Conservative party, was more cynical, but Fleury seems to have gauged the occasion about right. The emperor was delighted with the queen and her family, while Victoria was strongly impressed with Louis-Napoleon, taking care to write a long memorandum on his merits, especially noting his "indomitable courage, unflinching firmness of purpose, self-reliance, [and] perseverance."[2] She had kind words about Eugenie as well, and despite their vast differences in personality, they became lifelong friends.

This visit resulted in a reciprocal one, in August, of the British royal family to France, specifically to visit Paris's first Exposition Universelle, or World's Fair. It marked Britain's official recognition of Napoleon III's Second Empire.

~

Louis-Napoleon had been fascinated by the very first world's fair, held in London in 1851. He was especially impressed with the Crystal Palace, a huge cast-iron structure whose walls and ceiling were filled with the greatest area of plate glass ever before seen. Light flooded in through its ceiling and walls, amazing visitors and inspiring Louis-Napoleon to build one of his own—one that would be even better.

His idea for a world's fair quickly grew from a world's fair for agricultural and industrial products to one that included a world exhibition of fine arts. Fine arts were placed in a Palais des Beaux Arts at the far end of the site, along the Seine at Avenue Montaigne (although young Gustave Courbet—a pioneer in the new directions offered by Realism and miffed by the Salon's rejection of several of his paintings—held a one-man show in a specially constructed building that he called the Pavilion of Realism, near the fine arts pavilion). The chosen site for the centerpiece, the Palais de l'Industrie, lay between the Seine and the Champs-Elysées (it would be destroyed in 1900 to make way for the Grand Palais). Other structures were added along the Seine as exhibit requests poured in, but it was the Palais de l'Industrie in which the emperor was most absorbed, envisioning it as a structure that would outdo even the Crystal Palace.

As it happened, the end result was far from what the emperor had imagined. Although immense and well-lit from the acres of glass in its barrel-vaulted roof, the Palais de l'Industrie was sheathed in stone and appeared far heavier and less exciting than the Crystal Palace, which remained unchallenged as a forward-looking architectural wonder. In addition, the Palais was badly ventilated, miserably hot in the summer heat, and, even with its huge size, unable to accommodate all the exhibitions, some of which were sent to outlying exhibit halls.

Throughout the exposition, the French, as always, excelled at design, while the British remained the leaders in heavy industry and manufacturing (although it was a Frenchman who had just devised an industrial method for producing aluminum, and aluminum bars were exhibited for the first time at this exposition). But it was the fine arts that attracted the most visitors and created the most interest. As Maxime Du Camp put it, "For the first time the English school of painting was well represented," and works by German artists "revealed to our eyes the great decorative German school." As for French painters, the placement of works by Jean-Auguste-Dominique Ingres and Eugène Delacroix in the same room created a special stir.

At the heart of this agitation was the rivalry dividing the French school, especially between Ingres and Delacroix. While Ingres had for years been the bastion of Neoclassicism, holding off the rising tide of Romanticism, Delacroix had become the leader of the French Romantic school. One painted the coolly classical ideal, proclaiming the superiority of line over color, while the other portrayed the heroic, with a fervor for action and color. Still, both were extraordinary painters, and both received gold medals from the exposition jury. In the end, though, it was Ingres—as always—who received the most acclaim.

Neither artist had much respect for the other, although Delacroix buffered his criticism in wit. Ingres did not bother to hide his opinions and was especially down-putting when it came to Delacroix. As Du Camp tells the story, at some point during the exposition, a banker unwisely invited several artists, including Ingres and Delacroix, to dine with him. Ingres, who according to Du Camp "had a high opinion of himself" and thought that "after Raphael, the world had come to a standstill," was displeased to find Delacroix among the guests. Ingres rolled his eyes, expressed his impatience, and at the dinner's end, he approached Delacroix, coffee cup in hand. "Sir!" he said to him. "Drawing means honesty, it means honor!" And he became so excited that he spilled coffee down his shirtfront. At that, he exclaimed, "I am going; I will not stay here to be insulted any longer!"

Delacroix, for his part—coolly aristocratic, as usual—was more amused than offended by the incident and, according to Du Camp, had the good taste to stay above the fray. "Sometimes," Delacroix remarked of his rapidly exiting adversary, "it is difficult not to be exclusive when one is very gifted."[3]

~

Queen Victoria and Prince Albert arrived in Paris in August, in the midst of all the demolition going on throughout Paris. To hide the eyesores, false façades of wood and painted cardboard were put up along their route from the Gare de l'Est—linked, for the occasion, with the Gare du Nord, where they actually arrived (which at the moment was unattractively surrounded by blocks of housing under demolition). Some 800,000 people lined the lengthy crosstown route to their quarters at the Château de Saint-Cloud. After all, it was a momentous event—the first time a reigning British monarch had visited Paris in centuries.

The queen viewed the exposition, especially the products of British industry, and—at her insistence—visited the tomb of Napoleon I at the Invalides. There, as a summer thunderstorm darkened daylight to night, she paid her respects before the tomb of England's great enemy while the organ played "God Save the Queen." Later, Victoria wrote to her former tutor that "it was touching and pleasing in the extreme . . . to see old enmities wiped out over the tomb of Napoleon I, before whose coffin I stood (by torchlight) at the arm of Napoleon III, now my nearest and dearest ally."[4]

The emperor himself drove his royal guests around the streets of Paris, showing off his city to the newcomers. There were elegant state dinners, a ball at Versailles, and Haussmann outdid himself in providing a royal welcome at the Hôtel de Ville, for which the grand staircase was at last opened for use. Eight thousand guests were invited, and although the sovereigns gracefully bowed out before midnight, the party went on until morning.

To cap it off, the queen graciously agreed to give her name to the new avenue that had just been opened from the Place de l'Hôtel de Ville to the Place du Châtelet.

Fortunately, the royal visitors did not have to forage for hotel rooms, which were already at a premium by the time the exposition opened. Luxury accommodations were especially scarce: until the Pereire brothers' Grand Hôtel du Louvre opened, the only luxury hotel in town was the Meurice. The Hôtel du Louvre, which went up on property the Pereires had only recently acquired, between the Rues de Rivoli and Saint-Honoré at the Place du Palais Royal, was huge (the largest at that time in Europe), with seven hundred rooms and a dining room that accommodated three hundred. It was also luxurious, with many bathrooms, a pair of elevators, sumptuous carpets, boutiques on its ground and mezzanine floors, and a museum's worth of frescoes. Begun in August 1854, work proceeded on it round the clock—under electric arcs by night. But despite the Pereires' efforts, the Hôtel du Louvre was not finished in time for the exposition's opening (May 1, 1855), and no wonder. How could any such enterprise be completed within the time frame of eight months?

A partial opening took place in October 1855 (still record time), and after a few opening bumps, the Hôtel du Louvre became a chic meeting spot and location for elegant receptions as well as a popular destination for travelers. The press was flattering, describing the Grand Hôtel du Louvre as "a palace that visitors demand to visit, much like a monument."[5] The Pereires, who benefited greatly from the publicity, were suitably gratified.

That year, young Gustave Eiffel, who was making steady progress in his studies (although he was said to need improvement in technical drawing), asked his mother to buy him a season ticket for the Exposition Universelle. There, the future wizard of iron could not have missed seeing the iron-and-glass Palais de l'Industrie, although there is no indication that it made much of an impression on him.

By August, the young man had received his diploma, and with the prospect of running his uncle's successful vinegar factory no longer in the offing (due to severe political differences between Eiffel's Bonapartist father and republican uncle), he cast about for something else to do. Astonishingly, given his eventual career, he had chosen to specialize in chemistry rather than in metallurgy or mechanics, possibly because of the promise of the vinegar factory. Now he was willing to look in quite a different direction and apprenticed himself, on an unpaid basis, to his brother-in-law, who managed an iron foundry at Châtillon-sur-Seine.

Although young Eiffel was completely unprepared for this sort of work, he threw himself into learning as much as he could about all aspects of the iron-foundry business. At the same time, he looked for a permanent job, preferably in Paris, which had become the throbbing industrial and commercial center of France.

There were many other young or youngish men making their way in Paris that year, including Nadar, who was frantically busy trying to establish himself in photography—at a time when mass production of photographs had become a reality and competition among photographers was fierce. By this time, chief among Nadar's competitors was his uncooperative brother, Adrien, who had barred him from what was intended to be their joint studio and who refused to repay Nadar and Nadar's new wife the large sum that they had expended (from her dowry) for his training and equipment.

What really bothered Nadar, though, was the fact that Adrien was freely using the name "Nadar" to attract a bevy of fashionable clients. Nadar had established his pseudonym thanks to quite a lot of hard work, especially as a humorist and caricaturist, and along the way he had made important contacts in the press and with leading celebrities ("I had friendly relations," he later said, "with all the illustrious people of the time").[6] He had immediately seen the financial prospects that mass production offered for selling large quantities of photos of celebrities, but Adrien was cutting in on his clientele. Concerned above all about protecting his identity, Nadar sent bailiffs to seize Adrien's business cards at the printer and launched a lawsuit claiming trademark protection for his pseudonym. Life was tough enough without having to deal with an ingrate like Adrien.

Another that year who was striving for success in Paris was Jacques Offenbach, the German cellist and composer who from an early age had tried and failed to make his mark in Paris, each time returning to his home in Cologne. The son of a Jewish cantor who had grown up surrounded by music, Offenbach had left the Paris Conservatoire because he was bored. But despite his obvious musical talents, he failed to establish himself in Paris. Parked in a position as conductor at the Comédie-Française, where he was both overqualified and underappreciated, he kept trying, without success, to be accepted at the Opéra-Comique, even though by this time he had staged several short works in Paris.

It was the World's Fair that gave him his opportunity. Offenbach spotted an unoccupied little theater opposite the Palais de l'Industrie and requested permission to use it. He received the necessary consent, along with restrictions that included limiting the size of his prospective cast to three characters. Offenbach agreed and renamed the place the Théâtre des Bouffes-Parisiens. Assisted by Ludovic Halévy, a young civil servant with a gift for dialogue, he opened on July 5 with several one-acts, including *Les Deux Aveugles* (*The Two Blind Persons*), the first operetta ever performed in Paris. In it, two men pretending to be blind fight over the best spot for begging. The audience loved it, and it was still running a year later when the emperor asked for a special performance at the Tuileries Palace.

Offenbach could now resign from the Comédie-Française, and once the World's Fair was over, he moved his Bouffes-Parisiens to a larger hall, the Salle Choiseul, for the winter season. There, he began his extraordinary run of comic operas, mocking everyone from Victor Hugo and the Romantics to get-rich-quick stockbrokers and the importance of appearances in Parisian society.

He was still not out of the woods, financially speaking, but he would increasingly be a name to reckon with.

～

Another that year who was still striving for success was Charles Baudelaire, already in his midthirties and aching for recognition. Still bearing child-hood scars from the death of his beloved father, an amateur painter who was responsible for ordering pictures and statues for the Luxembourg palace, Baudelaire's unhappiness seems to have been rubbed raw by his rivalry with his stepfather for the affections of Baudelaire's mother. Whatever the cause, young Baudelaire—educated at the prestigious Lycée Louis-le-Grand in Paris but distinctly uninterested in the career in law or diplomacy that his stepfa-ther urged on him—went through his inheritance from his father in record time, playing the dandy, dressing expensively, frequenting brothels, and con-tracting syphilis en route. He also acquired a mistress, whom Nadar called Baudelaire's "black Venus" and who may have been a prostitute. In any case, she was not the sort of companion that Baudelaire's stepfather (a general and soon a senator) had in mind for his difficult stepson.

Despite the stepfather's efforts to dissuade him from this lifestyle (efforts that always involved stern lectures but also included sending him on a voyage to Calcutta, which he never completed), Baudelaire continued to spend freely and live dissolutely, but he began to write poetry as well. He also visited studios and museums with artist friends, listened to and joined in serious discussions on art, and began to write art criticism, beginning with his review of the Salon of 1845, in which he championed Romanticism, especially the work of Delacroix.

About this time, he also became acquainted with the writings of Edgar Allan Poe and began the difficult work of translating Poe into French—not, as he insisted, because he was a translator but because he found in Poe a kind of brother, someone who also believed in the natural evil of mankind. Baude-laire's series of essays passionately defending Poe had already appeared when selections from what would become his famous, or infamous, book of poetry, *Les Fleurs du mal* (*The Flowers of Evil*), were published in June 1855—just as the Exposition Universelle was opening.

Baudelaire—by this time poverty-stricken, hiding from creditors, and bro-ken in health—had returned to art criticism for the 1855 exposition. Once again he lauded Delacroix and Romanticism, but he completely ignored his friend Gustave Courbet. This, even though Courbet's one-man exhibit contained *L'Atelier du peintre* (*The Painter's Studio*), a huge canvas containing figures grouped around Courbet—figures that included Baudelaire. Despite the compliment, Baudelaire had already moved away from Courbet's poli-tics—the radical politics of 1848—as well as the emerging school of Realism that Courbet so emphatically espoused.

The publication of eighteen of Baudelaire's poems in *La Revue des Deux Mondes*, a longtime supporter of French romanticism, marked a moment of triumph for the impoverished and depressed poet. These were "a complete success," an enthusiastic Maxime Du Camp later wrote, and added that they "produced a great sensation." But this sensation was by no means entirely favorable. Du Camp added that "Baudelaire's skillful composition and the sonorous vigor of his verses were greatly admired, but more than one reader was shocked by the crudity of his ideas."[7]

Five months later, the critic Louis Goudall wrote a scathing review in *Le Figaro*, which only deepened Baudelaire's depression. "What emptiness around me!" he wrote his mother. "What blackness!"[8]

Earlier that same year, another poet, writer, and translator—although not quite so young as Baudelaire—had ended his life in a squalid quarter of Paris, hanging himself from the iron bars of a window in a dismal back alley. Like Baudelaire, this poet, Gérard de Nerval (the nom-de-plume of Gérard Labrunie), had gone through an inheritance, had led a Bohemian life, and had taken to some eye-popping doings (Baudelaire on at least one occasion dyed his hair green; Nerval took his pet lobster for walks). Like Baudelaire, Nerval played a critical role in the French Romantic movement, and like Baudelaire, he had a large pool of artistic and literary friends, including Alexandre Dumas *père* and Nadar as well as Théophile Gautier. And, much like Baudelaire, he had reached the depths of darkness of the soul.

But unlike Nerval, Baudelaire did not commit suicide.

"Paris changes! but nothing of my melancholy has lifted."[9] Baudelaire did not publish these words until 1857, but already he was grieving for the Paris that Georges Haussmann was destroying.

Haussmann indeed remained fully engaged in transforming the city. While working up a development plan for the space between the Hôtel de Ville and the Place du Châtelet, including the restoration and raised elevation underpinning the Tour Saint-Jacques and the creation of the first of Napoleon III's urban green spaces around it, he now was devoting much of his attention to work on the Left Bank. There, he focused on the Boulevards Saint-Michel and Saint-Germain, where in 1855 he was pleased to announce the achievement of the *Grande Croisée*. He also continued work on the Left Bank's Rue Jeanne d'Arc, a major thoroughfare reaching from Mount Saint-Geneviève and the Salpêtrière hospital to the Farmers-General wall at Place d'Italie, deep in what now is the thirteenth arrondissement.

In addition, Haussmann pressed forward with the Rue de Rennes thoroughfare, starting at Gare Montparnasse, which he and the emperor wanted to take all the way to and across the Seine via a new bridge. Since this meant the demolition of the Institut de France and the Pont des Arts, it was a nonstarter—the "immortals" of the Académie française as well as a host of others were not pleased.[10] Instead, the Rue de Rennes would slice its way through south-central Paris but would come to an abrupt stop at Boulevard Saint-Germain and Place Saint-Germain-des-Prés.

On the Right Bank, Haussmann now laid the groundwork for a Boulevard du Nord, later called the Boulevard de Magenta, to link the Gare de l'Est and the Gare du Nord along with a number of other streets along this route, to ease access to the railroad stations as well as to the Lariboisière hospital.

But thoroughfares and connections to the railways were just the beginning: Haussmann also wanted to improve the means of transportation for Parisians, and in early 1855, he made use of an imperial decree to merge eleven private-concession omnibus companies into a Compagnie Générale des Omnibus—a move that especially favored the Pereire brothers but also provided better service for the riders, offering modest fares, regular timetables, and a system for transfers throughout the city. These horse-drawn vehicles, now double-decker, usually seated fourteen below and twelve above, with the upstairs being in the open. Open-air seats cost less than those inside and attracted large numbers of workers, smokers, and anyone with limited funds. But the low ticket prices at either level (thirty centimes downstairs, fifteen centimes upstairs) offered something of a revolution in lifestyles for many Parisians, giving them an easy and inexpensive way to travel throughout the city.

The number of Parisians taking advantage of the new omnibus system showed that Haussmann had correctly gauged the demand as well as the price. The new Compagnie Générale des Omnibus owned 347 carriages, and among them, these lumbering vehicles carried a grand total of 36 million passengers in 1855 alone—an average of thirty-three trips per person per year. Within ten years, the Compagnie Générale would boast 664 omnibuses, which would carry 107 million passengers. By this time, each traveler was making an average of sixty trips per year—double the number of a decade before.

⌒

And where did all these people go? Many, or most, went to work, or to obligations of one sort or another, but many also were escaping their cramped and often dirty living quarters and heading for a variety of amusements, whether shops, theaters, or cafés.

Shops were becoming ever more delightful—and affordable—as Boucicaut progressively transformed his Le Bon Marché into a *grand magasin*, or department store, and others, such as Le Printemps and La Samaritaine, soon followed, offering the lower prices that mass production and bulk buying made possible. The Pereires created the Société des Galeries du Louvre for the boutiques in their Hôtel du Louvre; these soon became such a success that, known familiarly as "Au Louvre," they in turn combined and grew into one of the *grands magasins* of Paris. Later, this department store would expand into the hotel itself, which would eventually relocate to the other side of the Place du Palais Royal.

As for cafés, there were thousands of them, in every part of the city, each with its own loyal clientele. On the Boulevard des Italiens, in the heart of the Grands Boulevards, the fashionable Café de Paris attracted glittering after-theater crowds, while the literary set gathered at the Café Riche, and the prestigious Café Anglais drew those who enjoyed what was widely reputed to be the best food in the city. Writers and intellectuals gravitated to the Left Bank's Le Procope or the Café Voltaire (a favorite of Delacroix), while Edouard Manet and his friends met at the Café Guerbois, on Avenue de Clichy at the foot of Montmartre. Cafés provided the place and occasion for serious intellectual debate, drinking, or hijinks, depending on the clientele and the evening. And throughout the city there were countless neighborhood cafés, some little more than corner bars, where locals could gather, exchange news, and gossip.

~

Water was rarely an option for those with a thirst, nor was it readily available in which to bathe or launder. For despite the fact that a major river ran through it, Paris was a city that had always needed water—now, with its steadily growing population, more than ever.

The Seine (not yet dammed and controlled) was still a broad and shallow river that flooded regularly, leaving wide bogs and marshes along its lowland banks. It was also a river whose level lowered precipitately during the dry summer months, leaving behind a muddy detritus of shallow pools and ooze. It was to avoid the Seine's mud and floods that Paris's Roman conquerors built their homes and forum on the Left Bank hill of Mount Sainte-Geneviève, and it was to supplement their undependable and inconveniently located water supply that they built a lengthy aqueduct to bring in water from the south.

This aqueduct subsequently deteriorated and disappeared as the Roman Empire crumbled. Parisians had to fall back on Seine water, although a growing number began to dig wells—especially on the Right Bank, where the water table lay close to the surface. This water seemed clean but unfortunately was not. The very fact that it lay near the surface meant that it received the runoff from Paris's notoriously muddy and filthy streets, as well as seepage from its open sewers.

Until Haussmann, few drew a connection between the quality of water they drank and the epidemics that regularly swept the city. Instead, for centuries they merely drank up, with the more finicky either filtering the liquid or simply allowing it to settle before drinking.

For years, Paris had employed an extraordinary number of devices to step up its water supply, including aqueducts that tapped the northern springs of Belleville and Ménilmontant (neither being very productive or even drinkable) and the huge Samaritaine water pump on the Pont Neuf (dismantled in 1813) and its sister Notre-Dame pump on Pont Notre-Dame (removed in 1858). Along the way, steam pumps had their day, as well as Napoleon Bonaparte's grand Canal de l'Ourcq, which served as a navigation system as well as a supplier of drinking water.

By the 1830s, several entrepreneurs decided to take a new approach and proposed to tap into the pristine aquifer that lay deep below the city's surface. The idea was that this aquifer, caught between layers of impermeable rock and clay, could be reached by drilling. Unlike a regular well, an aquifer—if tapped in just the right spot—spurts upward. As it happened, Paris was sitting at the center of a huge geological basin containing an aquifer of formidable proportions. Prodded by various officials, the municipal council approved a large sum to tap this underground reservoir by drilling a series of artesian wells within city limits.

The first of these, the *puits de Grenelle* (begun in 1833 at what is now the intersection of Rues Valentin-Haüy and Bouchut, in the 15th arrondissement), encountered innumerable hardships until, after eight years and a depth of 538 meters, a sudden whistling sound pierced the air and a column of water dramatically shot up. Work then began, in 1855, on a well in Passy (at present-day Square Lamartine, in the 16th arrondissement). Two others followed, one at Place Hébert (in the Chapelle quarter of the 18th arrondissement) and another on the Butte-aux-Cailles (in the 13th arrondissement), both begun in 1863. The drilling in Passy reached water after six years, but the one at Place Hébert suffered a serious cave-in and did not become operational until 1888. The well on the Butte-aux-Cailles (interrupted by war as well as by internal squabbles) did not become operational until 1904.

By this time, it had become obvious that the Paris aquifer was not inexhaustible, as each additional well had noticeably depleted the force and flow of the others. But any disappointments over the artesian wells was significantly lessened by success elsewhere. Soon Paris would become the beneficiary of one of Haussmann's most daring—and successful—ideas.

Even before becoming prefect of the Seine, Haussmann had taken a great interest in the problems associated with public water, and although water's role in spreading epidemics was not yet widely known, he became convinced that something had to be done about Paris's water supply, which not only was insufficient and poorly distributed but also was cloudy and smelly. Quickly deciding against trying to draw more water from the Seine (which advocates planned to lightly filter and pump to reservoirs situated at the greatest possible height, for gravity distribution), he decided instead to investigate whether good-quality spring water could be brought into the city in quantities and at a sufficient height to be distributed to a large number of Parisians. In addition, Haussmann believed that it was necessary to provide adequate drains for wastewater, and he wanted to examine the whole related problem of sewage.

After consultations with the emperor, Haussmann called to Paris a former colleague, Eugène Belgrand, a civil engineer whose work he respected. At the time, Belgrand was in charge of river navigation in the lower Seine, and he was familiar with the waters of the Paris basin. Belgrand soon joined the Public Works Ministry of the Seine prefecture, and in 1854, he began to investigate the problems that Haussmann had outlined, first computing the springs in the Seine basin from which water could reach Paris at a sufficient height and then estimating the cost of channeling this water to Paris, filtering, and storing it there. Within months, Belgrand had his report on Haussmann's desk, and the prefect sent on his recommendations to the municipal council, which in early 1855 authorized Belgrand to continue his investigations.

It was the start of something big.

In the meantime, the spread of the telegraph for private communications was revolutionizing major parts of the city, while at the same time, Paris was undergoing its transformation into the City of Light. Gaslit streetlamps were rapidly spreading along the boulevards as well as on theater and shop fronts, and in 1855, Haussmann prompted a major improvement in gas supply by arm-twisting the various concessionary companies into forming a single Compagnie du Gaz, headed by the Pereire brothers. This not only gave the Pereires yet another area to monopolize, but it immeasurably improved the service.

Of course, all of the improvements that Haussmann was undertaking cost money, lots of it, and by spring of 1855, another major loan (of seventy-five million francs) was needed. This time, the city issued bonds with a face value of five hundred francs, repayable in fifty years at an interest rate of 3 percent. But to entice lenders sufficiently, it had become necessary to add something extra—in this case, each bond was entered into a twice-yearly lottery that would give out significant amounts of cash. This of course added considerably to the total real cost of the loan. The Pereires stepped up and ensured the success of the bond appeal, but the cost of borrowing was rising.

The Pereires had regularly served as Haussmann's dependable allies and had benefited greatly from the relationship. In 1855, they bought a magnificent mansion on prestigious Rue du Faubourg Saint-Honoré, a residence that rivaled the Rothschilds' mansion on nearby Rue Saint-Florentin. There, each Pereire family had its own apartments, and the sumptuously decorated mansion became a kind of museum for displaying the Pereires' growing collection of art.

But James de Rothschild had by no means given up the fight. The banking and railway boom had reached its peak in 1855, and now a plethora of demands on the economy, from the cost of the endless Crimean War to an unfortunately bad French harvest, placed the Banque de France under great strain. In a critical win for the Rothschilds in their rivalry with the Pereires, one of their own family, Alphonse de Rothschild (son of James), was now elected a regent of the Banque de France—the first Rothschild, and the first Jew, to hold the position. This now gave the Rothschilds a foothold at the Banque, which at the critical juncture of August 1855 chose to secretly buy thirty million francs of gold and twenty-five million of silver from the Rothschilds, to replenish its reserves.

The Pereires' seemingly invincible position was about to encounter major difficulties, starting with the center of their empire, the Crédit Mobilier.

∼

Money was at the heart of the enormous transformation that was tearing down the old and creating the new in Paris, even as pleasure and decadence were defining the city's image and appeal. One evening in August, the Goncourt brothers gave vent to their disgust, proclaiming that "we . . . are suffering from a moral indigestion brought on by debauchery." Later, in October—over "a couple of tankards of beer at Binding's"—they concluded that their moral dilemma was entirely women's fault. "Woman," they decided, "is an evil, stupid animal unless she is educated and civilized to a high degree." As far as they were concerned, women's only usefulness was for sex.[11]

The aristocratic Goncourts were hardly alone in their misogyny, which reflected a world in which women, even if placed on a pedestal, were generally viewed—and treated—as chattel. Those few who escaped these constraints usually were, like the extraordinary novelist George Sand (the *nom de plume* of Amantine-Lucile-Aurore Dupin), blessed with wealth, position, a liberal education, and an uncommon degree of strength and independence. Or, like some of the most famous courtesans of the day—such as the Russian-born Esther Lachmann, known during her Second Empire heyday as La Païva—they used their beauty and ability to manipulate men to rise out of poverty and into great wealth and influence. In La Païva's case, the mansion she built on the Champs-Elysées fairly dripped with money, featuring a surfeit of Italian Renaissance-style carvings along with a fabulous yellow onyx staircase and a gossip-inducing silver bathtub boasting three taps, the third providing either milk or champagne. But without comparable assets, a woman's lot in Paris of the Second Empire was not enviable.

The vast numbers, as well as the hierarchy, of sex workers in the mid-nineteenth-century City of Light is one indication of its women's plight. Shopgirls and factory workers illegally walked the streets by night to supplement their meager incomes, while registered prostitutes worked in around two hundred legal brothels and *maisons closes*.[12] Young dancers, singers, and actors, like Zola's gloriously endowed Nana, were in a more enviable position; if attractive, they could become courtesans, or *cocottes*, kept by wealthy protectors. If sufficiently clever, they could milk their protectors for all they were worth and become wealthy in their own right, retiring to a comfortable old age.

And then there was that in-between world, the demimonde, a term that Dumas *fils* introduced to Paris in his 1855 play, *Le Demi-Monde*. Dumas *fils* used the term to describe a woman who occupied a midway position between the worldly woman and the courtesan. Although it came to depict women who carried on the trade of love for money, Dumas himself used it to describe the half-world that contained mistresses "who do not present a bill the next morning," and he specifically included wives "put away" for infidelity and young girls such as the second wife in Zola's *The Kill*, who have compromised their virtue and desperately seek a husband—or a permanent protector.

Dumas *fils* was not sympathetic to such women. If *La Dame aux Camélias* found him in the preaching mode, then *Le Demi-Monde* revealed a savagery toward such women, whom he described as adventuresses—a kind of female whom any decent man must be prevented from marrying. In an early version of the play, he goes so far as to have the lead male character proclaim to the female character: "That kind of love which lays siege to another man's wife and forces her to adopt the low shifts of adultery and condemns her to an existence of daily lies . . . that kind of love I could never feel, especially not for you." He then adds, "It is from seeing you so pure, so loyal, so trusting that I have come to realize the terrible harm that such a love can do to a woman."

Still, while Dumas *fils* was moralizing on the stage, offstage he did the very thing he condemned and fell in love with a married woman, who left her husband for him. The woman was Nadejda von Knorring, an attractive young Russian princess then living apart from her husband in Paris. Dumas had already dallied with another married Russian aristocrat and come off the worst in the affair, having fruitlessly pursued her across Europe for almost a year. He wrote a novel based on the lady (his 1852 *The Lady of the Pearls*), but he claimed that adultery now disgusted him. Yet when the opportunity arose, he fell headlong into an affair with Nadejda. "What I love in her," he wrote family friend George Sand, "is that she is so completely a woman from the toes of her feet to the depths of her Slav soul." He told himself that he was improving the lady: "I delight," he told Sand—herself an adventuress by his standards—"in re-making this lovely creature who has been flawed by her country, her upbringing, the company she has kept, by coquetry, and above all, by idleness."[13]

Unfortunately, the prince refused to divorce Nadejda, and the czar stood behind him. Nadejda escaped with her jewels and her daughter, going to live in a villa in the south of France, where Dumas *fils* joined her.

Her mother paid for the villa.

The Exposition Universelle opened and closed with assassination attempts on the emperor. In late April, an Italian from the Papal States fired two shots at Louis-Napoleon while he was walking along the Champs-Elysées. The emperor had remained calm and kept walking, while his potential killer was arrested, tried, and executed on the exposition's opening day. Another attempt on the emperor's life, in September, ended safely enough for Louis-Napoleon when the would-be assassin's shots went wide.

That September, as the Exposition Universelle was winding down, the French—after a siege of 322 days—finally succeeded in capturing the fort of Sebastopol. Czar Alexander II struggled on for a time, but at length he agreed to peace negotiations, to be held early the following year in Paris. The emperor commemorated the long-awaited event with a Te Deum of thanksgiving at Notre-Dame, while the Boulevard du Centre now became the Boulevard de Sébastopol. Another major new thoroughfare, in northeastern Paris, would take the name Rue de Crimée.

All for the moment seemed well. Even though the war had been a disaster in terms of loss of life, the year ended in triumph, as French troops returning from the Crimea entered Paris.

Yet trouble was already brewing for France on the Italian peninsula, where—as in the German principalities—the tide of national unification was rising.

Empress Eugenie and her son, the Imperial Prince. Anonymous photographer. Private collection. © Jean Bernard / Bridgeman Images

CHAPTER SIX

~

What Goes Up . . .

(1856–1857)

Peace negotiations for ending the Crimean War were held in March 1856 in Paris—a tremendous coup for Louis-Napoleon, who was the first French ruler in many a year to host such an international gathering. The war had been a huge drain on France financially, and it had imposed a high cost in human terms as well (some 115,000 Allied soldiers were said to have died in the siege of Sebastopol alone). Nor could it be chalked up as a success in settling the tumultuous areas of the Balkans and eastern Mediterranean. Yet basking in popularity at home, and newly enjoying recognition and prestige abroad, the emperor now dreamed dreams—not of international conquest, but as supreme arbiter of Europe.

Louis-Napoleon's popularity received an even greater boost that March with the birth of the Imperial Prince, Napoleon Eugene Louis Jean Joseph Bonaparte. His father was ecstatic, rushing around and hugging everyone, while appropriate celebrations—including a 101-gun salute and the illumination of the *grands boulevards*—spread the emperor's joy throughout the city. He now had a son, and his dynastic future was assured.

Eugenie, who survived a grueling twenty-two hours of labor, had grimly done her duty and produced an heir. "You and the little one, you are everything for me," her grateful husband wrote her several months later, from the small spa town in the Vosges where he had gone to take the waters for his rheumatism. Yet, despite his devotion, Louis-Napoleon remained as unfaithful as ever, now taking a new mistress, the beautiful young Countess of Castiglione, who had recently arrived in Paris as wife of the ambassador from the Kingdom of Piedmont-Sardinia in northern Italy. Their affair lasted long enough to produce an illegitimate son (in time apprenticed to Louis-Napoleon's dentist), and it certainly reinforced Louis-Napoleon's connections with the Kingdom of Piedmont-Sardinia—which, unknown to him, had been the entire point.

What Louis-Napoleon had not known was that the Countess of Castiglione, despite her mere eighteen years of age, had already been the mistress of Victor Emmanuel, the King of Piedmont-Sardinia, whose prime minister (and the countess's cousin), Count Camillo Cavour, was determined to unite the Italian peninsula under Victor Emmanuel. This meant ousting the Austrians from northern Italy, which in turn required outside help, most particularly from the French. Enrolling the young countess in the service of Piedmont-Sardinia, Cavour sent her off to seduce Louis-Napoleon, who for his part thought that he had seduced the countess. "I have need of little distractions," he later told his cousin, the Princess Mathilde.[1]

Whether or not the Countess of Castiglione was bright enough to influence Louis-Napoleon (history has duly recorded that she was as empty-headed as she was beautiful), Louis-Napoleon was already favorably inclined toward Italian unification when he encountered her undisputable charms. In the end, Louis-Napoleon tired of the young lady and replaced her with the far more intelligent Countess Marianne de Walewska. As for Italian unification, it would not take much more to persuade the emperor of the French to get involved.

◠

While the emperor was rejoicing in his young offspring and dallying with lady friends, his capital was throbbing with the excitement of new wealth and the lure of profit.

The Pereire brothers' Crédit Mobilier reached its peak in 1856, when it handed out a breathtaking dividend of two hundred francs per share. By this time, the Bourse had become (in the words of Alexandre Dumas *fils*) "what the cathedral had been in the Middle Ages." A deputy in that year's Legislature agreed, adding that "the Bourse has become a sort of temple for the worship of stock gambling." Speculation on the market was all-absorbing—a new form of betting with the prospect of incalculable winnings. Nothing was sure, but everyone knew someone who had made a killing on the market, much like Zola's Saccard in *La Curée*, who took his loot from the expropriations game and dived into market speculation.

Some decried the influence of money in this new age, but money was also the root of productivity, taking the form of investment capital, whether in securities or joint stock companies. "Business," as Dumas *fils* famously put it, "is quite simple: it's other people's money."[2] The Pereire brothers had struck first with their Crédit Mobilier, which achieved huge success and now was spreading to other countries. But the Rothschilds were at last getting into the game, organizing a syndicate called the Réunion Financière and waging what amounted to a war on Crédit Mobilier.

Still, warnings of an economic slowdown were beginning to appear. All the demands for capital, whether from new banks or railway companies, could not be sustained, especially given the impact of the Crimean War on government borrowing. The first great wave of railway investment, and the prosperity that came with it, was already coming to a close. In 1856, the Banque de France, facing a shortfall of gold and silver, contemplated suspending the convertibility of the currency—something that the Rothschild regent, Alphonse, adamantly opposed. Instead, he and his father, James, succeeded in persuading the other regents to increase the discount rate and make larger purchases of gold and silver to maintain cash payments. Happily for the Rothschilds, its Paris house would provide the Banque de France with much of this gold—some 751 million francs of it—at a hefty rate of around 11 percent.

⌒

As the decade continued, the Second Empire continued to bring in wealth for many but brought suffering for many more. Wages were increasing, but so was the cost of living—especially rents.

Louis-Napoleon continued to believe that his role was to do good for those in need—a belief reinforced by his recognition that the workers of Paris and of France, now possessing the vote, constituted a significant portion of his support. Altruism and self-interest combined, and the emperor sent a considerable sum to the chief of police to open up a large number of soup kitchens, which in the span of a month distributed more than a million meals—not free of charge, but at a very low price.

The empress also joined in with her concern, using the 600,000 francs that the City of Paris had voted to purchase a valuable necklace for her, as a wedding gift, to establish a foundation to provide occupational training for poor girls.

Some, however, continued to do well. Gustave Eiffel was one of these, having had the luck to stumble upon a career in the railways at a time when they were the most dynamic industry around.

Until then, his life in Paris had been lackluster, largely because he had no idea of what he wanted to be or do. But then he chanced to visit the workshop of Charles Nepveu, near the Gare Saint-Lazare. Eiffel was making the rounds of several potential employers when he met Nepveu, who was a respected designer and maker of steam engines, rolling stock, and track. The two men hit it off, and Nepveu offered Eiffel the job of private secretary, with a great deal of freedom to become familiar with the company's extensive activities. It was now that something inside Eiffel suddenly ignited, and the young phenomenon rapidly emerged. Eiffel tore into the work, fascinated by what he saw and learned and eager to learn more. Unlike his previously easygoing approach to life, he now embarked on a routine that kept him at work for long hours, followed on Sundays by private lessons in economics at the Ecole des Mines (School of Mines).

Unfortunately Nepveu was not a good businessman, and he soon had to close his firm after suffering what appears to have been a breakdown. But he found a good position for Eiffel with the Pereire brothers' La Compagnie des Chemins de Fer de l'Ouest (by this time the Pereire brothers also owned the Gare Saint-Lazare as well as many of the principal French railway lines). The company immediately gave Eiffel considerable responsibilities, including the opportunity to work with its chief engineer, Eugène Flachat, who had just completed the first sheet-iron bridge in France (at Clichy), pioneering the use of sheet iron fixed by rivets rather than by pins and bolts.

By this time, Baltard's use of an iron framework for the construction of the iron-and-glass pavilions at Les Halles[3] had led the way for the use of iron in a wide range of structures in France, although it was not yet commonly used in bridges (Paris's Pont des Arts, dating from 1803, and the first Pont d'Austerlitz, from 1806, were some of the earliest French examples). Eiffel's own first design for his new employers was for a small (seventy-two-foot) cast-iron and sheet-iron bridge for the Saint-Germain Railway, which was quickly accepted.

While Eiffel was finding his footing with his new employer, Nepveu sold his own company to a larger Belgian one and was placed in charge of his own renamed firm. Late in 1856, he brought Eiffel back into the fold and gave him a senior position. When Nepveu won the contract for building a railroad bridge across the wide and turbulent Garonne river at Bordeaux, he made Eiffel (now age twenty-five) his assistant in the project. When the older man suddenly resigned, Eiffel was left with a bear of a project and a two-year deadline.

Eiffel brought many talents to the table, but one of his greatest was the recognition that iron as a building material required radically new design and construction methods. Wood and stone could accommodate an ad hoc approach to building operations, and throughout the centuries, cathedrals and castles alike had been argued over and reevaluated as they went up, sometimes surprisingly far into the process. But Eiffel completely rejected this trial-and-error approach, insisting that every component of his projects come ready for assembly, without any on-site adjustment or alternation. This revolutionary method, founded on exact mathematical calculations, may not have won instant converts, but Eiffel's iron bridges and buildings soon became renowned for their precision and reliability, even as they won admirers for their astonishing lightness and grace.

Eiffel began at the Garonne River by rising magnificently to the challenge, introducing new techniques (including hydraulic pile-driving into the riverbed) and demonstrating remarkable management abilities. He completed the project on time and without incident—an extraordinary accomplishment.

More would soon follow.

⌒

While Georges Haussmann's north-south artery continued to push southward across the Left Bank, other young men besides Eiffel were making their way in Paris. The Goncourt brothers, despite their wealth and privilege, were miserable as usual, thanks to the world's refusal to acknowledge their genius. Given the tension between their avant-garde literary production, with its unrelenting realism, and their politics, which were unabashedly conservative, they found themselves increasingly cynical observers of life around them. "At the present moment," they wrote in May 1856, "the world of petty journalism, the freemasonry of publicity reigns and governs and bars the way to any gentleman." And in October, they commented, with fashionable ennui: "Time cures one of everything—even of living."[4]

Twenty-four-year-old Edouard Manet, who also was blessed with family money and position, was considerably more optimistic as he left the studio of Thomas Couture to work on his own. He quickly installed himself in a studio in an untrendy area near the Gare Saint-Lazare, which he shared with Count Albert De Balleroy, another young painter of elegant taste, good family, and means. When they were not painting, the two frequented the Paris cafés together, both of them impeccably dressed as they strolled the boulevards, giving no evidence of the radical group of young artists to which they belonged.

Nadar, on the other hand, while he did not neglect the cafés, had to hustle to make a living, especially with his ingrate brother stealing his name and clients. In February, he registered his new company, Société de photographie artistique Nadar et Cie, with the Pereire brothers as his principal backers.

Modestly located on the Rue Saint-Lazare, Nadar's studio would benefit over the years from his growing art and antiques collection, and it soon became the heart of a successful business—especially as Nadar charged high prices and paid little rent, even while photographing some of the most important cultural figures of the day.

His brother, Adrien, continued to use the name "Nadar," much to Nadar's dismay, which a court in April ruled that he could do. Adrien was maddening, displaying photos by his brother in his own studio windows and telling clients that he was the true Nadar. At last, deciding that he could take no more of this, Nadar launched a formal appeal, organizing a campaign in the press to promote himself and his own studio as the true Nadar. It would take the better part of a year, but in late 1857, Nadar won his case. After that, his own career would continue to soar, as he established himself as the greatest portrait photographer of his age. Adrien and his studio disappeared from history.

With a world's fair just ended and a glittering international congress held to mop up after the Crimean War, not to mention the birth of the imperial prince, Paris by 1856 had seen more than its share of spectacle. Evidence of splendor was everywhere, as Louis-Napoleon was careful to provide the hoi polloi with plenty to occupy it. His concern with social issues and educational reform may have been real, but at the top of his agenda was retaining his position in power. And this meant maintaining order.

Order trumped everything else, as Maxime Du Camp was about to find out. Late in 1856, the *Revue de Paris*, which he and three others (including Théophile Gautier) had revived in 1851, was set to continue publishing a serialized version of Gustave Flaubert's remarkable new novel, *Madame Bovary*. The *Revue de Paris*, now under the leadership of Du Camp, Léon Laurent-Pichat, and Louis Ulbach, had established itself on the Paris literary scene, having published works by Gautier, Lamartine, Musset, and George Sand as well as by Baudelaire and the Goncourt brothers. But early in November, one of Du Camp's friends—who was in a position to know—informed him that the *Revue* was about to be placed under police ban. Du Camp, who was well aware that the *Revue* was under close surveillance, having already received several cautions, knew that "censure might mean suppression." At this point, he tried to encourage Flaubert to self-censor, leaving out any passage "which might be dangerous, or, at least, bear the semblance of danger."

Madame Bovary, as Du Camp explained in his memoirs, "is a novel of extraordinary power." As a result, "it startled people, and they were scandalized by what they thought improper." Flaubert, however, was adamantly opposed to changing anything. As Du Camp put it, "To help those he loved he would not have hesitated had the effort meant his own ruin, . . . but rather than change a sentence long pondered over . . . he would have broken with his dearest friend." In response, Flaubert argued, "You're prosecuting details, but it's the whole of it that offends. The work's brutality lies at its heart, not at its surface."[5]

Still, the *Revue* was indisputably in danger. "It should not be forgotten," Du Camp went on, "that we were living in 1856, and that the periodical press existed, or rather expired, under despotic rule." The long arm of the Police Correctionnelle soon reached out, indicting Flaubert, Laurent-Pichat (representing the *Revue*), and the printer on grounds of "outrage to public morality." In January 1857, the case went to trial in the Sixth Chamber, where Flaubert, son of a prominent surgeon, sat on the bench "usually set apart for thieves, cheats, rowdies, and disreputable women." Du Camp, who had not been named in the indictment and was in the audience, listened as the prosecutor argued that, while the book may have had literary merit, it was morally repugnant. Even though Flaubert had not described any actual eroticism, which took place beyond the reader's gaze, the prosecutor argued that adultery itself, undeniably front and center in *Madame Bovary*, undermined the family and the social order.

The defense began by describing Flaubert's most estimable family and then turned the court's attention to the serious character of the author, a man who—far from indulging in cheap eroticism—had spent years of somber study on the book in question. Rather than writing a salacious novel that undermined family life, it most powerfully portrayed the hazards that threatened it.

In the end, after acknowledging that Flaubert was duly respectful of propriety and religious morality and that his book had not been written to pander to sensationalism, the tribunal ruled in Flaubert's favor and acquitted the defendants of all charges and without costs. "The *Revue de Paris* had won a victory," Du Camp wrote, "Flaubert a triumph." Thanks to the trial and the publicity it generated, Flaubert became famous and *Madame Bovary* "had a prodigious success."[6]

Flaubert now was proclaimed by his literary colleagues as the leader of the Realist school of literature. This term, however, offended him, and according to Du Camp, "he never accepted it." As Flaubert later told George Sand: "I despise what is usually called Realism, and yet I have been made one of its high priests."[7]

Flaubert's friend Baudelaire had a similar aversion to the term "Realist" and, like Flaubert, believed that Realism's great failing was that it lacked the beauty that was critical to great art. In his October 1857 review of *Madame Bovary*, Baudelaire defined Realism as "a repulsive insult flung in the face of every analyst, a vague and elastic word which . . . signifies not a new means of creation, but a minute description of minor details."[8]

Only a few months after Flaubert, Baudelaire also ran afoul of the official guardians of morality, who attacked as obscene his volume of poetry, *Les Fleurs du Mal* (*The Flowers of Evil*), published in June 1857. In July, when he realized that prosecution was likely, he wrote his editor, "Quickly, hide the whole edition and hide it carefully."[9] In late August, the poet appeared before the same court as Flaubert, facing the same charges from the same prosecutor. Six of the poems in particular had drawn the prosecutor's attention, and unlike Flaubert, Baudelaire was convicted and fined.

These six poems would not be restored to the book for almost a century.

～

"There has never been an age so full of humbug," the Goncourt brothers wrote in early January 1857, as the Flaubert case was coming to trial. They, too, had been hauled up before the same court in 1853, and although they had been admonished, they had been acquitted. Still, their literary journal had been shut down, and this still rankled.

As they discussed this latest travesty with Théophile Gautier, who now was editor of the influential review *L'Artiste*, Gautier remarked that he was embarrassed for what his profession had become. "For the paltry sums which I have to earn because otherwise I should starve to death," he told them, "I say only half or a quarter of what I think—and even then I risk being hauled into court with every sentence I write."

Rumblings on censorship were by now a favored topic among Parisian writers, especially this year, which had seen both Flaubert and Baudelaire brought before the police court. In October, after Baudelaire was fined and six of his poems suppressed, the Goncourts had supper at the table next to him at the Café Riche. "He was without cravat," they noted disapprovingly, "his shirt open at the neck and his head shaved, just as if he were going to be guillotined." But they talked, as was expected with café dining, during which Baudelaire denied, "with some obstinacy and a certain harsh anger, that he has offended morality with his verse."[10]

Repression was rampant throughout Paris and throughout all of France, linked inextricably with the police and with the Roman Catholic Church. According to the prominent philosopher Victor Cousin, "No one dares to speak in the provinces or to write in Paris. The bourgeoisie . . . thinks only of making money."[11]

While the Church stood firm in protecting the moral order, the regime in turn was careful to stay in the good graces of the Church. Napoleon III and Haussmann not only carved out roads and arteries through Paris, they also built or rebuilt churches, temples, and synagogues—the most notable being the complete renovation of Notre-Dame, but also including the restoration of Saint-Germain-des-Prés and the construction of more than a dozen other churches, including Saint-Augustin and the completion of Sainte Clotilde.

Despite the official code of morality, which the police enforced for everyone else, Louis-Napoleon was free to enjoy his mistresses, while his guests and court were free to disport themselves however they wished—whether at the Tuileries (for the winter) or at Saint-Cloud (for the summer), with residences at Fontainebleau or Biarritz in between. It was a glittering, vulgar, and frequently debauched life, but without a free press to report it, the truth about the emperor and those around him never appeared. The emperor, empress, and their young son often posed for official photographs looking like a proper bourgeois family, but the reality was starkly different. And while the French bourgeoisie, whether Protestant or Catholic, held staunchly to their morality, for many others, adultery was a way of life.

At midcentury, life for the Parisian bourgeoisie—especially for bourgeois women—consisted of a predictable set of rules staunchly adhered to. Certainly the *haute bourgeoisie* family of Berthe Morisot, although more inclined toward the artistic than were other families of their station, had a conventional middle-class attitude toward what they regarded as the essentials of life, including property, occupation, social status, manners, and—most especially—morality.

Monsieur Morisot had harbored artistic inclinations as a youth and had hoped to become an architect, but yielding to bourgeois practicality, he had instead entered government service. There, he served as a prefect in several French cities, including Bourges, where Berthe was born in 1841. By 1857, he had become councilor of the Cour des Comptes (that is, the Court of

Audits, which audited most public institutions), located in Paris. The family, which included Berthe; her sisters, Yves and Edma; and their young brother, Tiburce, moved to what then were the western outskirts of Paris, in Passy.

There, when Berthe was sixteen, Madame Morisot brought her three daughters to the painter Paul Charles Chocarne-Moreau for lessons. Their brother, Tiburce, afterward wrote about this unfortunate introduction to art. To begin with, the portrait in the place of honor at the room's center featured a young woman with elegant hairstyle who was, as the sisters noted, most surprisingly nude to the waist. Sitting on a patch of grass dotted with immaculate daisies, her arms were raised "in a gesture of supplication," and her gaze "was fixed tearfully on a superlatively blue sky dotted with superlatively white clouds." This masterwork was titled *Invocation,* and whether or not that year's Salon's visitors had found it as unintentionally humorous as did the Morisots, it had not found a buyer there—much to Chocarne's dismay.

In any case, Chocarne set the three Morisot sisters to work with lessons in crosshatching—calling to mind (this is Tiburce again) "the dreadful landscapes in the showcases of shops that sell funerary articles." What a wretched time they had in Chocarne's studio, and how gloomy their trip was back to Passy, escorted by their father, who led the three sisters, "in cloaks, long skirts, and bonnets tied under the chin, a little flock reduced to a stupor by the Chocarne instruction." From the Rue de Lille on the Left Bank, they would walk to the Place de la Concorde, where they boarded a horse-drawn omnibus that ran on rails between Paris and Saint-Cloud. Debarking at the foot of the hill of Trocadéro (or of Chaillot), they climbed to their residence on what now is Rue Scheffer.

And that is the way it went, until Yves, the oldest sister, announced that if this was drawing, she would rather be a dressmaker.

But Berthe and Edma persisted in prompting their mother to find a better teacher, and soon Madame Morisot removed them from the tutelage of Monsieur Chocarne and took them to the painter Joseph Guichard, who quickly realized his pupils' talent. Indeed, not only did he recognize it, he was alarmed by it. According to brother Tiburce, Guichard took Madame Morisot aside and warned her that, given her daughters' talent, his teaching would not simply give Berthe and Edma the amateur drawing-room accomplishments so admired of young ladies in that era; in fact, the sisters would become painters. "Do you realize what this means?" he demanded, sounding more than a little distraught. "In the upper-class milieu to which you belong, this will be revolutionary, I might almost say catastrophic." In fact, he added, it would do no less than disrupt the "respectable and peaceful" Morisot home.[12]

Madame Morisot seemed to find him overly alarmist and, regardless of these warnings, told him to proceed. In that case, Guichard replied, he would apply for permission for the Morisot sisters to work in the Louvre, where he would give them lessons face-to-face with the masters.

⌒

While Berthe and Edma Morisot were embarking on their artistic training at the Louvre, Edouard Manet was traveling in Italy, accompanied by a sculptor friend, and Eugène Delacroix was at long last elected a member of the Académie des Beaux-Arts in the Institut de France. This considerable honor allowed Delacroix to serve on the prestigious Salon jury, but he was dismissive of the honor. He merely commented that he flattered himself that he could be of use there "because I shall be nearly alone in my opinion."[13]

In any case, neither he nor Ingres were represented in that year's Salon, leaving the field wide open for whatever was coming—most likely Realism, as many expected, given the increasingly heated debate over its merits.

In another part of town, eighteen-year-old composer Georges Bizet, by all accounts a brilliant student at the Conservatoire de Paris, won the prestigious Prix de Rome, allowing him three years of study in Rome. Unfortunately, his splendid beginning would not ensure an equally splendid career—as he would discover upon his return to Paris.

And as Bizet left for Rome, thirty-five-year-old Louis Pasteur moved to Paris, to head scientific studies at the Ecole Normale Supérieure—a move that enhanced his already-remarkable career but did not endear him to the school's students, who would stoutly resist his efforts to tighten up procedures and discipline.

In the midst of such to-ing and fro-ing, and the frequently frantic business of profit-making, Napoleon III decided to call an election for June 1857—dissolving the Legislature in April and shortening its life by nearly a year. Although the prospects for reelection of a Bonaparte majority were favorable, due to the prosperity that continued to buck the world monetary crisis and due as well to fond remembrances of the war's glorious outcome, the stakes still were high. Louis-Napoleon could not afford to show that he lost any support among the masses, which had turned out in his favor in 1852.

And so the government put the pressure on, especially on opposition candidates—as one of the opposition candidates, the poet François Ponsard, colorfully but privately described. "Mayors, police commissioners and rural policemen made the rustic herd vote as they wished," he complained in his private correspondence. "Those who carried my ballots were arrested and my posters torn up; my ballots were seized in voters' hands and even in peasants' houses, after their occupants were subjected to threats of all kinds." In addition, mayors were promised all sorts of desirable public assistance.[14]

Ponsard was a candidate in the Vienne, but opposition candidates ran the same gauntlet throughout France. Still, the republican opposition made inroads in some of the major towns, especially in central and eastern Paris, where it won five of the ten seats. Altogether, the opposition won 15 percent of the vote throughout France, indicating a growing malaise—largely from workers in large-scale industry. The government claimed great satisfaction with the outcome, although the rate of absenteeism was high, and the interior minister warned that "the whole point now is to find ways of reducing the number of malcontents from Paris to Lyons."

Unquestionably, the workers in Paris and other large towns remained hostile to the regime, and every year they showed a growing geographical split within the capital, with a republican working-class Paris demanding bread and a bourgeois Paris seeking order. Even Georges Haussmann could see that, despite the *grands travaux* and the benefits they brought workers, "a two-toned map representing how the majority of electors voted in each quartier would show Paris divided into two almost equal parts, as in the time of the barricades."[15]

〜

And that was before the financial crisis of 1857 hit.

Crédit Mobilier's star had already begun to wane, due to the slowdown that had sapped economies throughout Europe in the wake of the Crimean War. But the slowdown, and its impact on industry, was not the worst of it, for in August 1857, the crash came, originating in a financial panic in North America that triggered a domino effect of bank failures and stock market declines. Because of the increasing interconnectedness of the world economy, this financial panic quickly spread to Europe and beyond, penetrating even Second Empire France's booming prosperity.

The Pereire-Rothschild rivalry, always strong, had by now grown even more intense, with efforts to expand Crédit Mobilier–style banks internationally going hand-in-hand with efforts to grab railway concessions. This railway competition reached its peak in mid-1857, when the Pereires failed to block the fusion of their Grand-Central line with the Rothschild-controlled Paris-Orléans line—amounting to a major setback. The Pereires alleged that there had been a conspiracy against them, but from now on they would yield preeminence to the Rothschilds in the great European-wide race for railway concessions.

At the heart of this increasingly uneven struggle was the Pereires' chronic shortage of funds. While Rothschild was always certain of having sufficient capital of his own (or certainly of his family's), the Crédit Mobilier was not. This in turn would give Rothschild the advantage in this "duel of titans," which continued to play out throughout the remaining years of the Second Empire.

~

Financial uncertainty made any talk of another loan for Haussmann's projects for the moment unthinkable. And yet construction continued unabated on what Haussmann considered but the first step of his development of Paris.

As always, the prefect of the Seine was in a hurry. The Louvre-Tuileries complex, including the Place du Carrousel—now laid out as gardens—was officially inaugurated in August 1857, while on the Left Bank, the Boulevard Saint-Germain plowed eastward toward the Quai de la Tournelle, with its crossing of Boulevard Saint-Michel completed this same year.

On the Right Bank, another green space—the Square du Temple— opened in 1857, while Haussmann began to make inroads into the heart of the workers' quarters, in the eastern part of Paris, with the construction of Avenue Parmentier, beginning at Place Voltaire (now Place Léon Blum). Haussmann always protested that the wide boulevards he was carving through Paris did not have a military purpose, but it was indisputable that it would be far more difficult for the workers of Paris to construct barricades on broad avenues such as this and that such avenues would be far less hazardous for troops to march.

Crowning Haussmann's efforts this year was the opening of the Longchamp racetrack in April, after only eighteen months from start to finish. It was an instant success, drawing Parisians not only to the new racetrack but to the lovely paths, lakes, and woods of the Bois de Boulogne itself.

Haussmann's reward came in June of this same year, when the emperor made him a member of the Senate. From then on, Haussmann took the title of baron, from his maternal grandfather, who had been created a baron under the First Empire and whose only son had died without a male heir.

Georges Haussmann's enemies—and by now he had many—could only seethe in silence, for he was now Baron Haussmann and an imperial senator as well.

Demolition of Rue de la Barillerie for the piercing of Boulevard de Sébastopol. Engraving in Le Monde Illustrée, *10 September 1859.* © *Bridgeman Images*

~

CHAPTER SEVEN

More and More

(1858)

Whatever else the regime of Napoleon III could be accused of, it certainly wasn't lethargy.

Shrugging off the financial crisis of the year before, the government did not hesitate to intervene in support of railway construction, taking potentially risky steps such as guaranteeing the interest on companies' bonds. In addition, Georges (now Baron) Haussmann confronted the Council of State in what became an unfriendly wrangle to wrest more funds for yet another surge of public works in Paris.

The official end to what would be called the "First System" of redevelopment throughout the city had been marked that spring by the official opening of what by now was called the Boulevard de Sébastopol. Haussmann fully intended that a "Second System" would follow hard on the heels of the first, despite rising expenses—due in large part to the soaring prices of land purchases and the upward push of construction costs. Haussmann of course did get his way, as he usually did, resulting in a new agreement in March between the government and the city of Paris authorizing the staggering total of 180 million francs for the project. Under this arrangement, the city of Paris agreed, among other items, to build eighteen miles of new intra-city roads within ten years.[1]

Works under this agreement, and the huge loan it required, were not actually begun until 1860, thanks to growing opposition to Haussmann and his ever-more-extensive plans. In the Council of State, this opposition took shape in a modification of the law on compulsory purchases, making it more favorable to landowners and less favorable to the city, which as a result would suffer a distinct fall in revenues. In the Legislature, opponents managed to remove several planned operations and lower the government's share of the funding—thus raising the city's estimated share to more than one hundred and thirty million francs (closer to four hundred million francs in the end, due to huge cost overruns).

This growing unhappiness with Haussmann surfaced during the debates. Despite the citywide approval for his initial projects, this second set had, as far as many were concerned, gotten out of hand. Those who were uneasy about the Second System increasingly viewed Haussmann, and the emperor as well, as virtual megalomaniacs, carried away with their own power and grandeur. There also was a growing suspicion that both gentlemen were happily colluding with the speculators then thriving in Paris. At this point, however, the opposition still did not dare oppose the prefect directly and took cover by questioning him on his morals. After all, the fellow had actually been seen rather too many times with a particular dancer from the Opéra ballet, as well as with another dancer from the Opéra Comique.

This led to ribald jests, which reached the ears of Octavie Haussmann, the baron's long-suffering wife. Only the pleas of the equally long-suffering Empress Eugenie prevented Octavie from returning to Bordeaux for good.

Whereas the First System had dramatically cut into and reshaped the city's heart, from the Place du Carrousel, Place Saint-Germain-l'Auxerrois, and the Louvre colonnade to the Hôtel de Ville and the Place du Châtelet, the so-called Second System, as Haussmann conceived it, would reach farther into Paris. Even the slicing of the Boulevard de Sébastopol and the Boulevard Saint-Germain through the urban fabric had been done without much difficulty (with the exception, of course, of the impact on those who were displaced).

But now, Haussmann's Second System would dramatically transform whole neighborhoods throughout Paris. On the Right Bank, these transformations would extend from today's Place de la République to the Place de l'Etoile and the plain of Monceau, with significant alterations as well to eastern Paris. On the Left Bank, Haussmann would drive through Mount Sainte-Geneviève and the quarters of Saint-Jacques and Saint-Marcel, while the Ile de la Cité would emerge with scarcely a trace of its former self.

Adding to the chaos created by the destruction of houses that went with roadbuilding would be the upheaval produced by an army of trench diggers engaged in installing water and gas pipes as well as drains and sewage lines.

Haussmann had not overlooked anything in his far-reaching plans, and in 1858, in addition to his proposals for new roads, he presented the municipal council with the final results of Belgrand's investigations into providing Paris with good-quality water. According to Belgrand, the best and most plentiful supply of water was the Somme-Soude, which would require the construction of a twenty-six-mile aqueduct as well as more than one hundred miles of water mains. Already the municipal council (anticipating the need) had authorized the construction of a reservoir in Passy to hold this water, once it reached Paris. Soon after Haussmann's January 1858 report, the council (which was having a busy year) approved building another reservoir in northern Paris, at Buttes Chaumont, while yet a third was on the books for southern Paris, at Montsouris. Estimates for the total cost of these reservoirs alone came to twelve million francs.

And then there were all the pipes required to get the water to the people of Paris. Haussmann had at hand the results of one study, which provided for laying sixty-two miles of larger pipes and more than two hundred and fifty miles of smaller pipes, both for private consumption. He also called for forty-seven miles of larger pipes plus ninety-five miles of smaller pipes for street-cleaning, watering parks and gardens, and supplying fountains. All this, he estimated, would cost eight million francs.

This was not the end of it, for (based on English precedent) Haussmann now in addition proposed a sewer system to carry rain and wastewater from Paris to a point downstream on the Seine, as well as a system of sewers linked up with them. Already, Haussmann had doubled the city's sewer system, and now, in 1858, he called for many more miles of sewers (at an estimated cost of fifty million francs).

The municipal council, perhaps overwhelmed by Haussmann's research and proposals, took its time about replying and did not formally approve the diversion of water from the Somme-Soude until 1859. But at that time, it gave the prefect high marks for his work on water distribution and sewage in Paris.

The major projects that Haussmann proposed in 1858, and which would proceed throughout the 1860s, fell into several major categories. The first centered on what then was called the Place du Château-d'Eau and now is the Place de la République, which he envisioned as the base for redeveloping an entire poverty-stricken portion of Paris. This involved the creation of three major new thoroughfares radiating out from the newly important square: the Rue de Turbigo (heading southwest, through the volatile Arts et Métiers quarter and into the quarter adjoining Les Halles, site of the barricade memorialized in Victor Hugo's *Les Misérables*); the Boulevard de Magenta (taking a northwest course and linking the Place with both the Gare du Nord and Gare de l'Est); and the Boulevard du Prince Eugène (today's Boulevard Voltaire), which connected the Place du Trône—now the Place de la Nation—with today's Place de la République. All of these roadways improved traffic flow, but they just as unquestionably served as unimpeded avenues on which troops could march into the roiling heart of anti-imperial Paris.

Through this poverty-stricken area flowed the Canal Saint-Martin, which for several decades had connected (just above the Bassin de la Villette) with two other canals, the Ourcq and the Saint-Denis, to create a waterway cutting across one of the Seine's many wide-ranging loops and linking it to the river Ourcq. Although Napoleon Bonaparte had originally conceived of this canal network as a means of bringing the Ourcq's waters to the fountains of Paris (fountains for supplying the public with drinking water), it remained pristine only briefly. Soon the Industrial Revolution flooded in, blighting everything it touched. Where there had once been grassy banks, there now rose warehouses and foundries. Abject poverty quickly followed, accompanied by radical politics and a readiness for mob uprisings.

Haussmann viewed the Canal Saint-Martin with a critical eye, for it presented a kind of defensive moat between the potentially insurgent inhabitants to the east and order-restoring government troops marching in from the west. But the Canal Saint-Martin presented difficult technical problems, not the least the fact that where today's Boulevard Voltaire had to cross it, the canal stretched well above the road level. Eventually Haussmann and his engineering team decided against a bridge and instead chose to lower a large portion of the canal.

This not only eliminated three traffic-impeding locks, but it allowed Haussmann to cover over almost half the canal, from today's Place de la République to the Place de la Bastille. Boats could still navigate the canal underground through a series of tunnels, while aboveground, Haussmann created a wide promenade along today's Boulevards Jules-Ferry and Richard-Lenoir, with trees, gardens, and fountains. This of course was quite pleasant for those who could enjoy it (including, in time, George Simenon's famed Inspector Maigret, who lived with his wife on Boulevard Richard-Lenoir). But for most, life remained as difficult as ever, with the major difference being that (much to Louis-Napoleon's approval), an obstacle was now removed between the rabble-rousers of the eastern quarters and the soldiers he sent to subdue them.

~

In the process of all this improvement, the Place du Château-d'Eau, which began as a relatively small square with a large lion-bedecked fountain, was expanded into a major plaza that the Third Republic would rename the Place de la République—installing the huge monument featuring Marianne, the personification of Republican France, in the fountain's place.

Of course, Haussmann and the emperor were scarcely interested in promoting republicanism and had already taken care to erect a military barracks, named the Prince Eugène Barracks, in the Place du Château-d'Eau to assure proper military surveillance of this unruly area. These barracks (now quarters for the Republican Guard) were and remain huge, intended to accommodate more than three thousand men gathered from all over Paris. Their purpose was to respond rapidly to trouble in the flammable surrounding areas, especially the notorious Faubourg Saint-Antoine.

Another major new thoroughfare proposed for this eastern part of town was the wide and long Avenue Daumesnil. Leading from the Place de la Bastille to the Farmers-General wall and eventually to the Bois de Vincennes, Haussmann envisioned it as a kind of pendant to the Champs-Elysées, a poor-man's access route to his own pleasure grounds. The Bois de Vincennes, on the eastern edge of Paris, was about to be transformed, on the emperor's orders, into the workers' equivalent of the upper-class Bois de Boulogne on Paris's western side. After all, when the workers were behaving themselves, the emperor was inclined to be generous. As he put it, "The faubourg Saint-Antoine should also have its Hyde Park."[2]

Meanwhile, Haussmann was planning to clear and develop the area around the Place de l'Europe and the Gare Saint-Lazare and also was opening two new streets, the Rue de Rouen (now Rue Auber) and Rue Halévy, that nicely connected the Gare Saint-Lazare with the area directly to the southeast that would star the future Opéra. Haussmann had by now decided to place the new Opéra in this location.[3] But the whole project of the Opéra, especially its site, was still under wraps as far as Haussmann and Louis-Napoleon were concerned: after all, land prices could rise astronomically should word get out.

~

Continuing counterclockwise around the city to the west, Haussmann also had the plain of Monceau in his sights. This involved extending Boulevard Malesherbes in a northwest direction from the Church of the Madeleine all the way to the Monceau customs barrier in the Farmers-General wall, deviating slightly en route from the Haussmannian straight line to compensate for the necessary rise up to Monceau's elevation. Where the boulevard took a bend, Haussmann had the new Church of Saint-Augustin erected to provide an impressive vista at what appeared to be the boulevard's terminal point, as a pendant to La Madeleine. Haussmann's insistence on order and symmetry had another consequence: Saint-Augustin's outsized dome resulted from the prefect's requirement that it be visible all the way from the Arc de Triomphe.

This was Haussmann's part of town, where he was born—near the corner where Avenue de Friedland crosses the Rue du Faubourg Saint-Honoré.[4] There, it becomes Boulevard Haussmann, named by the emperor in the prefect's honor—one of the longest streets through what soon would become the elegant heart of Paris. Yet at the time that Haussmann was sending the Boulevard Malesherbes toward Monceau, he had to clean up a notorious quarter en route, a festering slum known as La Petite Pologne. Eugène Sue was well acquainted with the area and its terrors, which he depicted in his *Mysteries of Paris*. "There were no streets," he wrote, "but narrow alleys, no houses but ruins, no pavement but a small carpet of mud and dungheaps." From morning to night, one could hear the cries for help, which no one bothered to answer.[5]

In making way for progress, Haussmann would raze the entire quarter—which meant that a mass of lodgings would be destroyed. Although a large number would be constructed in their place, "there was a disconnect between the two programs, leading to a crisis in lodgings, which . . . favored speculation."[6] Speculation usually involved the Pereire brothers, and farther up the boulevard, toward Monceau, Haussmann would find the brothers' help invaluable. But this was of little concern to the original inhabitants of this dismal slum, who all-too-frequently found that, in the wake of widespread demolition, they had nowhere to go.

Monceau itself had a long and involved history, dating from the middle ages and before. Eventually, the lands had come into the hands of the Orléans family, a collateral line of French royalty that, in 1830, provided France with King Louis-Philippe. It was Louis-Philippe's father, Philippe, Duke of Orléans, who in the 1770s created a dreamy landscape garden on the site, complete with a colonnaded pool, winding paths, and numerous miniature temples and follies. The creation of the Farmers-General wall intruded along the garden's northern edge, but its customs barrier was disguised as a circular rotunda in the form of a tiny classical temple, and Philippe claimed its upper story for his own use.

Philippe, who attempted to reinvent himself as a champion of the common man during the Revolution, renaming himself Philippe Egalité, had
even cast his vote for his cousin Louis XVI's execution. But he soon followed
his king to the guillotine, losing his lands in the process. These were returned
to his family after the Restoration of the monarchy, but Louis-Napoleon
seized and nationalized them. Still, due to a plethora of complexities, by the
time Haussmann cast his eye on the park, half of it still belonged to the Orléans family, while the other half belonged to the state. As a result, Haussmann
now found that to continue Boulevard Malesherbes on its northwestern
course, he would have to make a major purchase on behalf of the city.

It was now that Emile Pereire stepped in, to prevent Haussmann the embarrassment of having to deal with the ousted royal family. This led to an amicable
agreement, and in gratitude, the city sold Pereire a large chunk of the land not
needed either for the road or for what Haussmann already envisioned as a new
(and smaller) public park. This, in turn, the Pereire brothers used to build the
elegant residential blocks on the Monceau plain. One of these, the luxurious
mansion of the Camondo banking family—Jewish bankers from Turkey who
moved to Paris in the late 1860s—would serve as the model domicile for Zola's
blatantly nouveau speculator, Saccard, in *La Curée*.[7]

⟿

Farther around the city to the west, Haussmann had already taken major
steps to establish the layout of the Place de l'Etoile,[8] which would become
possible after 1860, with the destruction of the Farmers-General wall.

He also planned two wide new boulevards for the nearby Chaillot and
Trocadéro quarter. The one (now Avenue George V) would lead from the
Pont de l'Alma toward the Champs-Elysées, while the other (now Avenue
du Président Wilson) would take traffic from the bridge westward toward the
Trocadéro and the Bois de Boulogne.

Haussmann's Second System also envisioned a multitude of new roads on
the Left Bank, starting at the Pont de l'Alma, where he envisioned two wide
avenues forking outward (Avenues Rapp and Bosquet). Plans also were in the
works to extend the Boulevard de la Tour-Maubourg to the Pont des Invalides,
where it would match up with what now is Avenue Franklin D. Roosevelt.

Farther to the east, in the Latin Quarter and territory to the southeast,
Boulevard Saint-Marcel and Boulevard de Port-Royal would complete the
line of inner boulevards on the Left Bank that Louis-Napoleon had featured
on his original color-coded map. Where these two boulevards met, another
boulevard, Arago, would lead from the Gobelins tapestry manufacturing
quarters to the Barrière d'Enfer (now Place Denfert-Rochereau), opening up

the *barrière* to the east. At the same time, Haussmann decided to continue today's Boulevard Raspail up to Boulevard du Montparnasse, opening up Place Denfert-Rochereau to the north.

To encircle Mount Sainte-Geneviève (hardly as formidable a rise as the name would suggest), Haussmann planned a wider avenue (Avenue des Gobelins) between today's Place d'Italie and the ancient Rue Mouffetard, which would link with a new road, Rue Monge, to the east, while other roads would join up with Boulevard Saint-Michel to the west. This, Haussmann thought with considerable pride, would open up the hitherto dense network of streets of the Latin Quarter (another area of troublesome opposition to imperial rule).

But it was on the Ile de la Cité that Haussmann's Second System would have an especially outsized impact, as virtually half the island would succumb to the wrecking ball. Both the Pont Saint-Michel (arched, narrow, and once lined with houses) and the equally narrow Pont au Change would be completely rebuilt. The old street that took traffic from the Pont au Change onto the island would be widened and become the Boulevard du Palais, while another new street, the Rue de Lutèce, would extend eastward from it, bordering a newly razed section that would become the police prefecture. Haussmann planned to carry on his demolition westward to the Pont Neuf, leveling Place Dauphine in the process, but he did not get that far.

Restoration continued on Sainte-Chapelle and Notre-Dame, and significant space would now be cleared around the cathedral, especially along its southern side, which at long last would be open to view, thanks to the demolition of the former archbishop's palace that had existed for centuries between the cathedral and the small southern arm of the Seine. Soon admirers would also be able to gaze at a full front view of the cathedral, thanks to Haussmann's insistence on demolishing whatever was necessary to expand the tiny parvis, or cathedral square, to its present size.

In addition to the former archbishop's palace, the charity hospital, the Hôtel-Dieu, had been squashed for centuries between Notre-Dame and the southern arm of the Seine. By now an enormous structure that had spread to both sides of the river's narrow arm, the Hôtel-Dieu was a dark and sinister edifice that crammed in some eight hundred patients, polluting the river with a deluge of hospital waste. Haussmann, who worried about hygiene, wanted to move it completely from the Ile de la Cité, which already was too crowded for his taste. But the emperor insisted on keeping a hospital in the city's center, which meant that in the end, the Hôtel-Dieu moved to the other side of the island, where it now overlooks the northern (and wider) arm of the Seine. To make space for the hospital, more demolition was necessary.

Present-day view of the courtyard of the Hôtel-Dieu, Ile de la Cité. © J. McAuliffe

By the late 1860s, when Haussmann had finished with the Ile de la Cité, its population had shrunk by 75 percent, from around twenty thousand to five thousand, and the island itself had become a virtual administrative center.

In addition to all his other activities, in 1858, Georges Haussmann condemned the River Bièvre to death.

Until this time, the Seine had not been the only river in Paris. While the Seine bisected Paris from east to west, the little Bièvre entered Paris from the south, winding its way through the Left Bank before depositing its waters in the Seine.

Once a bucolic stream where, according to legend, beaver thrived (possibly giving the watercourse its name), for centuries the Bièvre had meandered through a countryside dotted with ancient watermills and rustic villages. Within Paris, its waters—by now split into two arms, to better serve the watermills along the way—flowed past mills and gardens, its tree-lined banks providing shade and beauty.

But then, attracted to the Bièvre by its minerals, suitable for fixing dyes, the dyer Jean Gobelin set up shop in what now is the thirteenth arrondissement. By the seventeenth century, his small venture had become the renowned Gobelins tapestry workshops, attracting a plethora of tanners and dyers to the area. By the eighteenth century, Paris's Bièvre had grown dark and polluted, and even its upstream waters suffered from considerable contamination after Christophe-Philippe Oberkampf began to manufacture his famed toile print fabrics in the little riverside village of Jouy-en-Josas.

Industrialization completed what the early polluters began, and by the nineteenth century, the Bièvre had become little more than a fetid sewer that coursed its way through some of the most poverty-stricken parts of Paris. Two decades before Haussmann, efforts were made to construct an open-air canal along part of the river's path, but even this did not clean up the stinking mess, and so Haussmann—who was not inclined to tolerate messes—determined to relegate it underground, as a sewer. "The vile stream of the Bièvre," he announced, "will no longer pour its filthy waters into the Seine."[9]

His edict would arouse much opposition, especially in the industrial quarters through which the river passed. But by the end of the century, the city of Paris had dealt conclusively with the polluted and unhappy river, which now ran underground, in pipes.[10]

～

While Baron Haussmann was creating a massive construction zone throughout much of Paris, Berthe and Edma Morisot's quiet lives continued. Their copying sessions at the Louvre began, and there, for the first time, they met other pupils and friends of their teacher, including Félix Bracquemond and Henri Fantin-Latour.

This was at first exciting for the otherwise cloistered upper-class young women. But after two years, Berthe Morisot realized that she had gotten all she could from Guichard's teaching. Perhaps more importantly, she realized that she wanted to pursue her desire to work out of doors, in direct contradiction to the edicts of Guichard, who considered painting en plein air as "the negation of art."

And so in this way Berthe and Edma Morisot moved to yet another teacher— this time the master landscape and portrait painter Jean-Baptiste-Camille Corot, whose work anticipated the Impressionism to come.

⌒

Not far away, on the Left Bank, eighteen-year-old Emile Zola was also seeking what course his life should take but with far more despair than hope.

Although born in Paris, Zola had spent his formative years in southern France, in Aix-en-Provence, where he spent an idyllic boyhood with young Paul Cézanne, exploring the sun-washed Provençal countryside. His move back to the dark and dismal streets of Paris had followed the death of his engineer father, an imaginative but impractical man of Italian and Greek descent who had left the family virtually penniless. Still, among the father's belongings were stocks in a defunct company, which led to years of false hopes and legal wrangling on the part of Monsieur Zola's forlorn widow.

Madame Zola, the daughter of a poor Parisian tradesman, had returned to Paris in 1857 while pursuing her case through the courts, and now her son joined her, in grinding poverty, in a series of ever-more-decrepit Left Bank apartments. Friends tried to help, including a friend of Zola's father who managed to get a scholarship for the boy at the prestigious Lycée Saint-Louis, but there, Emile was totally out of his depth and miserable. "Being twentieth of sixty after being among the first in my class hurt me deeply," he wrote. "I lost heart and became a very mediocre student."[11]

Lonely and bored, Emile turned from his classical studies and submerged himself in the romantic literature of the period—Victor Hugo, George Sand, and Alfred de Musset. He knew that a baccalaureate would at least make it possible for him to enter law school, but what did it matter? He didn't really want to enter law school, even though it seemed the only option. Instead, the idea of becoming a writer increasingly enticed him, even though he despaired of ever making a living at it. And this did matter, especially since his mother's frantic appeals from one legal recourse to another had met with nothing but deaf ears and dead ends.

As their resources dwindled, he and his mother moved to ever smaller and more dismal quarters. Young Emile Zola, looking out on the dark and damp tenements lining the Left Bank streets where he lived, steadily dreamed of Provence and sunshine. It was the only thing that now made his life bearable.

⌒

While Baron Haussmann was busy decimating and re-creating Paris, the outside world, especially that trouble spot, the Italian peninsula, kept pressing its claims on imperial attention.

The year had begun with yet another assassination attempt on Louis-Napoleon, this time a carefully constructed plot to bomb the imperial carriage as the emperor and empress were arriving at the Opera (then on Rue Le Peletier). Louis-Napoleon, his face grazed by glass shards but otherwise unhurt, remained calm and, offering his arm to the empress, walked to their box—only pausing to tell Haussmann in a low voice to take care of the wounded. Haussmann immediately came to the rescue, making sure that all of the wounded were taken to the hospital or treated on the spot. Two already were dead, and six more would die, while the total of wounded would reach almost one hundred fifty.

The fomenter of the plot was Felice Orsini, of Romagna. Some say that he had hoped that killing the emperor would spark a revolution in France that would spread to Italy. Others argue that he wanted to punish Louis-Napoleon for forgetting and neglecting the Italian cause that he had so ardently supported in his youth. After all, in 1849, Louis-Napoleon as president of the Republic had sent French troops to overthrow the newborn Roman Republic and restore the pope (henceforth aided by a permanent garrison of French troops). This may well have been contrary to Louis-Napoleon's own personal preferences, but he had done it to keep the powerful Roman Catholic Church in France behind him as he navigated France's roiling internal politics.

Whatever the stew of causes that had impelled Orsini, the entire incident set off a furor at the highest levels, as officials realized how fragile was the thread—the life of the emperor—that held the Second Empire together. Reacting with fear-induced authoritarianism, the regime announced new repressive measures for public safety, with punishable offenses that included inciting others to oppose the emperor or his government. Clearly, these measures were intended to suppress the regime's small but fervent republican opposition. Under a new law, anyone who had been sentenced since 1848 for political activities could now be arrested, deported, and exiled without trial. Moreover, all candidates for office, even those not elected, were now required to take the oath of loyalty to the emperor.

This now led to by-elections that April, to fill the seats of those who refused to take this oath, and Paris took the opportunity to return two more republicans to the Legislature. These, along with three others (one from Lyons), would form the "Five" that led the anti-imperial republican opposition.

They swallowed hard and took the oath of loyalty but were determined to oppose the emperor with all possible constitutional means.

Still, it remained a dangerous time for any opposition to the regime. Maxime Du Camp's *Revue de Paris* was now suppressed by imperial decree for preparing to publish an account of a duel (*Le Coup de Jarnac*) from a portion of Jules Michelet's history of France. The minister of the interior had reasoned that this account could only be an allusion to Louis-Napoleon's 1851 coup and promptly shut down the *Revue de Paris*. Outraged, Du Camp could only write in later years that "to possess supreme authority, to be responsible to none, and to be able to destroy an enemy with a word, these are dangerous and tempting powers in the hands of mediocre men."[12]

Orsini was captured, sentenced to death, and went to the guillotine that March. And Louis-Napoleon—whether encouraged by Orsini's final courtroom plea (that the emperor remember his long-ago support of Italian liberation) or simply out of fear of further assassination attempts by Italian extremists—now showed renewed interest in Italian independence, especially if France received something in return. That July, the emperor met secretly with Piedmont's Cavour and promised to help liberate northern Italy from Austrian rule in return for Savoy and possibly Nice.

That December, Napoleon III concluded a defensive treaty with Piedmont-Sardinia. This had a hidden agenda, for Cavour, as Machiavellian as ever, secretly assured King Victor Emmanuel that, "not only shall we make war at the first opportunity, but we will seek a pretext."[13]

~

In the meantime, Baron Haussmann had been moving briskly ahead with his Second System, which he foresaw would require a new and very special fund in order to proceed with the kind of speed he wanted through the complexities of compensation payments to landowners and tenants. By late 1858 (thanks to the 180-million-franc agreement), he was able to persuade the emperor to create a special public works fund, the Caisse des Travaux de Paris, to permit expenditures for the Second System that would be offset by income at a later date.

But even this special fund had its constraints, which Haussmann would duly ignore. "Necessity knows no law" was his argument, and he had no intention of allowing anything to halt the transformation of Paris.

The emperor understood and continued to give his support. And for the time being—despite growing public opposition to Haussmann and his *grands travaux*—that was all the approval that Haussmann needed.

But for how much longer?

Napoleon III hands the decree to Baron Haussmann allowing the annexation of the suburban communes of Paris, June 1859. Painting by Adolphe Yvon. © Musée de la Ville de Paris, Musée Carnavalet, Paris, France / Bridgeman Images

CHAPTER EIGHT

~

Dreams of Glory

(1859)

Louis-Napoleon of course was no less inclined to plot than was Cavour, having spent his entire life at it, and the two together agreed on a plan to bait Austria into opening hostilities.

It worked rather well. Louis-Napoleon, who knew the importance of preparing public opinion, saw to it that a brochure (*L'Empereur Napoléon III et l'Italie*) circulated widely explaining that, while Napoleon I had conquered other nations in order to free them, Napoleon III intended to free other nations without conquering them. And that May, after Austria had taken the bait and attacked Piedmont-Sardinia, the emperor sent a message to his nation declaring that the war was one of liberation, "to give Italy back to itself." Wary of losing Catholic support, he also made sure to underscore that France now was heading for Italy, not to weaken the pope's power, but to protect it from foreign pressures.

Britain offered mediation, and worried sounds reverberated throughout Europe. But none of the participants were interested in calling the whole thing off, and—having secured Russia's promise not to intervene—Louis-Napoleon ignored Prussian growls to the east and went ahead, departing amid cheering crowds from the Gare de Lyon for points south.

Despite Louis-Napoleon's care to prepare public opinion, rather less care had been taken in preparing French troops for actual battle. Fortunately the Austrians were even less prepared, and the French won two bloody battles, at Magenta and Solferino, allowing the emperor to make yet another triumphal entry, this time into Milan alongside Piedmont-Sardinia's king, Victor

Emmanuel. But by now Prussian growls had become disturbingly louder, as the well-armed German state threatened to mobilize along the Rhine. At the same time, Louis-Napoleon discovered that he did not much care for war—or at least not for its bloody results. Viewing the wounded and the dead proved distressing for him, and he was now inclined to grab the spoils due him and go home.

Sensing Louis-Napoleon's desire to pack up and leave, the Austrians did quite well for themselves, despite their battlefield losses. Piedmont-Sardinia, to its disappointment, ended up with only Lombardy, while France received its prize of Nice and Savoy. But Austria kept its iron hand on the Venetia, while the duchies in central Italy were left to decide which way to go. The Papal States remained under the pope's control, although still protected by French troops.

Cavour was furious, regarding this as a betrayal of the first order, and promptly resigned. Realist as he was, he just as promptly returned to office, deciding to make the best of things and ensure that as much of Italy as possible went with Piedmont-Sardinia. Within two years, Piedmont-Sardinia would draw the Kingdom of Naples and the Papal States into what now had become the Kingdom of Italy, leaving Rome as a small separate state.

As for Emperor Napoleon III, he had had quite enough of war, but he thoroughly enjoyed the fruits of victory—especially the part where he led his triumphant army in a magnificent parade down the Champs-Elysées.

Back in Paris, military victories bestowed new names throughout the city—including Pont Solferino and, eventually, Boulevard de Magenta and Rue Magenta—while the emperor discovered that, in his absence, his wife had acquitted herself as regent rather more strongly than he had expected. According to Louis-Napoleon's uncle, Jerome Bonaparte, "[The Empress] shows in every instance and on every question a judgment that is clear, solid and nobly French."[1] Eugenie later recalled that this was her first intervention in the machinery of government, which she exercised "very seriously, with full consciousness of my responsibilities as well as of the powers of initiative that belonged to me." Louis-Napoleon seems not to have been entirely pleased by this development, which he would find difficult to reconcile with his own ideas of a woman's proper place—especially since, from now on, Eugenie, in her own words, "never ceased to take part in the general direction of public affairs."[2]

Baron Haussmann had also used the time of the emperor's absence to his advantage, especially in establishing his idea of what the Champs-Elysées should look like. Here, in the extended space between the Place de la Concorde and Rond-Point, he once again was at loggerheads with his rival, Hittorff, who had been architect for this portion of the promenade ever since the reign of Louis-Philippe. Hittorff had made the Champs-Elysées into a popular destination, but by the late 1850s, its lawns and trees had become a bit tired and in need of rejuvenation.

Haussmann now decided to smarten up the promenade, while at the same time giving the back of his hand to Hittorff. "I took it upon myself," he later wrote, "to authorize the removal of the withering trees remaining in those unfortunate damp rows." Taking advantage of the newly cleared ground, he then created enticing bowers of "choice trees and shrubs, and circular beds of plants and flowers." In addition, he put in fountains "to freshen the air with their gushing water."[3] None of this, he made clear, was Hittorff's doing.

Haussmann was pleased to note the emperor's surprise at "this unexpected change in the scenery." But in fact the emperor seems to have been more than a little annoyed by Haussmann's high-handed treatment of Hittorff, whom the emperor had chosen to supervise this work. Haussmann's behavior in general had become increasingly arrogant, and the emperor seems to have taken note of this.

Haussmann may have done a beautiful job of renovating the forty-six-acre strip of the Champs-Elysées, complete with theaters, cafés, and restaurants, but the emperor did not comment on it. His silence alone sent a clear message of disapproval.

⌒

Haussmann frequently was at odds with one official or another as he steamrolled ahead with what he wanted. By this time, he had benefited from a redistribution of powers that profited his prefecture at the expense of his Paris administrative rival, the prefect of police (which oddly enough had previously been responsible for road and sewer cleaning, street lighting, and the calculation and collection of municipal taxes).[4] But he also had encountered opposition from the Council of State, this time over the question of extending Paris's city limits.

Ever since the last wall around Paris—the Thiers fortifications—had been built in the early 1840s, the question had arisen of whether or not to incorporate into Paris those communes, or parts of communes, located between this new wall and the older Farmers-General wall within. After all, the Farmers-General wall, although not a bristling fortification like the Thiers defenses, nonetheless defined Paris city limits and controlled access to and from the city through its numerous toll gates, all of which were under military guard.

Why not simply move the tollhouses out to the new wall, incorporate every-thing between the walls into the City of Paris, and be done with it?

Many, however, were opposed, especially those living in these in-between districts, or suburban communes, who resisted the higher taxes and cost of living that incorporation into Paris would bring. Many Parisians also had concerns, especially about the high costs they anticipated from incorpora-tion, including the need to provide these largely rural areas with facilities such as lighted sidewalks, gas and water pipes, and drains and sewers. In ad-dition, many pointed to the high proportion of poverty among this area's in-habitants, who would be added to the city's already burgeoning mass of poor.

Haussmann, however, was insistent about incorporation, seeing it as a way to deal with the poor who surrounded Paris, profiting from its schools and hospitals without paying any duties or bearing any of the costs. The emperor needed persuading: he had not considered extending Paris's city limits on his original color-coded map, and this was a new idea. Back in 1856, he had appointed a commission (at Haussmann's prodding) to con-sider the question, which it did not satisfactorily resolve. But now, in 1859, Louis-Napoleon finally asked his minister of the interior to settle the ques-tion. This minister so enthusiastically endorsed the idea of incorporation that the emperor was won over.

Prompted by imperial resolve, the Council of State adopted the draft law on incorporation in April, passing it along to the Legislature, which en-acted it by an overwhelming majority. The Senate then voted unanimously in its favor. This being in the midst of Napoleon III's Italian campaign, the empress rather than the emperor signed the law in June, and it was put into effect late in the year. City taxes were levied on the new areas starting on January 1, 1860.

Paris grew enormously by this incorporation: its population increased by one-third (from 1.2 to 1.6 million), while its area more than doubled. This required an addition to its twelve arrondissements, or administrative units, to make a new total of twenty arrondissements. This resulted in a complete reordering, reshaping, and renumbering of the arrondissements themselves. Instead of the haphazard pattern that had grown up over the years, Hauss-mann now imposed a more logical order, which unfurled like a snail from the dense city center. The first arrondissement now encompassed the Louvre and Les Halles, while the twentieth, containing the ever-expanding cemetery of Père-Lachaise, completed the outer ring to the east.

Haussmann and, by now, the emperor had their sights on an even larger incorporation, extending Paris city limits to communes beyond the Thiers fortifications. But at this, Haussmann's enemies dug in their heels. Any further aggrandizement of Paris, they feared, would only further empower the prefect.

⁓

As the decade came to a close, and as Paris was expanding its city limits to encompass the surrounding countryside, France was expanding its influence in Italy and throughout the world.

By the decade's end, Louis-Napoleon had encouraged the development of a French colony in Senegal and had intervened to protect the local Christian community in the Syrian Levant—a move to curb Turkish power there that initiated France's presence in the Middle East. He also was looking with interest at the Far East, where in 1859, French sailors occupied Saigon, ostensibly to protect Catholic missionaries but leading to French expansion into Cochin-China (Vietnam), Cambodia, and Laos, where the French established colonies and protectorates throughout.

France under Napoleon III also put down the last of the uprisings in Algeria and now undertook to introduce modernity there, whether through irrigation or railroads. But the emperor had not yet thought through what he envisioned for Algeria's relationship to France, and for the time being, the military was fully in control.

Perhaps most interesting of all these worldwide developments were the activities of a former French diplomat, Ferdinand de Lesseps, who in 1859—despite considerable opposition, especially from Britain—began to realize his dream of linking the Mediterranean with the Red Sea by a canal across the Isthmus of Suez. Few were willing to help him with this formidable undertaking, and not surprisingly, the Baron de Rothschild's offer of financial assistance came at a hefty price—5 percent interest, a figure that appalled de Lesseps. "Five per cent!" he had cried, adding, "But for 200,000,000 [francs] that means 10,000,000 [francs]! Ten million francs of my shareholders' money for your devious channels! Thank you very much. . . . Our issue will be made without you."[5]

Rothschild had merely smiled and told de Lesseps that he would not succeed, but he was wrong. Of the 400,000 shares offered in de Lesseps's private company, more than half were quickly taken up, almost entirely by small French investors. For despite de Lesseps's efforts to make this an international endeavor, neither the English, the Americans, the Russians, nor the Austrians followed through and subscribed. In the end, it was French investors who carried his venture forward, giving the French control of the equity. The London *Globe* scoffed that "the principal shareholders are hotel waiters who have been deceived by the papers they have read, and petty grocery employees who have been beguiled by puffs."[6] Little people, it was true, but French people, buoyed by a surge of patriotism: as a result, the canal would be French.

And now, on April 25, 1859, Ferdinand de Lesseps struck the first ceremonial blow of the pickaxe, to begin work at Port Said. All in all, despite continued repression and the close watch of the police, the Second Empire of Napoleon III had reached what some already were calling its golden age.

In the spring of 1859, several years after leaving Thomas Couture's studio, twenty-seven-year-old Edouard Manet was ready to make his Salon début. The Salon was the official art exhibition of the Académie des Beaux-Arts, and Manet's submission was a painting he called *Absinthe Drinker*, a study of one of the Parisian characters he had met in the course of his strolls around the city—a ragpicker who existed, like so many others, on the margins of society.

Manet spoke of the painting's "naïveté, originality, sincerity," which he placed squarely in the tradition of seventeenth-century Dutch genre painting. But he was far more of a bomb-thrower than he was willing to admit, since he was in fact attempting to turn on its head the Salon's (and the Académie's) established hierarchy of acceptable and admired subjects. According to this, the historical, the mythical, and the religious were worthy of esteem, but everyday subjects most definitely were not. Manet's former art teacher, Couture, gave him due warning of what he was about to encounter and strongly criticized the painting. Much as Couture predicted, the Salon most emphatically turned down the painting, on the grounds that its subject matter was vulgar.

Manet was devastated—and furious. "I heard [the verdict] three days ago," he wrote his friend Antonin Proust. "I didn't want to tell you." But he had one comforting thought: "I've definitely been told that Delacroix liked it." Delacroix, who by now was a member of the Académie des Beaux-Arts and was thereby allowed to serve on the Salon jury, had not expected to make much of an impact there, and evidently he had not. Still, Delacroix's opinion mattered to Manet. "He's a horse of a different color from Couture," Manet told Proust. "I don't care for his technique. But he knows what he wants and gets it."[7]

Manet was not alone in his disappointment, for Henri Fantin-Latour and the American painter James Whistler had also been rejected from that year's Salon—along with a sufficient number of other young artists that a crowd of disappointed and angry rejectees soon gathered outside the Institut de France to protest. They at length dispersed under police persuasion, but artistic outsiders were clearly becoming less willing to bend to the will of the establishment.

By now Manet had met Baudelaire, who was eleven years older and by this time a well-entrenched rebel. Baudelaire had long advocated painting subjects other than the usual public and official ones, including "the thousands of floating existences—criminals and kept women—which drift about in the underworld of a great city." Baudelaire also stressed the essential role that imagination played in painting: "A good picture," he wrote in his review of the 1859 Salon, "which is a faithful equivalent of the dream which has begotten it, should be brought into being like a world"—that is, in a series of superimposed pictures.[8] Manet's practice of layering one version of a painting upon another followed closely Baudelaire's conception of the creative process. Whether it was a question of Baudelaire influencing Manet or Manet enjoying the friendship of someone with whom he had much in common, the friendship became a close one, which remained so until Baudelaire's untimely death.[9]

In the spring of 1859, young Oscar-Claude Monet arrived in Paris. He had been born there, in 1840, in the area of northern Paris near Notre-Dame de Lorette. But then his parents moved to Le Havre to work for his uncle, who ran a successful business selling ships' supplies.

Monet's mother reportedly was a talented artist as well as musician, and his older brother, Léon, was disciplined and studious. But young Claude was quite unlike his brother: according to their father, "he likes to sow disorder, does not listen to his professors, does not do his homework, instead fills his notebooks with grotesque caricature." Young Monet may have been, as friends reported, a happy and gregarious soul, but in later years, he agreed that he was "naturally undisciplined. Even in my childhood, I could never be got to obey rules."[10]

School felt like a prison to the youngster, and when he was not outdoors, he spent his time drawing fantastical ornaments and (influenced by what he saw of Nadar's work in *Le Journal amusant*) caricatures of his teachers and other local notables. Some of these made their way to a Le Havre picture-dealer, who exhibited and sold them. Finding that he could earn good money with his caricatures, young Monet left school in 1857, probably without getting his baccalaureate. By this time his mother and uncle had both died,

Claude Monet, 1861. Photograph by Carjat

his father had taken over the firm, and his aunt—a woman with a private income and a deep interest in the arts—was now devoting increasing attention to her nephew.

Others as well took an interest in the lad, including the local landscape painter Eugène Boudin, who invited him to come along on outdoors sketching trips. Later, Monet recalled that this experience was a revelation to him. "I watched more attentively," he recalled, "and then it was if a veil had been torn aside. . . . I grasped what painting could be." His revelation may not have been quite so sudden as this, since on another occasion Monet recalled that "Boudin, with untiring kindness, set about educating me. Eventually my eyes were opened, I understood nature; I learned to love it at the same time."[11]

However long the process, Monet learned Boudin's lessons well, and by 1859, he felt ready to apply for a state-supported scholarship to study in Paris. His father, who may have expected his son to study at the Ecole des Beaux-Arts, was for the moment swayed by his son's enthusiasm. But the municipal council (deciding that despite Monet's evident talent he was insufficiently serious) rejected the young man's application. Despite this, he decided to head for Paris, equipped with letters of introduction to several painters whom he expected would give him advice. His father, for the moment mollified, agreed to provide a monthly allowance.

And so Claude Monet arrived in Paris in the spring of 1859, where he moved around from place to place and tried to focus on his career. This meant visiting the Salon and paying calls on the artists to whom he had letters of introduction—in the expectation that he would find good advice as well as a suitable artist's studio in which to enroll, en route to success in the Salon.

Writing Boudin, he told him that he had visited the Salon ("some nice Corots and . . . some awful Diaz," he noted, adding that "Monsieur Lhuillier's [sic] picture is way off the mark"). He also visited several painters, including Constant Troyon, who looked at two still lifes Monet brought him and judged that the color was "all right" and "the effect is correct," but that it all came too easily to him. "If you want my advice," he told Monet, "and want to go in for art seriously, begin by joining a studio which specializes in figure painting"—in other words, "learn to draw." At the same time, Troyon encouraged Monet to "do some copying at the Louvre" and "go to the country from time to time and make studies." First then, in the order of priorities, would be some work in Paris (Troyon recommended Thomas Couture's atelier, where Manet had gone), then a return to Le Havre to study landscape, followed by a permanent move to Paris. Kindly, Troyon told the young man to "come and see me often: show me what you're doing and with enough courage you'll make it."[12]

Based on this response, Monet's father and aunt agreed to more financial support. The idea was to enter Thomas Couture's atelier, who would prepare the young man for the Ecole des Beaux-Arts. But Monet's interview with Couture went badly—possibly because the master offered criticism to which the young man objected. In any case, not long after, Monet referred to Couture as "that bad-tempered fellow."[13]

Instead, Monet chose the Académie Suisse (named after its founder, Charles Suisse), whose pupils had included Delacroix, Corot, and Courbet. Located on the Ile de la Cité near the Pont Saint-Michel, this particular academy was known for its lack of regimentation and restrictions. It was quite unlike traditional ateliers, where the students began by drawing first from engravings and then progressing to drawing from plaster casts before being allowed access to life classes—that is, with live models. Permission to paint came only after complete mastery over drawing. Instead, for a fixed monthly sum, the Académie Suisse allowed each student to use whatever medium he wished to depict a male model (for three weeks) and a female model (for one week).

Monet, who entered the academy in early 1860, seems to have enjoyed the freedom, and it was now that he probably met and became friends with Camille Pissarro, who arrived at the Académie Suisse that spring. It was also clear that Monet enjoyed partying, especially at the Bavarian-style Brasserie des Martyrs, which was located all too conveniently near his most recent lodging, on the seventh floor of an apartment on Rue Jean-Baptiste Pigalle. Later in life, Monet told the art critic Gustave Geffroy, "I used to go to the notorious Brasserie in the Rue des Martyrs, where I wasted a lot of time; it did me the greatest harm."[14]

In any case, Monet's output during his first stay in Paris was neither sizable nor remarkable.

That year, Nadar—whose caricatures Monet had admired—exhibited sixty of his photographic portraits of notable Parisians, thus staking his claim for photography on turf hitherto owned by portrait painters. The show was a great success, with one critic writing that "the whole constellation, literary, artistic, dramatic, political . . . of our era has filed through his studio." This, the critic continued, made this extraordinary series of portraits "the Pantheon . . . of our generation."[15]

At the other end of the spectrum, young Emile Zola was having one of the worst years of his life. He twice failed the baccalaureate examination, including a second try in Marseilles (after a month of convalescence in Aix), which he failed even more miserably than the first. After his return to Paris in November, he had no plans or possibilities—only a dismal future ahead.

Fifteen-year-old Sarah Bernhardt was also having a difficult year. She had become so ill after an attention-getting escapade that she had been sent home from her convent school. There she endured the machinations of her mother, Youle, who had worked her way via the bedposts into financial security and who now had similar plans for her daughters. Youle had taken due note of the fact that Sarah was growing up, and this meant openly encouraging the men who regularly flocked to the Bernhardt abode in their decidedly nonmarital interest in the girl. As the Goncourt brothers waspishly pointed out in their journal: "Overheard in Brabant's restaurant," they noted: "The Sarah Bernhardt family, now *there's* a family! The mother made whores of her daughters as soon as they turned thirteen."[16]

Was Bernhardt beautiful? Although her eyes were described as "flashing" and "unforgettable," she was also considered thin—ridiculously so, in fact, according to the well-upholstered standards of the day. Still, she was undeniably attractive, not the least because of the intensity of her gaze, the grace of her bearing, and her air of reckless gaiety. The Duke de Morny, the emperor's powerful and wealthy half-brother, who was one of Youle's protectors, had no doubt about Sarah's future: she should be an actress, he declared. But Sarah was having none of it. Attracted by the emotional intensity and ritual of the Roman Catholic Church, she had decided to become a nun.

Morny thought that Sarah might change her mind if she could experience an evening at the Comédie-Française and recommended that she and her mother share a box with a mutual friend, Alexandre Dumas *père*. Sarah was willing, and as the curtain went up, she experienced a moment of almost religious intensity. Even as a child she had realized that she "could not exist . . . without a passion of some kind," and now, as the curtain was raised, she thought that she might faint—"It was as though the curtain of my future life were being raised." The play reduced her to tears (which annoyed her mother), and eventually she became so caught up in the drama that she burst into loud sobs, attracting the attention of much of the audience. "This," she concluded, "was the début of my artistic life!"[17]

According to one account, on the way home she fell asleep in Dumas's carriage. He carried her to her room, where she heard him tell her, "*Bonsoir, petite étoile.*"[18]

Sarah had indeed been converted, and Dumas, in saying good night to his "little star," may have anticipated her star-studded future. But this future still remained a long way off, even with the assistance of the Duke de Morny, who used his influence to ensure Sarah's entrance into the Conservatoire de Musique et de Déclamation—Paris's Conservatory of Music and Drama.

By now, her dreams of the convent were completely forgotten.

Demolition of the barriers of the Farmers-General wall for the construction of the Place de l'Etoile (today's Place Charles de Gaulle), with the Arc de Triomphe in the background. Engraving in Le Monde Illustrée, *18 February 1860. © Bridgeman Images*

CHAPTER NINE

~

Suddenly Larger

(1860)

On January 1, 1860, Paris suddenly became a vastly larger city. Overnight, its surface area more than doubled and its boundaries moved from the old Farmers-General tax wall to the more recent Thiers fortifications, located about a mile outside the tax wall. In the process, Paris enlarged its population by one-third, annexing the eleven whole and thirteen partial suburban communes surrounding it (the Thiers fortifications having sliced through these partial communes). The city now was divided into twenty rather than twelve arrondissements—ones that bore no resemblance, either in shape or numerical order, to the original twelve.

Haussmann in fact would have preferred to extend Paris city limits even farther, to include the notorious Zone along the outer reaches of the Thiers fortifications, a no-man's-land where building was not allowed and where ragpickers and other detritus from society washed up. It was in this forbidding wasteland that Napoleon III planned to build a wide ring road and a tree-lined promenade. Beyond this, the prefect and the emperor now had dreams of extending Paris to include the entire department of the Seine. But Haussmann's growing number of enemies feared that further enlargement of the city would inevitably enlarge Haussmann's own power, and they put a stop to expansion beyond the actual fortifications.

Given the realities, Haussmann moved quickly to establish Paris city limits at the Thiers fortification line, demolishing the Farmers-General wall and launching the newly enlarged Paris.[1] This included doubling the width of the military road that ran alongside the Thiers fortifications and turning it into the outermost ring of boulevards surrounding the city. These became the Boulevards des Maréchaux (Marshals' Boulevards), bearing the names of military leaders of the First Empire. The destruction of the Farmers-General wall created yet another ring of boulevards, known as the Outer Boulevards, between the Boulevards des Maréchaux and the Grands Boulevards—a line of boulevards with a series of names such as Courcelles, Clichy, and Rochechouart that marked the dividing point between the old Paris and the new.

Next on Haussmann's agenda was elevation to full ministerial rank, as minister for Paris. But here, he would encounter stout opposition from his enemies.

～

"This is no longer the Paris I used to know," Théophile Gautier told the Goncourt brothers one evening in August. "It's Philadelphia, St Petersburg, anything you like, but not Paris."

The Goncourt brothers mournfully agreed. "Our Paris," they wrote that November, "the Paris in which we were born, the Paris of the manners of 1830 to 1848, is disappearing." Indeed, they lamented, "these new boulevards . . . make one think of London or some Babylon of the future." They added that it was difficult to live in a world of change—"the soul feels as uncomfortable as a man who moves into a new house before the plaster is dry."[2]

They of course were referring to changes in morals and manners as well as in streets and buildings, but the physical changes themselves were sufficient to upset those wed to the old order.

Baron Haussmann was now embarked on his Second System, the money for which had just become available after considerable foot-dragging in the Legislature—the result of a small but growing legislative opposition to both the prefect himself and to the enormous expenses he was incurring. This opposition reflected public opinion, for while a preponderance of Parisians, especially among the bourgeoisie, had approved of Haussmann's First System of *grands travaux*, viewing them as a much-needed improvement of the city, the magnitude of Haussmann's Second System now struck many as unnecessary and dangerously expensive. It was thus against a background of wary approval that demolition and construction now began anew throughout the city, largely at the hands of private companies but propelled by the prefect of the Seine and his emperor.

An early target was the Place de l'Etoile, on which Haussmann had been itching to get his hands ever since his run-in with Hittorff over the plans back in 1854. Despite a few disappointments, Haussmann's plans had won out, and now he at long last had the opportunity of putting them into place. No sooner had the tollhouses and barriers of the Farmers-General wall gone down than the earth-movers got to work, creating the twelve-armed star and enormous circular space that the Place de l'Etoile (now Place Charles-de-Gaulle) soon became.

Symmetry and straightness of line was at the heart of Haussmann's vision here, as it was everywhere, with the size, façades, and placement of the town houses surrounding the Place tightly controlled. But as for the twelve roads themselves, he had a job of it, not only in updating the old roads that still rambled through the area but in creating new ones that linked up with the rest of his fledgling network, all the while obtaining the symmetrical arrangement he wanted. This involved building new roads and opening, extending, and straightening others until he had the star-like arrangement he had envisioned, radiating out from the Arc de Triomphe.

While construction was tearing up large portions of Paris, the emperor—mindful of the importance of his support from the working classes—was insistent that lower-income areas receive their share of benefits, most especially in green spaces. The western and wealthier portion of the city had already received the Bois de Boulogne; legislation in 1860 now ceded the Bois de Vincennes to the city, to provide a public area for walks and enjoyment for residents of eastern Paris (with the stipulation that the city retain the area's military installations, including the castle and fort of Vincennes). Haussmann did not share the emperor's enthusiasm for green spaces for the hoi polloi, but mindful of his emperor's desires, he pushed forward efforts to provide parks and gardens throughout the city. By the decade's end, these would include the spectacular park of Buttes-Chaumont in the north and the lovely Parc Montsouris in the south, as well as other smaller parks or squares throughout the city, especially (such as the Square des Batignolles or the Square de la Place du Commerce) in the newly accessed arrondissements.

Doubling the size of Paris and adding almost half a million new consumers also meant that Haussmann and Belgrand would have to rethink their strategy for supplying water to the city—especially as the new portions of

Paris now included the heights of Montmartre and Belleville, which rose well above the highest points within the former city limits.

This was a big topic of discussion among Parisians throughout the year, since Paris's current water supply—from the Ourcq canal as well as from the ancient aqueducts of Belleville and Le Pré-Saint-Gervais to the northeast and the equally ancient one from Rungis to the south, along with the Seine's murky contribution and some inadequate spurts from the artesian wells of Grenelle and Passy—did not come close to providing what was necessary. Proposals for pumping more water from the Seine or for diverting water from the Loire were roundly rejected, and to meet the immediate need, Haussmann decided to focus on diverting water from the River Dhuys, while studying the possibilities of channeling water from the Vanne as well as from the Somme-Soude. Belgrand and his men soon concluded that water from the Dhuys could be channeled to a new reservoir at Ménilmontant, from where it could be pumped up to Montmartre and Belleville and then allowed to flow downward to thirsty citizens by force of gravity. Within a remarkably short period, water from the Dhuys would begin to flow into Paris.

Who would be in charge of this water was another question, but Haussmann did not hesitate to establish at the outset that the municipality's responsibility was limited to channeling the river water to the city, creating separate distribution networks (for public and private use) after it arrived, and administering the water for public use, including sewers. Water for private use would be managed by a private company (the Compagnie Générale des Eaux), under the prefect's control, with regulations (including a minimum daily volume, for which the company paid) that encouraged the company to make landlords bring water up to the highest floors.

Haussmann did not intend that control over Paris's water slip from his hands; he simply did not want the bother of having to administer it.

By this time, the Rothschilds, with their multinational business empire, had withstood the Pereire brothers' challenge, not only in France but across Europe. By 1860, the Rothschilds were once more the foremost lenders to European governments, and in 1864, Baron Rothschild would benefit from the creation of a new bank, the Société Générale de Crédit Industriel et Commercial, which became France's foremost deposit bank as well as a major commercial bank heavily involved in industrial investment, construction, and public works. Rothschild did not figure openly among the bank's leaders (the same group that had formed the Réunion Financière), but his role in challenging the Pereires with this syndicate was understood. The Pereires, according to one biographer, had lost a major battle here.[3]

But the Pereire brothers were far from down and out. Baron Rothschild may have been on better terms with the emperor now than he had been in the past, but the Pereires still had Georges Haussmann's ear, especially when it came to negotiating the terms for new loans, where they proved willing and even eager to lower their commission to well below that demanded by Rothschild.

And so the Pereires continued to make their mark on Paris, not only on the seventeenth arrondissement, where Boulevard Pereire remains a testament to their extensive activities on the Monceau Plain, but also in the nearby Opéra quarter, where they made massive purchases well before this quarter was developed—causing a certain amount of talk about their remarkable good luck in real estate investments. Indeed, some were quite willing to attribute this run of good fortune to insider information—and information from the highest levels at that.

As early as 1858, soon after the assassination attempt on Louis-Napoleon at the entrance to the old opera house on Rue Le Peletier, Haussmann decided that a new opera house was necessary—one that would provide a more secure entrance for the emperor—and determined on the site, just north of the Boulevard des Capucines's portion of the Grands Boulevards. But it was not until autumn of 1860 that the site of the new opera house was announced. With ill will mounting behind the scenes between rival architects, including Viollet-le-Duc (whom Empress Eugenie strongly favored), the minister for the arts sidestepped making a decision by opening a competition for architects to build this grand new opera house, one that would be a suitable jewel for the City of Light.

The result would not be what anyone had expected.

Affairs were developing unexpectedly in Italy as well. The citizens of Florence, Modena, Parma, and Bologna flat-out revolted against their rulers and voted to join Piedmont-Sardinia, even after Louis-Napoleon ordered Piedmont-Sardinia to give them up, and the four rebel city-states then decided to follow the banner of Giuseppe Garibaldi, whose republicanism alarmed the distinctly unrepublican French emperor.

Louis-Napoleon, along with the British, now agreed to the expansion of Piedmont-Sardinia, under its monarch, Victor Emmanuel, rather than admit Garibaldi to the table. In return, Louis-Napoleon demanded Nice and Savoy, whose citizens cheerfully supported the takeover by voting overwhelmingly to join France. But affairs in the Italian peninsula were far from settled. Naples now revolted, followed by Sicily, drawing Garibaldi and his large army of red-shirted volunteers to their aid. Landing in Sicily, Garibaldi captured Palermo and ousted its king, then crossed the Strait of Messina, sending the king of Naples fleeing.

Among those in Garibaldi's army were Maxime Du Camp and Alexandre Dumas *père*, both of whom—like so many intellectuals and literary figures of the time—were immensely attracted by the charismatic general and his cause of Italian unification. Dumas, who had already made Garibaldi's acquaintance and been won over, was sailing in his small schooner, the *Emma*, when he met up with Garibaldi in Sicily. Dumas, as Victor Hugo's eldest son, Charles, observed, had never been shy about moving into the center of things whenever great deeds were under way: "Revolutions are his concern." Charles added, "All nationalist parties are his party. . . . He offers, en passant, the advice of a much preoccupied man, implying that it had better be taken without delay, because he has twenty-five volumes to deliver before the end of the week." Dumas entered this particular historical event with his usual enthusiasm, buying guns for the cause (1,000 rifles and 550 carbines) with money he had originally intended for a trip around the Mediterranean.

Dumas by now was not a young man, but his energy amazed everyone, including his son. Upon the senior Dumas's nighttime return from Italy to Paris after an eight-day journey, the son admonished him to get some rest. The father protested, "I tired? —why I'm as fresh as a daisy!" He then proceeded to visit his friend Théophile Gautier, whom he awoke out of a sound sleep, and the two talked until four o'clock in the morning. Dumas *fils*, who by this time was worn out, persuaded his father to walk home with him, during which his father talked constantly. They reached home at six o'clock, at which point Dumas *père* asked for a lamp. Whatever for? the son asked. "To light [it]," the father replied. "I'm going to settle down to work."[4]

Maxime Du Camp was similarly flabbergasted by the senior Dumas's energy: "It seemed as if he could scarcely contain the life and energy ever ready to overflow all bounds." Even "after ten or eleven hours of conversation—and what conversation it was—he was as fresh as at the beginning."

As Michelet once said of Dumas, "He is an element of Nature, one of her original forces."[5]

After Sicily and Naples, Garibaldi's next step was to attack the Papal States from the south, which drew Piedmont-Sardinia into the fray. The Piedmontese forces now accomplished the double objective of blocking Garibaldi's army and defeating the papal forces that had arrayed against them. This led to the absorption of Naples and Sicily into the newly formed Kingdom of Italy.[6]

Since settling affairs in Italy the previous year, Louis-Napoleon had chosen not to intervene in the Italian imbroglio, except to claim Nice and Savoy. But although French forces still protected the pope in Rome, French Catholics (not to mention the pope) were dismayed by what they viewed as the emperor's double-dealing. Bologna, after all, had been part of the Papal States, but Louis-Napoleon merely published a pamphlet consoling the pope for his loss by proclaiming that "the smaller the territory the greater the sovereign." French Catholics became increasingly uneasy, and the members of the Académie Française, a bastion of conservatism, expressed its concerns by electing Jean-Baptiste Henri Lacordaire, a Dominican theologian, preacher, and writer, to join them.

Not only French Catholics were deserting their emperor. French industrialists, long accustomed to operating within the strong protectionist policies of the French state, were appalled by the emperor's dramatic break with tradition in signing a trade agreement with Britain, which he announced to an astonished public in early 1860. Although not a complete free-trade agreement, it amounted to something of a revolution in that both sides now agreed to lower their trade barriers. Louis-Napoleon, who had long supported free trade, had decided that it was time to lower trade barriers as much as possible, in the interest of stimulating, or restimulating, the economic expansion that had so far accompanied his reign but was showing worrisome signs of fading. As it happened, further commercial agreements followed with other European nations, including Prussia. But factory closings and mass layoffs signaled trouble, especially in the textile industries, where a "cotton famine" caused by the American Civil War severely affected the entire industry.

Now that Louis-Napoleon had alienated many Catholics as well as protectionists, he needed to cultivate other alliances. Under these circumstances, his half-brother, the Duke de Morny, advised him to make a major shift and liberalize his regime. Louis-Napoleon had already dipped a toe into the waters of reform the year before by granting amnesty to those convicted of political crimes (an amnesty that Victor Hugo proudly ignored, since "Napoleon the Little" was still on the throne). This was a small step, but late in 1860, the emperor took a larger one, restoring the "right of address" for the Legislature, thereby giving the deputies the right to respond to the emperor's speech at the opening session—a measure that involved changing the Constitution. For the first time, deputies at the start of each parliamentary session could now state their own views on that year's legislative program. In addition, three cabinet ministers were given the job of defending and explaining government policies to the Legislature, while newspapers were allowed to publish full transcripts of parliamentary debates.

Interestingly, Louis-Napoleon chose the moment to introduce these reforms at a time when Empress Eugenie was absent. For astonishingly, in mid-November, the empress suddenly disappeared.

The empress, of course, was ardently Catholic and just as ardently conservative. In addition, she had tasted independence and power during her five-month regency the year before, while the emperor was leading his armies in Italy. Her interests, her persuasions, and her politics—far more Catholic and conservative than those of her husband—conflicted on many points with the direction he was taking. It was already a difficult time for her, as she was in deep mourning for her sister, who had unexpectedly died. But in addition, Eugenie may well have been sick of her husband's relentless philandering, which he took little trouble to hide.

The empress left suddenly and without explanation, traveling incognito as the Countess of Pierrefonds—although those on the lookout for her could not have missed the regal style in which she traveled, accompanied by a retinue of two ladies-in-waiting, two gentlemen courtiers, and ten servants. She left for London and then traveled to Scotland. She did not return for a month, but when she did, her husband was waiting for her at Boulogne.

To all appearances, they were reconciled, but Eugenie had clearly used the time to consider her future role in this marriage. Empress, yes, but especially mother. She was appalled at the reforms her husband had initiated during her absence, viewing them as signs of weakness that would endanger her son's position when he came to power. For the past two years, she had insisted on attending her husband's twice-weekly Council of Ministers meetings; from now on, she would no longer be a mere spectator but would make her own contributions to the discussions. She would now dedicate herself to preserving the throne for her young son.

～

In the meantime, life in Paris went on. Georges Bizet, after three years in Rome, took his fourth year of the Prix de Rome in Paris, as he was allowed. The prize provided him with a modest income, at least until the end of 1861, and he reduced his expenses by moving back in with his parents, in the ninth arrondissement. His first choice, to have an opera of his accepted at one of the lyric theaters, was not immediately forthcoming, and he seems to have filled his days by teaching piano, harmony, and singing, as well as by working as an arranger and transcriber. But Paris could be intimidating to a sensitive soul like Bizet, and he had been "scared of coming back," as he wrote a friend from Italy. "I am scared of dealing with theatre directors and librettists," he confessed. "I'm scared of singers, I'm scared in a word, of the tacit civility of people saying nothing disagreeable to your face but stubbornly making sure you get nowhere."[7] The next few years would not be easy ones for him.

In another part of town, Berthe Morisot, having spent long hours with her sister copying art at the Louvre, had changed teachers, with the aim of working as much as possible out of doors and in nature. The sisters' new teacher, Jean-Baptiste-Camille Corot, quickly became a friend as well as a valued instructor, one who proved a useful guide in developing their talent. The sisters evidently paid no heed to Corot's critics, who thought he had lapsed into landscape painting because he could not draw figures.

Other young artists were also making their way, not always with success. Claude Monet had stayed on in Paris, with his father's reluctant approval, but he soon found his allowance diminished—not so much because of his failure to enter the atelier of Thomas Couture, but because of the birth of an out-of-wedlock child to his father, who now had significant new expenses to bear. Monet may not at first have been aware of this unexpected development, but he certainly was mindful of what loomed in November, when he turned twenty and became eligible for the draft. His fears proved all too real the following year when he drew a number in the draft lottery that committed him to seven years in the army. Choosing to join the Chasseurs d'Afrique (Monet later claimed that their colorful uniforms had attracted him), he soon would be stationed in Algeria.

Edouard Manet, eight years older than Monet and already well beyond any dangers from the draft, had by now moved into a studio in the unfashionable Batignolles quarter in newly annexed northwest Paris. There, he began living with Suzanne Leenhoff, a pianist of Dutch birth two years his senior, who may have been the model who at about this time posed nude for several of his paintings. Manet had made Leenhoff's acquaintance back when he was an art student; it was then that she came to live with his family to give piano lessons to him and his brother Eugène. Suzanne by now had an illegitimate son, who does not seem to have been Edouard's but may have been the offspring of Edouard's father. The possibilities for family strife over Edouard's relationship with Suzanne seem to have been considerable, but for the moment Edouard kept their relationship a secret.

While setting up his unorthodox household, Edouard continued to pursue his vision of truth in art, declaring to his friend Antonin Proust: "We've been perverted by all the artistic tricks of the trade. . . . Who's going to give us back a clear, direct kind of painting and do away with the frills?" Pondering this, he added, "The one true way is to go straight ahead, without worrying about what people are going to say."[8]

⌒

Other young strivers in Paris were doing well for themselves. Gustave Eiffel's reputation had spread rapidly following his remarkable role in supervising the bridge over the Garonne, and in 1860, he was promoted to engineer-general in his company's railway division, complete with a nice raise—including 5 percent of the profits of any projects he henceforth directed.

Nadar was also doing well, despite the fierce competition that already was growing among professional photographers in Paris. It was now that Nadar, with the financial backing of the Pereire brothers, left his modest Rue Saint-Lazare studio and established a far more glamorous one at 35 Boulevard des Capucines, in the heart of the emerging Opéra quarter. His brother Adrien had by 1860 gone bankrupt, and Nadar now paid off much of his brother's debt and bought up his equipment, even after expenditures on a huge and expensive renovation at the new address.

Some rose and others sank in the boomtown that was Second Empire Paris, a cutthroat metropolis that rewarded enterprise and hustle but mercilessly punished those who failed to make the grade. Emile Zola was by now among the latter group, having endured a lycée education without having attained the expected and necessary diploma. This unfortunately disqualified the young man for any reasonably lucrative white-collar work, while at the same time his education had not prepared him in any way for manual labor. Almost destitute, he and his mother—who still was hopelessly wed to her impossible dreams of financial restitution—left one dreary abode after another, finally settling in early 1860 in an eighth-floor garret at the top of 35 Rue Saint-Victor.

This was the heart of the area that Louis-Napoleon had chosen for his longed-for extension of Rue des Ecoles, where it crossed the newly formed Rue Monge. Haussmann had by now convinced the emperor that the Rue des Ecoles should stop at this point, its place in the grand scheme of things to be taken by the new Boulevard Saint-Germain. Located at the center of all this activity, Emile and his mother lived in a cacophony of roadbuilding surrounded by demolished houses. Soon number 35 Rue Saint-Victor would disappear into the rubble along with the rest.

But for now, young Zola needed a job. Not that he wanted one—he yearned to write. Yet extreme poverty forced the issue, and at last, the same friend of his father who had opened the doors for a *lycée* education found him employment as a low-level functionary at the Customs House. Here, at the Docks Napoléon, overlooking the Canal Saint-Martin, Zola collected his pittance of a salary and endured largely by gazing out the window and dreaming of Provence. "Before me," he wrote a friend, "stretches endless desert."[9]

After two months, he quit. But other jobs were not forthcoming, especially ones that would allow him to earn his living with his pen, and his situation—and that of his mother—was becoming desperate. By the year's end, his mother had moved to a dismal boardinghouse, while Emile moved to an attic room in the most squalid part of Rue Soufflot. There, he endured in quarters that resembled the interior of a coffin, where he looked out on a sooty wall and suffered from the damp. During the cold winter nights, he would incessantly write stories and poetry, all of these, according to one biographer, "alarmingly bad."[10]

Reduced to setting traps on the roof for sparrows and broiling them on the end of a curtain rod, he lived for days with his dreams and little else. And he wrote—badly, but he wrote.

⁓

Zola knew his subject intimately when he wrote, in *La Curée*, of the upheaval that Haussmann was creating throughout Paris. "When the first network is finished," his character Saccard notes, "the fun will begin. The second network will pierce the city in every direction. . . . The remains will disappear in clouds of plaster. . . . A cutting there," he added, "one further on, cuttings on every side, Paris slashed with sabre-cuts, its veins open."[11]

But as the decade progressed, Haussmann would no longer be able to ram his enormous projects through as before. No longer would an overwhelming majority of deputies be willing to give way to the emperor or, more specifically, to Haussmann. Republican opposition to imperial rule was growing, and Haussmann was a convenient target for those who wanted to attack the emperor without actually saying so.

In addition, Haussmann's own family affairs had opened him up to considerable criticism. His wife was rumored to have indiscreetly mentioned at dinner parties that her real estate purchases had been so silly because whenever her husband advised her to invest in a certain block, it was certain to be pulled down soon after (a rumor that one historian has called "without foundation," originating with "a disgruntled Orléanist").[12] Still, Haussmann's eldest daughter, Marie-Henriette, unquestionably created problems by falling in love with one of her father's young employees, leading to a hastily arranged marriage with a far wealthier and more suitable gentleman—a marriage that the Pereires may have had a hand in arranging and that, before it was over, involved both the municipal council and the emperor. Haussmann himself caused comment with his showgirls, while his youngest daughter, Valentine, a strong-minded beauty widely believed to be yet another of the emperor's favorites, would in mid-decade be married off hastily to provide a semblance of respectability to the birth of her son, whom most regarded as another of the emperor's illegitimate children.

But all of this, although admittedly rich stuff, was merely fodder for gossip. Haussmann's real problem was a more personal one. Autocratic by nature, he had become increasingly self-important with his years of success and power, marked by his easy access to the emperor. But the emperor would be decreasingly able to protect Haussmann. In part, this was the product of those new opportunities for opposition afforded the emperor's critics after 1860, when the Second Empire pivoted cautiously toward liberalism. This encouraged republican opposition, which now found a growing audience among those who were alarmed by the ever-larger loans that Haussmann's projects required. In addition, the French economy, whose expansion Louis-Napoleon had so strongly promoted, would not continue its remarkable growth into the empire's second decade. This in turn would undermine the very pillars on which both emperor and empire rested.

But perhaps most important was the health and strength of the emperor himself, which would markedly decline as the decade progressed. Haussmann would bear the brunt of Louis-Napoleon's physical decline, as the emperor became decreasingly able to deal with the host of problems that came his way. Increasingly, the transformation of Paris, and the prefect who was so staunchly driving it, would have to take second place in the emperor's mind to other concerns.

And so, in late 1860, when Haussmann pressed to be appointed minister for Paris, Louis-Napoleon—fearful of a violent reaction from Haussmann's enemies—did not give his prefect what he so dearly wanted. Instead, the emperor gave Haussmann the right to take part in any deliberations of the Council of Ministers affecting the city of Paris. And subsequently, the emperor tried to soften any blow by piling honors on Haussmann, including the Grand Cross of the Legion of Honor. It was now that the emperor named one of the major new thoroughfares in Paris as Boulevard Haussmann, in the prefect's honor.

But Haussmann was bitter about not attaining the rank of full minister, and years later, when writing his memoirs, he remarked that after this, his opponents in the government never missed an opportunity "to make me feel . . . that a distance still existed between us; that I was a mere prefect (thus, their subordinate)."[13]

Although Haussmann did not realize it, these enemies would in time bring about his downfall.

The Great Drawing Room of the Napoleon III Apartments, c.1861 (photo). © Louvre, Paris, France / Bridgeman Images

CHAPTER TEN

Turning Point

(1861)

From his contemporaries' perspective, the new decade promised ever-more-glittering success for Louis-Napoleon's empire. After almost a decade of rule, his Second Empire seemed more secure than ever. His country's economy was booming, and his position among the other European rulers was well established. Moreover, his health appeared good, and his energies, sexual and otherwise, remained undiminished.

Yet storm clouds loomed, which the emperor himself was quick to sense. Despite his long-held confidence in his destiny, Louis-Napoleon had begun to harbor darkened thoughts about the future. As early as 1859, he confided to his cousin, Prince Napoleon, that "nothing lasts for ever." He then added that he did not believe in the future.[1]

It was during the early 1860s that Louis-Napoleon began to send large sums of money to Nathaniel William John Strode, an Englishman whom the emperor had used as a go-between to repay his former mistress, Lizzie Howard, for the large sums she had spent on his election and 1851 coup. This second set of sums was recorded as gifts, but they were not for Lizzie. Only later it was discovered that around this time Strode bought and furnished a country house called Camden Place in Kent, which would in time serve as a home for the exiled emperor and empress. Even this early, Louis-Napoleon was contemplating a possible need for escape.

His regime still glittered with power and glory, but for those on the lookout for danger signs, its decline had already begun. For one thing, Louis-Napoleon's health was deteriorating, even though his condition—

gallstones, which would not be diagnosed for several more years—was not yet serious or incapacitating. Still, Louis-Napoleon's empire depended entirely on his person, especially since his heir was still a very young child. Any threat to the emperor, whether from assassins or disease, was a threat to the entire dazzling edifice.

Yet any impediments to Louis-Napoleon's health certainly did not limit his sexual adventures. Despite at least one bout with gonorrhea, he continued his avid pursuit of the ladies. According to the writer and historian Prosper Mérimée, who for years had been a friend and adviser to the emperor, Louis-Napoleon "likes to chase the girls. . . . He gets all excited and for a full two weeks can think of nothing or no one else. Then he immediately cools down and doesn't think about her again."[2] Following which, the whole fandango would begin all over with another woman.

Empress Eugenie was not pleased with her husband's behavior, which led to frequent altercations. According to observers, he was terrified of these encounters and would do anything to avoid them, save giving up the indiscretions that caused them. Louis-Napoleon did not give up his women, but he did give way to his wife on one important subject: from now on, Eugenie would exercise a great deal of political power, not only in attending meetings of the Council of Ministers but also by having an ongoing and commanding influence over her husband's decisions. Some quietly referred to her as the co-ruler of France, especially in her dealings with foreign ambassadors, with whom she now conducted her own private discussions.

In addition to feeling the effects of the emperor's declining health, the empire was beginning to suffer from its very success, or at least from its longevity. With more than a decade having passed since the failure of the Second Republic and the fear of anarchy that had catapulted Louis-Napoleon into power, his subjects no longer dreaded mob rule and devastation. The passage of a decade had brought a new generation of bourgeoisie to the fore, including many who were opposed to the Roman Catholic Church and who were equally opposed to the empire's constraints on their liberties.

At the same time, Louis-Napoleon had seriously undermined his support with conservative Catholics by his interventions in Italy, which had blown holes through the hitherto-sacred integrity of the thoroughly secular Papal States. And just as damaging, he had angered the significant group of protectionists among his supporters. Even the working class was emitting rumbles of discontent, as prices rose, misery increased, and the well-to-do were more ostentatiously well-to-do than ever.

The emperor responded by trying to shore up support among his more liberal subjects by making further concessions, such as those of late 1861, whereby the Legislature received a say over supplementary and special funds, hitherto raised by decree, as well as by other concessions that gave Parliament greater control over the budget—no small thing given Haussmann's enormous ongoing expenditures.

Still, Louis-Napoleon's Second Empire was far from being a parliamentary or a liberal regime, and his unpredictable and unsettling forays into foreign affairs only added to a growing sense of unease, both at home and abroad.

⌒

"Everyone distrusts him without knowing why," the Austrian ambassador, Prince Richard Metternich, wrote to his foreign secretary. Britain's ambassador, Lord Cowley, reported that "he must be a bold man who speculates upon the Emperor's intentions. . . . I must doubt whether he knows them himself."[3]

Louis-Napoleon was a schemer and had been from the outset. But now, his constant plotting and counterplotting had begun to undercut him with his staunchest allies, including Queen Victoria, who—despite her susceptibility to his charm—came to regard him as untrustworthy.

It was now that affairs in far-off Mexico came to the fore. These began that autumn when a Mexican diplomat, a childhood friend of Eugenie's, suggested that Louis-Napoleon should think seriously about founding a great Catholic empire in Mexico, with a European Catholic prince as emperor. Eugenie immediately thought of the young archduke of Austria, Maximilian, as the emperor-to-be, and her husband quickly saw the possibilities. After all, this scheme would prevent the predominantly Protestant United States from taking over Spain's former colonies of Latin America, which had recently won their independence. And the timing was right, since at the moment, the Americans were thoroughly mired in their bloody civil war and could be counted on paying little heed to affairs in Mexico. In addition, the idea appealed to Louis-Napoleon because it would involve the Austrian emperor's younger brother. According to Eugenie's later interviews with Maurice Paléologue, "In my husband's thoughts, the elevation of the Austrian archduke to the throne of Mexico, would one day serve him as an argument to obtain from [Austrian Emperor] Franz-Joseph the cessation [transfer] of Venice to Italy."[4]

Mexico had undergone decades of upheaval and corruption since its independence in 1821, until in 1858 Benito Juárez—a native Mexican lawyer and a reform-minded leader—became the constitutionally mandated president of Mexico. Prominent wealthy conservatives roundly opposed Juárez and his reforms, and their wild stories of Church property confiscated, large estates seized, nuns raped, and priests killed made the needed impression on the French emperor and his impressionable wife. Later, defending the whole debacle, Eugenie protested that "we were assured that the Mexican people hated the Republic and would hail with enthusiasm the proclamation of the monarchy" and that a Catholic prince with great allure such as Maximilian would be welcomed everywhere with open arms.[5]

Evidently neither Eugenie nor Louis-Napoleon knew that among those who had substantial financial interests at stake in Mexico was the Duke de Morny, Louis's half-brother, who had a lot of money to lose now that Juárez had suspended payments of foreign debts (the period was for two years, but many feared a far worse scenario).[6] And so, plunging ahead, France, along with Great Britain and Spain, signed an agreement aimed at forcing Mexico to pay all its foreign debts, now. Late in 1861, the three nations sent a joint naval force to seize the Mexican port of Veracruz, with the intent of scooping up incoming customs. The British and Spanish troops did not last long in Veracruz, departing in early 1862, but the two thousand French forces remained and, unaccountably, began to march (without reinforcements) to Mexico City.

This was taking place even as Maximilian, the would-be emperor, was still making up his mind on whether or not to accept the proposed imperial crown.

⁓

In the meantime, Baron Haussmann continued to rebuild Paris. Already, the church tower of Saint-Germain l'Auxerrois (which many confuse with its bell tower, of Saint-Bartholomew's Day infamy) was being completed, alongside a new *mairie* (town hall) in the Gothic mode, to complement the ancient church.[7]

To the northwest, Boulevard Malesherbes was inaugurated that summer, having already created considerable consternation since, in addition to razing the slums of La Petite Pologne, nicer homes close to the Madeleine were for the first time sacrificed to make way for progress. To the northeast, work continued on the Place du Château-d'Eau (today's Place de la République) and those streets radiating out from it, including Boulevard de Magenta, Rue de Turbigo, and Boulevard du Prince Eugène (today's Boulevard Voltaire)— the latter now one of the longest streets in the city and one that sliced through the impoverished eastern section of Paris.

Boulevard de Magenta linked the Place du Château-d'Eau with the Gare du Nord, and construction similarly ploughed on around another railroad station, the Gare Saint-Lazare, to provide it with a new square (the Place de l'Europe) and link it, by new boulevards (the Rue de Rome and the Rue Saint-Lazare) as well as by other streets, to central Paris.

Portions of the Orléans family's stamping grounds in Monceau were being turned into a landscape garden, while—thanks to the Pereire brothers—new luxury housing was going up on the rest. Not far away, the avenues radiating from l'Etoile were beginning to take shape around the Arc de Triomphe, as Avenue Kléber, Avenue de Bezons (now Avenue Wagram), Avenue Josephine (now Avenue Marceau), Avenue Prince-Jerome (now Avenue Mac-Mahon and its continuation into Avenue Niel), Avenue Essling (now Avenue Carnot), and Avenue de Saint-Cloud (which would become, much to his gratification, Avenue Victor-Hugo) were beginning to emerge. These were all in addition to the Champs-Elysées, the newly carved Avenue de l'Impératrice (now Avenue Foch), and the widened Boulevard de Neuilly (today's Avenue de la Grand Armée). Altogether, it made for quite an impressive dig.

On the Left Bank, the eastern portion of the Boulevard Saint-Germain was now completed all the way to the Quai de la Tournelle and the Seine, while a tussle over the route for the Boulevard Saint-Michel as it traveled southward was finally resolved. The problem with the route as planned was that it cut off a corner of the Luxembourg estate, whose palace held the Senate and whose grounds accommodated various Senate officers, some of whom would have been directly affected by the loss of several outbuildings, stables, and service buildings. At length, May 1861 brought a compromise by which one official's stables and another's house would be rebuilt elsewhere, while the Médicis fountain would be moved a bit and turned to face the gardens—a solution that generations of subsequent visitors to the gardens have appreciated.

In comparison with the residents of the Ile de la Cité, though, the grandees of the Luxembourg clearly resided in a privileged world. While Haussmann and his associates ran hither and thither to accommodate the dignitaries, no one thought much about the thousands of the Cité's residents who were being driven from their homes, however decrepit, during the vast upheaval accompanying the destruction and construction that then was forever changing the island.

The 1860 incorporation of the outer communes now presented a full range of problems and challenges for Haussmann, as it clearly required an entirely new system of development, a Third System, on Paris's outskirts—to provide new roads and public works within these areas and to link them with the railroads as well as with central Paris. Not coincidentally, these new byways, wide and straight, would continue Haussmann's imposition of order, whether artistic or military. After all, these were roads on which troops could easily march, giving the emperor control over what had previously been inaccessible strongholds in the heart of poverty-stricken Paris.

Up in the already construction-heavy zone of the Place du Château d'Eau, a new avenue (Avenue des Amandiers, now the Avenue de la République) would link the Place to the east with Ménilmontant at Père-Lachaise cemetery, while Avenue Parmentier would run parallel to the Canal Saint-Martin, crossing the Avenue des Amandiers and linking the Hôpital Saint-Louis (founded by Henri IV) with Boulevard Voltaire at what now is Place Léon Blum.

To the east, Haussmann now planned to complete the Place du Trône (today's Place de la Nation)—the destination of that all-important east-west artery, the Rue du Faubourg Saint-Antoine—with a starburst of roads from the Place's center. To the north and northwest, the prefect began to extend roads linking the Gare du Nord and the Gare Saint-Lazare with the new arrondissements and linked these railway stations with each other as well as with the Gare de l'Est.

Haussmann had plans as well for western Paris, especially around the Place du Trocadéro, in the Chaillot quarter, where developers were already hard at work, as well as with the future Place Victor-Hugo, from which he sent an array of new roads in yet another starburst pattern. In an adjoining western neighborhood, he took special interest in the Rond-Point des Champs-Elysées, where he once again established symmetry as well as connection by extending the Avenue d'Antin (now the Avenue Franklin D. Roosevelt) northward.

As for the Left Bank, Haussmann planned to open the Boulevard Saint-Germain's western section from the Rue du Bac all the way to the Pont de la Concorde, as well as to extend the Rue de Rennes northward to the Boulevard Saint-Germain, linking this western portion of the Left Bank with the Gare Montparnasse.

Perhaps most stunning of Haussmann's planned Third System, however, would be the quarter rising up around the new Opéra, a quarter whose shape was already beginning to emerge during the works of Haussmann's Second System.[8] The star of this new and ultimately glamorous quarter would be the opera house itself, which in turn bestowed renown on Charles Garnier when, in June 1861, he won the competition to become its architect.

It was a startling decision, as Garnier was young and relatively unknown, and he had beaten out far better-known candidates such as Viollet-le-Duc. Garnier, born in the rough Left Bank quarter of Rue Mouffetard, where his father pounded out a living as a blacksmith and wheelwright, had embarked on his artistic career at Paris's Ecole Gratuite de Dessin, a free school meant for the sons of workmen hoping for careers as craftsmen. From there, Garnier had progressed to the prestigious Ecole des Beaux-Arts, where he ultimately carried off the Prix de Rome. It was a brilliant beginning to a career that began to sag in the middle, until Garnier unexpectedly won the competition to design Paris's new opera house.

Garnier beat out 170 other architects based on his frank recognition of this opera house's basic purpose. Rather than directing attention to the stage and what went on there, Garnier's Opéra would showcase the audience, providing a glittering backdrop for the social encounters that constituted the true heart of a night at the Paris opera.

Excavation began that August and continued into the next year. The cornerstone would be laid in July 1862, but—as has gone down in legend— excavation had by this time become mired in technical difficulties, most especially the discovery of a subterranean tributary of the Seine that ran directly beneath the building.

Still, no one was about to give up. After all, the old opera house had burned, and everyone who had any say in the matter—and many of those who did not—agreed that Paris was not and could not be Paris without an opera house.

By now the Pereire brothers were especially busy in the new Opera quarter, where they had made massive purchases before it even began to take shape. As early as 1853 they had begun their land purchases there, expanding these dramatically as the decade came to a close. In early 1861, envisioning a hotel even larger and more luxurious than their Hôtel du Louvre, they began work on their Grand Hôtel de la Paix, which occupied the entire block across from the new Opéra and was so huge that its central courtyard could accommo- date six hundred people seated at tables beneath the courtyard's glass canopy. Many of its eight hundred rooms had private bathrooms, and other luxuries included a smoking room, a reading room with a wide selection of inter- national newspapers, a telephone and telegraph equipped with translators, doctors available day and night, and electric as well as gas lighting. Within a year, Nadar would be installed there in a his own photography salon, and the renowned Café de la Paix would open on the hotel's ground floor. Despite the size and complexity of this project, the hotel opened fifteen months after its cornerstone was laid.

It was, of course, a great success. The Pereires had accurately—and, many said, suspiciously—determined that a major center of Paris was going to develop here and put their claim in early. But the brothers had begun to encounter signs of trouble, among them the arrest earlier that year of one of their closest colleagues, Jules Mirès, who was sentenced to five years of prison for swindling. Mirès had already created a significant scandal when the General Railways Fund, of which he was the director, went bankrupt, and although he managed to get his sentence set aside, he would continue to skate close to the line, and the Pereires with him.

Haussmann's close connection to the Pereires did not help his reputation, which already suffered from his high-handedness as well as the mounting costs of his *grands travaux*. He was a close associate of entrepreneurs mired in corruption, and the smell of speculation and graft surrounded him. Despite Haussmann's insistence on his probity, his enemies had begun to circle. They had already prevented him from achieving a ministry; their attacks would now only escalate.

Even as the face of Paris continued to change, more seekers of fame and fortune continued to pour into the city, among them Emile Zola's boyhood friend, young Paul Cézanne, who arrived torn by doubts but lured by the possibility of studying art in this most remarkable of all cities. "Come, you'll see," Zola promised him, and Cézanne, accompanied by his irate father (who wanted his son to become a lawyer or a banker), arrived in April. Once the father left, Cézanne enrolled at the Atelier Suisse, where he learned little but at least did not have to fight any of the teachings of the traditional schools, to which he was deeply hostile. Much to Zola's delight, Cézanne also came equipped with a small but regular allowance from his worried parents. But he was not happy in Paris and soon returned to Aix. Zola was flummoxed by Cézanne's behavior, especially by his sudden rages and despair. "Paul may have the genius of a great painter," he wrote a mutual friend, "but he will never have the genius to become one."[9]

A future prime minister of France, Georges Clemenceau, also arrived in Paris that year, accompanied by his father. Born and raised in the remote reaches of the Vendée, near Nantes, Clemenceau, now twenty years old, was following in his well-born father's footsteps, both in his medical studies and in his ardent republicanism. His father immediately took him to see Henri Lefort, one of those who had tried to organize resistance in the streets of Paris following Louis-Napoleon's December 1851 coup. "My father was more concerned that I spend my time with Lefort than at the [medical] faculty," Clemenceau later recalled. "For through Lefort, who had known Victor Hugo, all doors opened."[10]

Doors did indeed open for Clemenceau, and soon the young man became a well-known habitué of the drawing-rooms of the liberal opposition as well as in the cafés and artists' ateliers of the Latin Quarter. He was an attractive as well as an ardent young man, and he managed a busy social life in addition to his medical studies and political activities, which included founding a weekly newssheet, Le Travail, with a group of other students. It took careful footwork to avoid the censors, and Clemenceau soon learned how to write reviews that only indirectly alluded to political subjects—although he sometimes came quite close to the line, as in an article he titled "The Martyrs of History," which began with Socrates and ended by praising the revolutionary leaders of 1793, including the Terror.

～

It was among the Bohemian society of the Left Bank that Clemenceau first met Claude Monet, who would become a lifelong friend. Clemenceau recalled that Monet "impressed me as a man of fervent enthusiasm, something of a bohemian." In particular, Clemenceau was struck by Monet's "large, passionate eyes, the slightly Arab curve of his nose, and a black beard in wild disorder."

As it happened, Clemenceau would not have much chance that year to become better acquainted with Monet, for Monet was about to leave Paris, courtesy of the army. That March he had drawn a number in the lottery for the National Service that determined his fate for the next seven years, although he was given his choice of where to serve. Deciding on the colorful Chasseurs d'Afrique, he soon was en route to Algeria.

His family had been willing to pay for his discharge, but on terms that Monet had flatly rejected: that he leave Paris and his dream of a career in art and return to Le Havre, to enter the family business. In addition to this negative propulsion, the romance of Algeria appealed to him. Years later, he would tell Gustave Geffroy that his time in the army "did me a great deal of good in every way; it made me less harum-scarum." In addition, the light there had a significant impact on him: "My vision gained so much," Monet later recalled. "It took a long time for the impressions of light and color that I received to sort themselves out; but the seeds of my future experiments were there."[11]

～

While Claude Monet was sorting out his life, Edouard Manet was still fighting the Salon and all it represented. After having had one painting rejected by the Salon in 1859, he submitted two in 1861 (skipping 1860, when there was no Salon): these were his Spanish Singer and a double portrait of his parents, both of which attracted a good deal of positive comment. The Spanish

Singer even won an honorable mention—the only official recognition that Manet would receive until the end of his life, when he received a second-class medal at the 1881 Salon.

In the meantime, Berthe Morisot and her sister Edma were delighted with their new teacher, Corot, and persuaded their parents to spend that summer of 1861 at a villa near his to the west of Paris. Back in Paris, Corot dined frequently with the Morisots, where he became almost one of the family.

In another part of town, the Goncourts, still despondent over their lack of success as novelists, continued to make biting and gossipy entries into the journal that in time would become their chief claim to fame. The untimely 1861 death of Henry Murger, the author who had given Bohemia its place in song and story, brought almost two thousand mourners to his funeral, including his old friend Nadar and an array of officialdom, but the Goncourts were not impressed. They had disparaged the fame Murger received with *La Vie de Bohème*, calling it the product of "the world of petty journalism, the free-masonry of publicity." And following the funeral, where they found much to mock, they denigrated the tributes Murger received in the press: "They have idealized everything about him," they wrote. "They have spoken not only of his talent, but also of his virtues, his heart, his dog. . . . Come now, to hell with this nonsense, this sentimentality, this publicity!"[12]

Still, the Goncourts' biting wit had its attractions, and conversation at the Goncourts' was predictably colorful. Early in January, for example, one friend regaled the brothers with a description of his recent encounter with Dumas *père*, just back from Italy. Dumas, radiating his usual bonhomie, had boasted with a chuckle that "if you locked me in my bedroom with five women, pens, paper, ink, and a play to be written, by the end of the hour I'd have written the five acts and had the five women."

Gustave Flaubert was a frequent visitor to the Goncourt residence, in the heart of what had become the ninth arrondissement—a quarter so teeming with artists, writers, and musicians that it was known as the "New Athens." Flaubert was no Dumas, and he had no intention of becoming one. "The story, the plot of a novel is of no interest to me," he told the Goncourts in March. "When I write a novel I aim at rendering a color, a shade." What color, then, did he have in mind for *Madame Bovary*? "Grey," he answered, "the moldy color of a wood-louse's existence."

Serious discussion such as this was valued, but wit and cutting remarks were the currency in which the Goncourts typically traded. The impressions of their mutual friend Théophile Gautier following an imperial house-party at Compiègne were typical. According to Gautier, everyone but the servants had behaved awkwardly. The bourgeoisie (among whom he classed the emperor and empress) do not "know quite how to behave." But the servants, who were remnants from the reigns of Charles X and Louis-Philippe, "are the only people who look as if they knew what a court was like."

As for Offenbach's "great little theater," the Bouffes-Parisiens, the Goncourts spent part of an evening with friends discussing "the place it occupies, the curiosity it arouses, the various worlds it touches upon, from the Jockey Club to the *demi-monde*." It was, they agreed, "a high-class place of ill repute, the home of the short skirt, the naughty song and the dirty joke." Yes, it was delightful, except for its tie-in with people like the Duke de Morny, Offenbach's patron, "the typical man of the Empire, steeped in all the corruption of Paris."[13]

More serious matters were afoot in the realm of grand opera, where the emperor—prodded by Princess Metternich of Austria—had requested a performance of Richard Wagner's *Tannhäuser*. Wagner's operas had never before been performed in Paris, and it required an unheard-of 164 rehearsals for orchestra and performers to prepare for opening night, on March 13. The audience, including some staunch anti-Wagernerians, was waiting, and opening night as well as the two subsequent performances were disrupted by whistling and shouts, peppered by scattered outbreaks of fighting. The uproar had several causes, among them the ire of some opera lovers at Wagner's refusal to introduce the usual ballet in the second act (he had agreed to introduce a ballet but insisted on putting it in the first act). Others were upset by Wagner's willingness to accept the patronage of members of the German aristocracy; after all, he was a rebel, was he not? Critics were annoyed by Wagner's talk of his music being that of the future, while musicians and composers were angered by the fact that the emperor was giving precedence to the music of a German over that of their own.

Mostly, though, the audience as a whole was unprepared for what it heard. After three performances, Wagner conceded defeat and withdrew *Tannhäuser*. It would be several decades before his music became fashionable in Paris.

Nadar, who opened his luxurious new studio in September 1861, welcomed many celebrities there, including Jacques Offenbach, whom he asked to play "La Marseillaise" on the studio's piano—flinging open the windows so that this rallying cry of revolution, banned by the Second Empire, could be heard on the streets. Offenbach complied but, according to the story, improvised sufficiently that he disguised it from any passing authorities, even while providing a delectable moment for Nadar and his left-leaning friends.

At the time, Nadar wanted to be the first to take photographs underground, using artificial light. His designated subjects were the Paris catacombs, into which he ventured in 1861, and the city's sewers, which he photographed several years later—much to the interest of the public, which rarely hazarded into such places.

Nadar was especially pleased with his sewer photos, which captured the new, spacious, and efficient tunnels put in place by Haussmann's man Belgrand, as a sort of underground counterpart to the prefect's aboveground thoroughfares. Gone, or going, was the damp and stinking labyrinth that would gain notoriety in Victor Hugo's *Les Misérables* as "the intestines of Paris."

Nadar was capturing on film the new Paris, even as Victor Hugo was memorializing the old.

The journalist and dramatist Charles-Edmond Chojecki returned to Paris in mid-June after spending several days with Victor Hugo in Brussels. It was an especially memorable occasion, for on the day Charles-Edmond arrived, Hugo announced that he had just finished *Les Misérables*—having traveled to Belgium that spring to visit the battlefield of Waterloo, the last missing piece of his huge novel. Summing up his long-awaited masterpiece, Hugo remarked to Charles-Edmond that "Dante . . . made an inferno out of poetry; I have tried to make one out of reality."[14]

Hugo had left off writing *Les Misérables* with the onset of revolution in February 1848 and had not taken up the manuscript again until April 1860—possibly prompted by Napoleon III's general offer of amnesty. Hugo had ignored the emperor's offer, but it may have reminded him that Napoleon le Petit (despite Hugo's fervent hopes and expectations) was still very much in power, even while Victor Hugo was not getting any younger. Following this wake-up call, Hugo spent months reviewing the original draft and writing a long preface, but he had not yet completed the story when, late in the year, he became seriously ill. Once recovered, he realized the importance of finishing his book while he still could. December 30, 1860, marked the date when he began the huge task of completing *Les Misérables*.

It was between January and March of 1861 that Hugo wrote most of the remainder of *Les Misérables*, with the exception of the lengthy section—the introduction to part II—on the battle of Waterloo, which he would not complete until later. It was during January 1861 that Hugo revised the rest of part II, set in Paris, which he had written all those years before. He relied on his own memory, but he also sent a journalist friend who was able to take advantage of the 1859 amnesty to do a careful study of the book's major Paris locations.

Paris was in a real sense one of the characters of Les Misérables, and Hugo, an inveterate walker, knew his city well. He was passionate about Paris. But he was well aware that Paris had changed dramatically since his departure—and, in his opinion, not for the better. He had been fighting "progress" for years, most notably with his campaign to save Notre-Dame de Paris, a campaign capped by his 1831 Notre-Dame de Paris, which portrayed the cathedral and the city around it in the full splendor of the past.

But the Paris Hugo depicted in Les Misérables was not one of splendor. His characters lived their lives in the tenements of what by 1860 had become the Left Bank's fifth and thirteenth arrondissements, as well as in the territory stretching from the Right Bank's Place de la Bastille (home of Gavroche's moldering plaster elephant) through the then-decrepit Marais to the quarters surrounding the ancient church of Saint-Merri and the markets of Les Halles (the latter quarter being the setting for the book's ill-fated barricade). Although Jean Valjean and Cosette would move to Rue Oudinot (called Rue Plumet in the book) in the more prosperous quarter near Les Invalides, where they gravitated to the pleasant Luxembourg Gardens, the book's focus is on the darkened slums to the south and east, with their open sewers, hunger, filth, and despair.

Hugo, writing in exile far from Paris, wrote Les Misérables as a kind of memory piece, but one with a purpose. By this time he had become an outspoken critic of the kind of society that could so devastatingly penalize someone like Jean Valjean for merely stealing a loaf of bread. Hugo's politics were of course complex; after all, his personal history had been buffeted by contradictions, and his politics had evolved with age and experience. As Théophile Gautier reminded the Goncourts, Hugo had been a royalist during the early part of his career, and even in 1848, he was no liberal and did not believe "in all that nonsense." In fact, continued Gautier, "he didn't get mixed up in that filthy business until later."[15]

Gautier was stating matters too simplistically, but overall, he had a point: the author of Les Misérables had changed from the man he had been twenty or thirty years earlier. Along the way, Victor Hugo had determined that poverty rather than evil character lay at the root of most social ills. And, carefully noting the changes wrought by Napoleon III and the Second Empire, Hugo concluded that in demolishing those slum-ridden narrow streets, Baron Haussmann had not diminished poverty—only the means to resist.

Cosette, from Les Misérables *by Victor Hugo. Original illustration by Emile Bayard.* © Les Misérables, *Emile Bayard / Lebrecht Authors / Bridgeman Images*

~

CHAPTER ELEVEN

Les Misérables de Paris

(1862)

*L*es *Misérables* was huge. Hugo likened it to a ship having "seven masts, five funnels," with "paddles [that] are a hundred feet across, and the lifeboats [that] are battleships." It was too big to enter any harbor and "will have to weather every storm on the open sea." As a result, "not a nail must be missing."[1]

Hugo had ratcheted up the price for this manuscript with a new and exceptionally eager Belgian publisher, who agreed to a sum higher than any ever before paid to an author (300,000 francs for eight years, including translation rights)—an amount equal to the annual salaries of more than one hundred civil servants. Hugo also made sure that the first print-run would be divided into several editions, to increase the appearance of the book's popularity. Part I of *Les Misérables* appeared on April 3, 1862, in more than a dozen cities in the Western world, in the wake of an impressive international advertising campaign (fed by Hugo's flood of press releases assuring everyone that this was not just a novel, but "the social and historical drama of the nineteenth century," as well as "a vast mirror reflecting the human race").[2] Translations soon followed, as did parts II and III on May 15.

What was especially striking about this book was its widespread appeal—not only to the usual readers of serious fiction but also, and especially, to the masses. On the morning of May 15, people from all social classes queued up to buy the newly released copies, some even bringing wheelbarrows. The word had spread that this was a good read—a great one, even—and the public responded with enthusiasm. Booksellers immediately sold out of thousands of copies of this latest installment, while factory workers set up subscriptions to share in a book that would have individually cost them far more than they could afford.

After all, word had spread that Les Misérables was a book that understood the poor and their struggles. It was a book to which the poor could relate.

⌇

Not everyone liked Les Misérables. Censorship in Napoleon III's France was always a danger—Hugo certainly had encountered and even invited it be-fore. But on this occasion he advised his publisher to play up Les Misérables' lengthy section on Waterloo in order to overcome French censorship by arousing patriotic sentiment. This seems to have done the job.

Still, the book offended and intended to offend. Alarmed members of the bourgeoisie took offense at the book's language (especially the unapologetic use of the previously unprintable word "merde"), which prompted its omis-sion in the English edition. Hugo's extensive and vivid discussion of the pur-pose as well as the contents of Paris's ancient sewers also offended many. But many more were alarmed by the book's message, that society and its institu-tions rather than those individuals caught in a corrupt system were to blame for criminal behavior. The Spanish publicly burned copies of Les Misérables, while the pope placed the book on the Church's Index of Proscribed Books— where it joined Madame Bovary and the novels of Stendhal and Balzac.

And then there were the literary critics, who were shocked by Les Mi-sérables. The Goncourts were predictably biting, relegating the novel to the kind of literature found in public reading rooms, and other critics followed suit. One described the morality of Les Misérables as "inane evangelism," while another called the book's egalitarian socialism "très dangereux," add-ing that "this book accusing society would be more aptly entitled The Epic of the Rabble."[3]

Madame Hugo, in Paris to give interviews, found it difficult to rally Hugo's literary friends and supporters, who unanimously turned down her invitation to dinner. As for Baudelaire, who early in his life had been a Hugo enthusiast, he detested the book, especially its message of progress and the natural good-ness of man. But this created a quandary, since Baudelaire still was in awe of Hugo, to whom he had dedicated three of his poems in Les Fleurs du Mal. Even more to the point, Baudelaire was badly in need of money and wanted to write a paying review but feared that a critical review might not be printed in the journal he had in mind. His solution was to write a review favorable enough to be published in Le Boulevard, without praising Les Misérables too much. Those close friends to whom he had already ridiculed the book, as well as critics ever after, could only regard his review as hypocritical.

⌒

The last two parts of Les Misérables went on sale on June 30, 1862. That September, Hugo's publisher threw a grand dinner party in Brussels to celebrate the book's success. Nadar, who was among those writers and journalists invited to the great bash, returned to Paris with reams of contraband—works by Hugo still banned in France, including Napoléon le Petit and a collection of poems attacking the Second Empire's corruption and decadence. It was a fitting gesture from the author of Les Misérables.

But despite Hugo's efforts to call attention to their plight, the poor of Paris remained poor, many of them desperately so. That same year, Baron Haussmann did some calculations and figured that if food prices (especially the price of bread) went up even slightly, more than 1,200,000 Parisians would be affected—that is, three-quarters of the population.

Given the bleak realities of life for the working poor, and even more so for those who were unemployed or unemployable, Parisians of the lower classes were becoming restive. Louis-Napoleon had always sympathized with the working poor but had done little or nothing for them. Now, with his wealthy supporters peeling away, it seemed to the emperor to be just the time to bolster his support from the other end of the economic spectrum by reinventing himself as a ruler favorably inclined to social reform.

The previous year, two industrial bankers with Saint-Simonian sympathies had launched an effort to subsidize French workers to visit the 1862 World's Fair in London, the idea being that they would be able to view the wonders of British industry up close and meet fellow British workers. The plan was successful, and French workers returned filled with enthusiasm for British trade unions, which had just won a fifty-five-hour week (a considerable decrease from the usual work week) plus wage guarantees. Instead of encountering opposition from Napoleon's regime, they were able to publish their reports under the emperor's patronage.

Activist French workers were now enthused about their prospects but divided on whether to align with the republicans in the Legislature or to go it alone with their own candidates. This remained a moot point at present, as no elections were taking place that year. In the meantime, a print-workers' strike, still illegal, caused consternation and convictions. The emperor took notice, and not only did he pardon the striking workers, but he sent a bill to the Legislature permitting nonviolent strikes—a bill that in early 1864 would pass with a large majority. Emile Ollivier, the republican legislator chosen to introduce the bill, received considerable criticism from his liberal colleagues for cooperating with the regime, but he merely replied: "I'll take something good from whichever hand it comes."[4]

For some, it was a pleasing development, but for others, it was annoying and confusing. As Théophile Gautier remarked one evening at the Goncourts, the emperor "wobbles from right to left, so that nobody knows what he wants to do." Worse, no one could comment on it, since "nowadays you aren't allowed to say anything at all."[5]

Business and politics continued to be closely aligned, and the emperor's support was critical in many of the great financial battles of the time. Until the 1860s, the Pereires had rocketed to success with the blessing of Louis-Napoleon and his right-hand men, Persigny, Morny, and Haussmann. But as the 1860s progressed, the Pereire brothers found such support seeping away. This was painfully evident as early as 1862, when the Pereires (who, unlike the Rothschilds, were always short of funds) tried to obtain permission for the Crédit Mobilier to issue bank notes throughout France—a concession that would have provided them with virtually unlimited credit. But the scheme collapsed in the face of Banque de France objections, and Louis-Napoleon seems to have kept his distance. In the years to come, Crédit Mobilier would increasingly find itself in financial difficulties, even as imperial support became ever more elusive.

In the meantime, the rift between the emperor and the Rothschilds had mended, and by late 1862—much to the Pereires' dismay—the emperor was seen attending a hunt at the Baron de Rothschild's château at Ferrières. The Pereires for their part continued to court trouble. That autumn, the Legislature voted in favor of a merger between the Pereire-controlled Société Immobilière and the Société des Ports de Marseille, in which they were shareholders. The whole thing, including the vote itself, smelled of collusion and corruption, and it continued to make its contentious way through the court system until 1865, when Emile Pereire and two of his colleagues would receive significant fines.

Still, word had it that the emperor himself had intervened to prevent a worse outcome, and Baron Haussmann continued to favor the Pereires, who despite their growing troubles had much to relish with the 1862 opening of their luxurious Grand Hôtel de la Paix in the heart of the newly emerging Opéra quarter. This hotel, a kind of palace for the people (or at least for those who could afford it), served as reassuringly solid testimony, for those who needed it, of the Pereires' vision and enterprise. In addition, the elegant and extremely popular Café de la Paix soon opened on the hotel's ground floor, providing its own kind of gilded counterbalance to the brothers' increasingly tarnished reputation.

That same year, the brothers built a large villa for themselves and their families in the forests of Armainvilliers, on land they had bought a decade before. Chalet Pereire, as they called it, was enormous, with two wings—one for each family—built around a central pavilion. Much to the annoyance of James de Rothschild, the Pereires established their far-from-modest villa near his château at Ferrières, which itself was impressively luxurious, with central heating, hot and cold running water, and silver baths in the principal bed-rooms. As one observer waggishly noted, the sumptuous Rothschild château united sixteenth-century vision with nineteenth-century money. Rothschild was annoyed by the Pereires' effrontery, as he viewed it, but he could be well consoled by the emperor's visit to Ferrières that December—displaying James de Rothschild's very public reconciliation with Napoleon III.

The Rothschilds may not have trusted Louis-Napoleon, but they were not about to be left out in the cold.

~

While small signs were beginning to appear that Napoleon III's empire in 1862 was not quite as blessed by fortune as it had been the decade before, Baron Haussmann was undeterred in his determination to continue the re-making of Paris.

Late in the year, he oversaw the inauguration of Boulevard du Prince Eugène (now Boulevard Voltaire), which took place with great ceremony. This long and important thoroughfare linked today's Place de la République with the Place de la Nation (then the Place du Trône), cutting a ramrod straight diagonal through the volatile eastern part of Paris. To commemorate the great event, an Arc de Triomphe was raised in the Place du Trône, along with other major architectural statements, including a monument to Napo-leon III's victorious armies.[6]

Haussmann also continued to create parks in places where parks had never been before, and he now cast his eyes northward, to the heights of Bel-leville, where a shantytown stretched through a huge garbage dump that had risen around former gypsum quarries. Despite enormous obstacles, the sixty-two-acre park of Buttes-Chaumont would emerge within five years, turning a major eyesore into one of the city's greatest beauty spots.

Baron Haussmann continued to reap accolades for his public works, and even though the emperor may not have seen his way clear to making Haussmann a minister of the empire, he did award him the Grand Cross of the Legion of Honor and named the major new roadway linking the Monceau area with the Grands Boulevards as Boulevard Haussmann—the name that it has kept.

But Haussmann was not satisfied. He remained bitter about the treatment he received from some of the emperor's closest advisers and carped about the difference in rank between him and them. With the passing years, this bitterness had become corrosive, and Haussmann was widely disliked for his arrogance and authoritarianism, especially for his inclination to take petty revenge wherever possible. Widely unpopular, Baron Haussmann would not find many friends in his corner, should he ever need them.

While Baron Haussmann was continuing to reshape and modernize Paris, other forces were simultaneously at work, bringing the city and its inhabitants into the modern world. The adoption of the rotary press was making large print runs possible, providing a powerful means for communicating the news of the day as well as for directing public opinion, even while the spread of the telegraph was shrinking distances and making the world a far smaller place.

The telegraph had at first been reserved for use by the state but from 1850 was available for private use, powered by a new electrical system that assured its uninterrupted functioning in any weather. By 1862, one journalist could write that the telegraph had revolutionized modern life, much as had the railways: "At present," he wrote, "one hour is enough for the prices in every stock exchange in Europe to become known in Paris and London."[7]

Streetlamps were spreading throughout Paris, making it truly the City of Light,[8] while Haussmann's efforts to create a new omnibus system continued to flourish, effectively linking residents throughout the city with one another. And Paris's "Little Railroad," the Petite Ceinture, continued to expand, while now moving passengers as well as freight around the city's circumference.

Paris was on the move, and Napoleon III's Second Empire had provided the impetus. But Second Empire Paris and France seemed less impressive to some, especially to Otto von Bismarck, whom King Wilhelm of Prussia had just appointed as his minister-president. Bismarck previously had been Wilhelm's minister to Paris, where he had taken it upon himself to understand the city and the country under Louis-Napoleon's rule. Parisians in particular he considered pleasure-loving and dissolute, no match for Prussia or Prussians.

"Viewed from a distance," Bismarck remarked of Louis-Napoleon's France, "it seems very impressive. Close at hand," he added, "you realize it is nothing."[9]

Already, Louis-Napoleon's France was showing surprising ineptness in its much-vaunted Mexican expedition. The young archduke, Maximilian, may have been a picture-book illustration of an emperor, but he was not born to rule, and he knew it. Still, his wife, Charlotte, loved the idea of being an empress and—along with Eugenie—continued to push the reluctant Maximilian to accept the role.

While Maximilian continued to vacillate, the French army kept moving toward Mexico City. En route, Juárez's troops decisively vanquished the French at Puebla, a defeat that should have alerted Louis-Napoleon to the dangers ahead. But Eugenie refused to acknowledge any setback, and Louis-Napoleon at length relented, sending almost twenty-five thousand troops to reinforce those already there. His hope was that sheer numbers alone would decide the future of Mexico in Maximilian's (and France's) favor.

While the French were being humiliated in Mexico, young Claude Monet had become ill with typhoid in Algeria and was sent back to France to recuperate. There, he was allowed a six-month leave, which he spent in his aunt's house in Le Havre. He still had five and one-half years of service left, but by the end of his leave, his aunt decided that a return to the army would be detrimental to his future. She was hesitant to give the young man his freedom, knowing how he had used and abused it in the past. Nonetheless, "I didn't want to reproach myself," she wrote a friend, "with either having stood in the way of his artistic career or leaving him too long in a bad school"—the latter being a reference to the army, which she feared would completely demoralize him.

The outcome was favorable: Monet's aunt bought out the remainder of his service (at a considerable sum), and the young man promptly returned to Paris, with his father's warning still ringing in his ears: "Get it into your head that you are going to work, seriously this time. . . . If you decide to be independent again, I shall cut off your allowance without a word. Am I making myself clear?"[10]

Back in Paris, Monet (at his family's urging) paid a visit to the successful society painter Auguste Toulmouche, who now was a relative, having married Monet's cousin. Later, Monet recalled that Toulmouche told him that he had talent but needed the discipline of studio work and recommended the studio of Charles Gleyre. Monet, having little choice in the matter, promptly followed this advice and entered the Gleyre Academy.

He was twenty-two years old.

～

That summer, Berthe and Edma Morisot vacationed in the Pyrenees, where they delighted in traveling by horseback and mule. Upon their return, they resumed work with Corot, and according to Berthe's grandson, Denis Rouart, "painting occupied them unremittingly in the year that followed."[11]

Another art form, etching, currently occupied James Whistler, who displayed his Thames etchings in Paris that summer. Baudelaire praised these for being as "subtle and as lively as improvisation . . . a chaos of fog, furnaces, and spiraling smoke; the profound and complex poetry of a vast city." Whistler, who was frustrated by the critics' unceasing resistance to his work, was unimpressed with the review and merely commented that Baudelaire had "said many poetic things about the Thames and nothing about the etchings themselves."[12]

Sarah Bernhardt was also experiencing disappointment. The year before, she had won only a second prize for tragedy and an honorable mention for comedy at the Conservatoire. Despite this, the Duke de Morny's influence won her an engagement at the Comédie-Française, where she experienced a true disaster in her debut in Racine's *Iphigénie*. Suffering from stage fright, which would stalk her throughout her career, she froze. Her performance did not improve in two subsequent roles, and the critics were unimpressed. One in particular trashed her performances. A close friend recalled that a humbled Bernhardt regretted mainly that she had not "swallowed her pride and allowed herself to be seduced by one or two of the critics"—a capitulation that "would have assured rave reviews and launched her career."[13]

～

That August, the Goncourt brothers were shocked to discover that their devoted housekeeper, Rose Malingre—who had died after serving them and their mother for a quarter of a century—had been living a double life. At first, their response to her death had been "What a loss, what a gap in our lives!" And then they discovered that she had regularly lied to them and robbed them, indulging in "a secret life of dreadful orgies, nights out, sensual frenzies." After concluding that she had become an alcoholic "in order to escape from herself," they were compassionate: "Poor woman," they wrote. "We forgive her." Yet they remained bitter at the duplicity and determined that "suspicion of the entire female sex has entered into our minds for the rest of our lives."[14]

Still, despite the swirl of fast living and degeneracy that has characterized these years, happy and loving relationships did take root and endure during the Second Empire. That summer, for example, Gustave Eiffel married Marie Gaudelet, a young woman from his hometown of Dijon. Although Eiffel conceded that seventeen-year-old Marie was far from stunning and possessed only a modest dowry, he loved her for her "great kindness, a steady humor and simple tastes."[15] Adding to his well-being, Eiffel received a promotion soon after his marriage, raising him to the position of director of the company's workshops in Clichy, on the northwest border of Paris.

Soon he and his new wife set up housekeeping in a large home on the Right Bank. Their marriage would be long and happy, and the family would eventually embrace three daughters and two sons.

Not all, of course, were happy or even moderately well-to-do in Second Empire Paris, and Edouard Manet—although himself well-off—was keenly aware of those who were less fortunate. In his 1862 lithograph, *The Balloon*, he depicted a giant balloon raised at the Fête de l'Empereur, held annually in honor of Louis-Napoleon's uncle, Napoleon Bonaparte. On this occasion, Louis-Napoleon distributed aid to the poor, and by his order, prizes dangled from the tops of poles, which the needy fought to climb. Unfortunately, these poles were soaped, making the ascent as difficult as possible, and in his lithograph, Manet depicted the dense crowds and the eager climbers as well as a lame person seated in the crowd's midst, unable to partake of the climb or prizes. The balloon, positioned in the lithograph's center, depicts the era's progress as well as its delight in display, but Manet—who placed his disabled man directly beneath the balloon—was more interested in portraying the downside of this progress.

Young Georges Clemenceau, who still was a full-time medical student, was also dismayed by the crushing poverty he saw around him. In a gesture of revolt against the Second Empire's neglect as well as its authoritarianism, he organized one of the few protest demonstrations of the period, held in the Place de la Bastille on February 24, the anniversary of the 1848 revolution. As it happened, he and his fellow students were unable to arouse the populace, and the demonstration fizzled as the police moved in.

Georges Clemenceau, 1869. © Tallandier / Bridgeman Images

Clemenceau escaped, but the police found him two days later in his lodgings, where they arrested him.

Despite his father's attempts to intervene, Clemenceau received a fine and a sentence of more than two months in the bleak Mazas prison. Once released, he visited friends in the more hospitable Sainte-Pélagie prison, the usual destination for political prisoners. There he became acquainted with the ardent republican Auguste Scheurer-Kestner, who—many years later—would play a key role with Clemenceau in the Dreyfus Affair. Clemenceau also, for a time, came under the spell of another Sainte-Pélagie inmate, the ardent revolutionary Louis Blanqui, whom he briefly assisted in Blanqui's sub-rosa activities.

In time, Clemenceau would also become an staunch ally of Emile Zola in their fight to defend Alfred Dreyfus, but this lay well in the future. In 1862, Clemenceau and Zola had only a passing acquaintance, linked by their common interest in the weekly newssheet *Le Travail*, to which Zola contributed. *Le Travail* did not survive the failed protest of February 24.

That autumn, Emile Zola's young friend from Aix, Paul Cézanne, gathered up his courage and returned to Paris, where he again enrolled in the Atelier Suisse and became friends with Camille Pissarro. Cézanne also encountered a number of other painters during this second Paris stay, including Pierre-Auguste Renoir, Alfred Sisley, Edgar Degas, Frédéric Bazille, and (upon his return to Paris) Claude Monet—acquaintances among the artistic avant-garde that bolstered Cézanne's confidence in his own decidedly avant-garde vision. Zola accompanied Cézanne in his visits to artists' studios throughout Paris, becoming acquainted with many of the city's young artists and, in the process, acquiring an artistic vocabulary as well as an appreciation for the newest of the new.

By 1862, Zola's horizons were widening on many fronts. Even before Cézanne's reappearance in Paris, he had acquired a job—best of all, a job in publishing. Thanks to the intervention of a family friend, he was accepted by Hachette and Company, which had already become a major force among French publishers. Zola began humbly enough in the packing department, but he was ecstatic.

"Saved from Bohemia!" he cried, and he never looked back.

Edouard Manet, 1850s. Private collection. © Roger-Viollet, Paris / Bridgeman Images

CHAPTER TWELVE

~

Scandal

(1863–1864)

The Salon, held annually after 1863 in May and June, was unquestionably the most important artistic event on the Paris calendar. Well aware of its significance, Edouard Manet had come to regard admission into the Salon as a personal crusade.

Although many thousands of people visited the Salon each year, where they viewed multitudes of paintings and sculptures crammed floor-to-ceiling into a Right Bank building near the Seine, these viewers—much to Manet's dismay—saw little of his output. Most of his major works were meant to be hung on the Salon's walls, but although he regularly submitted his best, most were rejected. Not until 1863 did he truly make his mark, and not even in the Salon itself, but in what was widely considered to be a sideshow—the Salon des Refusés.

How this happened was an unexpected result of the jury's decisions for the 1863 Salon, which had been even more severe than usual, rejecting more than half of the five thousand works submitted. These included Manet's *Le Déjeuner sur l'herbe* (*Luncheon on the Grass*) as well as his *Mademoiselle V. . . in the Costume of an Espada* (matador) and *Young Man in the Costume of a Majo* (matador).[1] Despite an uproar of protests, these *refusés* (rejects) were set aside, ready to be returned to their owners, when Napoleon III—who had learned of the brouhaha—visited the Salon and glimpsed some of the rejected works. Being politically if not culturally attuned, he noted that he could see little difference between what was accepted and what was not and decided to let the public make up its own mind. As a consequence, the rejected works now had a forum of their own, in another part of the huge building housing the Salon. This portion soon became known as the Salon des Refusés.

Admission to the Salon des Refusés was open to all those whose works had been refused, and almost eight hundred works now went up on these newly available walls. One enthusiast wrote that it was "a grand day, a day of supreme justice [when] the public was admitted to judge the judges."[2] Unfortunately, the public largely came to gape and gawk, and no painting drew more gasps and laughter than Manet's *Le Déjeuner sur l'herbe*, which quickly became the *succès de scandale* of the exhibition. After all, central to the painting is a completely unclothed young woman, while two completely clothed young men surround her (and the luncheon in question). Not only are the young men clothed, but they are clothed in modern dress rather than in Grecian togas—which would have been far more acceptable to this largely bourgeois and prudish audience, which found Manet's subject matter indecent and shocking, a sure sign of the decline of civilization.

Manet had intentionally painted contemporary Parisians rather than mythical nudes with flowing tresses and fluttering Cupids, and his bathing and lunching Parisians look natural, even matter-of-fact, rather than romantically or heroically posed. The public, made uncomfortable by this unheard-of nonchalance, jeered; and although not all the critics were hostile (and some chose to criticize Manet's technique rather than his subject), many either refused to review the *refusés* or joined in the attack. "One has to be doubly strong," commented Manet's friend Zacharie Astruc, "to keep erect beneath the tempest of fools, who rain down here by the million and scoff at everything outrageously."[3]

By contrast, Alfred Stevens's painting, *Palm Sunday*, which depicted a demurely dressed young woman placing sprigs of boxwood above the portraits of her parents, won rave reviews from one and all. Oddly enough, Stevens and Manet were good friends. Even odder, the probable model for Stevens's painting, his mistress Victorine Meurent, served as the nude model for Manet's *Le Déjeuner sur l'herbe*.

Controversy continued to surround Eugène Viollet-le-Duc, despite his formidable reputation as a restorer of ancient and decaying buildings, especially his decades-long work on restoring Notre-Dame de Paris. Criticism of both his methods and his results had dogged him throughout his career, especially the accusation that he had too frequently sacrificed historical accuracy to the spirit of an imagined past. Yet the scandal that erupted around him in the autumn of 1863 was especially virulent. Of course it should not have been unexpected: from the outset of his career Viollet-le-Duc had rebelled against the neoclassicism and lack of imagination at the Ecole des Beaux-Arts and, as a young man, had refused to attend this traditional destination for would-be architects. It was therefore all the more astonishing when, in 1863, Viollet-le-Duc was appointed as a professor at the very Ecole des Beaux-Arts that he had refused to attend.

Not surprisingly, the faculty there—led by Ingres—resisted this development, but word had it that Prosper Mérimée, a key figure in architectural restoration and a firm supporter of Viollet-le-Duc, had used his influence with the emperor to win the appointment. The outcome—according to Maxime Du Camp—was a major scandal. Prompted by the faculty, the students sent in a complaint; when this was disregarded, they erupted into major protests in the lecture hall and then outside, along Rue Bonaparte and the Pont des Arts.

After this, Viollet-le-Duc did not attempt to lecture to the students, who in any case refused to hear him: "Messieurs," was the only word he was able to utter to the students before the uproar began. But he continued his career in restoration, which reached a pinnacle on May 31, 1864, with the dedication of the completely restored Notre-Dame de Paris—an elaborate ceremony presided over by the archbishop of Paris.

That September brought the opening of Georges Bizet's first produced opera, *Les Pêcheurs de perles* (*The Pearl Fishers*), which took place just before his twenty-fifth birthday. It should have been a triumph, and indeed, for a brief moment—as Bizet was brought before the curtain to take his bow—it appeared to be so. But then the critics weighed in, including disparagement of his orchestration as "noisy" and "too colorful"—opprobrium that future aficionados of this work and Bizet's *Carmen* would find laughable. No less a figure than Hector Berlioz tried to come to the rescue, stating that the score for this opera "does M. Bizet great honor," but the public wasn't listening to Berlioz. *Les Pêcheurs de perles* closed after eighteen performances.

That same year, another brilliant young musician and composer, Camille Saint-Saëns, defied expectations by failing to win the Prix de Rome on his second try. By this time, Saint-Saëns had distinguished himself as a composer, as a pianist, and as one of the finest organists in Paris (at the churches of Saint-Merri and La Madeleine). "He knows everything, but lacks inexperience," Berlioz remarked dryly.[4]

Not only young strivers found Paris a tough place to make their mark. The month of August brought the death of Eugène Delacroix, a painter who, like Manet, had pushed the boundaries and who had remained much misunderstood by the general public throughout his life. From early in his career, Delacroix was criticized for not being able to draw, but increasingly his reputation grew as a master of color. In Maxime Du Camp's estimation, Delacroix's process of artistic creation "was more musical than plastic, and some of his works are symphonies rather than pictures."[5]

Yet this "chief of the revolutionary [Romantic] school of painting" seemed hardly a revolutionary in appearance or bearing. Elegant and reserved, aristocratic and un-bohemian, Delacroix lived in a different universe from the stereotypical renegade painter. The rumor had even taken hold that he was the illegitimate son of none other than Prince Talleyrand, and the patronage that Delacroix received from Talleyrand and Talleyrand's grandson, the Duke de Morny, seemed to bear this out—although Maxime Du Camp took issue with the rumor, claiming that there was no physical resemblance whatever between the men.

Those in lofty government circles made little effort to pay tribute to the deceased, but Manet, Baudelaire, and Henri Fantin-Latour were among those who did deeply value him and walked in his funeral procession. Baudelaire regarded the unsentimental and vividly realistic Delacroix as the first truly great modern painter, and in time, many others, including Cézanne, Van Gogh, Gauguin, and Picasso, would agree. Soon Fantin-Latour would paint a tribute to him, his 1864 *Homage to Delacroix*—a large painting with the admirers of Delacroix grouped around his portrait. These included Fantin-Latour, James Whistler, Edouard Manet, and Baudelaire.

Beaten down by years of criticism, Delacroix had once remarked to Du Camp: "What would I not give to come back in a hundred years and to know what is thought of me."[6] Future generations would validate him, but already the painters of a newly emerging way of looking at the world had found their hero.

∼

By spring of 1863, young Claude Monet was back in Paris and enrolled in the Montparnasse atelier of Charles Gleyre, on Rue Notre-Dame des Champs. There (unless the weather was too frigid, as it often was that winter of 1862–1863), the students worked from eight o'clock in the morning until around noon, when they partook of a gruel-covered chop and bread. This meager fare was cheap, costing fifteen sous, or less than one franc—a major consideration, since most of Gleyre's students were as impoverished as Monet. Afternoons they continued to work, with the goal of mastering drawing before they were allowed to launch into color.

Gleyre was a quiet and modest man, who emphasized the classical tradition but who nonetheless gave his students a good deal of freedom. Monet seemed to settle in here and soon became friends with several other young painters—Pierre-Auguste Renoir, Alfred Sisley, and especially Frédéric Bazille, a well-to-do young man who yearned to be an artist but whose parents wanted him to become a doctor. Monet was especially close to Bazille, and by the Easter holidays the two were vacationing and painting together in the nearby forest of Fontainebleau.

From Fontainebleau, Monet wrote another friend that he was staying on longer than he intended, as "it's so beautiful in spring, with everything turned green, the fine weather came and I couldn't resist the temptation of staying on longer"—even after the Salon had opened, drawing the others back to Paris. He had just received a letter from a friend of the painter Toulmouche, "who asked her to tell me that on no account should I stay any longer in the country, and above all that it was a grave mistake to have left the studio so soon." Monet had not abandoned the studio, he insisted, "but I found a thousand things to charm me here which I just could not resist."[7]

Bazille had described Monet as "pretty good at landscapes." This, however, was not an especially ringing compliment, given the low esteem in which landscape painting was then held. Landscape painting offered little in the way of a future to a young painter, as both Bazille and Monet knew. Still, landscapes and painting out-of-doors irresistibly attracted Monet, and despite his recent stint of good behavior, it was evident that he was about to break out and go his own way.

～

Back in Paris, young Sarah Bernhardt was encountering difficulties. Earlier in the year, during the Comédie-Française's annual celebration in Molière's honor, Sarah's little sister had caused a scene, and during the ensuing ruckus, Sarah slapped a leading lady. Sarah had refused to apologize, and after that, the Comédie-Française declined to give Sarah any further roles, terminating her contract. She would not return to the Comédie-Française for ten years.

With doors slammed on her in every direction, and her mother tired of supporting her, Sarah Bernhardt now turned to her mother's trade, as a courtesan. She was good at it, and soon she acquired a handsome young lover, an officer and leader of a group of fashionable men about town. He remained her lover for several months, until he was sent on military duty to Mexico.

But Bernhardt's true passion remained the theater, and soon she won some small parts at the Gymnase, a distinct step down from the Comédie-Française but still a fashionable-enough Paris theater. It was an opportunity for her to learn her craft as an actress, away from the unfriendly spotlight she had encountered at the Comédie-Française.

Yet the roles that Bernhardt played at the Gymnase did not satisfy her— these were comic or lightly dramatic, not tragic. And already, Sarah Bernhardt had decided that tragedy was where she was going to shine.

That May brought elections, which despite the requirement that all candidates take the loyalty oath, included many opposition candidates, especially republican opponents of the regime. These were not all of one accord, and the three hundred opposition candidates were often at odds with one another, not only between republicans and those who longed for a return to monarchy but also among the republicans themselves, who differed widely, from working-class rebels to those bourgeois who were willing to accept a reform-minded empire, so long as the reforms were what they had in mind.

Persigny, who had been successfully running elections for Louis-Napoleon ever since the Bonaparte heir had emerged on the electoral scene, was again in charge of this one, especially in composing the list of official candidates. This all-important stage, however, had become increasingly challenging, since there no longer were enough die-hard loyalists to fill the slots, and Persigny was resigned to having to accept more moderates. Yet once the lists were filled, he did his utmost to see that his candidates were elected, using the by-now time-tested methods of clamping down on the opposition press and urging the nation's prefects and local officials to do everything they could to dampen the opposition's ardor, including constituency gerrymandering and wholesale bribery.

Still, what was remarkable about this election was the diffidence with which many officials enforced their duties in supporting the government's candidates. The outcome was a surprising, if modest, defeat for Napoleon III's imperial rule. The opposition won in nearly all the major cities, including Marseille, Lyon, and Paris, and while the Legislature remained stuffed with official candidates, many of these were reliant on voters who were not as reliably pro-emperor as before. In addition, the working class had shown new strength, which it displayed not in support of the emperor—who despite his fine talk had done little for them—but on behalf of their own candidates.

Morny took a close look at the election results and decided that Louis-Napoleon should make further concessions, including greater freedom of speech and a program of social reforms. Instead, Louis-Napoleon merely carried out a cabinet reshuffle and, possibly at Eugenie's instigation, sacked Persigny, who in turn accused the emperor of being dominated by his wife. Eugenie may well have prompted Persigny's departure, since she had long resented his opposition to her, which had begun years before, when Persigny had summarily dismissed her as a bridal prospect on the grounds that she was not royal. Eugenie acknowledged the long-standing acrimony between them but attributed it to Persigny's jealousy: "He could not bear anybody between the Emperor and him."[8]

Morny, however, was looking at the bigger picture and concluded that something had to be done to deal with an unmistakably rising anti-imperial tide. The forces supporting democracy would only continue to grow, he observed, adding that "it is urgent to satisfy [democracy] if we do not want to be swept away by it."[9]

May 1863 saw authorization for a northward extension of Boulevard de Magenta (later renamed Boulevard Barbès), while drilling for artesian wells began in the Chapelle and Butte-aux-Cailles quarters[10] and work continued on the Opéra, whose masonry shell was rising steadily and now reached the first story.

In far-off Mexico, the French were buoyed by victory at the second battle of Puebla, which opened the road to Mexico City. French troops entered the city that June, where the residents received them unenthusiastically, while Juárez was forced to move to the countryside, where fighting turned to guerrilla resistance. Soon after, a so-called Assembly of Notables voted to offer the imperial crown to Maximilian and sent a delegation to convey the good news. But Maximilian still hesitated and at last asked that the Mexicans themselves vote on the question.

Maximilian, who naively thought that the outcome of such a vote would represent the will of the people, was not informed of the vote-rigging and bribery that brought in the necessary nationwide vote of approval. But even this was not enough to persuade the young man, who continued to agonize.

While Maximilian struggled over this decision, a number of financiers, most especially the Duke de Morny, looked on with considerable impatience. After all, there was a lot of money at stake.

That year, the left-wing journalist Georges Duchêne drew up a list of the richest and the most powerful French of the time and came up with 183 families—probably the origin of the so-called "200 families," a conspiracy theory originally referring to the 200 largest shareholders, largely Jewish and Protestant, of the Banque de France. In years to come, the "200 families" would be castigated by both the anti-oligarchic Communist and trade unionist left as well as by the anti-Semitic and anti-Freemason right for virtually all the ills of the times. Duchêne in fact was interested in illustrating the wide disparities between France's haves and have-nots, and of these 183 families, he singled out around thirty names of the "super rich," who included the Duke de Morny and the Pereires as well as the Rothschilds.

Without invoking the hyperbole of the so-called "200 families," it still was true that by now, certain wealthy and powerful families had come to hold an extraordinary degree of influence over France's economy—an influence that extended into other realms as well. By 1863, Emile Pereire sat on nineteen boards of directors, while Isaac sat on twelve, and their son and nephew Eugène on nine. For their part, the Rothschilds held twenty-seven seats on a variety of company boards.

One area where big financiers extended their sway was over the press, which gave them a powerful weapon for directing public opinion. The Second Empire had seen a boom in newspaper sales, especially at railway stations, and the introduction of the rotary press—complementing the extension of the railway network—made large print runs possible. In 1863, the wealthy banker Moïse Polydore Millaud founded *Le Petit Journal*, a cheap nonpolitical daily, which quickly became France's leading newspaper. Millaud's *Le Journal illustré* and *Le Soleil* soon followed, while other financiers owned leading imperialist papers, and the Rothschilds were said to be the financial backers of a newspaper with Orléanist leanings. Financial groups controlled the financial or stock market papers, and these newspapers regularly promoted the sale of these groups' securities. By the decade's end, Duchêne was able to document his assertion that "since 1852 the press has always been masterminded by certain financial powers."[11]

Publicity had always been Nadar's forte, and that autumn he made newspaper headlines with his new love, ballooning. In a publicity-garnering display in early October, he charged tickets of one franc apiece to watch his giant balloon go up from the Champ de Mars. Even though not as many people as he had anticipated showed up to watch the great event, the crowd nonetheless was substantial. After all, the balloon—designed by Louis and Jules Godard, part of balloonist Eugène Godard's family—was quite a spectacle. Twenty-two thousand yards of silk had been used to make its inner and outer envelopes, and when inflated, it was nearly as high as Notre-Dame and contained more than 200,000 cubic feet of gas (Nadar had persuaded the municipal gas company to lay a pipe to supply gas to the Champ de Mars). It carried a double-decker wicker cabin with six separate compartments, including a kitchen, a lavatory, bunk beds, a darkroom, and a wine cellar, and its observation deck was large enough for twenty.

Nadar had been drawn to ballooning by the possibilities for aerial photography as well as by the adventure and romance of air travel, and this first flight went smoothly enough, despite a rough landing twenty-five miles east of Paris. But his next flight, just weeks later, was a different matter. After some sixteen hours, during which the crew and passengers ate dinner on the upper deck, they decided to make a landing rather than risk being pushed out to sea. Unfortunately this attempted landing was a disaster. Encountering a gale, the balloon bounced and spun for almost thirty miles, just missed an oncoming train, and at last crashed into a forest. All nine passengers were injured, one of them seriously, but miraculously no one was killed.

Nadar, who knew a good publicity prospect when he saw one, commissioned a drawing of his giant balloon in the train's path—a vivid illustration that attracted headlines throughout Europe and even in North America. His balloon would fly again at various expositions, including the 1867 Paris exposition, and his own fame rose with it: not only did he become a widely known public figure, but he even served as model for a character in a Jules Verne fantasy, *From the Earth to the Moon.*

But eventually the costs became prohibitive—and in any case, Nadar's wife told him to stop. He had learned the hard way about balloons' limitations, but he nonetheless would find other uses for them, especially in wartime. That, however, lay in the future.

〜

The weather that winter of 1863–1864 was severe, affecting everything from Gleyre's academy, where the master was ill, to the Opéra, where construction came to a halt.

By February, though, the Opéra resumed its rise, with a surprisingly extensive, although hidden, use of iron to support its floors, vaults, and roofs—an unconventional departure in an otherwise conventional albeit opulent structure. Decorative stone for the building was now arriving, including rose and red granite, rose and red Jura stone, green porphyry, and an array of rose, yellow, and white limestone, in addition to marble shafts and blocks in an array of colors.

February also brought by-elections, in which labor began to flex its muscle. Earlier in the year, Adolph Thiers—a former prime minister under King Louis-Philippe and by now a staunch opponent of Louis-Napoleon Bonaparte—had made a major speech in which he demanded five "necessary freedoms," which he named as personal liberties, freedom of the press, free elections, legislative rights, and "ministerial responsibility." Thiers was no ally of the working classes, but his speech signaled a fresh push for reform. Labor militants in particular responded by fielding their own candidates for the by-elections, as they had the year before, and by issuing a manifesto proclaiming that the workers formed "a special class of citizens requiring direct representation."

This year's workers' candidates, although showing strength, still represented a distinct minority, but in the elections' aftermath, militant workers pushed Louis-Napoleon to make good on his earlier promise to permit nonviolent strikes. This became law that spring with large support, despite conservative opposition. In addition, that September the emperor allowed three representatives of the five-hundred-member strong French workers' movement to attend the inaugural meeting of the first Labor International.

But as many conservatives had feared, concessions now led to a wave of strikes, leading to clashes and worker demands for additional concessions, especially for their rights of association and assembly.

That March, Archduke Maximilian and his wife, Charlotte, paid a visit to Louis-Napoleon and Eugenie in Paris, where they were treated as the imperial couple that the French emperor and empress intended that they become. Adding to his legendary persuasiveness, Louis-Napoleon promised to keep a large contingent of French soldiers in Mexico, along with fighters from the French Foreign Legion. For his part, Maximilian saw no problem in pledging to repay, from the bankrupt Mexican treasury, all the debts owed to Britain, France, and Spain, in addition to reimbursing Louis-Napoleon for the considerable sum he had already expended on the French intervention.

Still, Maximilian resisted the call of empire, at least of a Mexican empire, in large part because he did not want to renounce his claims to the imperial Austro-Hungarian throne—a renunciation that his elder brother, Emperor Franz-Joseph, insisted upon should he accept the Mexican post. Louis-Napoleon and Eugenie despaired and told Maximilian, ever the gentleman, that he had committed himself and could not go back on his word. Franz-Joseph, who had his own reasons for seeing Maximilian leave the Old World for the New, also provided considerable pressure, and in April, after an emotional meeting between the two, Maximilian renounced his rights to the Austrian succession and accepted the throne that he had been persuaded to believe the Mexican people had offered him.

Soon after, the still-despondent archduke and his ebullient wife left for Mexico, where Maximilian promptly encountered a sea of difficulties with the French forces, exacerbated by frequent massacres from the guerrillas who surrounded them. In addition, the United States was not keen on these developments south of its border and was not inclined simply to sit by and watch.

In the meantime, in one of Louis-Napoleon's more positive achievements that year in foreign affairs, that August he sponsored the first Geneva Convention on the treatment of war wounded and the establishment of the Red Cross. The emperor of the French had acquired a distinct repugnance to warfare, based on his memories of the bloody battlefield at Solferino. Unfortunately, this would not be his last experience in battle.

～

That April, as buds and blossoms throughout Paris heralded the return of hope and spring, Sarah Bernhardt was seriously considering killing herself. She had recently appeared at the Gymnase in a light comedy in which even her mother said she looked ridiculous. Worse yet, she was pregnant, with no husband or lover to support her.

Instead, she impulsively left for Spain, taking a maid with her and leaving letters for her mother and the manager of the Gymnase Theatre asking them to forgive her and to "have pity on a poor crazy girl."[12] She spent a fortnight in Madrid, enjoying herself, until she received a telegram that her mother was very ill. After a hasty return to Paris, she and her mother were reunited and Sarah went to live nearby in her own apartment, taking her younger sister with her.

Nothing is said in her memoirs of the child that was born that December, her son, Maurice (who would not be mentioned in her memoirs until he was a toddler). Nor is anything said of the child's father. In later years, she would entertain her grandson-in-law and granddaughter with conflicting "true stories" that brimmed over with romance. Common to both, though, was the figure of the Belgian Prince de Ligne and a great love affair.

However romantic their liaison may have been, the prince most certainly did not recognize the child as his son, nor did he offer any support. Instead, according to a close friend of Bernhardt's, the prince merely informed her that "you must realize that if you sit on a pile of thorns, you can never know which one has pricked you."[13] Not until Bernhardt became

Sarah Bernhardt, c. 1860. Photograph by Nadar. © Bibliothèque de L'Arsenal, Paris, France / Bridgeman Images

famous did he reappear in her life, but, as her biographers point out, she neither forgot nor forgave him.

Bernhardt was twenty years old when Maurice was born, and now, with expensive tastes and no other income, she returned to a series of lovers to support her. It was around this time that she posed for Nadar, draped in dark velvet and in a white cloak; she also posed for him nude behind a fan. These portraits would in time become famous, even as her own fame grew.

Nadar was by now taking portraits of a raft of celebrities, including George Sand (who many at the time considered the greatest living French writer), making multiple copies that he sold at considerable profit to the public. He would do the same with his other celebrities, often, as in the case of Sand, becoming good friends along the way.

Nadar also continued to take photographs underground with only artificial illumination, putting his photographs of the Paris catacombs and the Paris sewers on public display. Haussmann's man for water, Belgrand, was especially pleased with the results of Nadar's sewer photographs, which clearly showed that the new system Belgrand was building was a far cry from the fetid and noxious underground through which Victor Hugo depicted Jean Valjean sloshing while carrying the wounded Marius to safety.

It was an especially good year for Belgrand, as water from the river Dhuys officially began to flow into Paris that autumn. Channeled to the new reservoir at Ménilmontant, it was then pumped up to the highest points of Montmartre and Belleville. From there it flowed down to the city by force of gravity, supplementing the haphazard and insufficient water supply for the city's inhabitants.

Aboveground, that summer Edouard Manet—who had startled his friends and family the year before by marrying his mistress and model, Suzanne Leenhoff[14]—experienced the unfamiliar thrill of success with his painting of a contemporary event, the sinking of a Confederate ship by a small U.S. gunboat off the coast of Cherbourg. Now a married man but still a man about town (with a remarkably tolerant wife), he now focused on seascapes while on holiday in Boulogne.

Manet by now was living on the Boulevard des Batignolles, bordering the newly annexed district of northwest Paris. There, in addition to frequenting the Café Tortoni on the Boulevard des Italiens, where he regularly lunched, Manet just as regularly gravitated to the Café Guerbois, located on the

Avenue de Clichy, just around the corner from his residence. Other artists had also found low-priced studios in the neighborhood and joined Manet at the Guerbois or in his nearby studio, as Fantin-Latour's 1870 A *Studio at Batignolles* would commemorate.

Among those who gathered at Manet's studio for their 1870 group portrait would be Claude Monet, although in 1864 the two had not yet met. But like Manet and most other Parisians who could afford it, Monet (despite his own impecuniousness) regularly got out of town for the holidays—heading that Easter for Fontainebleau and that summer for Honfleur, on the Normandy coast. Gleyre's academy closed that summer for lack of funds, but Bazille and Renoir stuck it out to the end. Monet did not. "I wonder what you could be doing in Paris in such beautiful weather," he wrote Bazille from Honfleur in July. "Each day I find something even more beautiful than the day before. It's enough to drive one crazy, I so want to do it all my head is bursting."

When summer ended and his stay was up, Monet found that he still could not leave. The landscape was becoming more and more beautiful, he told Bazille, and "I wouldn't have the heart to leave." Still on the coast of Normandy in October, he was painting forest scenes as well as boats and a still life of fish in a fisherman's basket. After that, he told Bazille, he was going to "turn out a few pictures to send wherever possible, given that now, first and foremost (unfortunately), I have to earn some money."[15]

This would become a familiar refrain, as Bazille came from a wealthy family and was inclined to help Monet out financially. In late 1864, though, when he and Monet were sharing a large flat with studio on the Left Bank, Monet was still able to help with the rent: Monet's father had consented to give his son some assistance. It was here that visitors such as Renoir and Sisley congregated, as well as Pissarro, Cézanne, and Fantin-Latour.

Monet, like so many others, would soon gravitate to the Batignolles neighborhood and the Café Guerbois, taking time to pose with other friends for Fantin-Latour's A *Studio at Batignolles* and Bazille's *Studio in the Rue de La Condamine*.

⁓

Increasingly drawn to painting outdoors, Edma and Berthe Morisot convinced their parents to spend that summer of 1864 in a picturesque converted windmill along the seaside cliffs of Normandy. There, Berthe took to exploring, carrying her art supplies in a knapsack and finding vantage points among the cliffs, where she feverishly worked to capture the particular time of day and the slant of the sun. Corot in the meantime wrote that Edma and Berthe should persevere, and that "Nature itself is the best of counselors."

Still, according to their brother, Tiburce, Corot found Edma more disciplined than Berthe, who "took liberties of which he disapproved."

Nonetheless, back in Paris, the sisters continued to paint, successfully submitting two paintings each to the 1864 Salon, where their work was graciously but indifferently received. Undaunted, they continued to paint in a garden studio their father built for them behind the house where the family moved in 1864, on Rue Franklin, after he was appointed chief councilor of the Cour des Comptes (the Court of Audits, which audited most public institutions).

There, the Morisots continued to entertain regularly with Tuesday dinners, inviting "no tiresome or boring people." Included as regular guests were the Ferry brothers, Charles and Jules, both of whom took a polite interest in Berthe and Edma, who in turn showed just as polite a disinterest in the pair. This was not surprising, Tiburce noted, "as these two strapping and somewhat burly fellows were completely lacking in elegance, in a period that carried social refinement to an extreme."

But Charles and Jules Ferry were undoubtedly intelligent and scintillating guests, who seemed to keep their ears open. As Tiburce noted, "It was from my father's candid talk . . . that Jules Ferry, not too discreetly, took material for his future pamphlet, *Les Comptes Fantastiques d'Haussmann*" (*The Fantastic Accounts of Haussmann*), which would help to destroy Haussmann's career even as it aided his own.[16]

Money, or lack of it, was increasingly becoming a problem for Georges Haussmann, most especially for the newly emerging Bois de Vincennes. Years later, writing his memoirs, Haussmann would complain about the cost of creating the Bois de Vincennes: "Exceeding all forecasts," he wrote, it "made a large breech in the city's finances."[17]

He had never been enthusiastic about this park, which he sourly pointed out was to be for the working classes of Paris's newly created eleventh and twelfth arrondissements, especially the workers of the fractious Faubourg Saint-Antoine. Louis-Napoleon, however, was a keen backer of the project, viewing this enormous green space on the eastern edge of Paris as part of his efforts to better the lives of Parisian workers, who largely inhabited the eastern portions of the city. He also had an interest in cajoling them, given their increasing discontent with imperial rule. After all, the rich were getting richer under Napoleon III, but the poor certainly were not benefiting from all the new wealth. Louis-Napoleon thought that a lovely park, where the workers and their families could stroll (during their admittedly limited leisure hours), would be of benefit both to them and to him.

The Bois de Vincennes had been a pleasure ground for royalty since the twelfth century, when Louis VII built a hunting lodge there. The forest's importance grew over the years, especially in the fourteenth century, when Jean II and Charles V erected the huge and heavily fortified Château de Vincennes, with its village of support buildings, a moated curtain wall, and a bullying keep or donjon that was the highest in France.

The castle was the product of the Hundred Years' War with England, but right through the nineteenth century it would serve as a fortress and prison, whose "guests" included such notables as Henri de Navarre (the future Henri IV), Denis Diderot, and the Marquis de Sade. By 1860, soon after Paris absorbed its surrounding suburbs, the emperor prompted the Legislature to cede the Bois de Vincennes to Paris on the condition that the city promptly convert it into a public area for walks—while keeping the castle and its surrounding military installations, including the camp and grounds used for army maneuvers. As with the Bois de Boulogne on the western edge of Paris, the more than two thousand acres of the Bois de Vincennes came with strict architectural stipulations as well as permission granted the city to sell almost three hundred of these acres to private purchasers.

But creating the elaborate system of artificial lakes as well as the extensive lawns and specimen trees that the landscaped areas required, in addition to grottoes, cascades, cafés, restaurants, and a racecourse—all of this cost money, and the money disappeared even more quickly in creating this Bois than in its twin across town. The Bois de Boulogne may have been bedeviled by an improperly set-out watercourse, but the Bois de Vincennes suffered most surprisingly from sandy soil, which made everything undertaken there far more difficult. By the time it was finished, in 1864, the Bois de Vincennes (according to Haussmann) cost five times more than the Bois de Boulogne; worse yet, its acres put up for public sale unsurprisingly brought in far less than the lands adjoining the far wealthier sections across town.

Haussmann could only grumble, even while, in the northern reaches of Paris, another expensive park, Buttes-Chaumont—in this case one he championed—continued to rise out of the detritus of a former garbage dump and quarry.

∿

October 1864 brought unexpected success to Emile Zola with his first publication—a volume of short stories that he titled *Les Contes à Ninon* (*Stories for Ninon*). The publisher (Hetzel and Lacroix) agreed to publish 1,500 copies, giving Zola a substantial royalty of twenty-five centimes per copy (far more than Hachette would have offered), while Zola agreed to publicize his work.

Already showing a decided flair for publicity, Zola energetically promoted his literary baby, using contacts he had made at Hachette and pushing magazine and newspaper editors to publish excerpts, insert blurbs, and review the book—preferably using review copy he had written on his own behalf. He was not shy about himself or his work, and he was relentless in pushing open doors and keeping them open.

As he knew, or at least suspected, the journalists he pursued were more inclined to use a piece already written than one that had to be composed from scratch, and of the many pieces that *Les Contes* elicited, most of them used Zola's own words to praise him. Still, despite the favorable reception, the book did not sell as well as Zola had hoped.

Yet despite this disappointment, Zola soldiered on. There was no stopping him now, and he already was halfway through writing his first novel, *La Confession de Claude*, by the time *Les Contes* appeared.

The Goncourt brothers were similarly determined in their pursuit of literary success, which they anticipated would arrive with their next book, *Germinie Lacerteux*, largely based on the life of their maid, Rose Malingre, whose hidden double life had led to her destruction. It was not a pretty subject, nor had the Goncourts intended it to be, and in researching its background they traveled to the farthest reaches of the city, near the fortifications, where they witnessed incredible violence in the midst of "wretched huts, the hovels of rag-pickers and gypsies."[18]

The Goncourts positioned themselves as leaders in the new literary Realism, with little regard for the full-blown Romanticism of a Victor Hugo. Hugo in turn was little impressed by the rising tide of Realism, led (despite his protests to the contrary) by Flaubert[19] as well as by the Goncourts—a trio already joined (in his own imagination) by Emile Zola.

Hugo had no regrets about what he wrote, how much he wrote, or how he wrote it. In a note in 1864, he simply expressed the wish that he hadn't started sooner. "What a shame I wasn't exiled earlier!" he wrote. "I would have done many things for which I now feel I shall not have time."[20]

Parc des Buttes-Chaumont. © J. McAuliffe

CHAPTER THIRTEEN

~

Death and Taxes

(1865)

That March brought the unexpected death of the Duke de Morny, Napoleon III's half-brother and the most influential as well as arguably the most able of all of the emperor's advisers. Although trailing a lengthy history of astute but shadowy business deals, along with a reputation as a womanizer and gambler, Morny had served his half-brother well, not only as president of the Legislature but especially as the emperor's personal adviser. Reporting the news to a colleague in London, Lord Cowley, Britain's ambassador to France, had this assessment of Morny: "He had it in him, if he had been honest, to have become a very great man."[1]

In the capacity of trusted adviser, the ever-realistic Morny had urged Louis-Napoleon to liberalize his regime, but now there was no one to take this position. From now on, the most influential man among the emperor's inner circle would be the austere and authoritarian Eugène Rouher, the emperor's minister of state, who would serve as a rock-hard opponent of liberalization—as well as an unrelenting foe of the increasingly difficult Georges Haussmann.

~

While Haussmann unquestionably was unpopular, stirring up animosity with his self-importance as well as with his bullying insistence on getting his way, it was the question of money—the money for the prefect's ever-more expensive and expansive city development—where the flash points between Haussmann and his enemies were growing.

Large-scale loans, in the form of bonds, were a necessity for Haussmann's *grands travaux*, since neither he nor the emperor wanted to increase taxes. Such loans needed the Legislature's approval, which was easily won during the Second Empire's early years. But the Legislature stalled over the loan of 1858, holding it up until 1860. Now in 1865, a third loan was required, in large part to pay for the enormous cost overruns of Haussmann's Second System. Haussmann did not present this loan for what it was but instead posed it as a necessity to pay for the costs incurred since 1860 for incorporating the many villages and communes around the outskirts of Paris. The Legislature gave its approval but only reluctantly, auguring dangers for Haussmann's future plans for Paris.

These included continued development of the spectacular park of Buttes-Chaumont in northeastern Paris as well as commencement of Parc Montsouris, a forty-acre landscape park with lake and other water features on the city's southern edge. Haussmann also received authorization to demolish the current Hôtel-Dieu, the huge hospital to the immediate south of Notre-Dame, and rebuild it (magnificently) in its present location, facing the northern arm of the Seine. In the process, much of the housing in the hospital's new location would be demolished, further diminishing the resident population of the Ile de la Cité, which was emerging as the center of government administration.

Water and sanitation continued to occupy Haussmann, who in his fourth and final report to the Paris municipal council in 1865 proposed diversion from the River Vanne to provide the amount of water the city's residents needed, as well as construction of a new reservoir to the south of the city, the Montsouris reservoir, adjoining the park of the same name.

It all was expensive. But whatever the cost, Haussmann (and the emperor) were determined that no taxes would be increased to pay for it.

By this time, accusations of favoritism and corruption were circulating pretty freely about Georges Haussmann, abetted by the circumstances surrounding the 1865 loan. Haussmann had not bothered to get competing bids to float the bond issue but simply handed the whole thing over to Crédit Mobilier and the Pereire brothers, who had offered a low commission rate of 1 percent to handle it. This created a hullabaloo when word got out, and the finance minister, Achille Fould (no friend of the Pereires or of Haussmann) complained that he had not even been consulted. Fould irately predicted that the bond issue would be unsuccessful, but he was wrong: it was a major suc-cess with the public, pulling in enough money to cover the huge deficit in Haussmann's Second System and offering him funds with which to proceed with further projects, under what would be called the Third System.

The Pereires for their part were beginning to suffer from the numerous shortcuts they had taken, with Haussmann's tacit or explicit approval, en route to their astonishing financial success. In February 1865, the court case begun several years earlier, involving suspicious circumstances surrounding a merger between the Pereires' Société Immobilière and the Société des Ports de Marseille, was decided against them. Had the emperor not intervened, they would have had to pay even heavier fines, but as it was, the verdict still took considerable wind out of the brothers' sails, forcing them to take more than usual precautions to avoid future encounters with the law.

The joke going around was that the Pereires had been sentenced to six years of forced honesty, but they did not see it as a joke. As for Haussmann, he was about to encounter his own financial difficulties.

While Haussmann was stirring up one ruckus after another, his younger daughter, Valentine, was doing her best to outdo him. She was beautiful and she was wild, offering plenty of tittle-tattle for gossips, especially after it was evident that she had become the emperor's favorite. The child she gave birth to in February 1865 was very likely the emperor's son, and Valentine's fiancé at the time refused to take responsibility for him. But the fiancé died, and Valentine ended up (wedded) in yet another man's arms.

It was all wonderfully spicy but not calculated to burnish the reputation of Valentine's family, especially not her father, whom many blamed for having placed Valentine directly in the emperor's notice in the first place.

Although Louis-Napoleon was continuing to behave much as he always had, chasing one female after another, by 1865 he was suffering from intermittent bouts of pain and a general decline in energy. While some blame this on the years he had spent in prison in the 1840s, following a failed coup attempt, others point to his condition of gallstones, which was first diagnosed in 1865 and attributed in part to his earlier attack of gonorrhea. At the time, the stone was not considered sufficiently serious to operate, and although Louis-Napoleon would suffer several severe attacks during the remaining years of the decade, he continued to behave normally in between. Still, by mid-decade, he had been weakened by the gonorrheal infection, and his general dissipation would have been enough to exhaust most men.

The carnival of luxury, self-indulgence, and pleasure that characterized the Second Empire was by now engulfing its ruling classes, most especially its charming emperor, a man who no longer saw any great need for action. "I never form distant plans," he now remarked. "I am governed by the exigencies of the moment." As one visitor recalled, "At first glance I took him for an opium addict. Not a bit of it; he himself is the drug, and you quickly come under his influence."[2]

Whether through weariness, penitence, or simply a recognition of Eugenie's inherent strength, Louis-Napoleon now increasingly allowed his wife to assume political power. Eugenie, for her part, was quick to push for and embrace this role, later recalling that from childhood she "had a taste for politics."[3] The question nonetheless remained whether a strong will and a taste for politics were sufficient.

At the same time, Prussia's energies were single-mindedly focused on obtaining German unity under Prussian leadership. That autumn, Bismarck met with Louis-Napoleon and Eugenie in Biarritz, with the aim of assuring France's neutrality in Prussia's coming war with Austria. Astonishingly, even after hours of long walks and talks, the French emperor exacted no price for his neutrality—a failure of vision and will that Bismarck viewed with contempt. A weak man, Bismarck concluded, "a sphinx without a riddle." The sphinx's wife, on the other hand, was (according to Bismarck) "the only man in [the French emperor's] government."[4]

Strength without a firm grasp on reality, however, was not proving an effective guide for French policy, most especially in Mexico. Eugenie had strongly urged her husband as well as Maximilian into the Mexican scheme, largely based on her response to some well-calculated horror stories as well as her grandiose dreams for the young Austrian couple, and now France was mired in a mess.

In fairness to the beleaguered principals, the Duke de Morny had also strongly advocated this course, strictly in his own self-interest, and then had died just when his shrewd political judgment would have been of most value. Instead, the principals in this doomed affair slogged on, defending a policy and a military commitment that were at heart indefensible.

By now France had more than thirty thousand troops in Mexico, propping up an emperor whom the Mexicans clearly did not want. Maximilian, despite his good intentions, was making a complete muddle of things, failing to win over a significant portion of the Mexican people while eradicating the corrupt existing power structure—the very landowners and clergy who were responsible for bringing him there. He wanted to help the people, and his new constitution set out a wide range of reforms, from establishing equality before the law to diminishing child labor, but he pleased no one, even as he offended many with his unapologetic foreignness and strict court protocol, straight from Vienna.

Although the French commander in Mexico continued to send optimistic reports, it was becoming clear that only the presence of French troops was keeping large parts of the country under Maximilian's control. Worse yet, now that its Civil War was concluded, the United States had begun to give significant aid to Juárez, who was engaging French troops with ever more frequent and bloody encounters.

Where and when would it stop? How long could France keep pouring financial and military support into what was emerging as an unwinnable morass?

Back in Paris, the harsh winter of 1865 prevented most work on the exterior of the new Opéra, but inside, the Grand Foyer and its adjacent salons received an iron superstructure that would support the foyer's suspended ceiling, while a ring of cast-iron columns reached the sixth level of the auditorium, followed by iron balcony platforms at each level. The substructure of the auditorium would be completed by the year's end.

The year was not good to Georges Bizet, whose ambitions continued to focus on opera. His grand opera *Ivan IV*, commissioned by the Théâtre Lyrique, encountered a variety of ill winds and never was produced. Meanwhile, the Goncourts' fourth novel, *Germinie Lacerteux*, published in early 1865, did not do well. Much to the brothers' dismay, it met with either neglect or disgust. Even their prestigious friend Princess Mathilde, cousin to the emperor, wrote them that the book "made her sick." Why, she wanted to know, would people like them, upstanding and reputable persons, write books like that?[5]

Alone among the reviewers, a young unknown by the name of Emile Zola had written enthusiastically about *Germinie Lacerteux*. He praised its "indomitable energy, [its] supreme disregard for the judgment of the timid and of fools, . . . [and] an artistic integrity rare in these times." Zola had not yet broken into the Paris literary scene and was writing for an out-of-town journal, the *Salut publique* of Lyon, but the Goncourts nonetheless were charmed. He had consoled them, they wrote, for the literary hypocrisy of the moment. Alone, he had understood what they wanted to accomplish.[6]

Again in September, Zola praised *Germinie Lacerteux*, this time in the pages of the *Messager de l'Europe*. When the Goncourts' stage play of contemporary life, *Henriette Maréchal*, appeared at the Comédie-Française in December, the playwrights still had not met the young critic, but they made sure that he received a complimentary seat to the production's opening night.

That evening the Goncourts were uncharacteristically excited ("The Theatre! We had got into the theatre!") and had every expectation of success. After all, they reasoned, the actors were so good that their performance alone would ensure a triumph. The brothers might well have realized what was coming when some of the actors backstage gave them peculiar smiles and said of the audience, "They aren't very affectionate tonight." But the Goncourts were anticipating a hit and were astonished when they began to hear catcalls and hisses. Soon much of the audience was doing its best to bring down the curtain.

Although the theater's management afterward insisted that they had seen nothing like it since the legendary uproar caused by Victor Hugo's *Hernani* in 1830, this was of little consolation to the brothers, who at length concluded that politics rather than the play's raw realism lay at the heart of the protest. They had paid tribute to Princess Mathilde in their preface, and they became convinced that the attacks came from writers and students of the Latin Quarter who decided that the play had passed the censors only because of the authors' friendship with the princess. The police had done little to quell the opening-night riot, possibly—as some conjectured—due to instructions from friends of Empress Eugenie, who was jealous of what amounted to Princess Mathilde's rival court. But the Goncourts preferred to blame a cabal of "envious, class-conscious Bohemians" and railed (in private) against "that new socialism of the beer-halls and Bohemia directed against all decent writers."

The next night went much better, but in the meantime Princess Mathilde had received threatening letters related to the play, saying that "her house would be the first to be burned down and that 'all her lovers' would be hanged." The Goncourts ignored the threat of house burning and instead took exception to the accusation about Mathilde's supposed lovers: this was absolute slander as far as they were concerned. In the three years that they had been frequenting the princess's salon, they had seen no one other than the princess's longtime lover, the Count de Nieuwerkerke, in her presence. This in turn led them to contemplate the "slanderous legends that are invented about the loves of princesses and queens."[7]

The next day, the theater removed *Henriette Maréchal* from production. But not before Emile Zola had seen and written about it, which he did with gusto. "I have lived an entire life in two hours," he wrote the Goncourts soon after opening night, "a life of struggle and of passion, . . . which has been for me the image of this modern life that we are hopelessly living."[8] Soon he had the opportunity to praise *Henriette Maréchal* in print (in a February 1866 issue of *L'Evénement*).

But the Goncourts remained disconsolate, and their spirits did not improve after hearing Alexandre Dumas *père* expound one evening on the current state of the theater. Holding forth at a dinner given by Princess Mathilde, Dumas remarked, "What can you expect, . . . when the only way to make money in the theatre nowadays is with tights that split?" One theater director, as Dumas told it, had made a fortune by telling his dancers to wear split-prone tights. Audiences loved it—until the censors put a stop to it. But the director in question certainly was onto something, according to Dumas. "Something spectacular," he added, "that's all you need."

This, however, provided little cheer for the Goncourts, who reflected: "Sickness, disease. That is the reproach which is constantly thrown at our books. But what is not sickness in this age of ours?"[9]

The year had been a big one for Zola, who not only set up housekeeping with his mistress, Alexandrine Meley, but also established good relations with the Goncourt brothers and began to dabble in journalism as a theater critic. In addition, he began to hold regular Thursday-evening gatherings, attended by Cézanne and Pissarro as well as by other friends.

In late November, Zola published his first novel, *La Confession de Claude*, which he described (in his publicity campaign) as "a psychological and physiological study, a tale of blood and tears that has Fall and Redemption as its lofty and pure moral." In this essentially autobiographical work, based on Zola's difficult life in the Latin Quarter, the young author explored the disillusionment experienced by a young poet mired in the sordid real world of Left Bank bohemia. He had consciously presented this as a moral tome, to evade the censors, but its subject matter offended many, even while Zola's inexperience as a writer put off the more discerning critics. "It is weak in certain places," Zola agreed. "It is the cry of a child who weeps and revolts against himself."[10]

Still, much to Zola's delight, he was being noticed. This included his employers at Hachette, who soon realized that Zola's public relations efforts involved publicizing his book on Hachette stationery, causing one critic to refer to it as "Hachette's little book." As a result, Zola and Hachette agreed to part company in the new year.

It was a potentially risky time for the young man, but the fundamental changes in his personality and lifestyle since coming to Hachette—from laziness and negligence to ambition, hard work, and drive—would serve him well in any career, including the one he most desired, as a man of letters. With utmost practicality, he wrote a friend that what he deemed essential henceforth was an adroitness that "is not a matter of lying to oneself, of being dishonest and providing a book for this or that taste. It is a matter, once the book is done, of not waiting for the public to come to you but of forcing it to caress or insult you." Yes, this might not be dignified, he conceded, but then added, "This is an impatient age."[11]

Much like the Goncourts, Flaubert, and Zola, who aimed at capturing the realities of modern life through their writing, Edouard Manet's goal was to capture reality with a paintbrush. With this as his aim and his guide, he once again attempted to breach the ramparts of the Salon in 1865, this time with two works—*Jesus Mocked by the Soldiers* and *Olympia*. Both were accepted, and both created an uproar—*Jesus Mocked by the Soldiers* for its unconventional portrayal of Jesus as a vulnerable and very human being and *Olympia* for its decidedly unromantic depiction of a cool and collected courtesan of Manet's own times.

Of the two, it is *Olympia* that has gone down in history for its break with tradition and for the pandemonium it created at the 1865 Salon. There is nothing respectable about Manet's courtesan: she is not partially concealed with carefully arranged drapery, nor is her direct gaze shielded from the viewer. She does not reference antiquity, nor is she surrounded by clouds and cherubs or depicted stepping delicately into virginal springs among flowers and butterflies. Instead, she calmly—and with an "I've seen everything" gaze—awaits her client, with a black maid behind her bearing flowers and a black cat crouched at her feet. In viewing Manet's worldly courtesan, startled female members of the ever-so-proper bourgeoisie would have realized, to their discomfort, that they had just seen the real thing.

Probably because he was aware of the storm he would set off, Manet had delayed showing *Olympia*—which he completed in 1863—until 1865. He was right: critics were furious, and the general public was so hostile that, according to *Le Figaro*, the Salon quickly moved it from its original position to the last room, where it hung so high that it was difficult to see.

Commenting on the public reaction, Manet told his friend Antonin Proust, "That kind, they need something frothy. I can't provide that particular article." But he was not so suavely impervious to the ridicule and abuse as he appeared. In a letter to Baudelaire, he wrote: "I wish I had you here, my dear Baudelaire, insults are beating down on me like hail, I've never been through anything like it. . . . All this uproar is upsetting, and obviously someone must be wrong."[12]

In response to the uproar, and perhaps reflecting his own doubts, Manet soon left Paris for Spain, "to go to *Maître* Velázquez for advice," as he put it. Soon after his arrival in Madrid, he encountered Théodore Duret, who quickly became a good friend (although Duret did not hesitate to rib Manet about the latter's objection to Spanish cuisine, which the very Parisian Manet found revolting). Together they visited the Prado, and Manet wrote his friend, the poet and sculptor Zacharie Astruc, that the work of Velázquez alone justified the journey: "He is the greatest artist of all. . . . I discovered in his work the fulfillment of my own ideals in painting, and the sight of those masterpieces gave me enormous hope and courage."[13]

At the same Salon where Manet had made such an unfavorable impact, Claude Monet's first submissions were hung, alphabetically, near Manet's (at least, until Manet's offending contributions were moved). Monet had submitted two seascapes, and they attracted a respectable amount of attention. They also caused some confusion between the painters' names, irritating Manet, who already was exasperated by the reception given his *Olympia*. It did not help that he found himself being complimented for paintings by another artist. "Who is this Monet whose name sounds just like mine and who is taking advantage of my notoriety?" he demanded.[14] Friends hoping to introduce the two artists decided to wait for a better time.

Soon Manet departed for Spain and Monet left Paris for nearby Chailly, where he was intent on producing a masterpiece, a *Luncheon on the Grass* of his own, with life-size figures in contemporary dress seated in the midst of a sun-filtered woods. Although there is no record of Monet's verbal response to Manet's *Luncheon on the Grass*, which he undoubtedly saw when visiting the 1863 Salon, the huge painting that Monet now envisioned can reasonably be believed to have been inspired by, or to have been a response to, Manet's work. Yet this would be a response with a significant difference: in Monet's *Luncheon on the Grass*, there would be no nudity—nothing racy or unrefined.

"Sometimes I am afraid of what I am getting myself into," Monet wrote Bazille in early May, summoning him to Chailly to pose. Bazille's height was essential to Monet's painting—he would serve as a model for at least four of the figures. Later that summer, still hard at work on his preliminary studies, Monet summoned Bazille once again to pose. "You promised to help me with my picture," he wrote testily. "You were supposed to come and pose for some figures and my picture depends on it." All of his studies for the painting were progressing well, Monet told Bazille, and "it's only the men that are missing now." The artist was worried and insistent: "I think only of my painting," he told Bazille, "and if I were to drop it, I think I'd go crazy."[15]

Not surprisingly, relations between the two men were becoming chilly, especially after Monet returned to Paris that autumn and found that Bazille was late in sending in his share of the rent. In the midst of financial worries, Monet nonetheless plugged on, transforming his final four-by-six-foot oil sketch to an immense canvas—fifteen feet high and twenty feet wide. Visitors crowded into the studio to admire the work, talking about the success it would bring Monet at the coming Salon.

But Monet did not submit the painting to the 1866 Salon, nor to the one that followed. Instead, the huge work remained unfinished. Possibly this was because it had become too difficult to complete; possibly it had also become too expensive. Certainly it had become excessively unwieldy, especially after Monet and Bazille were evicted from their spacious studio on Rue de Furstemberg: Monet's new abode (on the Right Bank's Rue Pigalle) was far smaller. In addition, there are accounts of how Gustave Courbet, whom Monet much admired, discouraged the young artist, essentially telling him that he had undertaken far more than he—or anyone—could possibly complete within a reasonable length of time.

Daniel Wildenstein suggests that, in addition to these concerns, Monet abandoned the project because "he had mastered the painting's real subject, the effects of light filtering through the foliage and playing on persons and objects."[16] Instead of striving to paint within the Academic tradition approved by the Académie des Beaux-Arts, Monet and his colleagues now would move in a new direction, one that they had only begun to glimpse.

As for his *Luncheon on the Grass*, Monet rolled up his enormous painting and left it in his landlord's basement, as security for unpaid rent. Years later, when he could afford to reclaim it, it had become moldy. He then cut it up and kept three fragments, of which only two have survived.[17]

～

Both Berthe and Edma Morisot submitted paintings to the 1865 Salon, and much as the year before, these were accepted. The sisters were in Chartres at the time, visiting an uncle, and it was their mother who first viewed the works in situ. "I had to go to a great deal of trouble to find Berthe's and Edma's pictures," she wrote their elder sister, Yves. "Berthe's *Chaudron* is all the less conspicuous because it is not hung in the hall of the M's [a reference to the alphabetical arrangement of the paintings]." Edma's *Pot de fleurs* "can barely be detected," she added. As for Berthe's other submission, *Femme*, her mother thought it was not well lighted, "at least in the mornings," but otherwise, it "does not look bad at all; I saw people point it out to one another."

Madame Morisot may not have been satisfied, but Berthe and Edma were doing reasonably well with their Salon submissions, at least in comparison with Manet—possibly because their entries were of subjects suitable for the Salon's staid audience. Yet the sisters were hardly free from criticism, in their case, from their mother. "It looks as though your paintings, particularly the flowers, are not varnished," Madame Morisot scolded Edma, soon after visiting the Salon. This, she said, was unacceptable: "This is being too careless of the appearance of a painting when the aim is to please untrained eyes susceptible to a first impression." In the future, she added, "you should show less contempt for ordinary people, even if they can make themselves heard only through your father or mother."[18]

The sisters, well knowing their mother, seemed undisturbed by her criticism. Madame Morisot indeed was proud of her daughters' paintings, even if she did not understand them.

～

That year another woman with a dream arrived in Paris. Louise Michel had come once before, in 1851, intending to teach, but her stay had been cut short by her mother's illness. Now she was going to try once more to live and work in the city of her dreams.

Born at the Château de Vroncourt in the Haute-Marne, to the northeast of Paris, Michel was the illegitimate daughter of one of the château's maids and, most probably, the landowner's son. We know little about the father, but Michel grew up regarding the landowner and his wife as her grandparents, and they in turn took it upon themselves to educate this precocious child by providing her with the writings of Voltaire and Rousseau and by encouraging her to question. Such a liberal education was uncommon during these years, especially for a female, and Michel blossomed under it, growing into a sensitive, observant, and caring young woman.

It is not clear whether Michel actually met Victor Hugo during her first stay in Paris, but in any case, she wrote to him throughout his exile. "Allow me to open my soul to you," she wrote, soon after her return to the Haute-Marne, as she was about to take the examination that would allow her to teach. "Please give me a word of hope."[19] Hugo replied and in time would write a moving tribute to her, in which he wrote of Michel's "forgetting of yourself to aid others" and his conviction that she was "incapable of all that is not heroism and virtue."[20]

But now, in 1865, Victor Hugo still was in exile, and Louise Michel once again had arrived in Paris, after spending the intervening years teaching at small schools in the Haute-Marne. During those years, she had experimented (as she would throughout her life) with teaching methods well in advance of their time, such as composing plays for her students to perform or bringing animals and birds into class for children to observe closely and to touch. It took her many years to save enough money to come back to Paris, but by 1865, a small bequest from her grandparents allowed her to return to the capital, where she taught in a day school in Montmartre.

Since childhood, Michel had ardently sympathized with the downtrodden, whether people or animals, but until this time she had not been actively involved in politics—although her memoirs record that, while in the Haute-Marne, she and a friend had placed mysterious marks on the doors of those who were bullying republicans, causing "the self-proclaimed defenders of law and order" to call her a "red," meaning a republican. She had by this time become a forthright opponent of Napoleon III and dreamed of going to Paris, where she would be "at the heart of affairs." But once there, she immersed herself in her teaching rather than in politics and dealt as best she could with her own poverty as well as that of the impoverished Parisians around her. She and her colleagues "knew quite well that teaching paid almost nothing," she later wrote, "but any other trade open to women offered less fulfillment."

She continued her reading, including Darwin's *On the Origin of Species*, and had a bad habit (as she was quick to admit) of buying books, even when she had little or no money. After all, as she put it, "It was hard to resist, for there were so many that tempted me and to me books were everything." But men, and marriage, offered no similar temptation: "There are enough tortured women in the world," she wrote, "without my becoming another one." She firmly retained this position, although she did concede that she was influenced by the fact that "those people who asked to marry me, although they are as dear to me as brothers, would be equally impossible as husbands."

Instead, a life of teaching and charity coupled with radical political activity called her, starting that autumn of 1865. For it was then that Louise Michel realized that, at that very moment, "the struggle against the Empire was intensifying."[21]

Not everyone was as taken with Victor Hugo as was Louise Michel. Charles Baudelaire in fact went to considerable effort during his stay in Brussels to avoid Hugo and his family, who were in residence there.

Baudelaire had come to Brussels in 1864 to give several lectures and to find a publisher for his works. After more than a year, though, things were not going well, and Baudelaire was feeling dismal. He hated Brussels, envied Hugo the fame that had eluded him, and found the very idea of Victor Hugo and Hugo's family more than he could stomach—even though Hugo himself was in Guernsey for much of Baudelaire's lengthy stay. But in May 1865, Baudelaire found himself with an invitation from Madame Hugo that he could not reasonably refuse: to dine with her and her sons, even though Madame struck him as "half-idiotic" and the two sons as "complete fools."

This dinner led to other invitations, some of which included Hugo, who irritated and bored Baudelaire with his godlike views of himself and his endless pontificating. But despite everything, Baudelaire came to like Madame Hugo, calling her a "decidedly a good woman."[22] For her part, Madame Hugo began to like and pity Baudelaire, who by now was suffering from ill health as well as from discouragement.

Manet, writing to Baudelaire in October, after his return from Spain, seems to have been trying to boost his friend's morale when he wrote that he was "delighted to hear that Victor Hugo can't do without you now" and added that he was not surprised: "He's bound to find the company of someone like you more attractive than that of his usual crowd of lionizers." Manet then hesitantly touched a sore spot: "Couldn't he put you in touch with his publishers?"[23]

But Hugo did not offer, and Baudelaire was not about to ask. It would have been too demeaning. Yet Baudelaire kept up the pretense of flattering Hugo, and Hugo continued to flatter Baudelaire, even though he was more honest with Charles Asselineau, a friend and future biographer of Baudelaire. "I met Baudelaire rather than knew him," Hugo frankly wrote Asselineau. "He often offended me and I must often have annoyed him. . . . I agree with all your praise, but with some reservations."[24]

～

While Nadar was embellishing his Boulevard des Capucines studio with a huge facsimile of his signature in ten-foot-high gaslit red glass tubing stretching fifty feet in length, a staunch opponent of Napoleon III was contemplating giving a huge statue representing liberty to the United States, as a potent symbol for the ideas that the Second Empire had suppressed.

The man was Edouard de Laboulaye, an esteemed French jurist, historian, and professor at the Collège de France, who had published a three-volume history of the United States and was considered an expert on America and its Constitution. Although firmly opposed to Napoleon III, Laboulaye had kept his opinions under wraps until the first signs of liberalization in the early 1860s, when he resumed teaching American history, using his lectures to criticize France's Second Empire and giving public lectures as well. Entering politics seemed a logical outgrowth, and although Laboulaye was unsuccessful in his bid for a seat in the Legislature, his platform of "Democracy and Liberty" marked him as a leader among the Empire's liberal opposition.

One evening in 1865, Laboulaye invited French sculptor Frédéric-Auguste Bartholdi to join him and a number of liberal politicians and intellectuals for dinner at Laboulaye's Normandy estate. There, the talk soon turned to recent events in the United States, including the Civil War, the abolition of slavery, and the assassination of President Lincoln. How, the various members of this select group wondered, could this young American nation maintain democracy in the face of the many obstacles it had encountered, while France, which had embraced so many of the same principles during its great revolution, had strayed so badly?

Laboulaye had a ready answer to this: Americans, he noted, were practical, while Frenchmen tended to become theoreticians, especially when drawing up constitutions. Conversation then turned to the friendship established between the two nations during the American Revolution, when France had given the American colonies essential financial and military aid. Evidently inspired by the discussion, Laboulaye offered an idea: that this friendship should be celebrated with some kind of symbolism, something that could be presented as a gift from the people of France to the American people. What about, he wondered, a statue representing liberty? This would serve not only as a tribute to the United States but also as a symbol for the ideas suppressed under France's Second Empire.

Bartholdi was intrigued. He was drawn to the idea of creating colossal statues and would soon propose the idea of a gigantic female figure holding a lamp for the entrance of the Suez Canal. But it would be several years before the idea of a Statue of Liberty would blossom.

In the meantime, Laboulaye and his republican friends would continue, to the best of their abilities, to try to uphold the light of liberty in Napoleon III's France.

Emile Zola, c.1865. Photograph by A. Pinsard. © Bibliothèque Nationale, Paris, France / Archives Charmet / Bridgeman Images

CHAPTER FOURTEEN

~

Crisis
(1866)

The year got off to a bad start with unmistakable signs of financial trouble ahead. The Pereires' glittering creation, Crédit Mobilier, had been experiencing uncertainties for some time, and now, in 1866, worrisome cracks were beginning to show through its façade. As the once-booming institution now cast about for capital, it was difficult not to perceive an uncharacteristic element of panic among its directors. Their alarm was justified: by the year's end, Crédit Mobilier would hardly be able to pay a dividend.

The Pereires were quick to blame the Rothschilds for their predicament, but the brothers seem to have brought much of the trouble upon themselves, whether through the activities of yet another of their creations, the Crédit Immobilier, or through their unsuccessful attempts to expand into the financial activities of several other foreign governments.

At the same time, evidence of worker discontent was growing, from strikes to the burgeoning membership of labor societies—especially the International Working Men's Association, founded only two years before and now rapidly expanding in France. The Duke de Morny may have disappeared from the scene, but a worried emperor was still inclined to offer concessions. That February, the minister of the interior advised prefects throughout the country to display more tolerance for strikers' meetings, while a law several months later revoked the article in the Code Civil that established the inequality of master and worker in the eyes of the law.

Yet despite such concessions, workers failed to gravitate to the regime. Living conditions remained harsh and wages low, prompting members of these labor societies, and especially of the International, to strongly support the republican opposition.

And then there was Mexico, where matters could hardly have been worse. With bloody massacres of French troops on the rise, the French press in early 1866 began to push strongly for withdrawal. Louis-Napoleon was inclined to agree and in January announced that, since Maximilian's regime was secure, he was about to order a phased withdrawal of the French expeditionary force there. In actuality, Maximilian's regime was anything but secure, but the emperor was taking the time-honored approach of declaring victory before leaving the scene of a disaster. Unfortunately, Louis-Napoleon was disinclined to commit himself irrevocably and dawdled for several months before actually giving the order to withdraw (10,000 men to leave in November, with another 10,000 the following March, and the remaining 14,000 the November after). Still, the commander of the French forces in Mexico advised Maximilian to get out as soon as possible. Unfortunately, Maximilian was adamant and refused. Instead, the beleaguered emperor sent his wife, Charlotte, to plead in person with Louis to delay the troop withdrawal and continue French support of the imperial Mexican regime.

Charlotte arrived at the French court in July, when Mexico was the last thing that Louis-Napoleon wanted to think about. He was ill again, and he was facing what amounted to an earthquake in international affairs: the mighty Prussian army had just defeated the Austrians in the battle of Sadowa, elevating Prussia to supremacy in Central Europe.

Even before becoming minister-president of Prussia in 1862, Otto von Bismarck had determined exactly how he wanted to proceed en route to establishing German unity under Prussia. Austria, although a declining state, was still wrapped in glory and still the major power in Central Europe. The previous autumn Bismarck had obtained Louis-Napoleon's tacit approval and agreement to French neutrality during what already was Bismarck's well-established plan for an upcoming Prussian war on Austria.

War broke out in June 1866, with the newly united Kingdom of Italy joining Prussia in the hope of receiving Venetia from a defeated Austria as its reward. Italian troops did not do well against their enemy, suffering a humiliating defeat in battle, but in the end it did not matter. Prussia's well-equipped and thoroughly modernized army, led by Count Helmuth von Moltke, annihilated the Austrian army in the Battle of Sadowa on July 3.

Austria sued for peace and handed over Venetia to Italy, with France serving as an intermediary in the exchange.

Suddenly the entire balance of power in Europe had changed. A little late to the party, Louis-Napoleon now attempted to win some territorial concessions on the Rhine's left bank from Prussia, but Bismarck was contemptuous. Others were contemptuous as well. Adolphe Thiers, by now a leading deputy of the opposition in the Legislature, remarked that "it is France who has been beaten at Sadowa."[1]

For her part, Empress Eugenie was devastated. Two days after Sadowa, at a hastily summoned meeting of the Council of Ministers, she listened as Foreign Secretary Edouard Drouyn de Lhuys recommended that France send troops to the Rhine in response to Prussia's muscular progress. When the interior minister disputed this, arguing that France would have no difficulty in obtaining territorial compensations through friendly negotiations with Prussia, Eugenie burst out: "When the Prussian armies are no longer tied up in Bohemia and can turn back against ourselves, Bismarck will simply laugh at our claims!" She even told the emperor, "Prussia did not scruple to throw a barrier in front of you after [your victory at] Solferino. Why should you worry over doing the same to her after Sadowa?"

Many years later, Eugenie told an interviewer: "The summer of 1866, after Sadowa, is the critical date, the date of doom for the Empire; it was during those months of July and August that our destiny was fixed!" Whether or not Bismarck would have pulled back if Louis-Napoleon had strongly opposed him after Sadowa, Eugenie and some of her husband's ministers firmly felt that this course was the only possible one. "At that moment," she said years afterward, "I felt the fate of France and the future of our destiny were at stake."[2]

But Louis-Napoleon—depressed and ill— refused to take action, any action at all, and now Eugenie thought seriously that her husband should abdicate in favor of their nine-year-old son, with her as regent.

It was at this unfortunate moment that Empress Charlotte arrived from Mexico.

Trying to protect her husband from this encounter, Eugenie at first met alone with Charlotte, assuring her that Louis-Napoleon was too ill to receive her. But Charlotte was distraught and not to be put off. Louis-Napoleon, accompanied by Eugenie, then received her—an excruciating encounter, during which he had to inform Charlotte that "Mexico is an abyss into which France is sliding. I must stop it." And he begged her to convince Maximilian to leave Mexico while he still could.

Charlotte, now sobbing, replied that he was condemning her and Maximilian to death. No, no, Louis-Napoleon insisted: they were both young, and there would be a new life for them back in Europe. At this, Charlotte retorted that her husband would not run away. As Louis-Napoleon continued his attempts to placate her, she suddenly screamed, "Blood and tears! . . . Both will flow again, and because of you! Rivers of Blood! And on your head!" And then she collapsed. When Eugenie tried to give her water, Charlotte seized the glass and threw the water at her, screaming, "Assassins! Leave me alone! I won't swallow your poisoned drink!"

She had gone mad.[3]

Despite the turbulence in affairs at home and abroad, and despite a new outbreak of cholera that struck Paris in the wake of the Austro-Prussian war, Haussmann's renewal of the city marched on.

In 1866, Boulevard de Magenta was finally completed as far as the outer boulevards, and a northward extension (later renamed Boulevard Barbès) was under way. The new Hôtel-Dieu hospital was now rising on the northern side of the Ile de la Cité, while construction continued on the Opéra throughout the winter, which turned out to be a mild one. Supplementary water from the River Vanne became closer to reality for Parisians, while at Belgrand's request, Haussmann purchased windmills on the River Marne and then set up two hydraulic machines to pump water from the Marne into the Canal de l'Ourcq.

All of this of course was expensive, but funds from the legislatively approved bond issue continued to support the *grands travaux*, while the municipal council approved Haussmann's portion of the city budget, as in the past. Unlike requests for state funding from the Legislature, which Louis-Napoleon had initiated for financing Paris's *grands travaux*, Haussmann did not have to justify his requests to the municipal council as work that would benefit the entire nation. In previous years, the municipal council had approved his portion of the budget with little ado. In 1866, it continued its approval; yet for the first time, a hint of trouble surfaced.

Somewhere in the depths of the national audit office, questions had arisen over alleged financial irregularities within the Haussmann administration. The city's treasury department was under the National Audit Office's control, and Haussmann viewed it balefully, as a "body that has forever been closed to progressive ideas," whose only purpose was "to tick off figures, to check additions down to the last centime," and to nitpick.[4]

Trouble had not yet materialized, but it was not far off.

～

It was now that Edouard Manet and his wife, Suzanne, moved in with Manet's widowed mother on Rue de Saint-Pétersbourg, near the Gare Saint-Lazare and the new Opéra quarter. Léon, Suzanne's illegitimate son, joined them—presented as always to the rest of the world as Suzanne's younger brother. Madame Manet and Suzanne enjoyed one another, and whether Léon was the son of Edouard's father or of Edouard himself—or of some other man previously in Suzanne's life—Edouard's mother did not seem overly concerned and was especially fond of the boy.

It was a busy and bustling household, where Edouard's mother surrounded herself with family and friends. Madame Manet was not inclined to solitude, and she often featured her daughter-in-law—an accomplished pianist—in musical evenings. Among those that Madame Manet invited to her twice-weekly soirées were a vibrant group of politicians, artists, writers, musicians, and composers, as well as personal family friends. This, plus the fortune that underpinned the entire family, made for a secure and pleasant home for Manet, who would never suffer, as did so many other painters, from poverty.

Even Manet's marriage seems to have been a happy one, whatever his man-about-town proclivities. Perhaps surprisingly, he and Suzanne longed for children of their own, as he indicated in writing to Zacharie Astruc. After congratulating Astruc "for the arrival of your heir," he added, "We would love the same thing to happen to us."[5]

And yet, despite his comforts and his security, Edouard Manet was frustrated and unhappy. That year, the Salon rejected both of his submissions (*The Tragic Actor* and *The Fifer*), which he had painted under the inspiration of his recent trip to Spain and, in particular, of Velázquez.

It was now that a friend introduced Manet to Emile Zola, who had begun to write art criticism for the weekly *L'Evénement*. Zola may have misunderstood Manet's work and modern painting in general; he may also have had his own career interests more in mind than Manet's when he took up Manet's cause. Still, Zola was the only one to come publicly to Manet's defense, and he did so with characteristic verve. Zola's subsequent article on Manet appeared in early May, as part of a series he called *Mon Salon*. "You know what effect Monsieur Manet's canvases produce at the Salon," he wrote. "Quite simply they burst open the wall. All around them stretch the sweets of the fashionable artistic confectioners, sugar-candy trees and pastry houses, gingerbread gentlemen, and ladies made of vanilla cream."[6]

"Monsieur Manet has a no-nonsense temperament which cuts clean," Zola continued. "He captures his figures alive." He especially liked Manet's rejected painting, *The Fifer*, whose exactness and simplicity made a strong impression on him. "He delineates his figures sharply . . . , rendering objects in all their vigor." Moreover, "his entire being compels him to see in patches, in simple elements charged with energy."[7]

Zola eviscerated the Salon as vigorously as he defended Monet, exposing the bargaining and the bribery involved in the selection process and scathingly depicting the artwork that was accepted. And what kind of works were accepted? he rhetorically asked. A dull lot, he answered, dreary and mediocre. While at the same time painters such as Manet, painters who were "strong, solid," and "the most living," were being rejected. It was scandalous!

Manet was delighted. Immediately after the article appeared, he wrote Zola: "I don't know where to find you to shake your hand and tell you how proud and happy I am to be championed by a man of your talent, what a splendid article , . . . a thousand thanks." He suggested meeting at the Café de Bade, where he regularly could be found from 4:30 to 7 p.m., "if that should suit you."[8]

The Café de Bade, or possibly the Café Guerbois, evidently suited, for the two now became friends. Manet, much to his gratification, had a champion, while Zola was on his way as a literary star of the avant-garde.

∿

Claude Monet, unlike Edouard Manet, did have two paintings accepted for the 1866 Salon. Since he was unable to complete his *Luncheon on the Grass* in time for the that year's Salon, he submitted *Le Pavé de Chailly*, which he had done the previous year, and a new painting—his remarkable full-length study *Camille*, or *The Woman with a Green Dress*.

Monet had by now moved to the Right Bank, where he began to paint this life-size female figure, posed indoors and clothed in a voluminous (and rented) green satin dress. His model was Camille-Léonie Doncieux, a nineteen-year-old Parisian, born in Lyon, who had recently become his mistress. Up against a tight deadline, Monet managed to finish the painting in time to get it to the Salon jury by the March 20 cutoff date (although probably not painted in the four days that legend has it).

Once on display, Monet's striking portrait attracted attention, much of it negative. One critic complained that "a dress is no more a painting than a sentence written correctly is a book" and demanded, "What does this outfit mean to me if I cannot understand the body beneath, . . . if the head is not a head, and the hand no more than a paw?" And, as the year before, viewers and critics alike confused Monet with Manet—not only because of the similarities in name but also because of the unconventional nature of the two painters' work. The caricaturist André Gill (of subsequent Lapin Agile fame) featured *Camille* with the caption: "Monet or Manet? —Monet. But it is to *Manet* that we owe this *Monet*; bravo! *Monet*; thank you! *Manet*."[9]

But Emile Zola did not confuse the two, while applauding both. Continuing his passionate support of Manet, he gave stellar marks to Monet as well. "Now there's a temperament," he wrote in *L'Evénement*. "There's a man among eunuchs!" Zola stood before Monet's *Woman with a Green Dress* and marveled at the contrast between it and the canvases displayed around it. "Here we have something more than a realist," he proclaimed. "We have a strong, subtle interpreter who has not gone wooden with his concern for detail."[10]

Not surprisingly, *L'Evénement's* readers were not all of a same mind, and angry letters flooded the editor, while some of its readers, evidently provoked beyond endurance, tore up the issue in front of the newspaper's office and stamped on the fragments. One irate soul even challenged Zola to a duel. *L'Evénement* thrived on scandal, but the flood of subscription cancellations convinced the editor that Zola could not go on in this vein. After just a few weeks of glory, Zola's art criticism in *L'Evénement* came to a halt. But he would soon publish his offending articles in pamphlet form as *Mon Salon*, which would have a life of its own.

Zola did meet Monet, while Monet and Manet did at last become friends, thanks to the intercession of Zacharie Astruc, who made it clear to Manet that the confusion between the two was not of Monet's making.

Monet in the meanwhile was encountering unexpected financial difficulties: his aunt had finally decided to put an end to the allowance she had regularly sent him. "I'm utterly shaken," he wrote the painter Amand Gautier, asking him to "placate my aunt for a little while longer" and adding that "I don't know quite how I could manage otherwise." Gautier, a friend of Monet's aunt, did indeed do exactly as Monet requested, writing the aunt and focusing on what he termed Monet's "Salon success." In addition, as an overjoyed Monet wrote Gautier, "no less than three people sent [the aunt] the *Evénement* [Zola's article] which you also sent," which delighted her— "She is congratulated at every turn." An ecstatic Monet thanked Gautier "from the bottom of my heart."[11]

Adding to his happiness, Monet sold several paintings based on his Salon showing, for a total of eight hundred francs. Still, *Camille* did not find a buyer, and his aunt had made it clear that, although renewing his allowance, she was not about to pay off his debts. Eight hundred francs represented a victory, but it would not go very far—especially now that Monet had another mouth to feed.

~

Among the young painters striving in new directions, Berthe Morisot continued to experience modest success at the Salon, once again having two paintings accepted in 1866. Camille Pissarro also had a landscape accepted at the 1866 Salon, as he had in every Salon but one since 1859. Edgar Degas, who showed for the first time at the 1865 Salon with an acceptable historic scene (*War Scene from the Middle Ages*), appeared at the 1866 Salon in a more audacious light, depicting a fallen jockey with galloping horses, all contoured in daringly sweeping outlines. Despite its calculated challenge to the tradition-bound, his entry was accepted but went unnoticed.

Pierre-Auguste Renoir, a fellow-student with Monet at the Gleyre academy, who had succeeded with his first try at the 1864 Salon, subsequently—after painting *en plein air* in the company of Monet, Bazille, and Sisley—became disillusioned with the acceptable style of Academic painting and destroyed his successful 1864 entry (called *La Esmeralda*). He scored with two submissions to the 1865 Salon (a portrait of Sisley's father and a landscape), but his 1866 submission, a landscape with two figures, was rejected. Enquiring hesitantly on its fate, in the guise of "a friend of Renoir," he was told (by one of the few jurors inclined to favor the "new" artists) that the painting had been solidly rejected. Still, the juror went on, "Tell your friend not to become discouraged, that there are great qualities in his picture. He should make a petition and request an exhibition of *Refusés*."

There had not been a sequel to the 1863 Salon des Refusés, and it is not known whether Renoir (or for that matter the disappointed Manet or Bazille) followed this advice; but Paul Cézanne most certainly did. Cézanne's submissions to the 1864 and 1865 Salons had been rejected, and his 1866 submission, the portrait of a friend, Anthony Valabrègue, struck one juror as having been "not only painted with a knife but even with a pistol." Expecting rejection and geared for a fight, Cézanne wrote the superintendent of fine arts, the well-connected Count de Nieuwerkerke (Princess Mathilde's longtime lover), of his disappointment. Not receiving an answer, he wrote again, not merely to request but to demand the chance to show his pictures to the public, despite their rejection by an "unfair judgment." He was not alone in this request, he told Nieuwerkerke, citing the many painters "in my position" who would all, if asked, "disown the jury." Yet even if he were alone, he demanded that the Salon des Refusés be reestablished.

Zola seems to have helped his boyhood friend Cézanne with this letter, which came at the same time that he began his weekly attacks on the Salon in *L'Evénement*, in which he may have received essential coaching from Cézanne. After all, Zola had long before admitted that he knew next to nothing about art. But this was a cause that he could commit to with a passion, and expertise—if not his own—was certainly available to him.

"What he asks is impossible," reads a marginal note that an official wrote on Cézanne's second letter. "We have come to realize how inconsistent with the dignity of art the exhibition of the *Refusés* was, and it will not be repeated."[12] The Salon des Refusés was not repeated, and the superintendent of fine arts does not appear to have answered either of Cézanne's letters.

But Cézanne may well have contributed essentials to the broadside that Zola launched against the Salon and in defense of Manet and Monet. Cézanne, however, was not among those whom Zola chose to praise, and in a later novel, *L'Oeuvre*, he would make it clear that he viewed his boyhood friend as an "incomplete genius." Still, if Zola owed Cézanne for assistance on his *L'Evénement* articles, he made a gesture toward repayment when he gathered together these articles into the pamphlet *Mon Salon*, which he dedicated to Cézanne.

Monet in the meantime had moved to a small village to the west of Paris, where he once again took up the challenge of creating a large painting of figures in a landscape. This time, the figures were all of women, who were clothed in the floating summer dresses of the time, and the physical challenges alone of creating such a huge painting were daunting: simply to reach every part of the canvas with his paintbrush, Monet found it necessary to dig a trench in his garden and set up a pulley system to raise and lower the canvas into and out of the trench. Despite such obstacles, and the recurring problem of debts, Monet completed *Women in the Garden* later in the year in Honfleur and submitted it to the 1867 Salon. But not before more problems, and bills, arose.

Gustave Flaubert, in the meanwhile, had been made a Chevalier of the Legion of Honor, probably at the urging of his friend Princess Mathilde. The honor may have pleased him, but he was not pleased that Pierre Alexis Ponson du Terrail, a popular writer whose work he despised, was decorated at the same time. Maxime Du Camp undertook to console Flaubert by telling him that in all probability Ponson du Terrail "was quite as much scandalized at being decorated in company with Gustave Flaubert"—a truth that Flaubert readily acknowledged.[13]

In another part of town, the master photographer Nadar—now at the top of his profession—was bored. Photography no longer inspired him, and he preferred the company of hot-air balloons or anything that flew. He could envision the possibilities for aerial military photography and land surveys, and he was determined to be the first to take photographs from the sky. But photographing celebrities had lost its charm.

Sarah Bernhardt was also bored. She had been on her own for two years now and longed to get back into the theater. Pulling strings, she managed to wangle an interview with the Théâtre de l'Odéon but on the condition that she behave herself. This meant controlling her temper and her indiscreet lifestyle. Hiding her annoyance, she outdid herself with charm but nonetheless managed to receive only a humiliating one-month contract. Still, the Odéon was France's second national theater, and it was a start. The director, who had encountered Bernhardt before, did not like anything about her, but the associate director was more amenable. And so she signed—fully intending to be a success.

Charles Baudelaire had by now come to despair of success. Still in Brussels, after his agent had led him to believe that a publisher was about to offer a contract, he learned to his disbelief that, after many months, the agent had not even approached the publisher in question. When a friend inquired on his behalf, the publisher promptly closed the door on all possibility of publication, ending all of Baudelaire's hopes.

His drinking increased, as did his use of opium, and in 1866—while still in Belgium—he suffered a massive stroke, followed by partial paralysis. Those concerned about him, including the Hugos, placed him in a nursing home in Brussels, and then in July 1866, friends brought him by private compartment in a train to Paris. There he entered a clinic, where for a brief time he entertained visitors and even attended dinners that Nadar arranged in his honor.

But soon, as death approached, Baudelaire withdrew from almost all contact with the outside world.

In the course of one of Haussmann's demolition projects, the city of Paris had condemned the school building that Louise Michel owned, with a colleague, on Rue du Château-d'Eau. Michel hoped that they would receive an indemnity for the building, but the reimbursement never materialized. She then bought a day school in Montmartre with money that her mother managed to scrape together. Michel and another teacher lived in the day school, and gradually, the number of her pupils increased. "For schoolmistresses," she recalled, "we were nearly comfortable," and "joy filled my heart."

Adding to her joy, Michel now began to attend classes at a Left Bank center on Rue Hautefeuille (6th) directed by two reform-minded republicans, Jules Favre and Eugène Pelletan. There, she and other schoolteachers continued their education with "free courses in elementary teaching, professional courses, readings to mothers of families, and a night course for young people who had to work." Those women who were young teachers or were preparing themselves to become teachers "were eager for this learning," Michel noted, as they had "only what they had been able to snatch here and there." Describing this vital atmosphere, Michel added, "A frenzy for knowledge possessed us."

At the Rue Hautefeuille center, there were lectures ranging from physics and chemistry to law. Teachers tried out new methods of instruction, and Michel taught many poor children there: "Young as they were," she later wrote, "they had to work all day, and if it hadn't been for the center on the rue Hautefeuille [where instruction continued up to ten o'clock at night], they would never have been in a class."

It was as she returned home late at night that Michel saw a Paris that most, except the destitute, did not see. "I have seen criminals and whores," she challenged her readers, "And spoken with them. Now I inquire / If you believe them made as now they are / To drag their rags in blood and mire, / Preordained, an evil race?" And she added, in pungent prose: "No one comes into the world with a knife in his hand to stab others, or with a card in her hand to sell herself."

Louise Michel had seen the darkness and wanted to shine a light on it, through teaching and education. "At the rue Hautefeuille in the long night of the Empire we had glimpses of a better world," she wrote. "It provided an untainted refuge in the middle of imperial Paris."[14]

OPENING OF THE PARIS EXHIBITION : ARRIVAL OF THE EMPEROR AND EMPRESS AT THE GRAND ENTRANCE.—SEE PAGE 366.
(Ouverture de l'Exposition Universelle : Arrivée de Leurs Majestés à la Grande Porte.)

Arrival of the Emperor and Empress at the Grand Entrance opening the 1867 Paris Exhibition (en-graving for The Illustrated London News, *13 April 1867). Private collection. © Look and Learn / Illustrated Papers Collection / Bridgeman Images*

CHAPTER FIFTEEN

~

A Setting Sun

(1867)

The year started badly, with Napoleon III receiving yet another brush-off from Bismarck. The French emperor had not learned from his unsuccessful attempt the year before to extricate a compensation along the Rhine in return for France's neutrality in Prussia's war with Austria. Now, in the new year, Louis-Napoleon received as little joy when he made his follow-up bid to Prussia, asking for French hegemony over Luxembourg. After a fairly major kerfuffle, in which Bismarck threatened war and Britain intervened, Louis-Napoleon backed off, his reputation none the better for the encounter. Those in the know began to remark quietly that a Franco-Prussian war was looking ever more likely.

Added to this, French Catholics were becoming alarmed over affairs in Rome where, the previous December, the emperor had withdrawn protective French troops after the Italian government agreed not to attack the pope. What, the devout wondered, would prevent the newly exposed Holy City from coming under attack from Garibaldi and his army of Italian nationalists?

As it turned out, the faithful were right to be worried: by autumn, Garibaldi was once again threatening the remnants of the Papal States. Reluctantly, Louis-Napoleon—concerned about undermining French-Italian friendship— sent French troops back to Rome. There, the French intervened in a firefight between papal forces and Garibaldi's men, inflicting heavy losses on Garibaldi's troops. Italian-French friendship, already frayed, now ended.

Two new, and hostile, powers now bordered France: Prussia and Italy. But this did not faze French conservatives, who applauded the emperor's minister of state, Eugène Rouher, when he proclaimed: "Never shall Italy lay hold of Rome. Never shall France support such violence to its honor, to the Catholic Church."

Louis-Napoleon is said to have congratulated Rouher for his speech, but then added: "In politics, you must not say *never*."[1]

And then there was the ongoing debacle in Mexico. Napoleon ordered the last French troops home that March, leaving behind some seven thousand dead Frenchmen on foreign soil and a naive young emperor whose situation was perilous. Soon, Maximilian and his remaining defenders were surrounded and besieged, and the would-be emperor of Mexico was forced to surrender.

On June 19, Maximilian was executed by firing squad. To the end, he was the very personification of nobility, voicing clearly before the shots rang out that his only wish was that his blood would "bring peace and happiness to my unhappy adopted fatherland."

The news of his death reached Paris on July 1, just as Louis-Napoleon was about to preside over a splendid ceremony at that year's glittering Universal Exposition. Pomp and circumstance reigned on the one hand but could not hide a bloody debacle, whose stain had made its mark. In the words of Philip Guedalla, an early historian of the empire, "The sky was still bright; but there was a strange chill upon the Empire. The clear dawn of 1852 seemed half a century away, and quite suddenly the Emperor had become an old man."[2]

That January, the Goncourts had noted the ongoing decline of civilization by remarking that there were no longer any chairs in the bookshops along the Seine's embankments. France, in their words, had been "the last bookseller who provided chairs where you could sit down and chat." But modern trade, as they put it, had been "all-devouring."

Despite their fears for the future of everything civilized, especially at the hands of Americans, whom the Goncourts feared were "destined to be the future conquerors of the world, . . . the Barbarians of civilization," the brothers were pleased when the elder, Edmond, received his admission to the Legion of Honor that September. Although his joy was incomplete, due to the absence of a similar recognition for Jules, Edmond nonetheless felt great pride in receiving the decoration, "which has that rare distinction of not having been asked for or solicited by so much as a single word or allusion, but obtained by a friend who thought of it by herself"—that is, Princess Mathilde.[3]

That year Georges Bizet once again suffered disappointment with yet another commissioned opera, *La Jolie Fille de Perth* (*The Fair Maid of Perth*), which was squeezed out of the prime summer exposition spot by Charles Gounod's *Roméo et Juliette* before at last making it to the stage late in the year, where it played for only eighteen performances. But that January, Sarah Bernhardt made her official debut at the Théâtre de l'Odéon. The part did not suit her, but soon after, she had a "veritable small triumph" (as she put it) in Racine's *Athalie*.

The Odéon was a Left Bank center for artists, intellectuals, and Sorbonne students, where anti-imperialism flourished and Victor Hugo and George Sand reigned supreme. It was therefore a notable break for Bernhardt when George Sand noticed her and awarded her with a small part in Sand's *Le Marquis de Villemer*, which Sand had dramatized from her novel with the help of Dumas *fils*.

Bernhardt loved her time at the Odéon. "Oh, that Odéon Theater!" she later enthused. "It is the theater I have loved most. . . . We thought of nothing but putting on plays, and we rehearsed morning, afternoon, and at all hours, and I liked that very much." Even her Spartan surroundings could not dampen her enthusiasm. "I always ran up the cold, cracked steps of the theater with veritable joy," she wrote, "and rushed up to my dressing-room." But it was the stage that delighted her the most—"to be once more in that infinite darkness with only a poor light." For her, there was "nothing more brilliant than that darkness."

As for George Sand, Bernhardt recalled her as "a sweet, charming creature, . . . [who] did not talk much, but smoked all the time." Bernhardt seems to have performed creditably in Sand's *Marquis de Villemer*, but it was in playing the role of Anna Danby in Alexandre Dumas's *Kean* in early 1868 that she elicited a review that first remarked on her voice, "her rich voice—that astonishing voice of hers." As a friend would later tell Bernhardt, "You are an original without trying to be so, " adding that "you have a natural harp in your throat."

Bernhardt was already striking some as extraordinary, "a creature apart"—which of course, as that friend pointed out, "is a crime of high treason against all that is commonplace."[4]

Early in January 1867, Zola published a long article in Manet's defense in *La Revue du XIX siècle*. Manet was delighted. "What a splendid New Year's gift you've made me," he wrote Zola. 'It comes just at the right moment." Once again, Manet had been treated shabbily by the Salon judges, and he now decided to hold a one-man exhibition at the upcoming Universal Exposition. "I have at least forty-odd pictures I can show," he added, and had been offered "sites in very good locations near the Champ de Mars." He promised Zola that he was "going to go all out."[5]

Yet even with boundless enthusiasm and support of friends like Zola it was a risky venture, as Gustave Courbet had discovered at the 1855 exposition. Sales and attendance for Courbet's one-man exhibition had been disappointing, and the members of the public who did show up had scoffed. Still, Courbet had emerged from the affair as a hero of the new school of Realist art and rapidly became a celebrity. Once again, at the upcoming 1867 exposition, Courbet planned a one-man exhibition, and this time, Manet planned to venture his reputation and a considerable fortune by joining him.

It was odd, Camille Pissarro later commented to his son Lucien, how Manet, "great painter that he was, had a petty side, he was crazy to be recognized by the constituted authorities." Despite his talent, despite the security that his life offered, "he believed in success, he longed for honors." In particular, Manet longed for recognition from the Salon, which in spite of his disappointments, he continued to regard as "the real field of battle."[6]

But given his treatment by the 1867 Salon judges, Manet decided on the radical step of a one-man show, held in a temporary pavilion of his own construction on the Place de l'Alma at Avenue Montaigne, diagonal from Courbet's own pavilion. This was no inexpensive venture: Manet had to ask his mother to advance him the funds to build the wooden pavilion and meet the exhibition's other expenses. Prepared to put the entirety of his work before the public, he exhibited fifty-three paintings, including *The Absinthe Drinker*, *Le Déjeuner sur l'herbe*, and *Olympia*. And he published a catalogue in which he (and probably some of his writer friends) set forth his aims as an artist, in which he presented himself as reasonable rather than radical. "M. Manet," it stated, "presumes neither to overthrow earlier painting nor to make it new. He has merely tried to be himself and not someone else."[7]

Unfortunately, as Courbet had already discovered, one-man exhibitions were not a good way to attract the attention of critics or the general public. Manet received praise from only one critic (Jules Claretie, in *L'Indépendance belge*), and members of the general public just as generally stayed away.

It was a disastrous experience for Manet, financially and in every other way—underscoring once again the difficulties in trying to win public recognition and success without the imprimatur of the Salon.

⌣

In late May, Claude Monet wrote Frédéric Bazille that "Manet's opening is in two days and he is in a frightful state." Courbet's opening was also due shortly, "but that's quite another story. Can you imagine, he's inviting every artist in Paris to the opening: he's sending three thousand invitations, and on top of that, every artist also gets a copy of his catalogue. Rest assured he's doing well."[8]

Monet himself was now in dire financial straits. By winter's end, he had come to live with Bazille, where he joined an equally broke Renoir. His prospects, and that of so many of his friends, looked bleak: that year's Salon jury had accepted none of the paintings Monet submitted and also rejected the paintings of Renoir, Bazille, Sisley, Pissarro, and Cézanne. Although Monet and others petitioned for a new Salon des Refusés, they had no luck. Even their attempt to organize an exhibit on private premises failed, leaving them to eke out the rest of the winter and spring as best they could. Only Bazille's last-minute intervention, by purchasing *Women in the Garden* at a remarkably high price (payable in fifty-franc monthly installments), brightened Monet's prospects, at least for the moment.

But still, Monet remained chronically out-of-pocket and out-of-sorts. He spent the spring painting views of Paris with Renoir and only occasionally looked in on his mistress, Camille Doncieux, who by now was pregnant and living separately from him. On contacting Monet's father on his friend's behalf, Bazille received the firm admonition that if young Monet wanted to succeed, "he must renounce his extravagant ideas and his past conduct."[9] As for Camille Doncieux, Monet's father was firm: Monet would have to leave her.

Monet did not completely abandon his mistress but nonetheless kept his distance, moving her to a room in a Batignolles apartment near that of her parents (who did not seem to have taken any interest in their disgraced daughter). He also arranged for the anticipated July delivery and planned to be present when it took place. But his interest seems to have been elsewhere, either with Manet's one-man show or with his own ever-pressing financial needs. Bazille had by now left for his parents' home in Montpellier, and Monet continued to press his friend for money. "I saw Camille yesterday," he wrote Bazille in late May. "I don't know what to do; she is ill, bedridden and penniless, or almost." Since he continued his plans to leave Paris shortly, to stay with his family in Normandy, "I have to remind you of your promise to send me fifty francs at least, for the first of the month"—the arrangement that Bazille had made in purchasing *Women in the Garden*.

After staying with his family for two weeks, Monet reported to Bazille that all was going well there: "Everyone is good to me and every brushstroke I do is admired." He was working hard and had twenty or so canvases "well under way." But then he switched to an appeal, to help "poor Camille," who "is so kind, a really good lass." His parents had warned that although he could stay with them as long as he liked, he would have to earn any money he needed. And as the baby was due in late July, he was writing Bazille "to ask you to send whatever you can, the more the better."[10]

Monet heard nothing from Bazille and continued to send him pleading and accusatory letters, although he juxtaposed pleas on Camille Doncieux's behalf with expressions of his own personal satisfaction: "All goes well here," he told Bazille, "work, family." Other than the imminent baby, "I could not be happier."[11]

The baby finally arrived on August 8, a boy whom Claude Monet recognized and registered as his legitimate son, Jean-Armand-Claude Monet. Zacharie Astruc stood by Monet and perjured himself by signing the official document, which in addition to stating the legitimacy of the child falsely gave the birth date as August 11, the father not having been present for the actual birth (Wildenstein says that Monet had not wished to "annoy his family" by being present at the child's birth).[12] Monet then promptly returned to his parents' home in Normandy, where he continued to press Bazille for money. "I really don't know what to say to you," he fired off on August 12; "you've shown such pig-headedness in not replying." Camille, he told Bazille, "has given birth to a big and beautiful boy, . . . and it pains me to think of his mother having nothing to eat." Monet continued with his grievances, telling Bazille that he had been forced "to borrow and received snubs from people I don't know, and I'm really angry with you." Neither he nor his mistress had "a penny of our own," and the entire situation was dismal. "It's all your fault," he admonished Bazille, "so hurry up and make amends and send me the money right away."[13]

Monet spent the summer and autumn painting in Normandy and then returned to Paris, where for the first time he painted winter ice floes on the Seine, in the western suburb of Bougival. But he and his mistress plus the baby were still living hand to mouth, and he continued to bombard Bazille with demands for money and accounts of their misery.

By now, Monet had unilaterally refashioned their agreement to one hundred francs per month, in addition to other sums he claimed that Bazille had promised him, but Bazille still did not desert his difficult friend. Instead, he invited him to share in the new studio he was moving to and persuaded a colleague to buy a Monet still life.

〜

Bougival's ice floes attracted Monet in the winter, but it was summertime when this little pleasure spot along the Seine was at its popular best, drawing those who wanted to take a dip in the river or drink and dance in its *guinguette* (as Renoir would later commemorate, in *Dance at Bougival*). Nearby recreational spots had by this time sprouted up west of Paris, as the railroad made it easier for folks of even modest means to escape their urban confines. Already, La Grenouillère, the famed floating café on the Seine's banks at Croissy-sur-Seine, and the Maison Fournaise on the Ile de Chatou were drawing pleasure-seekers.

These were not the sorts of people that a proper bourgeois woman such as Madame Morisot approved of. Writing to her daughter Berthe that August, Madame Morisot told her that Berthe's brother, Tiburce, had recently "gone to bathe [swim] at Bougival," where he encountered Jules Ferry. "They merely met and passed on," Madame Morisot added, "a little embarrassed no doubt at finding themselves at that place." And what sort of place was it? "It is said to be a very rustic little place," she went on, "used for rendezvous by a very frivolous society." Not only that, she added with a disapproving sniff, "if a man goes there alone, he returns in company of at least one other person."

Monet, Renoir, and Pissarro were about to launch into a new style of painting at La Grenouillère, and in time, Berthe Morisot would make a summer home for herself and her family at Bougival. But for the moment, only women of dubious reputation, or at least not of the upright bourgeoisie, could enjoy themselves at the guinguettes of Bougival and Croissy-sur-Seine.

Madame Morisot, despite herself, was a little envious. "Men indeed have all the advantages, and make life comfortable for themselves," she continued in her letter to Berthe. "I am not spiteful, but I hope there will be a compensation."[14]

〜

A more suitable destination for bourgeois enjoyment was that year's Exposition Universelle, or World's Fair, the first in Paris since 1855. As before, the emperor was intent on displaying his regime at its best, an empire still shining in glory. By the time the fair ended in November, ten million people had pushed through its entrance gates at the Champ de Mars to enter a massive iron-and-glass structure covering almost thirty-six acres, with gardens dispersed among galleries linked by walkways to the main building. Each gallery illustrated one aspect of industrial production, from raw materials to clothing, furniture, and the decorative arts, in which a bevy of objects, from rocking chairs to cannon, crowded displays of workers' homes and the latest in wallpaper. Gustave Eiffel, not yet a prominent name, was limited to relatively minor work on the Galerie des Beaux-Arts et d'Archéologie, but he also designed the main arch-girders for the Galerie des Machines, an enormous iron-framed ellipse. It was during this latter project that he—along with the director of the Conservatoire des Arts et Métiers—worked out calculations that Eiffel would use in his future wrought-iron constructions, including his famous tower.[15]

The exposition's gardens blossomed with restaurants and refreshment kiosks reflecting a world of gastronomy, whether beer from Strasbourg, Italian pasta, or Russian caviar, while in the surrounding park, visitors could revel in scenes of supposed lifestyles from far-off places (Arabs in a tent, Chinese women in a pagoda). Photographic studios did big business, while Nadar's *Le Géant* balloon flew for the last time, its owner—now deeply in debt—having had to sell it.

Louis-Napoleon was especially gratified by the number of crowned heads who showed up to enjoy the festivities, from the emperors of Russia and Austria to the kings of Prussia, Belgium, Sweden, Greece, and Portugal. Queen Victoria, still devastated by the death of Prince Albert several years earlier, did not attend this exposition, but her son and heir, Prince Albert, did not hesitate to partake of the delights of Paris. Throughout, Empress Eugenie presided with suitable brilliance, and Baron Haussmann provided a series of gala receptions at the Hôtel de Ville to honor the various members of royalty who trooped through. His reception of June 8, honoring King Wilhelm of Prussia and Czar Alexander of Russia, was especially dazzling, with eight thousand guests illuminated by seas of twinkling lights. "Before the queen that is Paris," the czar graciously observed, "we are no longer more than bourgeois."[16]

But all was not well in Louis-Napoleon's empire. For one thing, the emperor's health was not what it should have been, and he suffered yet another bad attack that summer. The Goncourts reported that when Louis-Napoleon asked Emile Ollivier—a moderate republican—to tell him frankly what the people were saying about him, Ollivier told him that "people thought his faculties were declining." At this, the emperor merely remarked impassively, "That is consistent with all the reports I have received."[17]

And then there was the trouble with Crédit Mobilier. Continuing to hemorrhage losses, by spring this huge financial institution was sufficiently foundering that the Pereires had to demean themselves by requesting a huge loan from their longtime foe, the Banque de France. There, they faced

Alphonse de Rothschild, who as regent was implacably opposed to granting their request. After all, for years he and his father, James, had denounced the Pereires' taste for adventure and their appetite for risk, in comparison with the Rothschilds' own steady prudence. In the end, pushed by Eugène Rouher (now minister of finance, who in turn was likely urged by the emperor), the Banque reluctantly agreed to a loan, but only on the condition that the Pereires and their friends resign.

Some felt sorry for the Pereires, including Rouher, who remarked that "they did not deserve the ferocious hatred with which they are being pursued." But many, especially the Rothschilds, were unsympathetic to their plight, and the Rothschilds—along with a number of disappointed shareholders—may have been responsible for the vehemence of the press coverage of the Pereires' financial failure, especially the persistent claims that the brothers were still able to pay, and should pay, their debts. Their former colleague Jules Mirès—himself under a considerable cloud for swindling—was especially scathing: "The Pereires," he wrote in 1868, "have indulged in an extraordinary game with the shares of Crédit Mobilier. . . . They have used and abused fictitious dividends, and . . . their shareholders have been ruined by their personal speculations."[18]

The Pereires rejected these charges, but the stain remained, even as the Rothschilds, among others, now ruthlessly proceeded to buy up the brothers' personal assets (including their mansion on Rue de Monceau, which the Rothschilds purchased for about one-third less than the Pereires had paid for it). Although the Pereires' Crédit Mobilier had played a decisive role in funding Napoleon III's vision for Paris and in shaping the city's financial institutions, its glory days were over. The Second Empire truly was a dog-eat-dog world, and the Pereires now were the ones being eaten.[19]

Georges Haussmann was also encountering trouble. That year, Haussmann found himself under attack, not only for having forced enormous numbers of families to leave their homes during the course of his rebuilding projects but also for violating the resting places of the dead. Opposition raged over his plans for cemeteries, from the move of several hundred tombs in Montmartre Cemetery (to provide a bridge for Rue Caulaincourt) to the need to find more burial space outside of Paris's new city limits. Soon the whole thing became such a hot potato that it would not be resolved until after Haussmann left office.

But it was finances where Haussmann's troubles were becoming especially fraught. Not only had his Second System incurred huge cost overruns, but his Third System now was encountering significant financial difficulties. Haussmann as always refused to consider tax increases, even though Louis-Napoleon was beginning to entertain thoughts of raising taxes on the rich while lowering duties on basic articles of consumption. Aghast, Haussmann talked him out of it, arguing that any raise in taxes would not even begin to make up the amounts required to continue and complete the *grands travaux*.

So where to get the money? Borrowing no longer was possible, with the Legislature and Council of State as well as Louis-Napoleon's finance minister and a newly influential James de Rothschild against it. The Société Générale, founded several years earlier by a group of financiers and industrialists in which James de Rothschild was quietly involved, now became a major player in Haussmann's schemes, enabling the prefect to find contractors to carry out the required work at a fixed (and high) price. Firms under contract operated under a complex and usually lucrative system involving compulsory purchase and eviction compensation as well as the purchase of surplus land, but payment from the city came with a job's completion—which of course could take years.

Haussmann was counting upon the length of time he had between the start and finish of these long-term projects to come up with the money. But still, the terms of these agreements created significant cash-flow problems. This in turn inspired Haussmann to authorize credit certificates against the final payment. These credit certificates amounted to loans without calling themselves such and gave Haussmann the kind of time he needed before payment was due. It was important that they not be called "loans," since the city could only legally borrow money with the Legislature's approval. Nonetheless, they were what they were, and adding to their essential illegality, these certificates were payable by Haussmann's invention, the Caisse des Travaux de Paris—the special public works fund created earlier to aid in inevitable cash-flow problems—which now was obligated for far more than its rules allowed.

The irregularities or even illegalities were massive, and despite Haussmann's efforts in December to present his request for a real loan to the Legislature, his public finances were coming unraveled. Adding to his woes, in December, Jules Ferry began to run a series of articles in *Le Temps* titled *Les Comptes fantastiques d'Haussmann* (*The Fantastic Accounts of Haussmann*), a play of words on Offenbach's popular *Les Contes fantastiques d'Hoffmann* (*The Fantastic Tales of Hoffmann*). Whether or not Ferry's dinners at the Morisots had given Ferry special ammunition, thanks to Berthe Morisot's well-informed father, these articles, and the pamphlet that Ferry made of them, would play a major role in destroying Haussmann's career, even as it assisted Ferry's own.

In any case, by year's end, Haussmann was in the unhappy position of wishing that he had retired soon after the World's Fair was over, in November, as he had wanted. Most unfortunately for him, the emperor had persuaded him to remain on.

～

Despite these obstacles, Haussmann soldiered on, intent on completing the vision he had for a new Paris. In the process, the old Paris that Manet loved was disappearing, and with it, the kinds of characters who occupied the derelict housing that Haussmann was so effectively destroying. Most of the street singers and ragpickers who captivated Manet in his strolls around the city had by now been forced outside the city limits, to exist in the wasteland of the Zone—a process that the 1867 World's Fair had accelerated, in the name of making the city a welcoming place for visitors. Paris, to Manet's mind, may have become a cleaner and more modern city, but in the course of its modernization, it had lost a considerable amount of what he considered to be its essence and its appeal.

In this, Manet was to some degree in agreement with both Victor Hugo and Charles Baudelaire, although Manet never romanticized his Paris. Rather, Manet painted in what Emile Zola termed a "Naturalist" style— differentiating him from Courbet, whose painting Zola and others termed "Realist." Naturalism, according to Zola, who early on embraced the term, was anti-Romantic to its core and drew its inspiration from exact observation and science, rejecting idealization or mythology to depict real people in real activities. How this differed from Realism was not always clear, but Manet appreciated Zola's positive publicity, and by year's end, he had begun to paint Zola's portrait as an expression of his thanks.

Zola in the meantime had published his first major novel, *Thérèse Raquin*, in which he depicted not the new and buzzing Paris of Georges Haussmann but the Paris of dirt, poverty, and darkness that he had come to know only too well. In this city of loneliness and degradation, he set his story of three misfits, genetically dictated psychological types whose actions were governed by their inherited temperaments. He, as the novelist, then probed these human beings and the society in which they lived, in much the same way that he believed a scientist probes experiments in a laboratory. "I have simply done on two living bodies," he observed, "the work which surgeons do on corpses."[20] Nature, in other words, governed his novel's action—here, leading directly and inevitably to death and destruction.

Flaubert's *Madame Bovary* as well as the Goncourt brothers' *Germinie Lacerteux* greatly impressed Zola, and he did not shy from the controversy, the scandal—and the attendant publicity—that might await his newest offering, much as it had enveloped Flaubert and the Goncourts. "The work is very dramatic, very poignant," he wrote the publisher Albert Lacroix of Brussels in September, whom he hoped would publish the book in its entirety now that the review *L'Artiste* was printing it in serial form. Upping his selling points, he added: "I am counting on a *success d'horreur* [a success based on horror]."[21] Lacroix, who specialized in publishing those authors, including Victor Hugo, who had been banned in Louis-Napoleon's France, agreed to take on this sizzling story of murder and self-destruction, and it appeared that autumn. Zola's sensational depiction of his characters, their setting, and their fate drew down criticism that the novel was bestial, putrid, and pornographic; but the ultimate endorsement, government prosecution, eluded him.

The government made no move to prosecute him.

Late that August, Victor Hugo's long-suffering wife, Adèle, died. Four days later, Charles Baudelaire breathed his last and was eloquently eulogized by Nadar, who had been faithful to him throughout the poet's long last illness.

"You spoke most eloquently in defense of our poor friend Baudelaire yesterday," Manet wrote Nadar, the day after the funeral. "I had already been touched by the loving care shown him in your home by you and your family."[22]

Manet seems to have been unmoved, however, by Zola's latest literary effort. "I've just finished *Thérèse Raquin*," he wrote Zola late in the year. After graciously extending his warmest congratulations, Manet offered the following faint praise: "It's a very well-constructed and very interesting novel."[23]

Praise was something that Georges Haussmann was also finding elusive. His extraordinary park of Buttes-Chaumont had opened earlier that year in northeastern Paris, having transformed the land around a massive played-out quarry to create a lake, a towering island topped by a small temple, several waterfalls, two dramatic bridges (one designed by Eiffel), and panoramic views where only shanties and a garbage dump had been. Haussmann brought Wilhelm of Prussia to visit the newly opened park when the king visited the World Exposition, only to see the monarch gaze in the distance and hear him remark thoughtfully: "It was through that gate that we entered in 1815." A somewhat disconcerted Haussmann could only reply, "Yes, but we have built some forts since then."[24]

The idea behind such a park in such a location was to provide Parisians of this part of the city, primarily workers, with a pleasant destination of their own. Louis-Napoleon had been wholeheartedly in support of the project, much as he was of yet another attempt at creating decent workers' housing—a large structure of contiguous housing on Avenue Daumesnil, deep in the twelfth arrondissement (a structure that the emperor was said to have had a personal hand in designing).[25]

Yet neither this nor the glorious park of Buttes-Chaumont made much of an impact on those they were meant to gratify, and Louis-Napoleon was disappointed by his failure to win over the working classes, especially since a poor wheat harvest that year led to bread shortages as winter approached. Worried about the ever-greater gains made by republicans in Paris and other towns throughout France, the emperor responded by making new concessions for the Legislature. The following year he would also abolish some of his restrictions on the press as well as the requirement for preliminary authorization for meetings, so long as they were neither political nor religious. But these were small gestures, and republicans and reformers perceived them as such.

As 1868 began, Lord Lyons, the new British ambassador, reported back to London that Emperor Napoleon's difficulties at home were growing. "The discontent is great," he wrote, "and the distress amongst the working classes severe." Unlike the opening years of Napoleon III's empire, "there is no glitter at home or abroad to divert public attention."[26]

As the sun began to set on his empire, the emperor was ill, tired, and bored.

The Rothschild country estate, the Château de Ferrières, 1855 (engraving). © Bridgeman Images

CHAPTER SIXTEEN

~

Twenty Years Later

(1868)

In July 1868, Austria's ambassador to France, Prince Metternich, reported that he had "never found the Emperor better, both in health and spirits, or more forthcoming, as he was during the short visit I have just paid." But during the same month, Britain's Lord Cowley reported that he had found Napoleon "aged and much depressed" and even considering abdication.[1]

There were good days and there were bad days, but the emperor's bad days were increasingly outnumbering his good ones. In 1866, he had firmly rejected Eugenie's urging to abdicate in favor of their young son, with her as regent. Now the idea of abdication was proving more attractive. Years later, Eugenie maintained that Louis-Napoleon had resolved, presumably around this time, to abdicate in 1874, when his son would be eighteen and of age to assume the imperial crown in his own right. According to her, the emperor had even planned where he and she would live in retirement—Pau in the winter and Biarritz in the summer. She made no mention that in these plans, her husband not only was making every effort to continue the empire and his line, but also was planning for his son's rule without Eugenie as regent.

Louis-Napoleon's physical deterioration was now manifesting itself in what most never would have predicted, a declining interest in women. His last mistress, the beautiful Countess Louise de Mercy-Argenteau, prettily conceded that she was the emperor's last love but firmly stated that she had never been his mistress. It had not been for unwillingness on her part.

The emperor was unhappy—about his aging and physical decline, but especially about his unpopularity, particularly in the towns. That May, in an attempt to mollify the growing republican opposition, he lifted certain restrictions on the press, and in June he abolished some of the restrictions on meetings, although only on those that were neither political nor religious in nature, making these concessions virtually meaningless. Although these reforms may have been intended as steps toward what Louis-Napoleon perceived as a "Liberal Empire," liberals were not moved to applaud.

Perhaps most ominously, the emperor's attempts to reform and strengthen the army now met with resistance and failure. Although French troops had won the battles of Magenta and Solferino back in 1859, they had done so only because their Austrian opponents had been even less prepared for war. During the following years, it would have been difficult to ignore the rising threat of a highly militarized Prussia, under the leadership of the rightly named "Iron Chancellor," Otto von Bismarck. France's current military system, established years earlier, required a seven-year military service; yet thanks to the common practice of buyouts (from which Claude Monet, among many others, had benefited), only a portion of the eligible conscripts ever showed up. This resulted in a lackluster army of some 400,000 indifferently trained men, most or all of whom were too poor to buy their way out. France had no trained reserves whatever.

Uncomfortably aware of the discrepancy between France's and Prussia's armed forces, Louis-Napoleon in 1867 instructed the minister of war, Marshal Niel, to come up with a solution. In response, Marshal Niel submitted a complicated bill that in essence provided for the call-up of all eligible conscripts and the creation of a mobile National Guard to defend the towns and France's borders—in addition to enforcing law and order at home. The resulting uproar united peasants, urban workers, and bourgeoisie alike. Conscription had always been unpopular, and in its newest incarnation, it aroused a tidal wave of opposition in the press as well as in the Legislature. When a less-offensive version became law in early 1868, its only innovation was a mobile National Guard, which in fact never saw light of day.

Nothing had been accomplished in readying France for what some already anticipated would be war with Europe's newest power, Bismarck's Prussia.

〜

On February 24, the twentieth anniversary of the 1848 Revolution's outbreak, the Goncourts reminisced over the explosion of popular sentiment they had witnessed on that day, including decapitated sculptures in the Tuileries gardens and a statue of Spartacus newly sporting a red bonnet. They had watched their local ironmonger hammer out the words "to the King" (following "Ironmonger") from the sign that hung over his shop. Now, they mused, the ironmonger's sign read "to the Emperor" instead of "to the King."

Had so little changed? Certainly the poverty had not. In May, the brothers visited a former mistress of Jules, who now served as a midwife in some of the poorer sections of Paris, areas that Haussmann had not yet eliminated. On this particular day, she was delivering a baby in a shack located at the far end of Boulevard de Magenta, a hut crunched in among a bevy of others that were leased to the poorest of Paris's poor. The planks forming the walls were coming apart, the floor was full of holes, and rats inundated the place, including the bed of the woman in labor, who was dead drunk, and her husband, likewise inebriated. Four children slept in a bed so small that they could not even stretch out, while two more children slept in a crate.

And who was the landlord of this "wretched shanty of civilization"? None other than the Baron James de Rothschild.[2]

Jules Ferry's s *Comptes fantastiques d'Haussmann*, attacking Haussmann and Haussmann's finances, continued to hammer at the prefect through May, focusing in particular on Haussmann's Third System. According to Ferry, the First System, now paid for, had the merit of opening up the center of Paris and creating more than five miles of new roads. The Second System had successfully linked the center of Paris to the outer portions of the city. But the Third System was a different matter and came under Ferry's fire for being "purely and simply M. Haussmann's personal system," an expression of ego comprising nothing more than "massive demolition" and equally massive development at an unjustifiable cost. This in turn was paid for through the mechanism of a financial vehicle—credit certificates—that Ferry blasted as completely illegal.[3]

No less withering was Ferry's attack on the social consequences of Haussmann's *grands travaux*. Although Ferry granted the importance of the First and Second Systems in opening up and connecting Paris, he weighed social costs against economic benefit and found that those who benefited most from the emperor's attempt to create wealth for all were the few who profited directly from the deals, often shady, behind the grand works. Those who suffered the most under the Second Empire, Ferry argued, were the workers, who remained mired in poverty and had been pushed en masse from their homes in the center of Paris to no-less-dilapidated quarters on the city's outskirts.

Others took up the same cry, and soon the National Audit Office stepped in, determining that the credit certificates were nothing more than disguised loans and that Haussmann's contract agreements with the Caisse des Travaux had been improper.

By year's end, Haussmann troubles were burgeoning, and they in turn threatened to spread their stain to Napoleon III himself and his empire.

It was in the thick of this that the Goncourts decided to leave the city and buy a house in the country, specifically in Auteuil—which in fact was within the farthest reaches of the city limits, as newly defined by the 1860 eradication of the Farmers-General wall.[4]

The brothers were at first delighted. "The sun was shining through the trees in the garden," they noted appreciatively, "and the lawn and the leaves were glittering under the rain of a garden hose." They made their purchase with beating hearts and went off, "intoxicated with happiness." The following month they moved in, still "not quite sure that this is not a dream."[5]

And then reality struck. The very next day they wrote that "unfortunately for us, who came here to escape from the noise of Paris," they now had other noises to contend with: "the noise of a horse in the house on the right, the noise of children in the house on the left," and perhaps worst of all, the noise of the Petite Ceinture—the little train that encircled the outskirts of Paris, whose "buckle" had finally closed the previous year with the completion of the last section from Gobelins to Auteuil. This was the portion that now ran across the street from the Goncourts' new house, its trains "rumbling and whistling and disturbing our insomnia."[6]

The Goncourts had traded the noise of Paris for the noise of the suburbs.

Despite their discomforts, the Goncourts did not hesitate to entertain literary friends in their new abode. That December they finally met up with Zola, "our admirer and pupil," who came to lunch. Zola, now twenty-eight, talked at length about how hard a life he had and how much he needed to find a publisher who would subsidize him and his mother sufficiently to free him up from those "foul ignoble articles I have to write these days." What he wanted was the financial freedom to write the massive novel he had in mind, one that he told the Goncourts would be the story of a family, in ten volumes. This would in fact emerge as Zola's masterwork, the Second Empire epic of two related families, the Rougons and the Macquarts, extending to twenty volumes.

But Zola did not yet know of the fame and success that awaited him, which (to their discomfort) would considerably outshine that of the Goncourts.

Edmond and Jules de Goncourt. Photograph by Nadar. © G. Dagli Orti / De Agostini Picture Library / Bridgeman Images

Now, during that December luncheon, he complained of his many enemies and of the difficulty he had in making a name for himself. The Goncourts, who had highly praised *Thérèse Raquin*, were interested to find their young author "waxy and anemic" and yet "a strapping young fellow," one who was "at once sturdy and puny." In all, they were struck by his divided nature—"an incomprehensible deep, complex character," as they put it. They added that they also found him "unhappy, worried, evasive, and disquieting."

Zola, for his part, expressed homage to his hosts: "We . . . the younger generation: we know that you are our masters, you and Flaubert."[7] But it would not be long before Zola would make his own way into the literary pantheon.

Earlier that year, Edouard Manet painted Emile Zola, probably as an expression of thanks to the young writer who had championed him. The sittings, which may have begun the previous November, continued into the new year, during which Zola recorded such gems from the artist as the following: "I can't do anything without the model. I don't know how to invent. . . . If I amount to anything today, I put it down to precise interpretation and faithful analysis."[8]

Among the books that Manet arranged on the desk before his sitter was Zola's brochure on Manet, whose title, *Manet*, became the artist's signature. Zola claimed to be delighted with the portrait, but later, a keen observer noted that it was not given a place of honor but hung in an inconspicuous spot in Zola's large Médan home. Possibly this was due to Zola's corpulence in later years, which was of sufficient embarrassment to him that he tried drastic measures to lose weight. The portrait was, indeed, of a man sufficiently thinner as to be virtually unrecognizable as Zola's younger self.

But for the moment, Zola remained thin and the 1868 Salon accepted Manet's Zola portrait, while Manet's congratulations on Zola's literary output became considerably warmer. "I'm in the middle of *Madeleine Férat*," he wrote Zola in late 1868, soon after publication of this story of obsession and destruction, "and don't want to wait till I've finished to congratulate you." But it was Zola's preface to the second edition of *Thérèse Raquin* that elicited Manet's unequivocal approval. "Bravo, my dear Zola," he wrote. "It's a splendid preface . . . and you are standing up not only for a group of writers but for a whole group of artists as well."[9]

It was during 1868 that Edouard Manet met Berthe Morisot. According to Morisot's grandson, Denis Rouart, Morisot admired Manet's work "for its freedom and sincerity" and had "long wished to meet him."[10] Their mutual friend Henri Fantin-Latour made the introduction, and soon Manet asked Morisot to pose, along with two other friends, for Le Balcon (The Balcony).

Edouard Manet and his two brothers, Eugène and Gustave, came from the sort of social milieu that would recommend them to the family of a sheltered young woman of the Parisian haute bourgeoisie such as Berthe Morisot. Both of the fathers were eminent in their respective fields, and upon his death in 1862, Monsieur Manet left his three sons with sufficient incomes for their financial independence. The Morisots and the Manets now began to socialize regularly, providing the Morisots with a new group of acquaintances, including musicians, art critics, and writers. It was there that Berthe Morisot first met Pierre Puvis de Chavannes and Edgar Degas as well as the Manet brothers.

Still, despite their position and connections, there was an element of danger to the Manet brothers, especially Edouard, that Madame Morisot found worrisome, even if her daughters did not. Elegant and sophisticated, Edouard was a ladies' man as well as a painter of provocative pictures. Not only was he a womanizer; he was a married man. To make matters worse, his marriage was hardly a conventional one, even though—shielded by the Manet family—Suzanne escaped the social ostracism one might expect.

And then there was the matter of the Manet brothers' politics. Madame Morisot and her husband were staunchly conservative, although constitutional monarchists rather than Bonapartists, but the Manet brothers were just as firmly anti-Bonapartist and anticlerical. Gustave was an outspoken republican, and Edouard, an admirer of Léon Gambetta, had also become involved in republican politics. Still, their mother's relative conservatism reassured the Morisot elders, who worried considerably about influences on their two still-unmarried daughters.[11]

Edouard Manet, as well as many others, had noticed the beautiful and talented Morisot sisters. Writing to Henri Fantin-Latour that August, he commented that he agreed with him that "the young Morisot girls are charming." He then added playfully, "It's a pity they're not men; but being women, they could still do something in the cause of painting by each marrying an academician and bringing discord into the camp of those old dodders." That, he conceded "would be asking for considerable self-sacrifice." In the meantime, he concluded, "give them my respects."[12]

⌒

That summer, Manet spent two months in Boulogne, with a brief excursion to London, where he failed to meet up with Whistler but was "enchanted by

London, by the welcome I got from everyone I visited." He was disappointed that Degas and Fantin-Latour had failed to come with him and added that, given the obstacles he had encountered in Paris, he was considering exhibiting in London the following year. But most of all, he thought that "if we resolved to stick together and above all not to get discouraged, we would be able to react against all this mediocrity which is only held together by consensus."[13]

This group of renegades had already begun to form, with Edouard Manet at its center. It included Claude Monet as well as Emile Zola, who had published another laudatory article about Monet that spring, prompted by the Salon's refusal of yet another Monet painting (*The Jetty at Le Havre*). Zola focused on it and Monet's *Women in the Garden*, which the Salon had refused the year before. Probably on Zola's recommendation, Monet took Camille Doncieux and their son to Bettencourt that spring, where Zola had already established himself for the warm months with his mistress, Alexandrine.

Since the beginning of the year, Monet had survived largely by leaning on Bazille for funds. January, by his own account, saw him, Camille, and the baby freezing and without a fire in Paris. Friends once again came to the rescue, and he then returned (without his mistress and child) to his family for two months, ignoring the winter cold to paint out-of-doors. As a columnist from Le Havre observed (on a day cold enough "to crack the pebbles"): "We saw a foot warmer, then an easel, then a man huddled in three overcoats, wearing gloves, and with his face half-frozen." This was Monet, working in the open air to study the effects of snow.[14]

By spring, Monet had moved, with Camille and their child, to an inn on the outskirts of Bettencourt, in Normandy. There, he painted avidly until the innkeeper threw him out ("without a shirt on my back") for non-payment. He immediately turned to Bazille, telling him that "I must have been born under an unlucky star" and asking Bazille "to come speedily to my rescue if you can." Monet's family had refused to do anything more for him, and he even alluded to a suicide attempt ("I was so upset yesterday that I was stupid enough to hurl myself into the water").[15]

Besides Bazille, Monet had another possible source of funding—a well-to-do art lover in Le Havre by the name of Louis-Joachim Gaudibert, who in late summer commissioned Monet to paint his wife (*Madame Gaudibert*). This portrait, now recognized as a masterpiece, was at the time praised only by its sponsor, and Monet's other works that autumn were dismissed by the jury for a Le Havre exposition—although much to Monet's satisfaction and relief, Gaudibert bought the paintings he had exhibited there.

October brought the news that the director of *L'Artiste* had purchased *Camille* and intended to donate it to the Palais du Luxembourg, which (unlike the Louvre) was the official state repository for contemporary paintings. In the end, *Camille* was sold at auction, but not before a Le Havre critic derided the painting and its subject, whom he smeared as a harlot. By this time even Gaudibert was unwilling to receive Camille Doncieux, and Monet's family remained adamant on the matter. Writing to Bazille in late October, Monet (by now ensconced, without Camille, in the Gaudibert château) was enjoying the château's hospitality but railed against the series of "disappointments, insults, hopes, renewed disappointments" he had undergone. At length he exploded to Bazille: "Painting is no good, and I have definitely given up all hopes of glory."[16]

Still, Gaudibert's continued patronage, and in particular Gaudibert's purchase of Monet's exhibition paintings, now allowed the painter to rejoin his mistress and son for a few weeks in nearby Etretat. "I'm very happy, very delighted," he wrote Bazille in December. "I spend my time out-of-doors on the shingle when the weather's stormy . . . ; otherwise I go into the country which is so lovely here." Thanks to Gaudibert, Monet could for a time live this peaceful existence, surrounded by his "dear little family."[17]

Unfortunately, this little bit of heaven did not last.

Gustave Eiffel, on the other hand, was doing well. That year, he signed deeds of partnership with a young and well-to-do German engineer, Théophile Seyrig, to form G. Eiffel et Compagnie with a capital of 200,000 francs—Seyrig having contributed more than half of the capitalization. It represented a giant step for Eiffel, even though his firm's business would for many years consist largely of unremarkable commissions, largely railway bridges, many of which were scattered throughout France's colonies.

It was while he was building up his expertise in bridges that Eiffel developed his experience in dealing with iron, both in his designs and in his methods of assembly. Soon he would become known for his rigorous planning and execution, all based on equally rigorous mathematical calculation.

But all the while he earned his living by building bridge after bridge, Eiffel dreamed of something more—iron-framed buildings and even other structures. For this genius with iron would in time build not only the tower bearing his name but also the internal structure of Frédéric Bartholdi's Statue of Liberty.

While the young were finding their way with varying degrees of success, the empire itself was aging, and with it, some of its most distinctive figures.

Despite the contempt of society leaders such as Princess Mathilde, great courtesans such as La Païva continued to hold sway. According to the Goncourts, Princess Mathilde protested "the dominion enjoyed by these women, honored by the company of philosophers, men of letters, scientists, and thinkers." She was right, in that La Païva, even in old age, continued to attract the very philosophers, men of letters, scientists, and thinkers whom the princess resented for flocking around the courtesan.

By 1868, Russian-born La Païva had lost her beauty but none of her powers of attraction. "She is always the same," the Goncourts noted, "disagreeable, unpleasant." And yet they—and many others—continued to patronize her at her extraordinary mansion on the Champs-Elysées. Dripping with emeralds one cold winter evening, the old courtesan presided over a dinner table discussion in which she expounded what the Goncourts found to be a "frightening theory of will-power." She insisted that "there were no such things as fortuitous circumstances, that one created one's own circumstances, and that unfortunate people were so only because they did not want to stop being unfortunate." When called upon to support her theory, she spoke of a woman who, in order to attain an unspecified goal, shut herself up for three years, scarcely eating, and entirely focused on a plan that she was developing.

La Païva then concluded, "I was that woman."[18] There was no need to ask her to name her goal—or her plan.

That November, James de Rothschild died. The last of the five Rothschild brothers, sons of the empire's founder, James had steered the family firm through multiple storms during the course of his long and eventful career. He had given the Paris house an additional and all-important role as an industrial investment bank, whose railroad empire added mightily to the house's fortunes, and he had, in the end, defeated the Rothschilds' great challengers, the Pereires.

By the time of his death at age seventy-six, James was enormously rich and powerful, and in recognition of this, his funeral figured as a major event in Paris. His grandnephew, Leo, reported with awe that "all Paris came to pay their respects," and Leo's brother Natty related that he had never seen "such an assembly of people as came to the Rue Lafitte this morning." Some four thousand people passed through the drawing room, he added breathlessly; "they say there were six thousand people in the court yard, and from the Rue Lafitte to Père-Lachaise [the burial site on the eastern edge of Paris] the wheels are lined five deep on both sides." Even *The Times*'s Paris correspondent was uncharacteristically impressed: not within his memory had he seen the streets more crowded.[19]

Many telegrams of sympathy came from around the globe, most especially from heads of state, including the exiled Orléans family. But Napoleon III did not attend, sending a representative in his place. Other leading political figures also thought it best to follow their emperor's lead and keep their distance.

Despite a definite mending of relations in recent years between James de Rothschild and the emperor, James had never taken to either Louis-Napoleon or to his empire. Recognizing this fact, the emperor chose not to pay his respects in person—a slight that did not seem to overly disturb the Rothschild family.

Around the same time, Maxime Du Camp dined alone with George Sand, by now considered one of the masters of French literature. The famed author was then sixty-four years old and, as Du Camp put it, "very talkative," even "disposed to confide in me more fully than I desired."

Sand's long life, during which she had lived boldly and exactly as she chose, was legendary, as had been her beauty. Now, Du Camp observed, "there was nothing left of her former beauty." But this hardly mattered. After a long conversation, "a masterful smile passed over her face which seemed to express pride in her own influence and acknowledged supremacy."

She then added, "I regret nothing."[20]

Berthe Morisot, 1869. Photograph by Pierre Petit. Private collection. © Archives Charmet / Bridgeman Images

CHAPTER SEVENTEEN

~

Haussmann in Trouble

(1869)

Debates in the Legislature on the finances of Haussmann's *grands travaux* began that February and continued, through eleven sessions, into March. Not only were Haussmann's opponents angered by the huge costs of his operations (tackling in particular his theory of productive expenditure), but they also accused him of embezzlement, of bribery, and of using inside information for his own and his associates' profit. Stories that had circulated underground now surfaced openly about figures altered in certain reports and bribes offered in the form of "commissions" to the powerful prefect of the Seine.

Unquestionably, with so much money involved, there were multiple possibilities for irregularities, most especially involving those who stood to benefit from municipal contracts. An area attracting particular scrutiny was the difference between purchase price and compensation payment for expropriated property, which could be considerable if those in possession of crystal balls (or a friend in City Hall) bought up property well in advance of the government's publicized decision to acquire the property in question. Whether this involved inside knowledge or was simply a shrewd guess, it was enough to make certain individuals, such as the Pereires, very rich indeed.

But had it benefited Haussmann? He would spend many years in retirement writing his memoirs, in which he defended himself and his expenditures at great length and in even greater detail. His honor meant much to him, and he was at pains to defend it as well as the unparalleled changes he had wrought in the city he loved. Central to his thinking then, and at the time of his prefecture, was the concept that Paris "is not the exclusive domain of Parisians," but belonged to—and was the glory of—the entire nation. Not only was Paris the "universal home of Letters, Science, and the Arts," but it was the converging point of great roads, railroads, and telegraphs. Laws, decrees, decisions, and orders originated and spread from there, and the sum total of all this creativity and activity made Paris the very soul of France, "its head and its heart." As such, it was the worthy recipient of whatever measures were necessary to improve and beautify it.[1] Moreover, if any failure in management had occurred in the service of this queen of cities, Haussmann was more than ready to defend these as the inevitable results of a huge enterprise boldly undertaken as a necessity and under the severe constraints of time.

Yet members of the Legislature were no longer inclined to acquiesce to Haussmann or his *grands travaux*, and although in effect acquitting the prefect for lack of solid proof, they firmly settled up the outstanding credit certificates and shut down the Caisse des Travaux.

It was clear that Haussmann would not be prefect of the Seine much longer.

During the Legislature's debates, Eugène Rouher—in his capacity of serving the emperor—had made it clear that Napoleon III bore no responsibility for whatever irregularities of accounts and management were under discussion. As for the future, Rouher assured the Legislature that "there will be no more contracting out, no more discounting of bills, no more disguised loans," and certainly no more credit certificates. "We have accomplished a great endeavor," he assured the deputies. "If there was also some irregularity of management, this will be forgotten and the grandeur of the enterprise will remain in the memory."[2]

Yet even if the emperor was not implicated in the affair, he certainly was not burnished by it—especially as the mounting attacks on Haussmann could also be understood as surreptitious attacks on him. As May elections approached, Louis-Napoleon's prestige continued to decline, even while the political climate throughout the nation—particularly in its cities and towns—had substantially changed, in part encouraged by the liberalization of assembly and press, albeit small, that had occurred the year before.

These spring elections did not go well for the emperor. The number of angry young republicans had proliferated, as had their meetings and assemblies, while the opposition press had similarly burgeoned. The 1851 *coup d'état*, hitherto sacrosanct, now came under attack, with new leaders such as Léon Gambetta denouncing it as a crime and its victims as martyrs. Under this withering criticism of both emperor and empire, prefects and mayors showed less enthusiasm for turning out the vote for official candidates, while some candidates, even though blessed by official imprimatur, were reluctant to display the fact.

Pro-government candidates still won the majority of votes but by a significantly smaller margin than ever before. The emperor and his candidates retained the loyalty of rural voters, but Paris and other cities and towns now were swinging ever more strongly toward republicanism, including candidates who irreconcilably opposed the regime.

It may not have amounted to a complete disaster for the emperor, but it certainly was far from the kind of victory he wanted and needed. Louis-Napoleon no longer could claim to be the absolute ruler of France. Bonapartists now were a minority in the Legislature, although still a sizable one, while the majority consisted of a volatile mix of moderates largely opposed to the regime but willing to support it should it move toward parliamentary government. Given this situation, the emperor at first hesitated, but then, pushed by liberals at the Legislature's opening session on July 6, he promised to yield to their demands for concessions. Several days later, the emperor responded by giving the Legislature further rights and by sacking his severely conservative minister, Eugène Rouher, replacing him with the more moderate Adolphe de Forcade La Roquette.

A transitional government was now appointed to carry out reforms, which would result the following year in the creation of a bicameral parliamentary system, with significant powers for the legislative body and constraints on the emperor. A new government, with the moderate republican Emile Ollivier in its ranks, would form in early 1870.

In the meantime, Haussmann clung to his job and Louis-Napoleon battled illness, suffering another bad attack that summer. Rumors spread that he was dying, and the stock market took fright, causing shares on the stock exchange to plummet. But the reports of the emperor's imminent demise had been exaggerated. As in the past, he quickly recovered, and soon he could be seen riding in the Bois de Boulogne. Later that autumn, the wife of one of his ministers reported how impressive the emperor's good health appeared to be and how he astonished his guests at his Compiègne château with his "gaiety and high spirits," leading them in a whirling dance that lasted for nearly two hours.

At the time of this particular house party, Eugenie was representing the emperor at the ceremonial opening of the Suez Canal. Largely funded by a sea of small French investors, the resulting achievement was a French one, even if not one that the government had underwritten, and the empress accordingly presided over the November ceremonies in Egypt. Later in life, she told an interviewer that this occasion remained with her as one of the most dazzling experiences in her life. "There was a real Egyptian sky," she recalled, "a light of enchantment, a resplendence as of dreams. . . . My yacht, *L'Aigle*, at once took the head of the procession. . . . The spectacle was so supremely magnificent, and proclaimed so proudly the greatness of the French regime, that I could contain myself no longer, I was exultant."

Such a spectacle momentarily distracted the empress from troubles at home, which she was quick to enumerate: "Outside the gates, a threatening Prussia, a thankless Italy, and the other powers sulking or spiteful . . . and within, disaffection and restlessness." Eugenie especially resented the press, "ignoble in its insolence and bad faith," as well as "continual strikes, riotous manifestations." In particular, she singled out Henri Rochefort's paper, *La Lanterne*, for contributing to "a wind of madness" that was "sweeping over France."[3]

Victor Hugo called Henri Rochefort his "third son." Born into an aristocratic and ultra-royalist family, Rochefort had veered sharply left in his politics, and by 1868, he had founded a newspaper, *La Lanterne*, that did not hesitate to reveal the shipworms that infested Napoleon III's empire. Rochefort idolized Victor Hugo, and when *La Lanterne* quickly earned Rochefort a fine and prison sentence, he fled to Brussels, where he set up *La Lanterne* in exile and met Hugo.

In the meantime, although censorship still stalked the press, Victor Hugo's sons, Charles and François-Victor, along with Auguste Vacquerie and Paul Meurice, agreed to take advantage of the reform that allowed newspapers to be published without official consent and founded a newspaper that Victor Hugo named *Le Rappel*—a word of many meanings, one of which was "a reminder."

Not only did *Le Rappel* publish Hugo's speeches and messages, but it supported republican candidates in the May elections, including Léon Gambetta and Rochefort himself. Soon the paper felt the force of official displeasure, when its offices were trashed and its editors threatened with imprisonment. Still, the tide of republicanism in Paris and other French cities continued to rise. Rochefort and Gambetta were elected, and when the police tried to shut down *Le Rappel* on the night of June 10, a large crowd of Parisians quickly mobilized in protest. In the process, some of the angriest erected the first street barricade seen in Paris since 1851.

Despite rumors that Victor Hugo was about to return, Napoleon III's nemesis remained safely outside of France, where he urged all protests to remain peaceful. That September, Hugo chaired a peace conference in Lausanne.

"To perpetuate war is to perpetuate tyranny," he said in his opening speech. "The logic is impeccable."[4]

∽

The 1867 execution of Archduke Maximilian, which followed France's withdrawal of military support, had quickly emerged as yet one more target for republican critics of Napoleon III and his regime. Edouard Manet, who was steadily embracing republican politics, found himself drawn to the subject of Maximilian's demise and, soon after the execution, decided to make it the subject of a history painting.

He began work on a large canvas that summer, probably based on a detailed account published in Le Figaro, and then began another full-scale version in September, followed by a smaller version and yet another large painting. In his final version, Manet clothed the firing squad in the uniforms of French soldiers—graphically illustrating where he felt responsibility for the tragedy lay.

Manet had every intention of submitting his final version to the 1869 Salon, but he was unofficially advised that it would not be accepted. Clearly the subject was politically sensitive. Still, Manet was disinclined to follow rules, whether political or artistic, and proceeded to make a lithograph, or print, of Execution to popularize the painting.

When Manet's printer presented the lithograph for copyright registration, he learned that it was banned. Manet promptly wrote Zola that he "had thought they could stop it from being published but not from being printed," and he appealed to his friend "to write a few lines about this ludicrously small-minded procedure." Manet took the approach that "we are surprised at the action of the authorities in banning a purely artistic work." Zola responded and, in his report on the ban, pointed out the French uniforms of the soldiers: "You understand the horror and anger of the censors. . . . An artist dared to put before their eyes so cruel an irony: France shooting Maximilian!"[5]

Soon matters escalated, and Manet's "Maximilian affair" became "more complicated," as he informed art critic Philippe Burty. Frightened, the printer asked Manet for permission to erase the image from the lithographic stone, but Manet refused. The printer then refused to give the stone back. "I should imagine," Manet continued, "one can't destroy a printing block, stone, etc., without a court order, and without publication there can be no punishable offense."[6]

Soon after, the Chronique des Arts published a letter from Manet providing details of the ban and the events that followed, along with the editor's comments on the gravity of the questions involved. Shortly afterward, the printer returned the stone to Manet.

The painting would not be shown in public for ten years, when it was exhibited in the United States. The lithograph would not be printed until after Manet's death.

Edouard Manet may have failed to exhibit *Execution* at the 1869 Salon, but he had two other paintings that successfully navigated that year's Salon jury: *Le Déjeuner dans l'atelier* (*The Luncheon in the Studio*) and *Le Balcon* (*The Balcony*). *Luncheon in the Studio* features his wife's son, Léon Leenhoff, standing before a luncheon table, while *The Balcony* depicts three figures, including a stunning dark-haired woman seated in front. The woman was Berthe Morisot.

This was the first time Morisot had posed for Manet, and her dark beauty evidently captivated him. Yet the painting itself, which paid homage to Goya's *Les Manolas au balcon*, did not captivate Salon viewers. Critics agreed that it was mysterious and even unsettling and pointed to the ambiguous relationship between its three figures. "One doesn't quite know what these good people are doing on the balcony," one critic wrote, while another complained about the complete absence of connection between the figures. Manet in turn had found it difficult to create *The Balcony* and was plagued with doubts about his work—as Madame Morisot commented in early spring to her daughter Edma: "Manet looks like a madman: he hopes that his picture will be a success, then all of a sudden he is filled with doubts that cast him down."[7]

The Salon accepted both *The Luncheon in the Studio* and *The Balcony*, but Manet's doubts continued. The Salon opened in early May, and Berthe Morisot immediately wrote her sister, "I don't have to tell you that one of the first things I did was to go to Room M. There I found Manet, . . . looking dazed. He begged me to go and see his painting, as he did not dare move a step." He alternated between laughter and worry, "assuring everybody that his picture was very bad, and adding in the same breath that it would be a great success."

And what did Morisot think of how Manet painted her in *The Balcony*? Well, she thought that he had made her "more strange than ugly" but admitted that "the epithet of *femme fatale* has been circulating among the curious." As for her opinion of Manet's painting in general, Morisot found that his works produced "the impression of a wild or even a somewhat unripe fruit," although she did not "in the least dislike them." Still, she preferred Manet's portrait of Zola.

As for Manet himself, she thought "he has a decidedly charming temperament, I like it very much."[8]

∽

Both Berthe and Edma Morisot seem to have enjoyed Edouard Manet's company, as well as that of his artist friends. In March, Edma told Berthe somewhat flippantly that "it is disheartening that one cannot depend on artists. My infatuation for Manet is over." Still, she admitted that she was curious to know what Monsieur Degas thought of her and added, "When I think of any of these artists, I tell myself that a quarter hour of their conversation is worth as much as many sterling qualities."[9]

Only a few weeks earlier, Edma Morisot had wed, breaking up the close working and personal relationship between the two sisters and effectively removing Edma from the Paris art scene. Edma's husband was Adolphe Pontillon, a naval officer who brought her to live far from Paris, in Brittany. From there, she wrote frequent letters to her sister, assuring her of her husband's goodness and kindness and hoping that he was "not aware of the void that I feel without you." But despite her kind husband and her efforts to acclimate to far-off Brittany, Edma was bored and missed Berthe, her family, and Paris. Berthe in turn wrote that "if we go on in this way, my dear Edma, we shall no longer be good for anything. You cry on receiving my letters, and I did just the same thing this morning."

"Come now," Berthe Morisot went on, "the lot you have chosen is not the worst one. You have a serious attachment, and a man's heart utterly devoted to you. . . . Remember that it is sad to be alone; . . . a woman has an immense need of affection."[10]

Yet even as aware as she was of her own need for affection, and aware as well that she was approaching the age of thirty, when she would be consigned to the dreaded category of "old maid," Berthe Morisot continued to hold marriage at arm's length—enduring chaperones for every outing and remaining resignedly in her parents' home. Driven by an increasingly clear and radical vision of what to paint and how, she was appalled by her sister's inability to paint after she wed. Men unquestionably found Morisot's dark beauty attractive, but with the single exception of the forty-five-year-old painter Pierre Puvis de Chavannes, whom she found stuffy, her talent and intelligence kept most suitors at bay.

And then there was Edouard Manet. Manet seemed fascinated by Berthe Morisot, and his Le Balcon was only the first of his many paintings of her. More recent generations have speculated about an affair between the two, but even the rule-breaking Edouard Manet would not have dared to break the iron-clad constraints governing his class in society: men could, with reasonable discretion, do as they pleased, but affairs simply were not acceptable for an unmarried woman of Paris's *haute bourgeoisie*. Presiding over her still-unwed chick, Madame Morisot continued to chaperone her daughter to and through all her social contacts, including sittings for Manet, and Berthe Morisot quietly put up with it.

Despite the drawbacks of continued maidenhood, Morisot found the prospect of marriage unsettling. That May, she regaled her sister with an account of a suitor: "I have missed my chance, dear Edma," she wrote, "and you may congratulate me on having got rid so quickly of all my agitations." Fortunately, she added, the suitor in question "turned out to be completely ludicrous." Surprised but not disappointed, Morisot now felt "free of all anxiety," and she quickly renewed her interest in visiting her sister in Brittany as well as in what she might paint while there.

"Men incline to believe that they fill all of one's life," she had written Edma in April. "But as for me, I think that no matter how much affection a woman has for her husband, it is not easy for her to break with a life of work." Edma concurred: "The longer I'm married," she told Berthe, "the more convinced I am that you wouldn't be satisfied with this arrangement on the same conditions. Do your utmost with your charm and your skill to find something that suits you."[11]

As it turned out, Berthe Morisot would do exactly that.[12] In the meantime, although Madame Morisot longed to see her third daughter wed, she did not seem inclined to marry her off to just anyone. Tellingly, on one notable occasion (perhaps the very one that Berthe described to Edma), Madame Morisot told Berthe to go upstairs to dress for a suitor's expected visit. When Berthe was slow in returning, Madame Morisot suddenly appeared before her. "How long," she demanded, "are you going to leave me face to face with that idiot?"[13]

By this time, Georges Bizet was far more enthused about marriage than he had ever expected. Geneviève Halévy, the daughter of his composition teacher, had turned the world around for him. "No more evenings out!" he had written a friend in 1867. "No more dissipation! No more mistresses! That's all over! . . . I've met an adorable girl and I adore her! In two years time she'll be my wife!"[14] Her well-to-do family had serious doubts about her marrying a not very successful composer, with a lifestyle that bordered on the bohemian. Bizet in turn could have had doubts about the mental instability that ran through the mother's side of Geneviève's family. But oblivious to shadows, a thoroughly besotted Bizet promised to reform, and in May 1869, he and Halévy announced their engagement. They were married shortly thereafter, with the bride bringing a happily substantial dowry to enhance their marriage.

～

That winter of 1868–1869, Claude Monet painted the effects of sunlight on snow in *The Magpie*, which he submitted—along with a seascape—to that year's Salon. Both were rejected, adding to his increasing misery.[15]

Monet's family, most especially his aunt, had refused to subsidize him further, especially in light of his open liaison with Camille Doncieux, while Monsieur Gaudibert had already done as much as he could or was willing to do. And so at winter's end, Monet returned to Paris, where once again Bazille took him in. Camille's family at last agreed to help their daughter (as Bazille put it, "They're not overjoyed, but they don't want their daughter to starve"). But the Salon's untimely rejection only added to Monet's woes. As he put it, in a begging letter to Arsène Houssaye (director of *L'Artiste* and inspector-general of fine arts, who had purchased *Camille*): "That fatal rejection [from the Salon] has virtually taken the bread out of my mouth." He added, "I am in quite a desperate state," and hoped that Houssaye would be willing to purchase "a few of the canvases I was able to save from the bailiffs."[16]

Unfortunately Houssaye does not seem to have received the letter, and at length Monet moved with his mistress and baby Jean to a small cottage to the west of Paris, near Bougival and Chatou. Even here his resources were inadequate, and food and fuel were running out. Renoir, who was living with his parents in nearby Voisins, on the outskirts of Louveciennes, often came to walk along the Seine with Monet, bringing bread with him. "Some days they don't get to eat," he wrote Bazille.[17]

Yet throughout these difficult days, Monet continued to paint. "I have a dream," he wrote Bazille late that September, envisioning the magic glow of light on water that enveloped the Grenouillère, that famed floating café on the banks of the Seine in nearby Croissy-sur-Seine.[18] Renoir shared this dream, and that summer the two artists painted this scene together—a view of the Grenouillère's tiny island, known as the Flowerpot or the Camembert, surrounded by light-infused and gently rippling water, which the boats and swimmers set in motion. Monet sensed that he was on the brink of an artistic breakthrough—a breakthrough that would be reinforced the following winter after Renoir returned to Paris, when Monet painted snow-covered landscapes with Pissarro in nearby Louveciennes.

But life still was hard. Monet returned occasionally to Paris that autumn, to contact potential buyers or to meet with friends at the Café Guerbois. It was during one or more of these visits that he posed with Renoir, Bazille, Zola and others grouped around Edouard Manet at his easel for Fantin-Latour's *A Studio at Les Batignolles*. Soon after, Bazille painted the same group of friends in *The Studio on the Rue de la Condamine*.

It was all quite convivial-looking. But Monet's mistress and their child remained back in the small cottage outside of Paris, and a long, cold winter lay ahead.

∼

It was a dismal winter for the Goncourt brothers as well. Not only had their latest book, *Madame Gervaisais*, attracted little attention—"not a single letter, not a single word, not the slightest comment from anybody"—but the health of the younger brother, Jules, was rapidly declining. Edmond put in his claim for sympathy ("both of us are ailing, casting inquiring glances at each other and measuring each other's sufferings"),[19] but it was Jules whose condition was clearly becoming the more serious.

That autumn, as it became evident that Jules was suffering from syphilis, the Goncourts' good friend Princess Mathilde offered the lodge at her château, Catinat, as a quiet place where the brothers could escape from the noise of their Auteuil house. Unfortunately, even there a volley of noise pursued them: the local church had begun to try out the bells that the princess had given them, ringing them incessantly.

"The agony of being ill and unable to be ill at home, of having to drag one's pain and weakness from one place to another," was clearly more than either of them could bear.[20]

∼

Following his December 1868 luncheon with the Goncourts, Zola had continued to cultivate the brothers, promising some much-needed publicity for *Madame Gervaisais*. Keeping himself resolutely in the swim of everything important to his career, he also introduced himself to Flaubert,[21] maintained numerous engagements with his Café Guerbois friends, and continued to publish a barrage of articles. Most importantly, he submitted the first master plan of his Rougon-Macquart series to the Brussels publisher, Lacroix. It was an exhausting life, but Zola rose to the occasion, summoning up the energy for which he would become legendary.

Meanwhile, Alexandre Dumas *père*, who also was renowned for his astonishing energy, was now reaching the end of his extraordinary life. Dumas was a fighter, but with his strength and health abandoning him, he took his doctor's advice and retreated that summer to the seashore. There, even in decline,

Dumas found the strength to put yet one more of his many talents into play, writing a cookbook—his wide-ranging and delightful *Dictionnaire de cuisine.* Dumas had been as enthusiastic a cook as he had been an eater, and his extensive travels fed his culinary experience, from North African bazaars to sturgeon fishing on the Caspian Sea. He could not resist telling stories, whether about chocolate or turkey, while his advice (see for example his entry on keeping eggs fresh) gives an insight into a very different pre-refrigeration era.[22]

Returning to Paris, Dumas noted that the Opéra had just completed its façade and wrote Charles Garnier to compliment him on it. "It is perfect," he told Garnier. "Let people talk, if they must." But then he added that "only one thing slightly bothers the eye, and unhappily it is the only thing that you could not modify." This of course was the "N" and the "E" on the façade. This tribute to emperor and empire, he observed, "will be modified . . . by time."[23]

The Opéra's façade was indeed drawing considerable attention, including some observations from young Auguste Rodin. A thrice-rejected candidate for the Ecole des Beaux-Arts, largely because his emerging naturalism was completely out of step with acceptable tradition, Rodin was now employed in the building trades, where he provided ornamentation for edifices such as La Païva's mansion on the Champs-Elysées. He was among the crowd that day who eagerly awaited the unveiling of the four large sculptural groups flanking the Opéra's entrance. Of the four, the single group that drew his attention was *La Danse,* by Jean-Baptiste Carpeaux, which Rodin considered to be a masterpiece. Others, however, were not of the same mind, objecting to what they viewed as the work's unabashedly naked figures. "What rage, what shrieks, what real or false indignation!" came from those who embraced the "cold mortality" of the "formulas of the academies," Rodin noted contemptuously. Much to Rodin's disdain, these critics considered Carpeaux to be a bad sculptor, and Rodin noted that the head of one atelier even dismissed a student who was overly enthusiastic about Carpeaux.[24]

But Dumas did not involve himself in such disputes, especially not when he had so little time left. Restricted to his apartment and his bed, he dreamed of new novels and reread his own works. His judgment on *The Three Musketeers?* "It is good," he told his son, Dumas *fils.* What about *The Count of Monte-Cristo?* He thought a bit. "It is not as good as *Les Mousquetaires,*" he observed.[25]

～

In another part of town, life for Sarah Bernhardt was just beginning. A trouser role as an ardent minstrel boy in *Le Passant,* an otherwise forgettable tear-jerker, had brought sudden stardom to her and to the young playwright and poet, François Coppée. "I had become the adored queen of the students," she recalled in her memoirs, "and I used to receive little bouquets of violets, sonnets, and long, long poems." Showers of flowers greeted her on arriving at the theater, and the emperor even requested a performance at the Tuileries.

Much to Bernhardt's professed embarrassment, the emperor caught her unawares ahead of time in a small drawing-room, practicing her three required curtsies. As Bernhardt described him, Napoleon was amused and charming, as only he could be. "I liked him much better like this," she later wrote, "than in his portraits. He had such fine eyes, which he half closed while looking through his long lashes." As for his smile, it was "sad and rather mocking," while his voice was "faint, but seductive." Louis-Napoleon seems to have been in full seduction mode.

As for the empress, Bernhardt thought her very beautiful—more beautiful than her portrait. But her voice most unfortunately was rough and hard, giving Bernhardt a shock. "From that moment," she recalled, "I felt ill at ease with her, in spite of her graciousness and her kindness."

The Prince Imperial, age thirteen, was a different matter. "He was delicious," Bernhardt wrote, "with his magnificent eyes with heavy lids like those of his mother, and with his father's long eyelashes." Even better, he was witty—according to Bernhardt, much like his father, "who had the most refined, subtle, and at the same time the most generous wit."

After setting up for rehearsal, Bernhardt and two others were invited to view the palace. "Nothing could have been uglier than the private rooms," Bernhardt recalled, "with the exception of the Emperor's study and the staircases." Unfortunately, the palace "bored me terribly."[26]

Bernhardt's own apartment, on Rue Auber—alongside the rising Paris Opéra—was far more to her taste, furnished with a variety of luxurious items as well as with a number of antiques. By her own account, she had spent a fortune on furnishings and curiosities, including a tortoise whose back was covered with gold and set with topazes. But one evening, fire broke out, probably due to a misplaced lighted candle. Whatever the cause, the fire destroyed everything (including the tortoise) and ruined Bernhardt; for in addition to her personal loss, she was held responsible for damage to other apartments in the building. Worst of all, she was not insured, having put off signing the insurance papers.

Homeless and penniless, she was forced to go back to living with her mother. This in itself was humiliating, but in addition, she felt that she "could not live without comfort and luxury."[27] Fortunately her plight caught the attention of sympathizers, who arranged a gala benefit for her at the

Odéon. The proceeds were impressive, and Bernhardt was able to relocate comfortably on the Rue de Rome, where she would remain for several years.

～

Bernhardt's taste in men as well as in furnishings ran to the luxurious. Her frequent escort and lover at this time was Charles Haas, whom she described as "a most charming man, who was very intelligent and distinguished."[28]

This was an understatement. Haas, a sophisticated and renowned man about town and one of the few Jewish members of the Jockey Club, would in time serve as a model for Proust's Charles Swann, in *In Search of Lost Time*— much as Bernhardt would serve as an inspiration for Proust's actress Berma. Proust was not yet born when their affair took place, but it must have rattled the rafters at the time, as Bernhardt enticed Haas with numerous raunchy summonses, including a sketch of a four-poster bed beneath which she dashed off the words, "Come! Come!! Come!!!" She flattered and cajoled him with missives such as "I have a thousand lovers but only one who is the real thing." And she beseeched him with "Come, and give me your lips."[29]

Haas came for a time, but Bernhardt may have amounted to little more than a pleasant diversion for this man who had scores of beautiful women vying for him. She did not remain with him for long. Their affair soon ended, with Haas providing Bernhardt with a substantial and gentlemanly "loan."

Still, although neither party appears to have regarded it as an affair to remember, the two remained friends until Haas's death.

～

As the year and decade drew to a close, life and death continued to coexist in the usual way, while on the larger scale, the empire's own decline was moving toward center stage. It had been a long run—almost two decades—but perhaps inevitably, the empire that Louis-Napoleon Bonaparte had created was losing its energy, even as Louis-Napoleon himself was succumbing to illness and perhaps death.

He had seen much of his vision realized during his two decades of imperial rule, not the least being the completion of all of the major routes of France's modern railway network. But chief of all, there was Paris, the city of dreams—undeniably, he and Haussmann together had transformed the city, a legacy in which he took the greatest pride.

Yet much remained to be done, and as the new decade approached, neither Napoleon III nor Haussmann retained the political power nor the will to move and shake people and landscapes as they had before. Now, other forces both at home and abroad would determine the destiny of Paris and of France.

Meeting of Napoleon III with Bismarck, 2 September 1870, following the Battle of Sedan (photograph). © SZ Photo / Bridgeman Images

~

CHAPTER EIGHTEEN

Finale
(1870)

Louis-Napoleon Bonaparte did not casually abandon Georges Haussmann. Instead, as the new year opened, it became clear that the emperor had few options remaining—whether in governing his empire or in retaining Haussmann as prefect of the Seine.

The spring 1869 elections had given the emperor little choice. Despite his foot-dragging and general unwillingness to acknowledge that his position as absolute ruler of France no longer was viable, Louis-Napoleon now faced the political realities of a potent opposition. Eugenie had already glimpsed his limitations, and as she sailed that autumn to the opening ceremony of the Suez Canal, she had written him: "I do not believe that one can carry out two coups d'état in one reign."[1]

And so on January 1, 1870, at the traditional New Year's Day reception, Napoleon III at long last told members of the Legislature that, although the nation had bestowed on him and him alone the power of government, he now was willing to share this power with them. He then followed through by asking the moderate liberal, Emile Ollivier, to head up a new government.

It should have come as no surprise when one of Ollivier's first actions was to push Haussmann out the door. "The emperor wanted to keep Haussmann," Ollivier later wrote. "But it was quite impossible to keep him on. His administration, to which justice was not yet done, had caused too much of an outcry."[2]

Unfortunately for those who preferred it otherwise, Haussmann refused to go quietly. He would not resign, as the emperor wished, and adamantly held out for dismissal. Therefore, on January 6, 1870, an official decree was published relieving Haussmann of his duties. The emperor met personally with Haussmann and apologized at length. The empress (who saw in Haussmann's exit a welcome safety valve for popular discontent) conveyed her heartfelt condolences, while members of the municipal council expressed their deepest sympathy. According to the record of their last meeting with the former prefect, the council members attested to Haussmann's "high intelligence and tireless activity" and declared the honor they felt in having for so many years assisted this eminent administrator in the work of transforming Paris.[3]

Officials may have been duly proper in their accolades as they showed Haussmann the door, but throughout Paris, people responded with rejoicing—and disbelief. As the journalist and publisher Emile de Girardin put it, "History will not believe that the author of the transformation of Paris could have been dismissed."[4]

Haussmann himself presided over his departure ceremony with typical hauteur as well as with considerable dignity, telling the council members that he would always retain the memory of the "bonds of profound esteem, of reciprocal trust, that united us, rendering our immense task far easier." He concluded that he had the satisfaction of hoping that they would not forget this.

At that, the still-formidable Baron Georges Haussmann stiffly bowed and left—"with head high and heart firm," as he later put it.[5]

Years later, Jules Simon—one of Haussmann's foremost critics during the 1860s—wrote, "It is of little importance to us today that the accounts of Monsieur Haussmann were fantastic. He had undertaken to make Paris a magnificent city, and in this he completely succeeded." Haussmann was so taken with this unexpected compliment that he reproduced it in full in his memoirs.[6]

But at the time, Haussmann's ouster did not quench the simmering public unrest. For too many, overwhelming poverty was still an everyday presence, even though the average wage for workers had risen during the Second Empire, when work for the most part was plentiful. This was due to the unhappy fact that prices had also risen during these years, wiping out any gains in wages. In addition, the scale of capitalism had rapidly escalated, encouraging concentration, squeezing out small and medium-sized enterprises, and leaving workers well behind. By 1870, wages had not even begun to keep up with profits, and the gap between the rich and the poor had dramatically widened.

As for the emperor's liberal reforms, they did not touch the urban masses, nor had they been intended to do so. Rather, Louis-Napoleon had aimed at satisfying the bourgeoisie, especially its conservative businessmen and clerics. Left behind in the scramble for wealth and profits, the poor simmered and the nascent labor movement took strength, expressed in a growing number of strikes. Early in 1870, the most massive one to date erupted after the death of a republican journalist, Victor Noir, who was killed in a duel with the emperor's cousin, Prince Pierre Bonaparte. The journalist had challenged the prince, but nonetheless, duels were supposed to let off steam, not result in serious injury let alone death. The republican opposition quickly compared Noir's death with the death of the Republic in 1851. Henri Rochefort editorialized that "for eighteen years France has been in the bloodstained hands of these ruffians who, not content with gunning down republicans in the street, draw them into vile traps in order to slit their throats at home." He concluded, "People of France, do you really not think there has been enough of it?"[7]

The government arrested the prince (who was no favorite of the emperor's) but also prosecuted and jailed Rochefort and impounded the newspaper in which he had published. None of this had any impact on the popular outcry. On the day of the funeral, huge demonstrations—as many as one hundred thousand people—showed up, alarming the emperor and the forces of law and order. Ollivier sent out the troops, and the regime hunkered down, under verbal assault from republicans and revolutionaries alike.

Yet despite facing a growing opposition on the streets and a diminution of his imperial power as the bicameral parliamentary system began to take shape, Louis-Napoleon was not about to give up his empire without a fight, however charming he might be about it. Reform there might be, but it must be understood as coming from his gracious dispensation. That spring, he went over the heads of his ministers and deputies to his old standby, the people of France—including, most importantly, those rural areas where his support had always been strongest—and asked them to vote on whether they approved of "the liberal reforms in the Constitution carried out since 1860 by the Emperor with the cooperation of the great bodies of the State." Further, he asked voters whether they wished to ratify the decree of April 1870 that henceforth divided power between the emperor and a bicameral parliament.

It was a deft ploy, since the voters could not accept the liberal reforms the emperor offered without endorsing the emperor. Victor Hugo irately responded that the true question was "Can arsenic be rendered edible?"[8] His comment appeared in Paris in Le Rappel and other papers, leading to a warrant for his arrest and yet another prison sentence for his sons.

But despite consternation on the left, the response—powered by the rural vote—was an overwhelming Yes.[9] This represented a victory not only for the emperor's model of a more liberal empire, but also—and most importantly—for the emperor himself and for the continuation of his line. As Louis-Napoleon reportedly told his young son: "My child, your coronation is assured with this plebiscite. More than ever we can look to the future without fear." Others reported that the emperor gleefully remarked, "I'm back to my old score."[10]

∿

Others were just as confident of France's future under the present regime. As Emile Ollivier announced in late June, "At no epoch has the peace of Europe been more assured."[11]

Charges against Haussmann appeared to have been forgotten, and the former prefect exited into comfortable retirement in the south of France. Back in Paris, Edouard Manet managed to get himself into a duel with his friend Louis Edmond Duranty, a writer and art critic who had temporarily enraged Manet with a review that Manet considered insultingly unenthusiastic. Manet's mother begged Fantin-Latour to help keep Manet away from the Café Guerbois, where the ruckus had taken place, but Manet had by then recovered his usual urbanity. As he told his friend Antonin Proust, he and Duranty "have wondered ever since how we could have been silly enough to want to run each other through."[12]

Manet by now was recognized as leader of the group of younger artists whom Fantin-Latour depicted in his group portrait that included Renoir, Bazille, and Monet as well as Zola, all surrounding Manet at work in his studio. Fantin exhibited A Studio in the Batignolles at that year's Salon, while Manet showed a portrait of his promising new student, Eva Gonzalès, as well as a joint portrait of his friend Zacharie Astruc and Astruc's wife that he called The Music Lesson. "Manet is in despair about where he is placed," Berthe Morisot wrote her sister Edma that May. "However, his two paintings look well," she commented, adding, "As usual, they attract much attention."[13] Not all of the attention was positive, as Morisot was well aware.

Morisot herself endured considerable doubt and consternation in the run-up to the 1870 Salon. She was coming to realize that she possessed an ability and need for expression that far outstripped the conventional amateurism that her social standing and gender permitted. Although the Salon had opened its prestigious doors to her earlier and most conservative paintings, she now was developing a far more unconventional way of painting—attempting with ever quicker and looser brushstrokes to capture the fleeting moments of everyday life, many of them radically out-of-doors.

Much to Morisot's dismay, even Edouard Manet did not quite grasp what she was after and criticized her most recent work as being "unfinished." This included her recent landscape, The Harbor at Lorient, which Morisot planned to submit to that year's Salon, along with her *Portrait of the Artist's Mother and Sister*. Manet praised *The Harbor at Lorient*, albeit with reservations. But the *Portrait of the Artist's Mother and Sister* was entirely a different matter.

Edma Morisot Pontillon, married and pregnant, had returned to Paris the previous winter for the birth of her first child, where Berthe Morisot had painted her, along with their mother. By the time Manet saw the painting, Puvis de Chavannes had already seen and critiqued it, telling Morisot that "the head [of Madame Morisot] was not done and could not be done." Given this, Morisot wrote her sister, "I took it out; I did it over again."

And then came Edouard Manet's critique. He liked the painting, thought it very good except for a few places, and promptly took up the brushes to put in a couple of accents. But "once started," Morisot mourned, "nothing could stop him; from the skirt he went to the bust, from the bust to the head, from the head to the background." He joked, laughed, and kept at it until late that afternoon, when the mover was waiting to take it to the Salon. Much to Morisot's despair, Manet had turned her painting into "the prettiest caricature that was ever seen," leaving her to hope that it would be rejected.[14]

It was not rejected, and despite her mother's efforts to calm the waters by recalling the offending painting (prompted by Morisot's insistence that "she would rather be at the bottom of the river than learn that her picture had been accepted"), Morisot went ahead and showed it. "Having got over my first emotion," she wrote Edma, "I find that one always derives benefit from exhibiting one's work, however mediocre it may be." But Morisot's health was suffering from tension and anxiety as well as from overwork. She wasn't eating properly, her mother reported, adding that, in fact, she wasn't eating much at all: "It disgusts her to swallow anything." For her part, Morisot told her sister that "I feel a great weight on my stomach, and I am disgusted for all time with painters and with friendship."

Morisot would continue to have what may have been an eating disorder for much of her life, and in contrast to the fulsome hourglass figures admired at the time, she was considered by some to be unpleasantly thin. The twenty-first century would take issue with this assessment, and Edouard Manet certainly disagreed, painting her again and again, but her mother was worried. "I have meat juice made for her every day," Madame Morisot told Edma and then gave the written equivalent of a sigh. "Oh, well! . . . "[15]

⌒

Sarah Bernhardt was another who was considered to be thin to the point of skinniness. Her portraits show what the twenty-first century would view as a pleasingly slim and elegant woman, but her detractors (of whom there were many) could be downright nasty about it. Cartoonists portrayed her as a scrawny-legged chicken or, as one acquaintance put it, a "little stick with the sponge on the top"[16]—this being a reference to her curly red hair, which tended to frizz.

Bernhardt responded by making fun of herself. On one occasion, she laughingly declined an umbrella by proclaiming, "Oh, I am so thin I cannot get wet! I pass between the drops." But her best response to her critics was her success. This had become ever more evident when, early in 1870, she was given the lead in George Sand's new play, *L'Autre*. Sand, too, had acerbic comments about Bernhardt, remarking in her journal that Bernhardt was "stupid, but she has a charming nature" and "interprets her role like the great tart she is."[17] But Bernhardt, who would not have known about Sand's journal, in any case had no need to worry about such slights. She was a triumph in *L'Autre* and was ready to move on to other triumphs when history suddenly intervened.

⁓

All was quiet when, on July 3, startling news broke that the recently vacant throne of Spain had been offered to, and accepted by, Prince Leopold of Hohenzollern-Sigmaringen. The most riveting element of this long name was "Hohenzollern," for the king of Prussia was head of the ancient House of Hohenzollern—a family that in times past had produced a noteworthy number of princes, monarchs, and emperors. The French were properly alarmed: Bismarck clearly was behind the offer to Leopold, and it was even clearer that a German prince ruling Spain would mean trouble. As Louis-Napoleon later put it to an interviewer, "The proud blood of Spain would have accepted no foreign masters, and the difficulties of the situation confronting Prince Leopold in a few years would have induced Germany itself to assume the supreme power in order to support him."

Whether or not others in France were alert to the dangers of proud Spanish blood (with which Louis-Napoleon, wed to a Spaniard, was well accustomed), France's leaders were alert to the dangers of Germanic encirclement. The French government immediately demanded, and obtained, the withdrawal of Leopold's candidacy. In addition to official diplomatic channels, Louis-Napoleon had quietly worked behind the scenes, urging those with access to the young prince's ear to tell him that world peace depended upon his renunciation of the Spanish throne.

Peace was the outcome, for the moment. But it was difficult to quench the strong feelings that had emerged on both sides. Bismarck reportedly felt humiliated by the withdrawal and contemplated resignation, while at the height of the confrontation, the deputies in France's Legislature had erupted with "*Vive la France! Vive l'Empereur!*" and even "*À Berlin!*" Public opinion strongly supported this belligerent bluster, to the extent that when Ollivier announced the news of Prince Leopold's withdrawal, it was met with a collective shrug. After all, most of the deputies (along with much of France) believed that it was only what could be expected, given the superiority of France's army over all others. Indeed, when the emperor asked his war minister whether the French army was prepared for war, the war minister (Marshal Edmond Le Boeuf) replied: "If the war were to last for a year, we would not need to buy a gaiter-button!"[18]

Unfortunately, his reply became public and only increased the level of bellicosity in the Legislature, whose deputies pushed for iron-clad guarantees, in writing, from Prussia's King Wilhelm. The French ambassador pressed Wilhelm, who was surprised and taken aback. The king then telegrammed Bismarck, in Ems, with a detailed description of the meeting. Bismarck in turn edited the telegram in ways calculated to insult the French and released it. The Ems telegram, as it became known, served as a deliberate affront to Gallic pride.

On July 19, as a wave of patriotism swept Paris, France declared war on Prussia.

By this time, Claude Monet was a married man, having married his mistress, Camille Doncieux. Opinion differs on whether he married for money (a small dowry in his wife's future) or to escape military service in the coming war. The dowry was indeed small and for the most part remained out of Monet's reach until the death of Camille Monet's father. But it could well have figured in Monet's calculations, for he still was in severe financial straits. This situation was only worsened by the Salon's rejection, once again, of his entries—all the more galling since it had accepted entries from Bazille, Renoir, Manet, and Pissarro. As for military service, Monet was unable to produce the proper papers showing that he had satisfied its requirements. His marriage provided a certain amount of protection, although not complete, against being called up.

In any case, love alone may not have been a sufficient reason for Monet to acquire a wife. After all, Camille Doncieux already was his mistress and showed no signs of straying. Still, despite his family's disapproval, he married her on June 28, 1870, in the town hall of Paris's eighth arrondissement, just as war fever was rising. The witnesses included Gustave Manet, Edouard's young brother, and the painter Gustave Courbet.

Monet and his small family now traveled to Trouville, where he painted the last carefree days of empire, with parasol-shaded ladies and dapper gentlemen strolling the seafront promenade. Before departing Bougival, and without a thought to war, he had taken care to deposit a number of his paintings with Pissarro, to keep them from falling into his creditors' hands. As he would find out, leaving these paintings with his colleague would not protect them from other, more malicious, intruders.

The French were thrilled with the prospect of war, and war was equally to Bismarck's liking, providing the most direct means of completing German unification around a solid Prussian core.

Louis-Napoleon, however, was once again ill and in great pain, leaving Eugenie as the real ruler of France. For several months before this, Emile Ollivier—bolstered by his fellow reformers' hostility toward the empress— had insisted that Eugenie stop attending meetings of the Council of Ministers. But now, once again, she was present, most importantly when the decision was made to go to war. Determined to do her duty, she viewed war with Prussia as the only possible option, a necessary war that would uphold national honor, revive the glow of empire, and assure her son's future, with herself by his side.

As for the emperor, Eugenie insisted that he take personal command of the army and ride at the head of his troops. Yet by now, although few knew it, Louis-Napoleon was in such pain that he was unable for any length of time to sit on a horse. Still, he did his duty, and on July 28, he and the fourteen-year-old Prince Imperial left for the front—on a train.

The emperor's proclamation to the army rang with optimism and conviction: "Whatever road we may take beyond our frontiers," he told his troops, "we shall find glorious traces of our fathers. We will prove ourselves worthy of them." Unfortunately, despite the emperor's fine words, the French army in no way measured up to these expectations and certainly was not comparable to the well-oiled machine that Bismarck had created in Prussia. Undermanned, disorganized, and short of just about everything, including even their outdated munitions, the French in addition were without allies and minus leaders of any quality. Bismarck, on the other hand, had well-trained troops equipped with arms far superior to those of the French. In addition, he made good use of France's declaration of war on Prussia to unite the south German states into an alliance with the Prussia-dominated North German Confederation, giving him a clear numerical superiority.

Not surprisingly, defeat followed defeat for the French, with a huge loss of French lives, while back in Paris, the empress—whom the emperor had appointed regent in his absence—formed a new Council of Ministers more to her liking and fiercely opposed any attempts to relieve the emperor of his duties at the front. When Ollivier resigned, some proposed bringing Haussmann back into the government, but Haussmann made his acceptance contingent upon the emperor's return to Paris, which Eugenie stoutly resisted. Haussmann then remained in Paris and took his place in the Senate.

By August 6, the Germans had stopped a brief French offensive, crossed the Rhine, and now were tearing their way into France, with enormous French losses. Louis-Napoleon telegrammed Eugenie of these reverses and urged her to prepare to defend Paris, but she told Prosper Mérimée, "We shall dispute every foot of ground. The Prussians do not know what they are in for." Mérimée in turn wrote a friend far more realistically: "All may still be put right," he remarked, "but it would need something like a miracle."

This miracle was not forthcoming. Certainly Louis-Napoleon, incapacitated as he was, could not bring it about. Badgered by Eugenie, he decided against returning to Paris; but then, under pressure from his Council of War to hand over command of the army, he argued that he must first consult with the regent, meaning Eugenie. At this point, his exasperated cousin, Prince Napoleon, furiously reminded him that he, Louis-Napoleon, was the sovereign. At this, Louis-Napoleon merely sighed, "I seem to have abdicated."[19]

On August 8, as news poured in of yet another major defeat, Frédéric Bazille enlisted in the 3rd Zouave Regiment. Manet would soon enlist as a volunteer gunner in the National Guard, and Renoir would be drafted. Georges Bizet, as a winner of the Prix de Rome, was entitled to escape military service, but he and fellow composer Jules Massenet nonetheless signed up. On the other hand, Claude Monet continued to paint holiday scenes, to all appearances as unconcerned about current events as the lighthearted holidaying crowd he depicted.

Georges Clemenceau, in the meanwhile, had returned to Paris after an absence of several years and promptly dived into the politics of the time. After completing his medical studies, he had traveled with his father to England, where they met Herbert Spencer and John Stuart Mill. Clemenceau now crossed the Atlantic and traveled throughout America, writing on American politics for Le Temps. Fascinated by America, he refused to return to France when his father summoned him—leading to the end of his allowance. Strapped for cash, he then taught for a time at a girls' finishing school in Connecticut. There, he met the beautiful eighteen-year-old Mary Plummer, whom he married and brought back to France with him, settling at his parents' home in the Vendée and practicing medicine in the locality. Within a year, she presented him with their first child, a daughter. Two other children would follow.

But Clemenceau was dissatisfied with his home life in the provinces, and in August 1870, in the midst of France's ever-more-disastrous war with Prussia, he left his wife and child and returned to Paris. Here he settled in Montmartre and promptly became immersed in his city's turbulent politics.

⌇

While Parisians anxiously awaited news, the war—which already was going badly—suddenly became disastrous. Surrounded by German forces at the little town of Sedan, the badly battered main force of the French army surrendered on September 1, and Napoleon III, emperor of the French, was taken prisoner.

Word did not reach Paris until late on September 3, by which time Louis-Napoleon had been taken into exile. Yet even two days earlier, enough news had trickled through to give a warning of what was to come. On September 1, Edmond de Goncourt, invited to dinner with Princess Mathilde, arrived to find the curtains taken down and the princess in a daze. "If anybody had told me on the first of August what was going to happen," she told him, "I wouldn't have believed him." And the following day, coming out of the Louvre, Goncourt met the curator, who told him that he was about to leave for Brest, to escort a train filled with paintings from the Louvre that were being taken out of their frames, rolled up, and sent to safety.[20]

Jules de Goncourt had died the previous June, and distraught with grief, Edmond had decided to stop keeping their hitherto joint journal. But after several weeks, he decided to pick up his pen again, beginning with his brother's long decline and then, urged on by current events, continuing with the present. On the evening of September 3, he wrote of the impact that the news of French defeat and the emperor's capture made on his fellow Parisians. "Who can describe the consternation written on every face," he wrote, but he also noted "the menacing roar of the crowd, in which stupefaction has begun to give place to anger." Already, great crowds were beginning to move along the boulevards, shouting: "Down with the Empire!"

Would France perish, or would it save itself? Goncourt wondered, as the sounds of revolution filled the air. A major portion of the army had surrendered, and the emperor had vanished into German hands, but Paris had not

given up. The heart of France was still beating, and Parisians were determined to resist to the last.

The next day, Goncourt described the scene as the republican deputies,
led by Léon Gambetta, made their way to the Hôtel de Ville, where they
proclaimed the Republic and formed a provisional government of national
defense. Among the vast crowd outside, cheers went up. "There was shouting
and cheering; hats were thrown into the air, . . . [and] all around one could
hear people greeting each other with the excited words, 'It's happened!'"
Throughout Paris, and especially at the Tuileries, memories of emperor and
empire were quickly disappearing. Already, sheets of newspaper hid the gilt
N's, and wreaths of greens were being hung to replace missing eagles.[21]

Eugenie, facing a hostile crowd that surged around the Tuileries, soon gave
up on her idea of staying in Paris and agreed to escape, via a tunnel connecting the Tuileries to the Louvre. There, she and a loyal companion hailed a
passing cab, which drove them to the house of Louis-Napoleon's dentist, a
longtime friend who gave them shelter for the night. Early the next morning, she and her companion left in the dentist's own carriage, with passports
describing her as an invalid being taken to England. Pounding their way to
the coast, they made it to Deauville, where an Englishman provided transportation on his yacht to the Isle of Wight.

The last vestiges of the Second Empire were rapidly disappearing. But
Germany, under Bismarck, still threatened, and Paris, even though surrounded by the enemy, was holding out.

Léon Gambetta leaving Place Saint-Pierre, Montmartre, by hot-air balloon on 7 October 1870, during the siege of Paris. Painting by Jules Didier and Jacques Guiaud. © Musée de la Ville de Paris, Musée Carnavalet, Paris, France / G. Dagli Orti / De Agostini Picture Library / Bridgeman Images

CHAPTER NINETEEN

~

An End and a Beginning

(1870–1871)

The morning after the Republic was declared, Victor Hugo appeared at the Brussels train station and requested a ticket to Paris. "I have been waiting for this moment for nineteen years," he told the young journalist who was with him.[1]

He crossed the border into France at four o'clock in the afternoon, and that evening he arrived at the Gare du Nord, where he was greeted by a huge cheering crowd. Never one to shy from an audience, Hugo pushed his way into a café, where he spoke from a balcony. "Citizens," he told them, "I have come to do my duty." He had come, he added, "to defend Paris, to protect Paris"—a sacred trust. After that, he climbed into an open carriage, from where he spoke again to the fervent crowd before making his way to the house of a friend, near Place Pigalle.

There the young mayor of Montmartre, Georges Clemenceau, warmly welcomed him.

~

Filled with republican ideas and ideals, Clemenceau had returned a month earlier to Paris, where he immediately became immersed in politics, with special attention to the emergence of a Republic. Given his many friends in the new government, it perhaps was no surprise when Clemenceau was appointed mayor of Montmartre.

At that time, Montmartre consisted of its steep hill, or Butte, on the northern edge of Paris and was the second most populous arrondissement, or district, in the city. It also was the home for many of Paris's poorest residents. Scarred by quarries on its southern slope and still open on top (this was before Sacré-Coeur), Montmartre in 1870 was steeply pitched and poverty-stricken, networked with unpaved narrow streets and a jumble of houses filled to brimming with many of those who had been expelled by Haussmann's *grands travaux* from Paris's center.

Clemenceau's left-wing politics and devotion to his constituents would win him widespread support during the difficult months ahead—especially from Louise Michel, with whom he worked to help the most destitute of Montmartre's residents. Together they organized distribution centers for food and medicine and started up free schools for the children.

He would soon open a dispensary where, for two days a week, he cared for Montmartre's impoverished residents free of charge. But the appalling conditions he saw around him urged him to focus on his career in politics, where he thought he could bring about change. In time, his remarkable career as both a politician and journalist would culminate at the top, as prime minister of France, during the anguished years of yet another war with Germany.

Baron Haussmann's career, on the other hand, was over. Recognizing the dangers of remaining in Paris, he had prudently left for Bordeaux as the empire collapsed, fleeing with other officials of the Second Empire. But when it appeared that even Bordeaux might not be safe, he crossed the border into Italy, using an assumed name and false passport. Haussmann would remain there, in exile, until it seemed safe to return.

Many others, including the Rothschilds, found their lives completely disrupted by the war and the collapse of empire. For the first time in their family history, the Rothschilds suffered a severe rupture: the Frankfurt branch wholeheartedly supported Prussia, while the Paris branch unequivocally defended the French, with two of its younger members serving in the Garde Mobile. This led to severe reprisals when the Prussians occupied the family château at Ferrières en route to Paris. Whether or not the Prussians actually looted and pillaged the place (this is in dispute), they certainly behaved badly, and Bismarck seems to have taken malicious pleasure in the fact that the château they occupied was Jewish-owned.

Another whose life was upended was Sarah Bernhardt, whose flourishing theater career came to an abrupt halt as theaters closed and actors left for military duty. When the German army began to close in on Paris, she decided against leaving, although she managed to get her mother, sisters, and son to Le Havre and safety. She then decided that since the actresses at the

Comédie-Française had turned part of their theater into a hospital for the wounded, she could do the same at the Odéon.

Bernhardt pulled strings, got permission, and then hunted up supplies. Luckily, the handsome new prefect of police was charmed by her visit and was more than willing to round up the food and supplies she needed. Ten barrels of wine, thirty thousand eggs, and one hundred bags of coffee soon arrived at the Odéon, along with an unexpected five hundred pounds of chocolate, a gift from the Menier chocolate-makers. In response to her appeals, others presented her with a flood of supplies, including overcoats, slippers, and lint and linen for bandages.

The wounded began to flood in as well, forcing her to set up beds in the theater's auditorium, dressing rooms, foyer, and even the bar. The wounded were never-ending, even as the weather became colder and food became scarce.

But the worst days were yet to come.

～

Edouard Manet was ecstatic about the end of the Second Empire, but he recognized the perils that lay ahead. Skeptical of the new government's claims that the Prussians would grant an armistice to the new Republic, he and many others prepared for a siege. Remaining in Paris as a volunteer gunner in the National Guard, Manet nonetheless was not about to subject his family to the dangers and deprivation of staying. Instead, he promptly sent his wife, his mother, and his wife's son to safety in the south of France.

Manet also sent his most precious pictures into hiding with his friend Théodore Duret, who had offered to keep them safe. These included *Olympia*, *The Luncheon on the Grass*, *The Guitar Player*, *The Balcony*, and others. Scrawled along the side of his note to Duret were the words: "In the event of my death, you can take your choice of Moonlight or Reader, or if you prefer, you can ask for the Boy with the soap bubbles."[2]

Writing to Eva Gonzalès on September 10, Manet told her that many were hastily exiting the city. "It's a debacle," he wrote, "and people are storming the railway stations." Writing to his wife on September 11, he reported, "We're expecting the Prussians any day now." He continued to write her almost daily, even when on guard duty at the fortifications (the massive Thiers fortifications surrounding Paris). On September 20, he wrote, "There's fighting everywhere, all round Paris." By September 21, Prussian troops had surrounded Paris; soon after, he told her that "Paris is determined to defend itself to the last." On guard at the ramparts, "we heard the guns going all night long. We're getting quite used to the noise."[3]

Manet worried when he did not hear regularly from Suzanne and was "tormented by the thought that you're without news of us"—a situation which became all the more common once the Prussians closed their siege around Paris. From then on, all communications in and out of the city had to be carried out by balloon and homing pigeon, a formidable task.

At the war's onset, Nadar and two others had formed the No. 1 Compagnie des aérostiers (No. 1 Balloonists' Company) and proposed that they make tethered ascents from Montmartre to provide reconnaissance for the military. After the empire's fall and the continuation of the war, Nadar volunteered to assist his city during the siege. Without waiting for official sanction, he and his colleagues established a base on top of Montmartre and began their first tethered ascents before the Prussians completely encircled the city. Clemenceau, as mayor of Montmartre, at first objected, but then changed his mind and provided the balloonists with tents and straw to keep them warm at night.

The provisional government, which had escaped to Tours before the Prussian encirclement was complete, never read or acknowledged the observations Nadar and his colleagues made—marking French, Prussian, and unidentified troops on maps of the Paris region. But now, with Paris encircled, Nadar proposed that the balloons for the first time be untethered and float sacks of correspondence over the Prussian army toward Tours—in what amounted to the world's first air mail.

His idea was accepted, and on September 23, Le Neptune took off from Montmartre with more than two hundred and fifty pounds of mail and dispatches. Not only was the flight risky—the balloons were fragile, and the Prussians could easily use them for target practice—but the question remained, how to get news back? It was impossible to steer a balloon accurately enough to make a pinpoint landing in a besieged city.

The answer was homing pigeons. Le Neptune and the balloons that followed carried caged birds that flew back to the capital. But how to manage the weight of mail they must carry? Here, an especially ingenious solution presented itself. An unidentified engineer approached Nadar with the proposal to gather the Paris-bound correspondence and photograph it, shrinking it and sending the film—an early version of microfilm—by pigeon. Microfilm had in fact been invented a decade before, and its inventor was willing to fly to Tours by balloon with the requisite equipment. Film rolled into goose-quill tubes then was tied by silk thread to the homing pigeons.

In all, sixty-six balloons flew out of Paris during the siege, including the one that brought Gambetta out of Paris, in a failed attempt to organize new armies to come to Paris's rescue. Nearly one hundred thousand messages would make the return trips. Hundreds of pigeons gallantly served.

⌒

On September 25, Manet wrote Suzanne that a balloon carrying letters was due to leave the following day and that he had been promised that his to her would be on it. He sought to assure her that, although "it is still impossible to make firm predictions, . . . Paris is tremendously well defended. There are now four hundred thousand armed National Guardsmen, without counting the *Garde mobile* and the regiment. If the provinces came to our aid, I think we could get the better of the Prussians."

He also assured her that he was in good health, although he could not deny that the siege was beginning to pinch. "It's true that we can't have milk with our coffee now; the butchers are only open three days a week; people queue up outside from four in the morning, and there's nothing left for the latecomers."[4]

That was September. By October, smallpox had broken out, and food shortages were becoming more severe. Edmond de Goncourt went to get a card for his meat ration and noted that "horse-meat is sneaking slyly into the diet of the people of Paris." Milk was available only to children and the sick, and by November, Manet recorded that "horsemeat is a delicacy, donkey is exorbitantly expensive, [and] there are butchers' shops for dogs, cats, and rats." Later that month, Geneviève Bizet remarked that although she had "not yet eaten cat or dog or rat or mouse . . . I shall taste donkey for the first time today." And late in the year, Goncourt visited Roos's, the English butcher's shop on Boulevard Haussmann, where he saw "all sorts of weird remains. On the wall, hung in a place of honor, was the skinned trunk of young Pollux, the elephant at the zoo; and in the midst of name-less meats and unusual horns a boy was offering some camel's kidneys for sale." The butcher, much to his own irritation, had gotten less meat out of Pollux than he had expected.[5]

Manet and his colleagues may have bravely put up with deprivation, but working-class anger was soon boiling over. News that the remaining portion of the French army (under Marshal Bazaine) had surrendered at Metz, along with rumors that the government was making peace overtures to Bismarck, erupted in late October when the working-class battalions of the National Guard stormed the Hôtel de Ville and set up an insurrectional Commune. Goncourt, who was present on the Rue de Rivoli near the Hôtel de Ville, observed that "on every face could be seen distress at Bazaine's capitulation,

... and at the same time an angry and rashly heroic determination not to make peace."[6] This insurrection did not last, and soon bourgeois elements of the National Guard put an end to this early version of the Commune. But tensions between the government and the working classes remained, only to erupt far more bloodily in the spring.

Perhaps unexpectedly, Berthe Morisot and her parents decided to remain in Paris during the siege. Writing to her sister Edma in Brittany, Morisot told her that she had made up her mind to stay "because neither father nor mother told me firmly to leave," and she did not want to abandon them. And so she remained in besieged Paris, where life was dull if not at present dangerous, and with militia quartered in their studio, which prevented her from painting. The house, she wrote, was "dreary, empty, stripped bare." News of Prussian atrocities upset her, and she was suffering from nightmares. Worst of all, she had heard nothing of their brother, Tiburce, who was fighting on the front. Yet by September 25, she wrote Edma, "Would you believe that I am becoming accustomed to the sound of the cannon? It seems to me that I am now absolutely inured to war and capable of enduring anything."[7]

In mid-September, Edouard Manet and his brother Eugène paid the Morisots a visit, to see how they were faring. Both brothers clearly admired Berthe Morisot, but it was the unmarried brother, Eugène, who would soon begin a gentle courtship, which in time would lead to marriage. For now, he told Morisot very calmly "that he did not expect to come out of [the war] alive."[8]

Early on, Edouard Manet's friend Edgar Degas joined him in the artillery, where both served as volunteer gunners, while the other Manet brothers, Eugène and Gustave, along with the painter Antoine Guillemet, joined National Guard battle units and were waiting to go into action. But "a lot of cowards have left," Manet reported, including Zola and Fantin-Latour. "I don't think they'll be very well received on their return," he added.[9] Zola, who married his mistress as war approached, had headed south to Marseilles with his wife and mother as the Prussians closed in.

Another who was avoiding military duty was Claude Monet, who hung around Le Havre until November, when it became obvious that he would be drafted if he didn't get out of France. Sometime that month he took a boat for London, with his wife and son soon following. There he met up with Pissarro, whose house in Louveciennes had suffered greatly under Prussian occupation. Prussian soldiers had trashed the paintings that he and Monet had stored there, with Pissarro's losses by far the heavier of the two.

This London stay proved valuable to Monet, for it was there that he made the acquaintance of art dealer Paul Durand-Ruel, who also had fled France to England to escape the war. Durand-Ruel expressed an interest in acquiring some of Monet's paintings and soon would become a pivotal figure in Monet's career.

While Monet remained in safety, on November 18, his friend and benefactor, Frédéric Bazille, was killed in action, leading an assault on a German position. He was twenty-eight years old.

⁓

By year's end, suffering and deprivation within Paris had become unbearable. Edouard Manet, who by now had traded in his position as a gunner for that of a cavalry officer attached to the general staff, reported that there was little to eat and no more coal. Trees, house shutters, theater seats, and anything burnable were being chopped up for firewood, while the weather was growing increasingly frigid and smallpox was rapidly spreading. He wrote Suzanne, "I think of you all the time and have filled the bedroom with your portraits." "Paris is deathly sad," he wrote Eva Gonzalès that same day. "We have had more than enough."[10]

That December 5, Alexandre Dumas *père* died in his son's summerhouse in Normandy, surrounded by his son's family. He died quietly, leading George Sand to write, "He was the genius of life; he has not felt death." But Maxime Du Camp wrote, "He died during the war, clinging like so many others to illusive hopes, and believing that victory must revisit the French camp." Du Camp added, "He did not see Paris capitulate, nor the Commune, for the Gods loved him."[11]

⁓

Following a climactic pounding on Paris administered by Prussia's long-range siege guns, the French shuddered and at long last capitulated on January 28, 1871. "There was no way we could have held out any longer," Manet wrote his wife.[12] Hastily called elections quickly followed, in compliance with Bismarck's requirement for a legal authority to sign the peace. Thanks to France's rural voters, who constituted a majority of the electorate, the election returned a government heavily tilted toward advocates of peace, law and order, and monarchy. Adolphe Thiers became chief executive of this French Republic, which had all the appearances of being temporary.

The peace treaty required France to hand over Alsace and Lorraine as well as pay a huge war indemnity, accompanied by German occupation until

Prussian troops enter Paris through the Arc de Triomphe, 1871. © *Lebrecht History / Bridgeman Images*

the indemnity was paid in full. In addition, Bismarck insisted on a chest-thumping German victory march down the Champs-Elysées. But especially appalling to the French was Bismarck's thumb-in-the-eye pageantry arranged for his king, Wilhelm of Prussia, who now arrived on the scene to declare the birth of a new German Empire—and his own imperial status—from the Hall of Mirrors of that most French of all palaces, Louis XIV's Versailles. "This really marks the end of the greatness of France," Edmond de Goncourt wrote sorrowfully, responding to news of the event.[13]

In the meantime, with the future of the new Republic in doubt, the poor of Paris—simmering under the humiliating capitulation to Prussia as well as the threatened return of monarchy—suddenly erupted. They had not done well under two decades of empire and the Haussmannization of Paris, and they were more than ready to take affairs into their own hands.

For the most extreme, this meant burning the house down, and before long, an array of Parisian structures—including, most symbolically, the Tuileries palace and the Hôtel de Ville—went up in smoke, even while members of a new Commune struggled to establish their own more equitable government. But Thiers, who quickly removed his government—and its army—to the safety of Versailles, now prepared to fight the Commune and Communards.

After a wrenching war with Germany, the French were now at war with each other.

Louis-Napoleon remained comfortably imprisoned for several months in King Wilhelm's summer palace, where he—and Eugenie—negotiated until the last for a return to power. Yet having little to bargain with, he and his proposals barely warranted a shrug from either Bismarck or Wilhelm, while for their part, the French seemed little interested in having either of them back.

On March 1, the newly elected French assembly officially deposed Louis-Napoleon Bonaparte as emperor and declared him responsible for the nation's ignominious defeat. A few observers, including Maxime Du Camp, begged to differ. "The nation," he wrote, "had her fate in her own hands and this is what she has made of it."[14] But for the most part, Louis-Napoleon would go down in history, especially in French history, as the cause of France's humiliating defeat to Prussia.

Released from captivity, the former emperor joined Eugenie in the Georgian country house near London that he had presciently bought several years earlier, presumably as a bolt-hole if escape proved necessary. Remembering his youth in the court of his uncle, Napoleon Bonaparte, Louis-Napoleon had always mistrusted how long his glittering empire would last.

There he remained until his death two years later, following several operations. His son, the Imperial Prince, would die six years after that, as an officer in the British Army fighting in South Africa.

Eugenie lived to the age of ninety-four, spending much of her time at Cap Martin on the Mediterranean. Yet she sometimes returned to Paris where, strangely enough, she chose to stay at the Hôtel Continental, overlooking the Tuileries gardens. From her well-appointed rooms there, she could hardly avoid seeing the vast empty space where her palace, the Palais des Tuileries, once dominated the gardens' eastern end. The palace had disappeared, burned and gutted during the Commune uprising of 1871 and swept away by the Third Republic, which wanted no imperial memories to contend with.

A crusty and energetic old lady, the former empress was as tough in old age as she had been in her youth. Instead of indulging in delicate wistfulness, she simply remarked to her interviewer, Maurice Paléologue: "Heavens! How dearly we paid for our grandeurs!"[15]

Yet those who paid the highest price for the empire's grandeurs, and for their own dreams, were the poor of Paris, whose attempt to create an ideal Republic—the highly contentious but socially conscious Commune—came to a violent end that May.

Following the opening shots of revolt, members of the official French government, under Thiers, raced for the safety of Versailles, well beyond Paris's massive walls. Thiers, who had been responsible for building these fortifications in the first place and well knew their strengths and weaknesses, proceeded deliberately. Finally, after a lengthy cannon bombardment of western Paris and the capture of several of the fortification's nearby fortresses, government troops poured into the city.

Unquestionably, the Communards found it difficult to build and defend their barricades in the new Paris that Haussmann had created, with its wide and straight thoroughfares on which troops could march unimpeded. But one unforeseen consequence of Haussmann's slum clearance was the removal of Paris's poor from the center of town to its outskirts—to Montmartre, Belleville, and all those impoverished communities around Paris's periphery. Here, in their home territory, the Communards put up a fierce fight.

During that terrible week in May since known as "Bloody Week," reprisals triggered reprisals as fury and despair escalated. Seething at the brutality of Thiers's troops, Communards destroyed his mansion on Place Saint-Georges

(9th) and then set to work on other monuments linked with the ancien régime and both empires. Soon it seemed as if all Paris was burning, and the killing still went on. By the week's end, only a few pockets of resistance remained—the largest being the famed cemetery of Père-Lachaise, in the twentieth arrondissement. Here, a macabre nighttime gun battle took place among the tombstones, until by morning the remaining Communards had been driven into the cemetery's far southeastern corner. Lined up against the wall, all 147 were shot and buried in a communal grave. This site, now a place of pilgrimage, is marked only by a simple plaque dedicated "Aux Morts de la Commune, 21–28 Mai 1871."

At least twenty thousand Communards and their supporters died—a figure that dwarfs not only the Communards' own well-publicized executions but even the grisly body count of the Reign of Terror. This, and a Paris filled with smoking ruins, was the legacy of these terrible weeks and months.

Edouard Manet left Paris and rejoined his family soon after the capitulation but returned during the height of the Commune uprising, where he sketched some of the horrors he had witnessed: government soldiers firing at close range on a barricade ("The Barricade") and a body lying at the foot of a toppled barricade ("Civil War"). Manet was quick to sympathize with human suffering but was no Communard. Instead, he was an ardent supporter of a liberal republic, who was appalled by the violence and repression practiced by the government troops but who was equally unnerved by the Commune.

Sarah Bernhardt was also sympathetic to the downtrodden of Paris ("This war," she wrote afterward, "had hollowed out under their very feet a gulf of ruin and of mourning") but termed the Commune "wretched." She had nursed her wounded soldiers right through the Prussian bombardment but left immediately after the armistice, retrieving her mother and family from Germany (where they had inexplicably landed) and taking refuge just outside of Paris as it went up in flames. Venturing back after the Commune was crushed, she noted in her memoirs that everywhere one could smell the "bitter odor of smoke." Even in her own home, everything she touched left an unpleasant residue on her fingers. "What blood and ashes!" she wrote. "What women in mourning! What ruins!"[16]

Victor Hugo, for his part, heartily approved of the Commune, at least in theory, but was leery of its extremism. Leaving Paris in a hurry just as the Commune burst into being, he fled to Brussels and then to Luxembourg, not returning to Paris until the worst was over.

Louise Michel, on the other hand, gloried in the Commune uprising, mobilizing the women, organizing day care for the children, and fighting on the barricades. After the last of the Communard resistance was shot down, Michel was arrested and brought to trial. There she defiantly dared the court to kill her. "Since it seems that any heart which beats for liberty has the right only to a small lump of lead," she told the court, "I demand my share."[17] Instead of granting her wish, the court sentenced her to what it probably believed was a slower form of death—deportation to the harsh penal colony in France's South Pacific islands of New Caledonia. There she remained, defiantly surviving. Paris had not seen the last of the woman whom her antagonists derisively called the "Red Virgin."

〜

Berthe Morisot remained in Paris until the outbreak of the Commune, when she joined her sisters in Cherbourg. There, Edouard Manet wrote her after his own return to Paris. "What terrible events," he exclaimed, "and how are we going to come out of this? Each one lays the blame on his neighbor, but to tell the truth all of us are responsible for what has happened."[18]

It was an unusually generous view, and one not shared by many at the time—certainly not by Georges Haussmann, who had watched with horror as much of the city he had transformed was reduced to ashes. His response was to try to bring back Napoleon III and the empire. But the Third Republic—despite its rocky early years—rejected Bonapartism, even while it continued with many of Haussmann's plans for building and rebuilding Paris.

After some initial hesitation, the new republic finished the Opéra Garnier and the Avenue de l'Opéra leading to it; completed the Left Bank's major east-west artery, the Boulevard Saint-Germain; and continued to expand on Haussmann and Belgrand's revolutionary water and sewer system. At the same time, the new republic went to work to repair the damage inflicted during the Commune, most especially by rebuilding the burned-out Hôtel de Ville and the Palais de Justice.

France quickly paid off its war reparations, the German occupiers went home, and within a miraculously short time, Paris was back in business—ready to host a new epoch in creativity, the Belle Epoque. Out of the ashes of defeat would come Monet, Gauguin, Van Gogh, Matisse, and Picasso, while composers such as Debussy, Ravel, and Stravinsky would rock the musical world. Zola would provide literary fireworks, and Proust would dip his pen into his delicate teacup of memories, while that magician of iron, Gustave Eiffel, would defy a host of naysayers to build a tower that would identify Paris for all time.

Instead of death, there now was dawn—along with another chance to define and redefine Paris, city of dreams.

~

Notes

Selected sources are listed by chapter, in the approximate order in which they informed the text.

1. From Barricades to Bonaparte (1848–1851)

Maurice Agulhon, *The Republican Experiment, 1848–1852* (New York: Cambridge University Press, 1983); Graham Robb, *Victor Hugo: A Biography* (New York: Norton, 1997); Claude Schopp, *Alexander Dumas: Genius of Life* (New York: Franklin Watts, 1988); George Rudé, *The Crowd in History: A Study of Popular Disturbances in France and England, 1730–1848* (London: Lawrence and Wishart, 1981); Fenton Bresler, *Napoleon III: A Life* (London: HarperCollins, 1999); Maxime Du Camp, *Recollections of a Literary Life*, 2 vols. (London: Remington, 1893); Frederick Brown, *Flaubert: A Life* (London: Pimlico, 2007); Lois Boe Hyslop, *Baudelaire: Man of His Time* (New Haven, Conn.: Yale University Press, 1980); Michel Carmona, *Haussmann: His Life and Times, and the Making of Modern Paris* (Chicago: Ivan R. Dee, 2002); David H. Pinkney, *Napoleon III and the Rebuilding of Paris* (Princeton, N.J.: Princeton University Press, 1958); Edouard Manet, *Manet By Himself: Correspondence & Conversation, Paintings, Pastels, Prints & Drawings* (London: Macdonald, 1991); Kathleen Adler, *Manet* (Oxford, U.K.: Phaidon, 1986); Françoise Cachin, *Manet: Painter of Modern Life* (London: Thames and Hudson, 1995); Eugène Sue, *Mysteries of Paris*, vol. 1 (New York: Century, 1903).

1. Schopp, *Alexandre Dumas*, 359. Dumas was writing the playwright and theater director Hippolyte Hostein two days before the barricades went up.

2. Bresler, *Napoleon III*, 214–15. The second quote is quite possibly apocryphal, but nonetheless it sounds like him.

3. Bressler, *Napoleon III*, 215. Louis-Napoléon was writing to Narcisse Viellard on 11 May 1848.

4. By-elections take place to fill elected offices that have become vacant between general elections. Since candidates could run in more than one department, this necessitated by-elections in those departments they did not in the end choose to represent.

5. Du Camp, *Recollections of a Literary Life*, 1:265, 276. Disillusioned by the outcome of the 1848 revolution and the coup that followed, Baudelaire would withdraw from political life (see Hyslop, *Baudelaire*, 93).

6. Hugo, *Les Misérables*, 987–88, 990.

7. Du Camp, *Recollections of a Literary Life*, 1:266.

8. Carmona, *Haussmann*, 66; Du Camp, *Recollections of a Literary Life*, 1:265.

9. The priest and Christian socialist Hugues Felicité Robert de Lamennais, quoted in Agulhon, *Republican Experiment*, 62.

10. Hugo quoted in Carmona, *Haussmann*, 68. The Battle of Austerlitz is widely considered to be Napoleon Bonaparte's greatest victory. The newspaper, *L'Evénement*, owned by Hugo's sons and two friends and supporters, would enthusiastically endorse Louis-Napoleon in the December 1848 presidential election.

11. Bresler, *Napoleon III*, 217.

12. Agulhon, *Republican Experiment*, 69.

13. Du Camp, *Recollections of a Literary Life*, 1:276.

14. Hugo quoted in Agulhon, *Republican Experiment*, 73.

15. Dickens quoted in Robb, *Victor Hugo*, 245.

16. Edouard Manet to Jules De Jouy, 26 February [1849]; Edouard Manet to Auguste Manet, 22 March 1849, both in *Manet By Himself*, 24, 25.

17. Du Camp, *Recollections of a Literary Life*, 1:292; Louis-Napoleon quoted in Carmona, *Haussmann*, 84.

18. Du Camp, *Recollections of a Literary Life*, 1:292.

19. Sue, *Mysteries of Paris*, 1:11.

20. Robb, *Victor Hugo*, 290.

21. Du Camp, *Recollections of a Literary Life*, II:23.

22. Hugo quoted in Agulhon, *Republican Experiment*, 136.

23. Du Camp, *Recollections of a Literary Life*, 2:24.

24. Bresler, *Napoleon III*, 233.

25. For Du Camp's account, see his *Recollections of a Literary Life*, 2:24–26.

2. Blood and Empire (1852)

Du Camp, *Recollections of a Literary Life*; Agulhon, *Republican Experiment*; Bresler, *Napoleon III*; Carmona, *Haussmann*; Pinkney, *Napoleon III and the Rebuilding of Paris*;

Victor Hugo, *Napoleon the Little* (New York: Athenaeum Society, 1909); Adler, *Manet*; David I. Harvie, *Eiffel: The Genius Who Reinvented Himself* (Gloucestershire, U.K.: Sutton, 2004); Edmond and Jules de Goncourt, *Pages from the Goncourt Journals* (New York: New York Review of Books, 2007); Schopp, *Alexandre Dumas*; Robb, *Victor Hugo*; André Maurois, *The Titans: A Three-Generation Biography of the Dumas* (New York: Harper, 1957); Emile Zola, *Au Bonheur des dames* (Berkeley: University of California Press, 1992); Charles Merruau, *Souvenirs de l'Hôtel de Ville de Paris, 1848–1852* (Paris: Plon, 1875); Bruno Carrière, *La Saga de la Petite Ceinture* (Paris: Vie du Rail, 1992); Alain Clément and Gilles Thomas, eds., *Atlas du Paris souterrain: la doublure sombre de la Ville lumière* (Paris: Parigramme, 2001); Guy Fargette, *Emile et Isaac Pereire: L'esprit d'entreprise au XIXème siècle* (Paris: L'Harmattan, 2001); Félix Nadar, *When I Was A Photographer* (Cambridge, Mass.: MIT Press, 2015); Niall Ferguson, *The House of Rothschild*, 2 vols. (New York: Viking, 1998–1999); Alain Plessis, *Rise and Fall of the Second Empire, 1852–1871* (New York: Cambridge University Press, 1987); Henri Murger, *The Bohemians of the Latin Quarter* (Philadelphia: University of Pennsylvania Press, 2004); Robert Baldick, *The First Bohemian: The Life of Henry Murger* (London: H Hamilton, 1961); André Tuilier, *Histoire de l'Université de Paris et de la Sorbonne*, 2 vols. (Paris: Nouvelle Librarie de France, 1994).

1. For Du Camp's account, see his *Recollections of a Literary Life*, 2:26–27.
2. Du Camp, *Recollections of a Literary Life*, 2:28; Hugo, *Napoleon the Little*, 121.
3. Eiffel quoted in Harvie, *Eiffel*, 7.
4. Goncourt, Dec. 1851, in *Journals*, 1–2.
5. Goncourt, Dec. 1851, in *Journals*, 3.
6. Dumas to writer Paul Bocage, quoted in Schopp, *Alexandre Dumas*, 385.
7. Maurois, *The Titans*, 188.
8. Du Camp, *Recollections of a Literary Life*, 2:29.
9. Merruau, *Souvenirs de l'Hôtel de Ville de Paris*, 497. Hugo's remark is from *Napoleon the Little*, 13.
10. Agulhon, *Republican Experiment*, 173.
11. Du Camp, *Reflections on a Literary Life*, 2:33, 42–43, and 53.
12. Pinkney, *Napoleon III and the Rebuilding of Paris*, 3.
13. Today, the RER runs on a portion of the Petite Ceinture's right-of-way, but for the most part, the Petite Ceinture remains a ghost of the past, its tracks closed off and neglected.
14. Nadar, *When I Was A Photographer*, 204.
15. Ferguson, *House of Rothschild*, 2:xxii.
16. Persigny quoted in Carmona, *Haussmann*, 262.
17. Hugo, *Napoleon the Little*, 12, 27, 30, 293.
18. Robb, *Victor Hugo*, 323.
19. Du Camp, who quoted Louis-Napoleon, notes that the prince-president was repeating a saying by Louis Antoine de Saint-Just (*Recollections of a Literary Life*, 2:23).

20. Murger, *Bohemians of the Latin Quarter*, xxiii, xxiv.
21. Murger, *Bohemians of the Latin Quarter*, 392.
22. Tuilier, *Histoire de l'Université de Paris et de la Sorbonne*, 2:362–63.

3. Enter Haussmann (1853)

Georges Haussmann, *Mémoires: edition intégrale* (Paris: Seuil, 2000); Carmona, *Haussmann*; Alain Plessis, *The Rise and Fall of the Second Empire, 1852–1871* (New York: Cambridge University Press, 1987); Pierre Pinon, *Atlas du Paris Haussmannien: La Ville en heritage du Second Empire à nos jours* (Paris: Parigramme, 2016); Pinkney, *Napoleon III and the Rebuilding of Paris*; Nadar, *When I Was A Photographer*; Sarah Kennel, *Charles Marville: Photographer of Paris* (Washington, D.C.: National Gallery of Art, 2013); Bresler, *Napoleon III*; Béatrice de Andia, ed., *Les Enceintes de Paris* (Paris: Action Artistique de la Ville de Paris, 2001); Charles Merruau, *Souvenirs de l'Hôtel de Ville de Paris, 1848–1852* (Paris: Plon, 1875); Alain Erlande-Brandenburg, *Notre-Dame de Paris* (New York: Harry N. Abrams, 1998); Georges and Olivier Poisson, *Eugène Viollet-le-Duc* (Paris: Picard, 2014); Bayle St. John, *The Purple Tints of Paris: Character and Manners in the New Empire*, 2 vols. (London: Chapman & Hall, 1854); Emile Zola, *La Curée* (New York: Boni & Liveright, 1924); Frederick Brown, *Zola: A Life* (New York: Papermac, 1997); Maurois, *The Titans*; Schopp, *Alexandre Dumas*; Goncourt, *Journals*.

1. Haussmann, *Memoires*, 81. Haussmann also credited his grandfather's example for his own "moderation of character . . . and a personal disinterestedness which caused me to prefer less vain satisfactions than fortune and honors, satisfactions which remain assured, even in misfortune, by a clear conscience and a legitimate pride in a great task loyally accomplished" (*Memoirs*, 81). Haussmann, writing in retirement, was defending himself, his career, and his honor.
2. Haussmann, *Memoires*, 75.
3. Haussmann, *Memoires*, 357.
4. See Bresler, *Napoleon III*, 265, 266. 268, 269, and 270, for all quotations in this section.
5. Plessis, *Rise and Fall of the Second Empire*, 6, 9; Bresler, *Napoleon III*, 226–27.
6. These are the Rotonde de la Villette; the small rotunda at the northern entrance to Parc Monceau; Place Denfert-Rochereau, where one now serves as an entrance to the Catacombs; and the two columns at the Place de la Nation, which dramatically mark the old Barrière du Trône tollgate.
7. Carmona, *Haussmann*, 144.
8. The first floor in French architecture is not the ground floor but what would be the second floor in American design.
9. Haussmann, *Memoires*, 795, 796–97.
10. Pinon, *Atlas du Paris Haussmannien*, 139. See Haussmann, *Memoirs*, 826.
11. Nadar, *When I Was A Photographer*, 211.

12. Carmona, *Haussmann*, 159. See also Pinon, *Atlas du Paris Haussmannien*, 89.

13. Dumas quoted in Carmona, *Haussmann*, 249–50. Nerval's body was found hanging from a bar of the cellar window on the morning of 25 January 1855. Dumas had been one of his closest friends.

14. Haussmann retained the tower's original elevation by placing it on an enormous pedestal surrounded by a small park, the first of many small parks or squares that Napoleon III would introduce into Paris. The difference in elevations between the tower and its surrounding area can be seen from the stair steps leading from nearby Rue St-Bon up to Rue de la Verrerie, a difference of almost five feet.

15. Haussmann, *Memoires*, 1072.

16. Only one of Baltard's pavilions still exists and can be found in a park in Nogent-sur-Marne, on the eastern outskirts of Paris (see photo).

17. Pinon, *Atlas du Paris Haussmannien*, 87.

18. Haussmann, *Memoires*, 471–72.

19. Merruau, *Souvenirs*, 366.

20. Erlande-Brandenburg, *Notre-Dame de Paris*, 212. Erlande-Brandenburg, a specialist on Gothic and Romanesque art, was director of the Musée de Cluny and president of the Société Française d'Archéologie.

21. Lassus died in 1857.

22. Following the tragic fire of April 2019, Notre-Dame will reemerge but by necessity will be extensively rebuilt, with an entirely new spire.

23. Erlande-Brandenburg, *Notre-Dame de Paris*, 58, 219, 225.

24. St. John, *Purple Tints of Paris*, 1:7.

25. Zola, *La Curée*, 15, 18, 29, 27.

26. Schopp, *Alexandre Dumas*, 409.

27. Goncourt, 20 Feb. 1853, in *Journals*, 11–12.

4. A Nonessential War (1854)

Plessis, *Rise and Fall of the Second Empire*; Bresler, *Napoleon III*; St. John, *Purple Tints of Paris*, vol. 1; Haussmann, *Mémoires*; Carmona, *Haussmann*; Pinon, *Atlas du Paris Haussmannien*; Pinkney, *Napoleon III and the Rebuilding of Paris*; Fargette, *Emile et Isaac Pereire*; Jean-Pierre Rigouard, *La Petite Ceinture: Memoire en Images* (Saint-Cyr-sur-Loire, France: Editions Alan Sutton, 2012); Clément and Thomas, *Atlas du Paris souterrain*; Goncourt, *Journals*; Nadar, *When I Was A Photographer*; Adam Begley, *The Great Nadar: The Man Behind the Camera* (New York: Tim Duggan, 2017); Arthur Gold and Robert Fizdale, *The Divine Sarah: A Life of Sarah Bernhardt* (New York: Vintage, 1991).

1. See Plessis, *Rise and Fall of the Second Empire*, 141.

2. St. John, *Purple Tints of Paris*, 1:16.

3. Haussmann, *Memoires*, 825.

4. Haussmann, *Memoires*, 838.

5. Originally called the Compagnie des Immeubles et de l'Hôtel de la Rue de Rivoli, it changed its name to the Compagnie Immobilière in 1859.

6. Both the Cité Napoléon and the Villa Daumesnil are now gated apartment complexes.

7. Pinon, *Atlas du Paris Haussmannien*, 31.

8. Goncourt, [undated, 1854], in *Journals*, 14.

9. Nadar, *When I Was A Photographer*, 203.

10. Begley, *Great Nadar*, 12–13.

11. Gold and Fizdale, *Divine Sarah*, 22.

5. A Queen Visits (1855)

Haussmann, *Mémoires*; Carmona, *Haussmann*; Bresler, *Napoleon III*; Plessis, *Rise and Fall of the Second Empire*; Maurice de Fleury, *La société du second empire: D'après les mémoires contemporains et des documents nouveaux*, vol. 1 (Paris: A. Michel, 1917); Harvie, *Eiffel*; Adler, *Manet*; Du Camp, *Recollections of a Literary Life*, vol. 2; John Rewald, *The History of Impressionism* (New York: Museum of Modern Art, 1987); Michele Hannoosh, *Painting and the Journal of Eugène Delacroix* (Princeton, N.J.: Princeton University Press, 1995); Fargette, *Emile et Isaac Pereire*; Begley, *The Great Nadar*; Hyslop, *Baudelaire*; Charles Baudelaire, *Baudelaire: A Self-Portrait: Selected Letters* (New York: Oxford University Press, 1957); Charles Baudelaire, *The Flowers of Evil* (Middletown, Conn.: Wesleyan University Press, 2006); Siegfried Kracauer, *Jacques Offenbach and the Paris of His Time* (New York: Zone Books, 2002); Pinon, *Atlas du Paris Haussmannien*; Pinkney, *Napoleon III and the Rebuilding of Paris*; Mary McAuliffe, *Twilight of the Belle Epoque: The Paris of Picasso, Stravinsky, Proust, Renault, Marie Curie, Gertrude Stein, and Their Friends, through the Great War* (Lanham, Md.: Rowman & Littlefield, 2014); Laure Beaumont-Maillet, *L'Eau à Paris* (Paris: Hazan, 1991); Mary McAuliffe, *Dawn of the Belle Epoque: The Paris of Monet, Zola, Bernhardt, Eiffel, Debussy, Clemenceau, and Their Friends* (Lanham, Md.: Rowman & Littlefield, 2011); Ferguson, *House of Rothschild*, vol. 2; Goncourt, *Journals*; Alain Corbin, *Women for Hire: Prostitution and Sexuality in France after 1850* (Cambridge, Mass.: Harvard University Press, 1990); Emile Zola, *Nana* (Hammondsworth, U.K.: Penguin, 1972); Maurois, *Titans*; Marianne and Claude Schopp, *Dumas fils, ou L'anti-Oedipe: biographie* (Paris: Phébus, 2017).

1. Fleury, *Société du second empire*, 1:214–15.

2. Bresler, *Napoleon III*, 283.

3. Du Camp, *Recollections of a Literary Life*, 2: 218, 221–22.

4. Bresler, *Napoleon III*, 283.

5. Fargette, *Emile et Isaac Pereire*, 188.

6. Begley, *The Great Nadar*, 76.

7. Du Camp, *Recollections of a Literary Life*, 2:66.

8. Baudelaire to [Mme Aupick], undated, in *Baudelaire: A Self-Portrait*, 99.

9. Excerpt from Baudelaire, "The Swan" (from "Parisian Scenes"), in *Fleurs des Mal* (translated by Keith Waldrop), 116.

10. A half-century later, the "immortels" put a stop to the most direct route for the construction of Métro line four, which as a result had to take a considerable jog around the Institut de France (see McAuliffe, *Twilight of the Belle Epoque*, 165).

11. Goncourt, Aug. 1855 and 13 Oct. 1855, both in *Journals*, 17 and 18.

12. The registered prostitutes underwent various regulations, such as health checks. Strictly speaking, even registered prostitutes were not legal but tolerated (see Corbin, *Women for Hire*, xviii).

13. Maurois, *Titans*, 296, 297–98.

6. What Goes Up . . . (1856–1857)

Plessis, *Rise and Fall of the Second Empire*; Carmona, *Haussmann*; Haussmann, *Mémoires*; Bresler, *Napoleon III*; Pinkney, *Napoleon III and the Rebuilding of Paris*; Fargette, *Emile et Isaac Pereire*; Ferguson, *House of Rothschild*, vol. 2; Zola, *La Curée*; Harvie, *Eiffel*; Goncourt, *Journals*; Adler, *Manet*; Begley, *Great Nadar*; Du Camp, *Recollections of a Literary Life*, vol. 2; Brown, *Flaubert*; Hyslop, *Baudelaire*; Baudelaire, *Baudelaire: A Self-Portrait*; Berthe Morisot, *Correspondence of Berthe Morisot, with Her Family and Her Friends Manet, Puvis de Chavannes, Degas, Monet, Renoir and Mallarmé* (London: Camden Press, 1986); Anne Higonnet, *Berthe Morisot* (New York: Harper & Row, 1990); Rewald, *History of Impressionism*; Ronald Anderson and Anne Koval, *James McNeill Whistler: Beyond the Myth* (New York: Carroll & Graf, 2002); Hugh Macdonald, *Bizet* (New York: Oxford University Press, 2014).

1. Bresler, *Napoleon III*, 287, 291.

2. Plessis, *Rise and Fall of the Second Empire*, 72, 73.

3. See chapter 3.

4. Goncourt, 10 May and 14 Oct. 1856, in *Journals*, 19.

5. Du Camp, *Recollections of a Literary Life*, 2:144, 145, 146; Brown, *Flaubert*, 325.

6. Du Camp, *Recollections of a Literary Life*, 2:147, 149, 150–51. The *Revue de Paris* would not last much longer, however, being officially suppressed by Imperial Decree in early 1858 (see chapter 7).

7. Du Camp, *Recollections of a Literary Life*, 2:151; Hyslop, *Baudelaire*, 164–65. As Flaubert remarked to Du Camp, "They accuse me of realism, that means to say of copying what I see before me and of being incapable of invention" (*Recollections of a Literary Life*, 2:152).

8. Hyslop, *Baudelaire*, 164.

9. Baudelaire to Poulet-Malassis, 11 July 1857, in *Baudelaire: A Self-Portrait: Selected Letters*, 125.

10. Goncourt, 7 and 20 Jan. 1857; Oct. 1857, all in *Journals*, 24, 25, 30–31.

11. Cousin quoted in Carmona, *Haussmann*, 271.

12. Morisot, *Correspondence*, 18–19.

13. Rewald, *History of Impressionism*, 31.
14. Ponsard quoted in Plessis, *Rise and Fall of the Second Empire*, 143.
15. Carmona, *Haussmann*, 271, 272.

7. More and More (1858)

Plessis, *Rise and Fall of the Second Empire*; Pinkney, *Napoleon III and the Rebuilding of Paris*; Carmona, *Haussmann*; Haussmann, *Mémoires*; Beaumont-Maillet, *L'eau à Paris*; McAuliffe, *Paris Discovered*; Christopher Curtis Mead, *Charles Garnier's Paris Opéra: Architectural Empathy and the Renaissance of French Classicism* (Cambridge, Mass.: MIT Press, 1991); Eugène Sue, *Mysteries of Paris*, vol. 5; Fargette, *Emile et Isaac Pereire*; Kennel, *Charles Marville*; Erlande-Brandenburg, *Notre-Dame de Paris*; Renaud Gagneux, Jean Anckaert, and Gérard Conte, *Sur les traces de la Bièvre parisienne: promenades au fil d'une Rivière disparue* (Paris: Parisgramme, 2002); Morisot, *Correspondence*; Higonnet, *Berthe Morisot*; Brown, *Zola*; Matthew Josephson, *Zola and His Time* (Garden City, N.Y.: Garden City Publishing, 1928); Bresler, *Napoleon III*; Du Camp, *Recollections of a Literary Life*, vol. 2.

1. According to Pinkney, Haussmann considered the distinctions between his First and Second Systems, or Networks, as "purely financial." The First, focused on the Rue de Rivoli, the Boulevard de Sébastopol, and the Boulevard Saint-Michel, along with streets accessory to them, was authorized before 1858 and built with financial aid from the state. The Second System, whose costs were shared by city and state, included only those streets specifically listed in the agreement of March 18, 1858, between the city and the state. A Third System would eventually follow and would include "all other streets built by the city alone without subsidy from the national government" (*Napoleon III and the Rebuilding of Paris*, 58–59).
2. Carmona, *Haussmann*, 288.
3. Mead, *Charles Garnier's Paris Opéra*, 55. According to Mead, "While the decree [of 14 November 1858, declaring the creation of Rues Auber and Halévy] did not include provision for the Rues Scribe, Meyerbeer, and Gluck, which would complete the network of streets around the future Opéra, or the avenue Napoléon [to become Avenue de l'Opéra] that would connect the Place de l'Opéra to the Louvre . . . their existence was implicit in 1858" (55).
4. The house no longer exists.
5. Sue, *Mysteries of Paris*, 5:211.
6. Fargette, *Emile et Isaac Pereire*, 169.
7. This mansion, at 63 Rue de Monceau, no longer exists. In 1911, the Camondos replaced it with a far more elegant and classically inspired model, which is now open to the public, along with the Camondos' collections of art, china, and furnishings. The last members of the Camondo family were deported and murdered in Auschwitz in 1944.
8. See chapter 4.

9. Gagneux, *Sur les traces de la Bièvre parisienne*, 51.

10. Efforts to revive the Bièvre have been successful upstream, outside of Paris, but have encountered enormous difficulties within the city—although several spots have been eyed as possibilities for rehabilitation. These include Parc Kellermann, Square René-Le Gall, Rue Berbier-du-Mets, and the annex of the Museum of Natural History.

11. Brown, *Zola*, 47.

12. Du Camp, *Recollections of a Literary Life*, 2:157. Du Camp now went to the *Revue des Deux Mondes*.

13. Bressler, *Napoleon III*, 296.

8. Dreams of Glory (1859)

Plessis, *Rise and Fall of the Second Empire*; Carona, *Haussmann*; Haussmann, *Mémoires*; Pinkney, *Napoleon III and the Rebuilding of Paris*; Bresler, *Napoleon III*; Maurice Paléologue, *The Tragic Empress: A Record of Intimate Talks with the Empress Eugénie, 1901–1919* (New York: Harper & Brothers, 1928); Charles Beatty, *De Lesseps of Suez: The Man and His Times* (New York: Harper, 1956); Manet, *Manet By Himself*; Adler, *Manet*; Cachin, *Manet*; Baudelaire, *Baudelaire: A Self-Portrait*; Stanley Weintraub, *Whistler: A Biography* (Cambridge, Mass.: Da Capo Press, 2001); Anderson and Koval, *James McNeill Whistler*; Daniel Wildenstein, *Monet, or the Triumph of Impression*, vol. 1 (Cologne, Germany: Taschen/Wildenstein Institute, 1999); Ruth Butler, *Hidden in the Shadow of the Master: The Model-Wives of Cézanne, Monet, and Rodin* (New Haven, Conn.: Yale University Press, 2008); Claude Monet, *Monet By Himself: Paintings, Drawings, Pastels, Letters* (London: Macdonald Orbis, 1989); Rewald, *History of Impressionism*; Begley, *Great Nadar*; Brown, *Zola*; Gold and Fizdale, *Divine Sarah*; Bernhardt, *Memories of My Life*.

1. Jerome Bonaparte quoted in Bresler, *Napoleon III*, 302.

2. Paléologue, *Tragic Empress*, 63, 66. Asked at what period did she begin to sit regularly at the Council of Ministers, Eugenie replied that she "never sat there regularly. I was only present for important deliberations. It was chiefly after 1866 that I was often seen there" (66–67).

3. Haussmann, *Mémoires*, 928–29.

4. In 1859, Napoleon transferred these services to the Prefecture of the Seine.

5. Beatty quoting from De Lesseps's memoirs, *De Lesseps of Suez*, 175.

6. Beatty, *De Lesseps of Suez*, 187.

7. Manet to Antonin Proust, as recorded by Proust, in *Manet By Himself*, 28.

8. Quoted in Adler, *Manet*, 28, 29.

9. Baudelaire made Manet's acquaintance in 1859 and immediately recognized his worth, coming to his defense in two articles published in 1862 (see *Baudelaire: A Self-Portrait*, 192).

10. Butler, *Hidden in the Shadow of the Master*, 98–99; Wildenstein, *Monet*, 11.

11. Wildenstein, *Monet*, 18.
12. Monet to Boudin, 19 May 1859, in *Monet By Himself*, 18.
13. Wildenstein, *Monet*, 25.
14. Wildenstein, *Monet*, 31.
15. Begley, *Great Nadar*, 81.
16. Gold and Fizdale, *Divine Sarah*, 26.
17. Bernhardt, *Memories of My Life*, 39, 60.
18. Gold and Fizdale, *Divine Sarah*, 32.

9. Suddenly Larger (1860)

Plessis, *Rise and Fall of the Second Empire*; Carmona, *Haussmann*; Haussmann, *Mémoires*; Pinkney, *Napoleon III and the Rebuilding of Paris*; Pinon, *Atlas du Paris Haussmannien*; Fargette, *Emile et Isaac Pereire*; Ferguson, *House of Rothschild*, vol. 2; Mead, *Charles Garnier's Paris Opéra*; Bresler, *Napoleon III*; Schopp, *Alexandre Dumas*; Maurois, *The Titans*; Du Camp, *Recollections of a Literary Life*, vol. 2; Macdonald, *Bizet*; Morisot, *Correspondence of Berthe Morisot*; Rewald, *History of Impressionism*; Wildenstein, *Monet*; Manet, *Manet By Himself*; Harvie, *Eiffel*; Begley, *The Great Nadar*; Brown, *Zola*; Josephson, *Zola and His Time*; Zola, *La Curée*.

1. Four toll barriers are all that remain of this wall (see chapter 3, note 6).
2. Goncourt, 24 Aug. and 18 Nov. 1860, in *Journals*, 53.
3. Fargette, *Emile et Isaac Pereire*, 118–19.
4. Maurois, *The Titans*, 322–23, 329.
5. Du Camp, *Recollections of a Literary Life*, II:179.
6. Only the Venetia (still under Austrian control) and Rome itself (guarded by French forces) remained outside the new Kingdom of Italy.
7. Macdonald, *Bizet*, 58.
8. Manet recorded by Antonin Proust [1858–1860], in *Manet by Himself*, 29.
9. Brown, *Zola*, 69.
10. Josephson, *Zola and his Time*, 59.
11. Zola, *La Curée*, 81.
12. Pinkney, *Napoleon III and the Rebuilding of Paris*, 212–13.
13. Haussmann, *Mémoires*, 578.

10. Turning Point (1861)

Bresler, *Napoleon III*; Plessis, *Rise and Fall of the Second Empire*; Carmona, *Haussmann*; Haussmann, *Mémoires*; Paléologue, *Tragic Empress*; McAuliffe, *Dawn of the Belle Epoque*; Mead, *Charles Garnier's Paris Opéra*; Fargette, *Emile et Isaac Pereire*; Brown, *Zola*; Josephson, *Zola and His Time*; Jack D. Ellis, *Early Life of Georges Clemenceau, 1841–1893* (Lawrence: Regents Press of Kansas, 1980); David Robin Watson, *Georges Clemenceau: A Political Biography* (New York: David McKay, 1974); Wildenstein, *Monet*, vol. 1; Manet, *Manet by Himself*; Adler, *Manet*; Cachin, *Manet*; Rewald, *History of Impressionism*; Hyslop, *Baudelaire*; Morisot, *Correspondence of Berthe Morisot*; Goncourt, *Journals*; Baldick, *First Bohemian*; Begley, *The Great Nadar*; Beaumont-Maillet, *L'Eau à Paris*; Robb, *Victor Hugo*; David Bellos, *The Novel of the Century: The Extraordinary Adventure of* Les Misérables (New York: Farrar, Straus and Giroux, 2017); Victor Hugo, *Les Misérables* (New York: Penguin, 1985); Danielle Chadych and Charlotte Lacour-Veyranne, *Paris au temps des* Misérables *de Victor Hugo* (Paris: Paris-Musées, 2008).

1. Bresler, *Napoleon III*, 304–5.
2. Mérimée quoted in Bresler, *Napoleon III*, 330.
3. Bresler, *Napoleon III*, 307.
4. Paléologue, *Tragic Empress*, 92.
5. Paléologue, *Tragic Empress*, 94. "Alas!" Eugenie continued. "We were mistaken about the resistance and the complications in store for us. Or rather, we were misled" (Paléologue, *Tragic Empress*, 93).
6. Many years afterward, Eugenie continued to argue that, "as for the allegation that the Mexican expedition was undertaken at [Morny's] prompting and for base motives, that is a calumny of which he should be entirely cleared. The improper influence of the Jecker bonds counted for nothing in our intervention of Mexico; it merely hooked itself on exactly as you will always find villainies creeping into the noblest enterprises" (Paléologue, *Tragic Empress*, 74).
7. This is the *mairie* of what had become the first arrondissement.
8. See chapter 7, note 3.
9. Josephson, *Zola and His Time*, 62.
10. Watson, *Georges Clemenceau*, 22.
11. Wildenstein, *Monet*, 29, 36–37.
12. Goncourt, 10 May 1856, in *Journals*, 19; Baldick, *First Bohemian*, 184.
13. Goncourt, 28 Jan., 17 March, 10 Oct., and 28 Nov. 1861, all in *Journals*, 57, 58, , 64–65.
14. Goncourt, 12 June 1861, in *Journals*, 61.
15. Goncourt, 20 July 1863, in *Journals*, 87.

11. Les Misérables de Paris (1862)

Hugo, *Les Misérables*; McAuliffe, *Dawn of the Belle Epoque*; Robb, *Victor Hugo*; Bellos, *Novel of the Century*; Chadych and Lacour-Veyranne, *Paris au temps des* Misérables *de Victor Hugo*; Goncourt, *Journals*; Hyslop, *Baudelaire*; Begley, *Great Nadar*; Plessis, *Rise and Fall of the Second Empire*; Carmona, *Haussmann*; Haussmann, *Mémoires*; Fargette, *Emile et Isaac Pereire*; Ferguson, *House of Rothschild*, vol. 2; Clément and Thomas, *Atlas du Paris souterrain*; Carrière, *Saga de la Petite Ceinture*; Bresler, *Napoleon III*; Wildenstein, *Monet*, vol. 1; Rewald, *History of Impressionism*; Morisot, *Correspondence*; Anderson and Koval, *James McNeill Whistler*; Weintraub, *Whistler*; Gold and

Fizdale, *Divine Sarah*; Harvie, *Eiffel*; Adler, *Manet*; Watson, *Georges Clemenceau*; Ellis, *Early Life of Georges Clemenceau*; Brown, *Zola*; Josephson, *Zola and His Time*.

1. Hugo quoted in Robb, *Victor Hugo*, 374.
2. Robb, *Victor Hugo*, 377.
3. Quoted in Hyslop, *Baudelaire*, 157.
4. Olivier quoted in Carmona, *Haussmann*, 341.
5. Goncourts, 1 March 1862, in *Journals*, 69.
6. These disappeared with the Third Republic.
7. Carmona, *Haussmann*, 268.
8. During the following decade, more than fifteen thousand gas lamps would be added to Paris's streets, doubling the number in use (Pinkney, *Napoleon III and the Rebuilding of Paris*, 72).
9. Bresler, *Napoleon III*, 315.
10. Wildenstein, *Monet*, 1:40, 42.
11. Morisot, *Correspondence*, 20.
12. Weintraub, *Whistler*, 77; Anderson and Koval, *James McNeill Whistler*, 123.
13. Marie Colombier quoted in Gold and Fizdale, *Divine Sarah*, 54.
14. Goncourt, 16 and 21 Aug. 1862, in *Journals*, 74–76.
15. Harvie, *Eiffel*, 35.

12. Scandal (1863–1864)

Manet, *Manet by Himself*; Adler, *Manet*; Cachin, *Manet*; Rewald, *History of Impressionism*; Plessis, *Rise and Fall of the Second Empire*; Poisson, *Eugène Viollet-le-Duc*; Du Camp, *Recollections of a Literary Life*, vol. 2; Hannoosh, *Painting and the Journal of Eugène Delacroix*; Erlande-Brandenburg, *Notre-Dame de Paris*; Macdonald, *Bizet*; Hyslop, *Baudelaire*; Anderson and Koval, *James McNeill Whistler*; Wildenstein, *Monet*, vol. 1; Monet, *Monet by Himself*; Gold and Fizdale, *Divine Sarah*; Bernhardt, *Memories of My Life*; Bresler, *Napoleon III*; Beaumont-Maillet, *L'eau à Paris*; Begley, *Great Nadar*; Mead, *Charles Garnier's Paris Opéra*; Baudelaire, *Baudelaire: A Self-Portrait*; Morisot, *Correspondence*; Carmona, *Haussmann*; Haussmann, *Memoires*; Pinon, *Atlas du Paris Haussmannien*; Emile Zola, *Correspondance*, vol. 1 (Montréal, Canada: Presses de l'Université de Montréal, 1978); Goncourt, *Journals*; Robb, *Victor Hugo*.

1. In both *Mademoiselle V. . . in the Costume of an Espada* and *Young Man in the Costume of a Majo* (modeled respectively by Victorine Meurent and Manet's younger brother Gustave), the same costume was thriftily used. Victorine Meurent also posed for the nude featured in *Le Déjeuner sur l'herbe*.
2. Adler, *Manet*, 48.
3. Rewald, *History of Impressionism*, 83.
4. Widely quoted. See Macdonald, *Bizet*, 111, for one example.

5. Du Camp, *Reflections of a Literary Life*, 2:208.

6. Du Camp, *Reflections of a Literary Life*, 2:211. The 2018 blockbuster exhibition on Delacroix shown at both the Louvre and New York's Metropolitan Museum of Art was an emphatic answer to Delacroix's self-questioning.

7. Monet to Amand Gautier, 23 May 1863, in *Monet by Himself*, 19.

8. Bresler, *Napoleon III*, 317.

9. Morny quoted in Plessis, *Rise and Fall of the Second Empire*, 158–59.

10. It would be 1888 and 1904 respectively until they reached water.

11. Quoted in Plessis, *Rise and Fall of the Second Empire*, 81.

12. Bernhardt, *Memories of My Life*, 117.

13. Gold and Fizdale, *Divine Sarah*, 62–63.

14. Baudelaire wrote: "Manet has just told me the most unexpected news. He is leaving this evening for Holland from where he will bring back a *wife*. However, he has several excuses; for it seems that his wife is beautiful, very kind, and a very great artist [musician]. So many treasures in one woman is monstrous, don't you think?" (Baudelaire to Etienne Carjat, 6 Oct. 1863, in *Baudelaire: A Self-Portrait*, 192).

15. Monet to Frédéric Bazille, 15 July [1864], 26 August, and 14 October 1864, all in *Monet by Himself*, 20–22.

16. Morisot, *Correspondence*, 21–23.

17. Haussmann, *Mémoires*, 917.

18. Goncourt, 8 May 1864, in *Journals*, 98–99.

19. See chapter 6 note 7.

20. Robb, *Victor Hugo*, 329.

13. Death and Taxes (1865)

Bresler, *Napoleon III*; Paléologue, *Tragic Empress*; Plessis, *Rise and Fall of the Second Empire*; Carmona, *Haussmann*; Pinkney, *Napoleon III and the Rebuilding of Paris*; Pinon, *Atlas du Paris Haussmannien*; Mead, *Charles Garnier's Paris Opéra*; Macdonald, *Bizet*; Goncourt, *Journals*; Zola, *Correspondance*, vol. 1; Josephson, *Zola and His Time*; Brown, *Zola*; Adler, *Manet*; Manet, *Manet by Himself*; Baudelaire, *Baudelaire: A Self-Portrait*; Cachin, *Manet*; McAuliffe, *Dawn of the Belle Epoque*; Wildenstein, *Monet*, vol. 1; Monet, *Monet by Himself*; Butler, *Hidden in the Shadow of the Master*; Morisot, *Correspondence of Berthe Morisot*; Higonnet, *Berthe Morisot*; Louise Michel, *Louise Michel* (Melbourne N.Y.: Ocean Press, 2004); Louise Michel, *The Red Virgin: The Memoirs of Louise Michel* (Tuscaloosa: University of Alabama Press, 1981); Hyslop, *Baudelaire*; Begley, *Great Nadar*; Cara Sutherland, *The Statue of Liberty* (New York: Museum of the City of New York and Barnes & Noble Books, 2003); Walter D. Gray, *Interpreting American Democracy in France: The Career of Edouard Laboulaye, 1811–1883* (Newark: University of Delaware Press, 1994).

1. Quoted in Bresler, *Napoleon III*, 334.

2. Quoted in Bresler, *Napoleon III*, 331.

3. Paléologue, *Tragic Empress*, 61. "What stirred me," she told Paléologue, "was the broad questions, where national interest, national prestige, were at stake" (62).

4. Bresler, *Napoleon III*, 340.

5. Goncourt, 7 August 1865, in *Journals*, 107.

6. Zola to Edmond and Jules de Goncourt, 3 Feb. 1865, in *Correspondance*, 1:405 note 3; Goncourts to Zola, 27 Feb. 1865, in Zola, *Correspondance*, 1:405 note 3.

7. Goncourt, 5 and 6 Dec. 1865, in *Journals*, 110–12, 113–14. See also 113 note 1.

8. Zola to Edmond and Jules Goncourt, 7 Dec. 1865, in Zola, *Correspondance*, 426–27.

9. Goncourt, 14 Feb. and 27 June 1866, in *Journals*, 116, 117.

10. Brown, *Zola*, 122; Josephson, *Zola and His Time*, 94.

11. Quoted in Josephson, *Zola and His Time*, 98.

12. Manet, as recorded by Antonin Proust; Manet to Baudelaire, [early May 1865], both in *Manet by Himself*, 33. Baudelaire replied, "I must endeavor to prove to you your own worth" (Baudelaire to Manet, 11 May 1865, in *Baudelaire: A Self-Portrait*, 221). Several years after Manet's death, Claude Monet set about raising the money to give *Olympia* to the state, to hang in the Louvre. This is a painting, Monet wrote to the minister of public instruction, "in which [Manet] is seen at the height of his glorious struggle, master of his vision and of his craft." It was "unacceptable that such a work should not have its place in our national collections." The Louvre turned it down, but the Musée du Luxembourg accepted it until the Louvre at length opened its doors—on the order of Georges Clemenceau, who by then was prime minister of France. Thanks to Monet and his good friend Clemenceau, *Olympia* now hangs in the Musée d'Orsay (see McAuliffe, *Dawn of the Belle Epoque*, 198).

13. Manet to Zacharie Astruc, 23? Aug. [1865] and 17 Sept. [1865], both in *Manet by Himself*, 34, 36.

14. Manet recorded by Théodore Duret, [at the Salon of 1865], in *Manet by Himself*, 33.

15. Wildenstein, *Monet*, 1:58; Monet to Frédéric Bazille, [July or early Aug. 1865], in *Monet by Himself*, 23.

16. Wildenstein, *Monet*, 1:59.

17. Now in the Musée d'Orsay, Paris. The oil sketch is in the Pushkin Museum, Moscow.

18. Morisot, *Correspondence*, 24.

19. Michel to Victor Hugo, in *Louise Michel*, 32, 35.

20. Hugo, *Viro Major*, in *Louise Michel*, 25.

21. Michel, *Memoirs*, 31, 39, 40, 44.

22. Baudelaire to his mother, 3 Nov. 1865 and 16 Feb. 1866, both in *Baudelaire: A Self-Portrait*, 226.

23. Manet to Baudelaire, [ca. 25 October 1865], in *Manet by Himself*, 37.

24. Hugo quoted in Hyslop, *Baudelaire*, 163.

14. Crisis (1866)

Ferguson, *House of Rothschild*, vol. 2; Fargette, *Emile et Isaac Pereire*; Plessis, *Rise and Fall of the Second Empire*; Carmona, *Haussmann*; Pinkney, *Napoleon III and the Rebuilding of Paris*; Bresler, *Napoleon III*; Paléologue, *Tragic Empress*; Mead, *Charles Garnier's Paris Opéra*; Manet, *Manet by Himself*; Adler, *Manet*; Cachin, *Manet*; Brown, *Zola*; Josephson, *Zola and His Time*; Wildenstein, *Monet*, vol. 1; Butler, *Hidden in the Shadow of the Master*; Monet, *Monet by Himself*; Rewald, *History of Impressionism*; Du Camp, *Recollections of a Literary Life*, vol. 2; Brown, *Flaubert*; Begley, *Great Nadar*; Gold and Fizdale, *Divine Sarah*; Bernhardt, *Memories of My Life*; Baudelaire, *Self-Portrait*; Michel, *Memoires*.

1. Thiers quoted in Bresler, *Napoleon III*, 340.
2. Paléologue, *Tragic Empress*, 102, 105, 106.
3. Bresler, *Napoleon III*, 343, 344. After a subsequent visit to the pope in Rome, during which she screamed that her attendants were trying to poison her, Charlotte was taken back to her native Belgium, where she spent the remainder of her long life in total insanity.
4. Carmona, *Haussmann*, 211.
5. Manet to Zacharie Astruc, [23? August 1865], in *Manet by Himself*, 34.
6. Quoted in Adler, *Manet*, 135.
7. Brown, *Zola*, 135; Cachin, *Manet* 69.
8. Manet to Emile Zola, 7 May [1866], in *Manet by Himself*, 38.
9. Butler, *Hidden in the Shadow of the Master*, 116; introduction, *Manet by Himself*, 8.
10. Brown, *Zola*, 135.
11. Monet to Amand Gautier, [early April 1866] and 22 May 1866, in *Monet by Himself*, 23.
12. Quoted in Rewald, *History of Impressionism*, 142.
13. Du Camp, *Recollections of a Literary Life*, 2:268.
14. Michel, *Memoirs*, 45, 47–49.

15. A Setting Sun (1867)

Plessis, *Rise and Fall of the Second Empire*; Carmona, *Haussmann*; Pinkney, *Napoleon III and the Rebuilding of Paris*; Bresler, *Napoleon III*; Philip Guedalla, *The Second Empire: Bonapartism, the Prince, the President, the Emperor* (New York: G. P. Putnam's Sons, 1922); Goncourt, *Journals*; Macdonald, *Bizet*; Gold and Fizdale, *Divine Sarah*; Bernhardt, *Memories of My Life*; Manet, *Manet by Himself*; Adler, *Manet*; Brown, *Zola*; Camille Pissarro, *Letters to His Son Lucien* (Santa Barbara, Calif.: Peregrine Smith, 1981); Wildenstein, *Monet*, vol. 1; Butler, *Hidden in the Shadow of the Master*;

Morisot, *Correspondence*; Bresler, *Napoleon III*; Harvie, *Eiffel*; Begley, *Great Nadar*; McAuliffe, *Dawn of the Belle Epoque*; Ferguson, *House of Rothschild*, vol. 2; Fargette, *Emile et Isaac Pereire*; Emile Zola, *Thérèse Raquin* (New York: Penguin, 2004); Zola, *Correspondance*, vol. 1; Josephson, *Zola and His Time*; Robb, *Victor Hugo*; Pinon, *Atlas du Paris Haussmannien*.

1. Quoted in Carmona, *Haussmann*, 357.
2. Guedalla, *Second Empire*, 363.
3. Goncourt, 2 Jan., 23 April, and 4 September 1867, all in *Journals*, 122, 126, and 129. Jules would die before his turn came.
4. Bernhardt, *Memories of My Life*, 132–34, 137, 332.
5. Manet to Zola, 2 Jan. [1867], in *Manet by Himself*, 41. Manet toyed with the idea of turning Zola's article into a pamphlet that he could sell at his exhibition but then decided against it, concluding that it would be in poor taste "to reprint such an outspoken eulogy of me and sell it at my own exhibition" (Manet to Zola, [Feb.–March 1867], in *Manet by Himself*, 42).
6. Pissarro to Lucien, 28 Dec. 1883, in *Letters to His Son Lucien*, 43; Manet quoted in Adler, *Manet*, 95.
7. Adler, *Manet*, 100. Either Zola or Zacharie Astruc may have authored or co-authored this statement with Manet.
8. Monet to Frédéric Bazille, [20 May 1867], in *Monet by Himself*, 24.
9. Butler, *Hidden in the Shadow of the Master*, 128.
10. Monet to Frédéric Bazille, [20 May 1867] and 25 June [1867], in *Monet by Himself*, 24.
11. Quoted in Butler, *Hidden in the Shadow of the Master*, 131.
12. Wildenstein, *Monet*, 1:67.
13. Monet to Frédéric Bazille, 12 Aug [1868], in *Monet by Himself*, 25.
14. Madame Morisot to Berthe Morisot, 19 Aug. 1867, in Morisot, *Correspondence*, 29.
15. This would be the starring attraction of the 1889 exposition. See McAuliffe, *Dawn of the Belle Epoque*.
16. Quoted in Carmona, *Haussmann*, 356.
17. Goncourt, 3 Feb. 1867, in *Journals*, 122.
18. Fargette, *Emile et Isaac Pereire*, 283, 285; Ferguson, *House of Rothschild*, 2:158.
19. The Pereires and Crédit Mobilier would attempt a comeback in the Third Republic, although not with marked success.
20. Quoted in Josephson, *Zola and His Time*, 117.
21. Zola to Albert Lacroix, 13 September 1867, in *Correspondance*, 1:523.
22. Manet to Nadar, 10 Sept. 1867, in *Manet by Himself*, 44.
23. Manet to Emile Zola, [late 1867], in *Manet by Himself*, 45.

24. Carmona, *Haussmann*, 356.

25. This now is a gated community, Villa Daumesnil. See chapter 4 for the Cité Napoléon (9th).

26. Bresler, *Napoleon III*, 347.

16. Twenty Years Later (1868)

Bresler, *Napoleon III*; Paléologue, *Tragic Empress*; Plessis, *Rise and Fall of the Second Empire*; Goncourt, *Journals*; Carmona, *Haussmann*; Pinkney, *Napoleon III and the Rebuilding of Paris*; Carrière, *Saga de la Petite Ceinture*; Clément and Thomas, *Atlas du Paris souterrain*; Brown, *Zola*; Josephson, *Zola in His Time*; Zola, *Correspondance*, vol. 2; Manet, *Manet by Himself*; Adler, *Manet*; Morisot, *Correspondence of Berthe Morisot*; Higonnet, *Berthe Morisot*; Wildenstein, *Monet*, vol. 1; Butler, *Hidden in the Shadow of the Master*; Monet, *Monet by Himself*; Harvie, *Eiffel*; Du Camp, *Recollections of a Literary Life*, vol. 2; Ferguson, *House of Rothschild*, vol. 2.

1. Bresler, *Napoleon III*, 327, 348. Lord Lyons, who replaced Cowley as Britain's ambassador to France, agreed.

2. Goncourt, 24 Feb. and 14 May 1868, in *Journals*, 135–37.

3. Carmona, *Haussmann*, 363.

4. Since 1860, Auteuil has been in Paris's 16th arrondissement.

5. Goncourt, 4 Aug. and 16 Sept.1868, both in *Journals*, 139–41.

6. Goncourt, 17 Sept. 1868, in *Journals*, 141. See also Carrière, *Saga de la Petite Ceinture*, 5; and Clément and Thomas, *Atlas du Paris souterrain*, 173, 174.

7. Goncourt, 14 Dec. 1868, in *Journals*, 144, 145. Soon after, Zola would write his first letter to Flaubert, enclosed with a copy of *Madeleine Férat*, in "homage to your great talent for observation and description" (Zola to Gustave Flaubert, 10 Jan. 1869, in Zola, *Correspondance*, 2:189–90).

8. Zola, for *L'Evénément illustré*, 10 May 1868, in *Manet by Himself*, 45.

9. Manet to Zola, [late April–May 1868?] and [Dec. 1868], in *Manet by Himself*, 45.

10. Morisot, *Correspondence*, 30.

11. In 1867, the Morisots' eldest daughter, Yves, became engaged to M. Gobillard, who now held the post of tax collector at Quimperlé, in Brittany.

12. Manet to Henri Fantin-Latour, 26 Aug. [1868], in *Manet by Himself*, 49.

13. Manet to Henri Fanti-Latour, [10? Aug. 1868] and 26 Aug. [1868], in *Manet by Himself*, 47, 49.

14. Wildenstein, *Monet*, 1:69.

15. Monet to Frédérick Bazille, 29 June [1868], in *Monet by Himself*, 26.

16. Quoted in Wildenstein, *Monet*, 1:74.

17. Monet to Frédéric Bazille, [December 1868], in *Monet by Himself*, 26.

18. Goncourt, 3 Jan. and 7 Aug. 1868, both in *Journals*, 134, 140.
19. Ferguson, *House of Rothschild*, 2:155.
20. Du Camp, *Recollections of a Literary Life*, 256.

17. Haussmann in Trouble (1869)

Haussmann, *Mémoires*; Pinkney, *Napoleon III and the Rebuilding of Paris*; Carmona, *Haussmann*; Plessis, *Rise and Fall of the Second Empire*; Bresler, *Napoleon III*; Paléologue, *Tragic Empress*; Robb, *Victor Hugo*; Manet, *Manet by Himself*; Adler, *Manet*; Cachin, *Manet*; Morisot, *Correspondence of Berthe Morisot*; Higonnet, *Berthe Morisot*; Macdonald, *Bizet*; Wildenstein, *Monet*, vol. 1; Monet, *Monet by Himself*; Daniel Wildenstein, *Claude Monet: Biographie et catalogue raisonné*, vol. 1 (Paris: Bibliothèque des Arts, 1974–1991); Goncourt, *Journals*; Zola, *Correspondance*, vol. 2; Brown, *Zola*; Schopp, *Alexandre Dumas*; Alexandre Dumas, *Mon dictionnaire de cuisine* (Paris: Bartillat, 2011); Ruth Butler, *Rodin: The Shape of Genius* (New Haven, Conn.: Yale University Press, 1993); Meade, *Charles Garnier's Paris Opéra*; Bernhardt, *Memories of My Life*; Gold and Fizdale, *Divine Sarah*.

1. Haussmann, *Mémoires*, 557.
2. Carmona, *Haussmann*, 364.
3. Paléologue, *Tragic Empress*, 17–18.
4. Quoted in Robb, *Victor Hugo*, 434.
5. Manet to Emile Zola, [Jan. 1869]; Manet to Théodore Duret, [early Feb.? 1869], both in *Manet by Himself*, 50; Adler, *Manet*, 116.
6. Manet to Philippe Burty, 18 Feb. [1869], in *Manet by Himself*, 50.
7. Morisot, *Correspondence*, 34.
8. Berthe Morisot to Edma Pontillon, 2 May 1869, in Morisot, *Correspondence*, 35–36.
9. Edma Pontillon to Berthe Morisot, 21 March 1869, in Morisot, *Correspondence*, 33. Edma Pontillon's "infatuation" should only be taken as it was then used, in the lightest sense.
10. Edma Pontillon to Berthe Morisot, [early March, 1869]; Berthe Morisot to Edma Pontillon, 19 March 1869, both in Morisot, *Correspondence*, 32–33.
11. Berthe Morisot to Edma Pontillon, 23 April and 11 May 1869, in Morisot, *Correspondence*, 34, 38; Edma Pontillon quoted in Higonnet, *Berthe Morisot*, 53.
12. See McAuliffe, *Dawn of the Belle Epoque*, 51–52.
13. This story was told by Madame Léouzon-Leduc, whose mother had arranged the introduction (see Morisot, *Correspondence*, 43).
14. Macdonald, *Bizet*, 140.
15. Jean-Léon Gérôme, a new member of the Salon jury, considered Monet and his colleagues a "gang of lunatics" and would continue to mount attacks against them in the years to come (see Wildenstein, *Monet*, 1:77; and McAuliffe, *Dawn of the Belle Epoque*).

16. Wildenstein, *Monet*, 1:76; Monet to Arsène Houssaye, 2 June 1869, in Monet, *Monet by Himself*, 27.

17. Wildenstein, *Monet*, 1:78.

18. Monet to Bazille, 25 Sept. 1869, in Wildenstein, *Monet, Biographie et catalogue raisonné*, 1:427.

19. Goncourt, 15 Jan. and 22 Feb. 1869, both in *Journals*, 148, 150.

20. Goncourt, 15 Jan., 22 Feb., and 1 Nov. 1869, all in *Journals*, 148, 150, 156.

21. See chapter 16 note 7.

22. For keeping eggs fresh: "Bury them in the ashes of new wood in which is mixed branches of juniper, laurel, and other aromatics, along with very dry and fine sand" (*Dictionnaire de Cuisine*, 451–52).

23. Schopp, *Alexandre Dumas*, 483.

24. Butler, *Rodin*, 62.

25. Schopp, *Alexandre Dumas*, 486.

26. Bernhardt, *Memories of My Life*, 142–44, 147.

27. Bernhardt, *Memories of My Life*, 157.

28. Bernhardt, *Memories of My Life*, 148.

29. Gold and Fizdale, *Divine Sarah*, 78.

18. Finale (1870)

Bresler, *Napoleon III*; Plessis, *Rise and Fall of the Second Empire*; Carmona, *Haussmann*; Pinkney, *Napoleon III and the Rebuilding of Paris*; Robb, *Victor Hugo*; Manet, *Manet by Himself*; Morisot, *Correspondence of Berthe Morisot*; Higonnet, *Berthe Morisot*; Bernhardt, *Memories of My Life*; Gold and Fizdale, *Divine Sarah*; Wildenstein, *Monet*, vol. 1; Butler, *Hidden in the Shadow of the Master*; Watson, *Georges Clemenceau*; McAuliffe, *Dawn of the Belle Epoque*.

1. Eugenie quoted in Bressler, *Napoleon III*, 351.

2. Ollivier quoted in Carmona, *Haussmann*, 365–66.

3. Haussmann, *Memoires*, 547.

4. Carmona, *Haussmann*, 366.

5. Haussmann, *Memoires*, 548, 771.

6. Haussmann, *Memoires*, 434. Simon published this accolade in the May 1882 *Le Gaulois*.

7. Rochefort quoted in Carmona, *Haussmann*, 368.

8. Robb, *Victor Hugo*, 438.

9. The majority in the largest cities, especially Paris, voted against.

10. Bressler, *Napoleon III*, 351–52; Plessis, *Rise and Fall of the Second Empire*, 166.

11. Bressler, *Napoleon III*, 353.

12. As recorded by Antonin Proust, [23 Feb. 1870], in Manet, *Manet by Himself*, 51.

13. Berthe Morisot to Edma Pontillon, [May 1870], in Morisot, *Correspondence*, 51.

14. Berthe Morisot to Edma Pontillon, [March 1870], in Morisot, *Correspondence*, 48.

15. Berthe Morisot to Edma Pontillon, [March and May 1870]; Madame Morisot to Edma Pontillon, 22 March 1870, all in Morisot, *Correspondence*, 49, 51, 52.

16. Bernhardt, *Memories of My Life*, 339.

17. Bernhardt, *Memories of My Life*, 299; Gold and Fizdale, *Divine Sarah*, 80.

18. Bressler, *Napoleon III*, 359, 361n.

19. Bressler, *Napoleon III*, 366, 368, 369.

20. Goncourt, 1 and 2 Sept. 1870, in *Journals*, 168–69. There was a similar, if more massive, evacuation during World War II (McAuliffe, *Paris on the Brink*, 250–52).

21. Goncourt, 3 and 4 Sept. 1870, in *Journals*, 169, 170.

19. An End and a Beginning (1870–1871)

Robb, *Victor Hugo*; Watson, *Georges Clemenceau*; Carmona, *Haussmann*; Ferguson, *House of Rothschild*, vol. 2; Bernhardt, *Memories of My Life*; Gold and Fizdale, *Divine Sarah*; Adler, *Manet*; Manet, *Manet by Himself*; Macdonald, *Bizet*; Goncourt, *Journals*; Begley, *Great Nadar*; Morisot, *Correspondence of Berthe Morisot*; Higonnet, *Berthe Morisot*; Brown, *Zola*; Wildenstein, *Monet*, vol. 1; Schopp, *Alexandre Dumas*; Du Camp, *Recollections of a Literary Life*, vol. 2; Paléologue, *Tragic Empress*; Michel, *Memoirs*.

1. Robb, *Victor Hugo*, 44.

2. Manet to Théodore Duret, [15 or 16 Sept. 1870], in *Manet by Himself*, 56.

3. Manet to Eva Gonzalès, 10 Sept. [1870]; Manet to Suzanne Manet, [11 Sept. 1870], 20 [September 1870]; 24 [September 1870], [25 (26?) Sept. 1870], and 30 Sept. [1870], all in *Manet by Himself*, 55, 57, 58.

4. Manet to Suzanne Manet, [25 (26?) Sept. 1870] and 30 Sept. [1870], both in *Manet by Himself*, 58.

5. Goncourt, 1 and 10 Oct. 1870; 31 Dec. 1870, all in *Journals*, 174, 175, 179–80; Manet to Eva Gonzalès, 19 Nov. [1870], in *Manet by Himself*, 60; Macdonald, *Bizet*, 169.

6. Goncourt, 31 Oct. 1870, in *Journals*, 176–77.

7. Morisot to Edma Pontillon, 18 and 25 Sept. 1870, in Morisot, *Correspondence*, 53–55. Tiburce was taken prisoner but escaped and returned to France, where he rejoined the army (see letter from Edma Pontillon, 19 Feb. 1871, in Morisot, *Correspondence*, 60).

8. Morisot to Edma Pontillon, [mid-September], in Morisot, *Correspondence*, 54.

9. Manet to Eva Gonzalès, 19 Nov. [1870], in *Manet by Himself*, 60. Yet Manet, not one to hold a grudge, immediately wrote a friendly letter to Zola as soon as he heard from him in February, giving him the news and reassuring him that not much damage had been done to his house (Manet to Emile Zola, 9 Feb. 1871, in *Manet by Himself*, 65).

10. Manet to Suzanne Manet, 19 and 22 Nov. [1870]; Manet to Eva Gonzalès, 19 Nov. [1870], both in *Manet by Himself*, 60 and 61.

11. Sand quoted in Schopp, *Alexandre Dumas*, 488; Du Camp, *Recollections of a Literary Life*, II:190.

12. Manet to Suzanne Manet, 30 Jan. [1871], in *Manet by Himself*, 65.

13. Goncourt, 30 Jan. 1871, in *Journals*, 183.

14. Du Camp, *Recollections of a Literary Life*, II:365.

15. Paléologue, *Tragic Empress*, 111.

16. Bernhardt, *Memories of My Life*, 227, 233–34.

17. Michel, *Memoirs*, 87.

18. Manet to Berthe Morisot, 10 June 1871, in Morisot, *Correspondence*, 74.

Bibliography

Adler, Kathleen. *Manet*. Oxford, U.K.: Phaidon, 1986.

Agulhon, Maurice. *The Republican Experiment, 1848–1852*. Translated by Janet Lloyd. New York: Cambridge University Press, 1983.

Anderson, Ronald, and Anne Koval. *James McNeill Whistler: Beyond the Myth*. New York: Carroll & Graf, 2002.

Andia, Béatrice de, ed. *Les Enceintes de Paris*. Paris: Action Artistique de la Ville de Paris, 2001.

Baldick, Robert. *The First Bohemian: The Life of Henry Murger*. London: H. Hamilton, 1961.

Baudelaire, Charles. *Baudelaire: A Self-Portrait: Selected Letters*. Translated and edited by Lois Boe Hyslop and Francis E. Hyslop Jr. New York: Oxford University Press, 1957.

———. *The Flowers of Evil*. Translated by Keith Waldrop. Middletown, Conn.: Wesleyan University Press, 2006.

Beatty, Charles. *De Lesseps of Suez: The Man and His Times*. New York: Harper, 1956.

Beaumont-Maillet, Laure. *L'eau à Paris*. Paris: Hazan 1991.

Begley, Adam. *The Great Nadar: The Man Behind the Camera*. New York: Tim Duggan Books, 2017.

Bellos, David. *The Novel of the Century: The Extraordinary Adventure of Les Misérables*. New York: Farrar, Straus and Giroux, 2017.

Bernhardt, Sarah. *Memories of My Life: Being My Personal, Professional, and Social Recollections as Woman and Artist*. New York: D. Appleton, 1907.

Bresler, Fenton. *Napoleon III: A Life*. London: HarperCollins, 1999.

Brown, Frederick. *Flaubert: A Life*. London: Pimlico, 2007.

———. *Zola: A Life*. New York: Papermac, 1997.

Butler, Ruth. *Hidden in the Shadow of the Master: The Model-Wives of Cézanne, Monet, and Rodin.* New Haven, Conn.: Yale University Press, 2008.

———. *Rodin: The Shape of Genius.* New Haven, Conn.: Yale University Press, 1993.

Cachin, Françoise. *Manet: Painter of Modern Life.* Translated by Rachel Kaplan. London: Thames and Hudson, 1995.

Carmona, Michel. *Haussmann: His Life and Times, and the Making of Modern Paris.* Translated by Patrick Cailler. Chicago: Ivan R. Dee, 2002.

Carrière, Bruno. *La Saga de la Petite Ceinture.* Paris: Vie du Rail, 1992.

Chadych, Danielle, and Charlotte Lacour-Veyranne. *Paris au temps des* Misérables *de Victor Hugo.* Musée Carnavalet, 10 Oct. 2008–1 Feb. 2009. Paris: Paris-Musées, 2008.

Clément, Alain, and Gilles Thomas, eds. *Atlas du Paris souterrain: la doublure sombre de la Ville lumière.* Paris: Parigramme, 2001.

Corbin, Alain. *Women for Hire: Prostitution and Sexuality in France after 1850.* Translated by Alan Sheridan. Cambridge, Mass.: Harvard University Press, 1990.

Du Camp, Maxime. *Recollections of a Literary Life.* 2 vols. Translated. London: Remington, 1893.

Dumas, Alexandre. *Mon dictionnaire de cuisine.* Paris: Bartillat, 2011. First published 1873.

Ellis, Jack D. *The Early Life of Georges Clemenceau, 1841–1893.* Lawrence: Regents Press of Kansas, 1980.

Erlande-Brandenburg, Alain. *Notre-Dame de Paris.* Translated by John Goodman. New York: Harry N. Abrams, 1998.

Fargette, Guy. *Emile et Isaac Pereire: L'esprit d'entreprise au XIXème siècle.* Paris: L'Harmattan, 2001.

Ferguson, Niall. *The House of Rothschild.* 2 vols. New York: Viking: 1998–1999.

Flaubert, Gustave. *Madame Bovary.* Translated by Eleanor Marx Aveling. New York: Barnes & Noble Classics, 2005. First published 1856.

Fleury, Maurice de. *La société du second empire: D'après les mémoires contemporains et des documents nouveaux.* 4 vols. Paris: A. Michel, 1917.

Gagneux, Renaud, Jean Anckaert, and Gérard Conte. *Sur les traces de la Bièvre parisienne: promenades au fil d'une rivière disparue.* Paris: Parisgramme, 2002.

Gold, Arthur, and Robert Fizdale. *The Divine Sarah: A Life of Sarah Bernhardt.* New York: Vintage, 1991.

Goncourt, Edmond de, and Jules de Goncourt. *Pages from the Goncourt Journals.* Edited and translated by Robert Baldick. New York: New York Review of Books, 2007.

Gray, Walter D. *Interpreting American Democracy in France: The Career of Edouard Laboulaye, 1811–1883.* Newark: University of Delaware Press, 1994.

Guedalla, Philip. *The Second Empire: Bonapartism, the Prince, the President, the Emperor.* New York: G. P. Putnam's Sons, 1922.

Hannoosh, Michele. *Painting and the* Journal *of Eugène Delacroix.* Princeton, N.J.: Princeton University Press, 1995.

Harvie, David I. *Eiffel: The Genius Who Reinvented Himself.* Gloucestershire, U.K.: Sutton, 2004.

Haussmann, Georges. *Mémoires: édition intégrale.* Vols. 1–3. Paris: Seuil, 2000. First published 1893.

Higonnet, Anne. *Berthe Morisot.* New York: Harper & Row, 1990.

Hugo, Victor. *Les Misérables.* Translated by Norman Denny. New York: Penguin, 1985. First published 1862.

———. *Napoleon the Little.* Translated by George Burnham Ives. New York: Athenaeum Society, 1909. First published 1852.

Hyslop, Lois Boe. *Baudelaire: Man of His Time.* New Haven, Conn.: Yale University Press, 1980.

Josephson, Matthew. *Zola and His Time.* Garden City, N.Y.: Garden City Publishing, 1928.

Kennel, Sarah. *Charles Marville: Photographer of Paris.* Washington, D.C.: National Gallery of Art, 2013.

Kracauer, Siegfried. *Jacques Offenbach and the Paris of His Time.* Translated by Gwenda David and Eric Mosbacher. New York: Zone Books, 2002. First published 1937.

Lesseps, Ferdinand de. *Recollections of Forty Years.* Translated by B. Pitman. New York: D. Appleton, 1888.

Macdonald, Hugh. *Bizet.* New York: Oxford University Press, 2014.

Manet, Edouard. *Manet by Himself: Correspondence & Conversation, Paintings, Pastels, Prints & Drawings.* Edited by Juliet Wilson-Bareau. Translated. London: Macdonald, 1991.

Maurois, André. *The Titans: A Three-Generation Biography of the Dumas.* Translated by Gerard Hopkins. New York: Harper, 1957.

McAuliffe, Mary. *Dawn of the Belle Epoque: The Paris of Monet, Zola, Bernhardt, Eiffel, Debussy, Clemenceau, and Their Friends.* Lanham, Md.: Rowman & Littlefield, 2011.

———. *Paris Discovered: Explorations in the City of Light.* Hightstown, N.J.: Princeton Book Company, 2006.

———. *Twilight of the Belle Epoque: The Paris of Picasso, Stravinsky, Proust, Renault, Marie Curie, Gertrude Stein, and Their Friends, through the Great War.* Lanham, Md.: Rowman & Littlefield, 2014.

Mead, Christopher Curtis. *Charles Garnier's Paris Opéra: Architectural Empathy and the Renaissance of French Classicism.* Cambridge, Mass.: MIT Press, 1991.

Merruau, Charles. *Souvenirs de l'Hôtel de Ville de Paris, 1848–1852.* Paris: Plon, 1875.

Michel, Louise. *Louise Michel.* Edited by Nic Maclellan. Melbourne, N.Y.: Ocean Press, 2004.

———. *The Red Virgin: The Memoirs of Louise Michel.* Edited and translated by Bullitt Lowry and Elizabeth Ellington Gunter. Tuscaloosa: University of Alabama Press, 1981.

Miller, Michael Barry. *The Bon Marché: Bourgeois Culture and the Department Store, 1869–1920.* Princeton, N.J.: Princeton University Press, 1981.

Monet, Claude. *Monet by Himself: Paintings, Drawings, Pastels, Letters.* Edited by Richard Kendall. Translations by Bridget Strevens Romer. London: Macdonald Orbis, 1989.

Morisot, Berthe. *The Correspondence of Berthe Morisot, with Her Family and Her Friends Manet, Puvis de Chavannes, Degas, Monet, Renoir and Mallarmé.* Edited by Denis Rouart. Translated by Betty W. Hubbard. London: Camden Press, 1986.

Murger, Henri. *The Bohemians of the Latin Quarter.* Translated by Ellen Marriage and John Selwyn. Philadelphia: University of Pennsylvania Press, 2004.

Nadar, Félix. *When I Was a Photographer.* Translated by Edouardo Cadava and Liana Theodoratou. Cambridge, Mass.: MIT Press, 2015.

Paléologue, Maurice. *The Tragic Empress: A Record of Intimate Talks with the Empress Eugénie, 1901–1919.* Translated by Hamish Miles. New York: Harper & Brothers, 1928.

Pinkney, David H. *Napoleon III and the Rebuilding of Paris.* Princeton, N.J.: Princeton University Press, 1958.

Pinon, Pierre. *Atlas du Paris Haussmannien: La Ville en heritage du Second Empire à nos jours.* Paris: Parigramme, 2016.

Pissarro, Camille. *Letters to His Son Lucien.* Edited by John Rewald, with assistance of Lucien Pissarro. Translated by Lionel Abel. Santa Barbara, Calif.: Peregrine Smith, 1981. First published 1944.

Plessis, Alain. *The Rise and Fall of the Second Empire, 1852–1871.* Translated by Jonathan Mandelbaum. New York: Cambridge University Press, 1987.

Poisson, Georges, and Olivier Poisson. *Eugène Viollet-le-Duc.* Paris: Picard, 2014.

Rewald, John. *The History of Impressionism.* New York: Museum of Modern Art, 1987. First published 1946.

Rigouard, Jean-Pierre. *La Petite Ceinture: Memoire en Images.* Saint-Cyr-sur-Loire, France: Editions Alan Sutton, 2012.

Robb, Graham. *Victor Hugo: A Biography.* New York: Norton, 1997.

Rudé, George. *The Crowd in History: A Study of Popular Disturbances in France and England, 1730–1848.* London: Lawrence and Wishart, 1981.

Schopp, Claude. *Alexandre Dumas: Genius of Life.* Translated by A. J. Koch. New York: Franklin Watts, 1988.

Schopp, Marianne, and Claude Schopp. *Dumas fils, ou L'anti-Oedipe: biographie.* Paris: Phébus, 2017.

St. John, Bayle. *The Purple Tints of Paris: Character and Manners in the New Empire.* 2 vols. London: Chapman & Hall, 1854.

Sue, Eugène. *The Mysteries of Paris.* 6 vols. New York: Century, 1903.

Sutherland, Cara. *The Statue of Liberty.* New York: The Museum of the City of New York and Barnes & Noble Books, 2003.

Tuilier, André. *Histoire de l'Université de Paris et de la Sorbonne.* 2 vols. Paris: Nouvelle Librarie de France, 1994.

Watson, David Robin. *Georges Clemenceau: A Political Biography.* New York: David McKay, 1974.

Weintraub, Stanley. *Whistler: A Biography*. Cambridge, Mass.: Da Capo Press, 2001. First published 1974.

Wildenstein, Daniel. *Claude Monet: Biographie et catalogue raisonné*. 5 vols. Paris: Bibliothèque des Arts, 1974–1991.

———. *Monet, or the Triumph of Impressionism*. Vol. 1. Translated by Chris Miller and Peter Snowdon. Cologne, Germany: Taschen/Wildenstein Institute, 1999.

Zola, Emile. *Au Bonheur des dames (The Ladies' Paradise)*. Translated by Kristin Ross. Berkeley: University of California Press, 1992.

———. *Correspondance*. Vols. 1 & 2. Edited by B. H. Bakker. Montréal, Canada: Presses de l'Université de Montréal, 1978.

———. *La Curée (The Kill)*. Translated by Alexander Teixeira De Mattos. New York: Boni and Liveright, 1924.

———. *Nana*. Translated by George Holden. Hammondsworth, U.K.: Penguin, 1972.

———. *Thérèse Raquin*. Translated by Robin Buss. New York: Penguin, 2004.

Index

Page references for illustrations are italicized.

~

About the Author

Mary McAuliffe holds a PhD in history from the University of Maryland, has taught at several universities, and has lectured at the Smithsonian Institution, the Barnes Foundation, and the Frick Pittsburgh. She has traveled extensively in France, and for many years, she was a regular contributor to *Paris Notes*. Her books include *Paris Discovered, Dawn of the Belle Epoque, Twilight of the Belle Epoque, When Paris Sizzled, Paris on the Brink,* and *Clash of Crowns*. She lives in New York City with her husband and shares her insights about and photos of Paris with her readers on her Paris Facebook photo blog (www.ParisMSM.com).